8/03

POWER PLAY

To the policy makers of an earlier era who had the good sense to place essential services in public hands

POWER PLAY

The Fight to Control the World's Electricity

SHARON BEDER

THE NEW PRESS

NEW YORK
LONDON

Originally published in Australia by Scribe Publications Pty Ltd, 2003
Published in the United States by The New Press, New York, 2003
Distributed by W. W. Norton & Company, Inc., New York

ISBN 1-56584-808-X (hc.)
CIP data available

The New Press was established in 1990 as a not-for-profit alternative to
the large, commercial publishing houses currently dominating the book
publishing industry. The New Press operates in the public interest rather
than for private gain, and is committed to publishing, in innovative ways,
works of educational, cultural, and community value that are often deemed
insufficiently profitable.

The New Press
38 Greene Street, 4th floor
New York, NY 10013
www.thenewpress.com

In the United Kingdom:
6 Salem Road
London W2 4BU

Printed in the United States of America

10   9   8   7   6   5   4   3   2   1

Acknowledgments

I would like to thank Truda Gray, Jasmin Sydee, and Jim Green for their research assistance, which was facilitated by an Australian Research Council grant. I am particularly indebted to Richard Gosden, who has tirelessly provided support, encouragement, research assistance, proof reading, and feedback throughout the writing of this book.

Contents

Tables and Figures

Abbreviations

ABARE	Australian Bureau of Agricultural and Resource Economics
AC	alternating current
ACCC	Australian Consumer and Competition Commission
ACCI	Australian Chamber of Commerce and Industry
ACT	Australian Capital Territory
ACTEW	ACT Electricity and Water Authority
ACTU	Australian Council of Trade Unions
ADB	Asian Development Bank
AEF	American Economic Foundation (US)
AEP	American Electric Power
AGL	Australian Gas Light
ALP	Australian Labor Party
ANEEL	Agência Nacional de Energia Elétrica (Brazil)
ANWR	Arctic National Wildlife Refuge
APEC	Asia Pacific Economic Cooperation forum
ASI	Adam Smith Institute (UK)
BCA	Business Council of Australia
BJP	Bharatiya Janata Party (India)
C&L	Coopers & Lybrand
CBI	Confederation of British Industry
CCGT	combined cycle gas turbine
CEA	Central Electricity Authority (India)
CEB	Central Electricity Board (UK)
CEGB	Central Electricity Generating Board (UK)
CEO	Chief Executive Officer
CHP	combined heat and power
COAG	Council of Australian Governments
CPS	Centre for Policy Studies (UK)
CPUC	California Public Utilities Commission
CSE	Citizens for a Sound Economy
DC	direct current
DGES	Director General of Electricity Supply (UK)
DOE	Department of Energy (US)
DPC	Dabhol Power Corporation
DSM	Demand-Side Management
ECA	export credit agency
EdF	Electricité de France

Abbreviations

EEI	Edison Electric Institute (US)
EPAC	Economic Planning Advisory Council (Australia)
ESAA	Electricity Supply Association of Australia
ESI	Electricity Supply Industry (Australia)
ETSA	Electricity Trust of South Australia
EU	European Union
EUAA	Energy Users Association of Australia
FDI	foreign direct investment
FEE	Foundation for Economic Education (US)
FERC	Federal Energy Regulatory Commission (US)
FPC	Federal Power Commission (US)
FTC	Federal Trade Commission (US)
FTCR	Foundation for Taxpayer and Consumer Rights (US)
GATS	General Agreement on Trade in Services
GE	General Electric
GLCT	Greater London and Counties Trust (UK)
HEC	Hydro-Electric Corporation (Australia)
IADB	Inter-American Development Bank
IEA	Institute of Economic Affairs (UK)
IMF	International Monetary Fund
INR	Industrial News Review (US)
IOU	investor-owned utility
IPA	Institute of Public Affairs (Australia)
IPP	Independent Power Producer
ISO	Independent System Operator (US)
kW	kilowatt of electricity
kWh	kilowatt hour of electricity - the amount of electricity consumed by ten 100 watt light globes in an hour
Light	Light Servicos de Electricidade (Brazil)
MAI	Multilateral Agreement on Investment
MSEB	Mahrashtra State Electricity Board
MW	Megawatt of electricity, equals one thousand kWs
MWh	Megawatt hour of electricity – one thousand times a kWh
M/A	Mergers and Acquisitons
Napocor	National Power Corporation of the Philippines
NCF	National Civic Federation (US)
NECA	National Electricity Code Administrator (Australia)
NELA	National Electric Light Association (US)
NEM	National Electricity Market (Australia)
NEMMCO	National Electricity Market Management Company (Australia)

Abbreviations

NETA	New Electricity Trading Arrangements (UK)
NGO	Non-government organisations
NRDC	Natural Resources Defense Council (US)
NSC	National Security Council (US)
NSW	New South Wales, Australia
OECD	Organisation for Economic Cooperation and Development
OFFER	Office of Electricity Regulation (UK)
OFGEM	Office of Gas and Electricity Markets (UK)
OPEC	Organisation of Petroleum Exporting Countries
OPIC	Overseas Private Investment Corporation (US)
PGE	Portland General Electric
PG&E	Pacific Gas & Electric
PPA	Power Purchase Agreement
PX	Power Exchange (US)
SEC	Securities & Exchange Commission (US)
SECV	State Electricity Commission of Victoria
SoCalEd	Southern California Edison Company
SCE	Southern California Edison Company
SMUD	Sacremento Municipal Utility District
SS	Shiva Sena Party (India)
PND	National Privatization Program (Brazil)
PUC	Public Utilities Commission (US)
PUHCA	Public Utility Holding Company Act
PURPA	Public Utility Regulatory Policy Act
R&D	Research and Development
REA	Rural Electrification Administration (US)
REC	Regional Electricity Company (UK)
SA	South Australia
TNC	Transnational Corporation
TURN	The Utility Reform Network (US)
TVA	Tennessee Valley Authority
UNDP	United Nations Development Program
USCSI	US Coalition of Service Industries
WA	Western Australia
WTO	World Trade Organisation
WWF	World Wildlife Fund

Throughout the text (apart from part four),
all dollar amounts referred to are in US currency.

POWER PLAY

Introduction

Power liberalisation generally means the loss of public authority and sovereignty over a strategic economic sector. Public assets fall to the hands of a few unaccountable and increasingly powerful multi-national corporations.
The Transnational Institute[1]

ELECTRICITY RATIONING IN BRAZIL ... Blackouts from California and New York to South Australia and Buenos Aires ... Mass protests in India, Africa, and across Latin America. Enron, the seventh-largest company in America, goes bankrupt ... And in Auckland, New Zealand, the central business district goes without power for weeks. Welcome to the brave new world of electricity deregulation and privatisation.

Dozens of governments have embarked on the pathway to electricity deregulation and privatisation since the mid-1990s.[2] It is referred to as 'liberalisation' by its advocates, who use the term to disguise what is in essence a massive shift of ownership and control of electricity from public to private hands, in the name of economic efficiency and in the cause of private profits.

The privatisation of electricity is not something that citizens have demanded or wanted. In general, there has been very little public participation in electricity-reform decisions; instead, as experience has built up, there have been a number of bitter protests. Popular uprisings have occurred in Argentina, India, Indonesia, and Ghana. Protests have halted privatisation proposals in Peru, Ecuador, and Paraguay. In the Dominican Republic, several people were killed during protests against blackouts imposed by privatised companies. In South Africa, thousands marched during a two-day

1

general strike to protest privatisation, which they labelled "born-again apartheid".[3]

In Korea, workers held a five-week strike to protest the sale of the national electricity system. In Papua New Guinea, thousands of students rallied against the planned privatisation of government services, including Elcom, the electricity authority. When riot police attempted to end the peaceful protest with tear gas, and shotgun and M-16 rifle fire, three students were killed and many injured, causing widespread rioting. In France, more than 40,000 protestors marched through Paris to protest against proposed privatisations. Even in China, workers are protesting the sale of a power plant in Henan province to a private company, and threatening to "block the state highway and lie on the railroad while the trains run over us".[4]

This book is not so much about why electricity privatisation is a bad idea —although it provides plenty of evidence to show that it is—but about how and why policy-makers came to think of it as a good idea. In 1979 Margaret Thatcher thought her party's privatisation plans to be too controversial to mention in the election campaign. Twenty years later it has become the accepted wisdom amongst governments and opinion leaders, with more than one hundred countries having privatised various government enterprises.[5]

'Liberalisation' has seen the goal of "reliable, universal electric service prices at a reasonable rate" replaced by the stated goal of consumer choice.[6] However, consumer choice refers to a very narrow choice of retail suppliers, all delivering the same product, rather than a citizen's choice about "whether electricity will be a commodity" produced, transported, and traded by private companies who "use their influence to maximise sales and expansion, or whether electricity will be seen as a nonprofit service tied to least-cost policies, efficiency, and meeting of unstimulated, uninflated electric needs".[7]

The term 'deregulation', when referring to electricity, is essentially a misnomer, since the changes involved are not really about getting rid of regulations: they are about replacing regulations that protect the public and the environment with rules to ensure the smooth running of the market and the electricity system. 'Privatisation' is the more accurate term, because what is happening in the case of deregulation is the privatisation of control over electricity provision. This use of the term is endorsed by the US Department of Energy (DOE), which says: "We treat privatization ... as any movement that diminishes public ownership and control and increases private ownership and control".[8]

The struggle over control of electricity dates back to the earliest days of electricity at the end of the nineteenth century. Nowhere was it more fiercely fought, however, than in the US in the early twentieth century (see part one). From the outset, private electricity companies in the US competed with municipal electricity suppliers by promoting the belief that public ownership of resources and essential services threatened the 'American way of life'.

To defend themselves against further public control of electricity supply and the loss of their own freedom to make profits, private power companies used all the techniques of agenda-setting, political influence, and public relations that we have come to associate with the modern corporation. Together they launched one of the largest nation-wide propaganda campaigns ever undertaken. The campaign utilised a wide range of public relations techniques, which involved schools, churches, banks, community groups, and the media promoting the industry view that private utilities represented free enterprise (see chapter 2).

A federal inquiry into the electricity industry (1928-34) provided a unique insight into its techniques of influence and agenda-setting. The secrets uncovered at that time reveal much about how the industry has worked, and continues to work, tirelessly behind the scenes, persuading the public and politicians to give private interests more and more control over public power. The struggles for public power in the 1920s and 1930s shaped the electricity system for decades to come. The establishment of publicly controlled electricity systems, including the Tennessee Valley Authority (TVA) projects and other federal hydroelectric schemes, and the rural electricity cooperatives, were fought every inch of the way (see chapter 3)

Shielded by their propaganda, the power companies grew into massive holding companies, forerunners of modern multinational corporations. Like Enron, these holding companies resorted to accounting tricks to manipulate their stock prices and rates of return, exploited subsidiaries, and came to dominate the electricity sector (see chapter 1). Then, during the Great Depression, some of these holding companies came crashing down. In 1932, when Samuel Insull's power company, along with its hundreds of subsidiaries and associated companies, went bankrupt, its employees and other shareholders who had invested their life savings in company stock lost everything.

The public disgust and disillusionment with the behaviour of those giant unregulated power companies allowed president Roosevelt to introduce legislation to rein in their power despite the vigorous opposition of the companies themselves. It took several decades for Americans to forget the lessons of the past and to allow this legislation to be weakened and repealed. Today's power companies are again becoming large, multi-limbed monsters engaging in the excesses and abuses that Roosevelt's legislation sought to prevent.

In the 1980s even the limited public control that governments exercised over electricity supply in the US came under attack. And in countries where electricity had been nationalised in the public interest, moves were made to privatise it. The reinvigoration of the struggle for private control of electricity was fostered by a new business-sponsored ideological movement that had emerged in the 1970s.

Neoliberalism

During the 1970s business interests promoted a combination of neoclassical economic theories and economic or market liberalism that came to be referred to as 'neoliberalism' in Europe, 'neoconservatism' in the US, and 'economic rationalism' or 'economic fundamentalism' in Australia.[9] It consisted of a basic policy formula involving government spending cuts, privatisation of government services and assets, and deregulation of business activities. All this was done in the name of free markets, competitiveness, efficiency, and economic growth. The public sector was broadly characterised as "bloated and inefficient".[10]

Neoclassical economic theories, which were largely a revival of the classical economic theories of Adam Smith and his nineteenth-century followers, were developed as a way of giving increased legitimacy to unrestrained market forces and increasing the potential for profit-making. These theories put great faith in the ability of markets to allocate resources efficiently and ensure optimum productivity.[11]

Liberalism was a philosophy that promoted the freedom of individuals to follow their own desires with a minimum of interference or constraint from society. Economic liberalism was a philosophy that was opposed to government intervention or regulation. The emphasis was on the freedom of the individual to make money rather than freedom from oppression, exploitation, and poverty.[12] Neoliberalist policies were supposed to be in the public interest; but, in reality, such policies were promoted by those who stood to gain most from them.

One of the first countries to adopt market-oriented reform was Chile. When General Pinochet ousted the democratically elected Marxist government of Salvador Allende in 1973, with the support of the Americans, he adopted policies that involved cutting the budget deficit, privatising state-owned businesses, and opening the economy to free trade. Chile separated its electricity authority into its component parts and sold them off in the 1980s, and was the first country to do so.[13] (Other countries had electricity systems that were wholly or largely owned by private firms, but Chile was the first government to mandate a change from government to private owner-ship.[14])

Britain was the first major industrialised country to follow suit in 1990 (see chapters 11 and 12). Both Chilean and British privatisation were experiments driven by business interests and shaped by a mix of neoliberal dogma and, in the case of Britain, pragmatic politics. Yet they became models for countries that followed. And many did, to varying degrees: from Sweden and Finland in the north to Australia (see part 4) and New Zealand in the south.

Deregulation in the US was pushed by large industrial consumers of electricity. Whilst electricity is a vital ingredient for most businesses and households, price has not traditionally been a major consideration, except for the very poorest households and the most energy-intensive industries. For the majority of businesses, electricity has been a minor cost. Therefore, "for most users, the key attributes are probably availability, reliability and quality of service, rather than price."[15] However, for some industries, price becomes a major consideration because they use so much of it: these are the industries that have been most keen on electricity-industry reform.

Deregulation in the US was also advocated by unregulated power companies trying to break into monopoly territories. They and the large industrial consumers used think tank-supplied neoliberal arguments to make their case in a way that did not appear to be self-interested. The first state to deregulate was California; it adopted many aspects of the UK model in its restructuring, including the use of a power pool to decide prices (see part 2).

In Europe, the European Commission has been pushing for the liberalisation of electricity. In December 1996 it issued a directive that required member nations to open up their markets to competition, beginning in 1999, with the aim of creating a single electricity market across Europe. The directive also required countries to allow private companies to provide generating facilities and to open access to their transmission and distribution networks without discrimination.[16] Some countries were already in advance of commission requirements (see table below).

The promised benefits of this competition were based on neoliberal assumptions that it would improve efficiency and service, foster innovation, and lower prices. The priority that the European Commission gives to competition is evident in its documents, where it encourages member nations to "pursue public policy considerations" such as environmental protection, so long as this doesn't limit the liberalisation process nor "restrict trade and competition more than necessary".[17]

Some countries, most notably France, resisted pressure from other EU nations and from business leaders within France to privatise its electricity. However, in 2002, with the election of a centre-right government, the French government at last agreed to open its markets and to partially privatise EdF. The partial privatisation is referred to by government ministers as 'opening of capital', so as not to alienate voters who associate privatisation with 'Anglo-Saxon' economic liberalism. The partial privatisation had been recommended by a right-wing think tank, Foundation Concorde, in a report commissioned by president Jacques Chirac.[18]

■ **Table i.1: Opening of the retail electricity market**

Country	Retail market opening	Full retail market opening
Austria	100%	2001
Australia	Some states	No date
Belgium	35%	2007
Denmark	90%	2003
Finland	100%	1997
France	30%	No date
Germany	100%	1998
Greece	30%	No date
Ireland	30%	2005
Italy	45%	No date
Netherlands	33%	2003
New Zealand	100%	1994
Norway	100%	1991
Portugal	30%	No date
Spain	54%	2003
Sweden	100%	1998
UK	100%	1998
US	Some states	No date

Source: European Commission. 'First Benchmarking Report on the Implementation of the Internal Electricity and Gas Market.' 2002, pp . 3, 19; International Energy Agency. 'Electricity Market Reform: California and After.' March 2000, p. 5.

In Latin America, Asia, and Africa electricity privatisation was often introduced because of pressure from the World Bank, the International Monetary Fund (IMF), and regional development banks—the agents of neoliberalism in the developing world. Since the 1980s the World Bank and IMF have required privatisation of public services as a condition of their loans, and have prescribed policies to open up the economies of developing countries for investment by multinational corporations (see chapter 16).

As a result, new markets have been opening up all over the world as developing countries invite multinational companies to provide their essential services. Privatisation has been adopted in virtually every Latin American country except Cuba. Between 1988 and 1993 approximately 2,700 state-owned enterprises in 95 countries were transferred to private hands.[19] In Asia privatisation has tended to take the form of investment by independent power companies (IPPs) who contract to provide electricity at a contracted price (see chapter 17).

The stated reasons for privatisation worldwide, as outlined by the US DOE, are:[20]

- raising revenue for the state;
- raising investment capital for the industry or company being privatised;
- reducing government's role in the economy;
- promoting wider share ownership;
- increasing efficiency;
- introducing greater competition; and
- exposing firms to market discipline.

It is interesting to note that 'consumer choice' is not included in their list, indicating that the emphasis on it in public is in order to sell the benefits of privatisation to consumers, but is not a genuine reason for its introduction.

Many of the above reasons are based on assumptions propagated by economists and think tank personnel rather than aims supported by empirical evidence. The goals of reducing the government's role in the economy and promoting wider share ownership are clearly ideologically based. The goal of economic efficiency is commonly extolled, but there is little evidence that privately owned electric companies are more efficient than publicly owned ones; certainly, the historical and contemporary evidence (presented in ensuing chapters) suggests that public utilities tend to offer cheaper electricity than privately owned ones.

The goals of introducing competition and exposing firms to market discipline are the neoliberal prescriptions for increasing efficiency, which are supposed to lower prices; but privatisation of electricity has often caused prices to increase, as future chapters will show. Where prices have fallen, they have more often than not been part of a more general downward trend that predated privatisation.[21]

This leaves only the goal of raising revenue, which seems to be the main pragmatic goal of politicians and governments. However, this has often turned out to be little more than a mirage because the loss of dividends and control over prices outweighs the financial gains. After deregulation, in general, according to the US-based Consumers Union, service standards decline, consumers lose ground, and the government has to spend billions of dollars on bailouts:[22]

> The marketplace has become more adversarial toward consumers. Absence of strict rules has inspired aggressive tactics, which have led competitors to respond in kind. Sellers have gained disproportionate power over buyers through widespread use of hidden charges, fine-print loopholes, ever-changing prices, and unauthorized switching of service.[23]

Nevertheless, pro-market think tanks, citing the goals listed above, have promoted the privatisation of public services worldwide to the general public through avenues such as the popular press, newsletters, journal articles, speeches, and education programs, and to specific government policy bodies through reports, consultancies, conferences, submissions, and visiting speakers.

In addition, management consultants, particularly the large multinationals such as Price Waterhouse (now PwC) and Peat, Marwick and Mitchell, have earned large sums of money for their advice and studies on how to restructure government enterprises and privatise them. As consultants to the multinational companies that would benefit from the privatisations, they were able to help their clients in the process.[24]

The promoters of privatisation all published reports selectively citing and describing privatisation success stories in the US, the UK, and Europe, and neglecting to tell of its social costs. They also wrote feasibility studies on privatisation, and held conferences that brought together politicians, bureaucrats, and private companies and consultants to discuss the wonders of privatisation.[25]

The success of privatisation advocates in convincing policy-makers has occurred despite the lack of empirical evidence of its benefits, and despite the opposition of communities that are often able to see through the spurious ideological arguments thought up by think tanks. This book will show how democratic impulses and mechanisms that would otherwise have prevented privatisation have been and are still being undermined.

The Uniqueness of Electricity

Whilst electricity has much in common with other privatised services, and even with commodities that have been more traditionally found in the marketplace, it also has some characteristics that make it unique and undermine its suitability as a commodity. The first is the physical need for supply and demand to be balanced at all times to prevent the electricity grid from being damaged. This means that supply and demand cannot be left automatically to the market; they require detailed oversight, which becomes more complex the more parties there are involved in supply. The costs of system coordination are higher in a market system than in one dominated by an integrated monopoly.[26]

A related issue is the interdependence of the system, which means that a major disturbance or damage in one part of the network can immediately affect other parts, thousands of kilometres away. "In a liberal competitive context, ground rules for access to the AC network for both generators and users must therefore be established, agreed and enforced."[27] This is another reason why regulations are necessary and rules established for use of the network.

Electricity cannot easily be stored as electricity. Its inputs can be stored, whether they are gas, coal, or water in a dam. But once it is dispatched on the network, electricity has to be used. Also, once dispatched, the network requires certain operating conditions, such as voltage and frequency, to be maintained. "These operating conditions are provided by what system operators call 'ancillary services'. In a monopoly system they are provided as a matter of course. In a competitive system they have to be bought and paid for, or they may not be provided."[28]

Electricity demand varies considerably according to the time of day, the day of the week, the weather, and other variables. But the inability to store electricity means that some expensive generating plants are idle part of the time, while they are needed at other times of peak demand. In a monopoly system the operator would use low-cost stations for baseload demand that "were designed to operate continuously, supplemented by higher-cost peak-load capacity in periods of higher demand."[29]

In a market there is no central planner choosing which plants to call on according to logic and marginal costs. Instead, "the central planner is replaced by price signals."[30] The owners of plant that are sitting idle most of the day require the price they get at peak time to compensate **them** for the periods of idle time. So even in a competitive market prices go up and down.

This price fluctuation has been exacerbated by the ease with which private companies can use their market power, or create artificial shortages of electricity, to force the price up to very high levels, even in times of lower demand. Electricity markets bring a disjuncture between price and the cost of production. Wherever deregulation has been introduced, wholesale electricity prices have spiked at hundreds of times the cost of production. *The Economist* noted that, "In future, firms will live or die based on how well they manage the volatility inherent in deregulated markets."[31]

It is not easy for the average consumer to respond to these price spikes by reducing her consumption when the price goes up. This is, first, because the average householder doesn't know when the wholesale price is soaring. Second, electricity retailers generally charge householders according to their total consumption, whenever it occurs. Third, the demand for electricity is not particularly flexible, because in modern societies electricity has become an essential service that cannot easily be curtailed, particularly since consumption depends on factors such as the energy-efficiency of electrical goods bought in the past and fixtures installed by landlords. If electricity fails, lights, computers, air conditioning, refrigeration, lifts, and traffic lights cannot work. Life-support systems close down.

The inelasticity of demand means that the market is unlikely to automatically send the right signals for conservation. And if electricity fails, even for a short time, the consequences are major for businesses, hospitals, and people who depend on electricity for life support or for their daily work.

The theory of the market assumes that supply and demand reach an equilibrium at a price that is mutually acceptable. In reality, because demand for electricity is not flexible, sellers have power over buyers: they know that they will have to buy their product, even if the price becomes unreasonable or exorbitant. The threat of blackouts can also be used as a form of blackmail to pressure governments to bail out utilities, change their policies, and/or increase regulated prices. It is this power of electricity providers that causes concern about the concentration of an electricity supply in the hands of a few large companies, particularly if those companies are foreign or simply irresponsible.

For consumers, choice does not mean much in terms of the actual product: one unit of electricity is exactly the same as another, whoever is supplying it and however it is generated. Since retailers are often unwilling or unable to compete on the basis of price, they seek their profits in other ways:

> the new electric industry is using big brother tactics such as cherry-picking the best customers, shifting costs from large industrial users to small commercial and residential users, gutting renewable energy programs, denying weaker companies access to transmission lines, withholding power to drive up prices, or digging the dirt on local government officials who try to look elsewhere for electric service for their constituents. The last-mentioned is so common the industry even has a name for it: 'competitive intelligence'.[32]

In Britain, London Electricity was fined £2 million for its "totally unacceptable" doorstep-selling techniques that included offering people gifts which were never delivered.[33]

The other unique aspect of electricity is the combination of long lead times and heavy capital expenditure that is often required to add capacity to the system. An electricity system depends on a physical infrastructure for transmission and distribution that is too expensive to duplicate. This means that transmission and distribution are necessarily monopoly functions. Until recently, economies of scale have also favoured large, capital-intensive generating plant, meaning that monopolies which incorporated generation, transmission, and distribution made sense, whether they were publicly or privately owned.

The traditional wisdom that larger power stations were more economical was being questioned by the 1980s, as new technologies introduced the possibility of competition from smaller stations in the generating sector. In the early 1990s, with gas prices down, combined cycle gas turbine (CCGT) plants became the technology of choice for electricity generation by private companies. They were cheap and relatively quick to build and operate, and they were flexible in that the amount of electricity they generated could be changed from hour to hour without increasing the cost of that electricity. They took two to three years to build, compared to six to eight years for a coal-fired plant, and cost about half as much. They could also be sited more flexibly, as gas could be delivered by pipe.[34]

Privatisation and deregulation of electricity around the world has been accompanied by restructuring of the industry to separate generation, transmission, distribution, and supply to enable competition in the generation and supply ends of the electricity chain (see following diagrams). However, in many countries the private companies have achieved an effective reintegration through mergers. In Britain, "[t]he retail supply industry is now completely integrated with the generation sector and consolidation is taking place into only a handful of companies."[35] The strategy of newly established private companies "has been to buy up possible competitors, despite governments' attempts to unbundle the electricity sector as a way to avoid monopolistic control of the market".[36]

Planning and Integration

Electricity as a system is more than the sum of its parts. Although the market is supposed to provide better incentives for efficiency and productivity in individual firms, it does not necessarily ensure that the whole system is developed in a balanced way, securing broad access for all citizens, smooth operation, and future planning.[37]

■ Figure i.1: Before restructuring

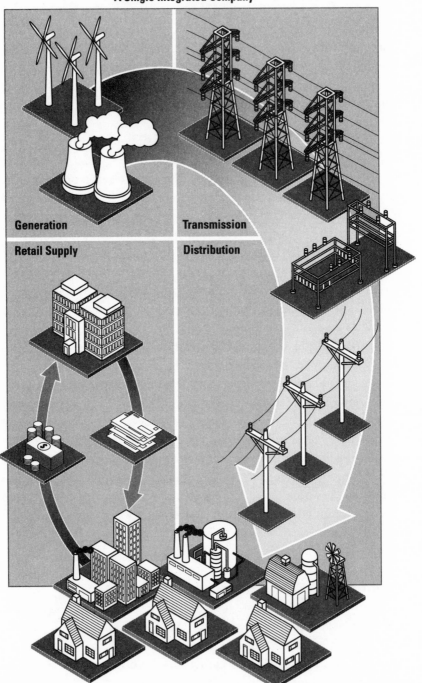

A Single Integrated Company

Generation

Transmission

Retail Supply

Distribution

■ Figure i.2: After restructuring

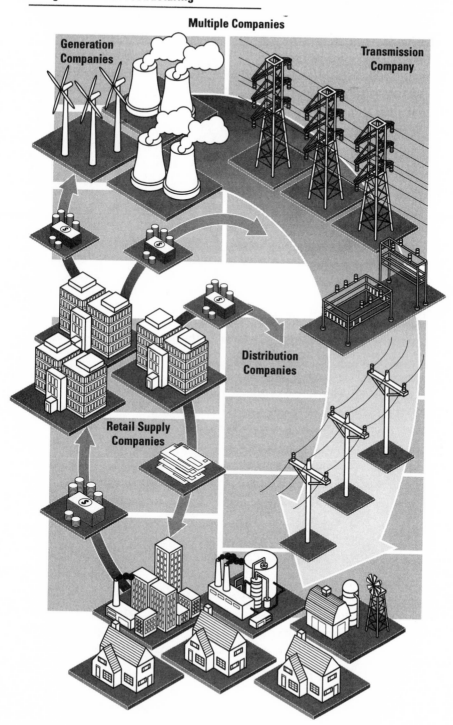

In public electricity systems, planning and long-term forecasting of demand is an essential part of guaranteeing a reliable electricity supply and avoiding the blackouts and crises that come with shortages. Because the large-scale power plants that ensured economies of scale took years to build and operated for 30 or more years,[38] expert forecasters had to take into consideration population growth, demand patterns, weather patterns, and future generation capacity. The need for long-term planning was a major reason for government intervention and coordination in many countries, either through ownership or regulation.

Many countries, including Britain (see chapter 10), nationalised their electricity industries in the mid-twentieth century because they recognised the benefits of government planning and coordination (see table below). It was also believed that governments "were best able to mobilize the large amounts of capital necessary to develop the sector and bear the long time horizons for recovery of costs."[39] Even in the system of regulated private monopolies in the US, the utilities were required to serve all customers in their area of franchise and to have generating capacity that would cover the next ten years.[40]

■ **Table i.2: Electricity nationalisation**

France	Austria	UK	India	Hungary	Italy	Quebec
1946	1947	1947	1948	1949	1962	1963

Often there was a tendency for government authorities to overestimate rather than underestimate future demand, particularly since there could be severe, adverse political consequences from failing to provide a reliable electricity supply, while the costs of oversupply were cushioned by the falling cost of electricity generation and transmission (at least until the advent of nuclear power). This meant there was generally always sufficient generation capacity to ensure security of supply.

Economies of scale combined with technological advances ensured that the electricity was reasonably priced, despite the maintenance of reserve capacity. And the cheap electricity promoted more consumption and further growth. However, in the 1970s electricity rates increased dramatically in many countries because of the costs of building nuclear power plants, rising interest rates, and the escalating costs of oil following the oil crisis.[41] As a result, the demand for electricity did not increase as much as it had previously; but governments and electric utilities failed to take account of this lowered growth rate quickly enough, and constructed more generating plant than was necessary. This was seen as a failure of government planning.

In the 1980s the need for planning began to take second place to the need to cut costs.[42] And in the 1990s, when electricity was liberalised, privatised, and deregulated, the planning function of government bureaucracies was abandoned altogether, surrendered to market forces.

Market forces were supposed to ensure that there were enough supplies because the market was assumed to have the ability to balance supply and demand through competition. It was thought that private companies would be unlikely to oversupply electricity as, in a competitive market, this would cost shareholders dearly. Rather, they would be interested in maximising profits; and, because they were competing with each other, they would have to minimise costs.

In practice, the market has turned out to be a rather poor mechanism for ensuring adequate supply. A government or a regulated monopoly can build reserve capacity to meet unusual peaks without much risk, because the costs can be spread over a large number of consumers over long periods of time. However, companies in a deregulated, competitive environment are loath to build reserve capacity in case they are not able to get an adequate return on their investment. System reliability is therefore compromised by the unwillingness of deregulated private companies to maintain and plan for reserve capacity in case of sudden rises in demand.[43]

The market system, which rewards companies in times of shortages with high prices, also encourages the premature retirement of generating facilities. In the UK, older power stations, constructed in the 1980s, were shut down before they had been paid off, although they could still operate. The decision to close plants, like the decision to build new ones, is up to the owners—and they make it on the basis of projected profits rather than on projected need.[44]

Analysts admit that an unplanned market tends to produce a pendulum effect between too much power and too little. Companies are reluctant to invest in new capacity until a prolonged period of shortage emerges; then they all rush to build new capacity, creating a glut for a period.[45] In a market, no one is responsible for planning or ensuring adequate generation or transmission facilities into the future. This does not matter with most commodities, but it can lead to crises in the case of the supply of electricity.

The Multinationals

Before privatisation and the rise of multinational electricity companies, "system planning, finance, operations and other decision-making took place within national borders". However, this changed in the late 1980s and 1990s

as independent power producers emerged to take advantage of the opportunities offered in various parts of the world by electricity 'liberalisation'.

Moreover, many newly fledged electricity companies created by privatization and
restructuring in the past decade are being progressively engulfed by a new breed of
voracious predator, the multinational electricity corporation, advancing across
national borders to buy up or take over smaller prey.[46]

In the US, mergers and acquisitions have expanded the horizontal reach of
the power corporations, vastly increasing their customer base.[47] Many companies, such as Enron, saw opportunities in international investment "to escape
from stringent US regulation into the comparatively deregulated market
context of countries where liberalization had progressed further, including the
UK, Argentina, Australia and Brazil". Many developing countries also offered
expanding electricity markets, whereas the size of the US market tended to be
more static.[48]

■ **Figure i.3: Mergers and acquisitions of utilities announced, 1992–1996**

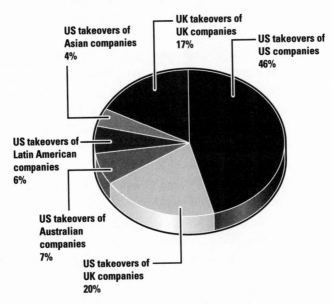

*Source : E.B. Flowers, U.S. Utility Mergers and the Restructuring of the New Global Power Industry, Westport,
Connecticut: Quorum Books. 1998, p. 4.*

There was some $70 billion worth of mergers announced worldwide
between 1992 and 1996, with 83 per cent of them undertaken by US
companies. Two-thirds of the international activity of the US companies

were takeovers. They were joined in the buying frenzy by newly privatised companies in the UK and even state-owned companies such as Electricité de France (EdF). The two large British companies, PowerGen and National Power, began a spree of overseas acquisitions in 1997 in Asia, Australia, Europe, and the US. European and Asian power companies have also joined in in recent years.[49]

Such expansion helps corporations to cut costs and spread expenses, but mainly it is done to increase profits—either by acquiring rival companies at home and so increasing their market power, or by finding overseas corporations that promise high rates of return on investment. This latter prompted US companies to purchase approximately half the available power companies in Britain and Australia as soon as they were privatised.[50]

The Transnational Institute observes:

Despite the frequent claim about the negative impacts of public monopolies, these are often recreated by private foreign companies that manage to assume control over the whole chain of production, transmission and distribution of electricity, undermining government efforts to introduce competition and keep some authority over prices, supply and environmental standards.[51]

In Europe, increasing concentration (see table i.3) means that electricity generation in the European Union is likely to be dominated by six or seven companies by 2005, according to the Transnational Institute. It claims that "these corporations are already exceptionally well placed to operate jointly or to form a cartel to pressure governments, control prices and limit competition."[52]

Mergers were also prompted by the convergence of electricity, coal, and gas markets as electricity companies sought to integrate their power source:

The coal, gas and electrical utilities industries mergers have created a new top tier of large national power marketing firms. These firms are willing to compete with the formerly monopolistic state utilities in most parts of the United States, selling whichever of the energy sources is the lowest cost.[53]

As the electricity and gas markets have converged, international electricity companies have diversified to create the 'integrated gas major'. Almost half of the largest gas and electricity firms "made 'convergence-related' acquisitions or major moves" at the end of the nineties. Oil companies have started taking the gas they used to burn off more seriously, and are acquiring power companies.

Even oil companies such as bp, Shell, and Texaco are buying up electricity companies.[54] "Some analysts now suggest that by the year 2010 the world electricity scene will be dominated by eight or even fewer global companies – electricity multinationals."[55]

■ Table i.3: Concentration in electricity market in European Union, 2002

Country	Share of three largest retail suppliers	Share of three largest generators
Austria	42%	68%
Belgium	100% (1 company)	97% (2 companies)
Denmark	32%	75% (2)
Finland	na	54%
France	96%	98%
Germany	62% (2)	63%
Greece	100% (1)	100% (1)
Ireland	97% (1)	97% (1)
Italy	93% (1)	79% (2)
Netherlands	80%	64%
Portugal	90% (1)	85%
Spain	94%	79%
Sweden	52%	77%
UK	37%	44%

Source: European Commission. 'First Benchmarking Report on the Implementation of the Internal Electricity and Gas Market.' 2002, pp . 3, 19.

Vertically and horizontally integrated companies that provide a full electricity and gas service, as well as water service from source to customer, are emerging. The Public Services Privatisation Research Unit claims:

> The multinationals are now prepared to take over virtually any part of public services. Generale des Eaux is the most dramatic example of this. In the UK, it operates water companies; hospitals; refuse collection services; waste-to-energy plants; housing management; financial administration; road and bridge building; car parks; cable television; mobile phones; and is bidding for a railway franchise. In France, it operates in all these areas plus television, catering, bus and rail transport, motorways, and electricity generating - and, now, education. In the rest of the world, it is acquiring a similar range of contracts.[56]

The problems associated with concentration of ownership in the industry are exacerbated because of the inability of national governments to control foreign owners. First, there is the problem that foreign owners are likely to send their profits back to their home countries rather than make further investment in their facilities or spend the money in the country where they earned it and stimulate the local economy.[57]

Second, whilst power companies are willing to turn off individual plants so as to increase the profits they make on other plants they continue to operate, foreign owners can turn off all their electricity generating capacity for political and other reasons, thereby cutting off an essential part of the economic system without governments being able to do anything about it. For example, Walt Patterson relates a situation that occurred in 1998 when Quebec was experiencing an electricity crisis. A private US company shut down its plant until it could get the price it wanted for its electricity.[58] US companies also shut down supply in the Dominican Republic to force the government to pay its debt to them (see chapter 17).

Companies such as the now-bankrupt Enron, that have no qualms about misleading shareholders, depriving employees of their pensions and life-savings, and manipulating prices (see chapters 8 & 9), cannot be expected to exercise their power over foreign governments responsibly. Patterson observes:

> Many analysts now believe that by 2020, and possibly sooner, most of the world's electricity systems may belong to fewer than a dozen electricity multinationals. Such a multinational will be able to exert almost irresistible leverage on governments and users, simply by the threat of shutting down a system unless its requirements are satisfied. Oil multinationals with a wide portfolio of activities in different parts of the world have never hesitated to suggest that they will withdraw from a particular concession or shut down a particular oilfield if government policy appears contrary to their interest. Electricity multinationals with similarly large portfolios will have a much more potent threat at their disposal ...[59]

Some argue that 'electricity multinationals' will become not merely 'power centres' but 'global centres', owning not only electricity systems within national borders but also systems extending across entire continents, probably including natural gas and telecommunications as well as electricity.[60] Given what is at stake, it is little wonder that the push for privatisation and deregulation has been strong and relentless, bulldozing citizen opposition out of the way.

This book demonstrates that, although arguments for privatisation and deregulation have inevitably been presented in terms of their public benefit, privatisation is really undertaken for the benefit of particular commercial interests at the expense of the public's. It shows how simplistic ideology and economic theory have been used to mask the pursuit of self-interest; how control of electricity has been wrested from public hands to create profit opportunities for investors and multinational corporations; and how an essential public service has been turned into a speculative commodity in the name of 'reform'.

PART ONE

Power Politics in the United States Before Deregulation

To UNDERSTAND THE LENGTHS to which private companies have been willing to go to gain control of the electricity supply, it is necessary to look back to the early decades of electricity development in the United States.

It was during the early twentieth century that the private companies and their trade associations developed their arsenal of political strategies and massive propaganda campaigns in their battle for control over electricity systems. It was these same strategies and public relations techniques that were later used to such good effect in the 1980s and 1990s to win the world's governments over to electricity privatisation, and to ensure that electricity was further deregulated in the United States.

To be effective, these strategies and techniques have to be secret. However, a federal inquiry into the electricity industry that ran from 1928 to 1934 exposed them in a way that has not occurred since. The revelations provide an insight into how private interests have managed to establish privatisation and deregulation of electricity as the accepted wisdom at government and policy-making levels despite widespread popular concern, and in many countries, outright opposition to it.

CHAPTER ONE

Utilities Set The Agenda, 1900–1925

They make a daily, hourly business of politics, raising up men in this ward or that, identifying them with their machines, promoting them from delegates to city convention to city offices. They are always at work protecting and building up a business interest that lives only through its political strength.
Tom Johnson, Mayor of Cleveland (1901-9) referring to electricity companies[1]

PROPONENTS OF DEREGULATION in the US in the 1990s attacked the state utility commissions, which regulated the electric companies, as inhibiting private enterprise and preventing competition. However, these same commissions were established as a result of sophisticated agenda-setting strategies on the part of private utilities in the early years of the twentieth century. The private utilities proposed and advocated state commissions as a way of legitimising private monopolies and blunting the call for public ownership and control of electricity.

From the outset, private electricity companies in the US competed with municipal electricity suppliers by promoting the belief that public ownership of resources and essential services threatened the 'American way of life'. They were concerned about the growth of publicly owned utilities and potential moves to take private utilities into public ownership or, at a minimum, have them heavily regulated.

The private companies and their business allies argued that public ownership was a socialist way of doing things. They argued that free enterprise was the best way to supply water and electricity. They also disliked the way that publicly owned utilities sought to promote social goals through the supply of electricity rather than treat it as a mere commodity. More public-minded individuals argued that electricity and water were essential resources whose cheap and reliable supply was necessary for community welfare and economic growth, and therefore were too important to be left to profit-oriented companies.[2]

The Challenge of Public Power

At the end of the nineteenth century, customers were increasingly unhappy with the poor service, high rates, and a disregard for safety that characterised many of the private utilities. As a result, public utilities gained in popularity; citizens campaigned to have the local government provide their electricity, and several councils took over electricity businesses. By 1888 about 53 cities and towns had municipal systems of electricity. A novel by Edward Bellamy, *Looking Backward*, which described a utopia of municipally owned or 'nationalised' utilities, sold well and gave rise to a number of 'nationalist' clubs, 150 of them by 1890 in 27 states. Public utilities were often set up in areas that were considered uneconomic by private utilities. In this way they made electricity more widely available to the common person.[3]

The private utility bosses opposed public utilities not only because they competed for business but also because they provided an invidious comparison to private utility operations. The public utilities tended to offer electricity at about half the cost of the private companies, and a level of service that was equal to or better than the private utilities.

In Detroit, citizens voted 15,282 to 1,745 for a municipal plant in 1893, but the Detroit Electric Light and Power Company, a subsidiary of General Electric, fought against it, wooing councillors and spreading propaganda. "If the city were to do its own lighting at about half what other companies bid, it would establish a bad precedent", general manager, William H. Fitzgerald, argued, "and other cities that are now lighted by companies owned by General Electric Company would be apt to follow Detroit's example". Indeed, when the city set up its own plant to power its street lights the annual cost went from $132 for each lamp to $63 within a few years.[4]

Some community leaders feared that private ownership of electricity would lead too easily to the corruption of local councils. A mayor of Cleveland, Ohio (1901-09) and campaigner for public power, Tom Johnson, argued that the power companies spent too much time and money attempting to promote sympathetic politicians and influence government in their own interests.[5] He argued for municipal ownership of electricity companies "because if you do not own them, they will in time own you. They will destroy your politics, corrupt your institutions and finally, destroy your liberties".[6]

When Cleveland citizens voted for a municipal electricity system, the private company that supplied most of Cleveland, the Cleveland Electric Light Company, mounted a major campaign of opposition that included giving funds to councillors and the city Republican committee. So, despite the public vote, the council voted against municipal ownership.[7]

The experience in Cleveland was repeated throughout the country where public power was contested in hundreds of towns and small cities. In Massachusetts, a number of cities and towns petitioned the state for the right to produce and distribute electricity and gas. They were opposed by 61 private gas and electricity companies. The attorney for the Boston Gas Light Company called the idea "an excursion into the dark socialistic jungle". The resulting 1891 legislation was not conducive to municipal ownership. It required any municipality wanting to set up its own company, to buy out any private utilities supplying the area. The council had to achieve a two-thirds majority in favour of it two years in a row, and then get majority support from residents. This gave the private utilities time to run their propaganda campaigns and bribe councillors; and then, if that failed, they could delay indefinitely by failing to agree on a price for the acquisition of their operations.[8]

McGuire and Granovetter note in their study of this period that, all over the US:

> Investor-owned utilities responded by attacking NFP [not-for-profit] advocates, bribing city officials, engaging in predatory pricing, convincing General Electric not to sell equipment to cities, or by getting bankers including J.P. Morgan and Marshall Field to sponsor capital boycotts against proposed NFP electric firms.[9]

Despite these tactics, more than 700 public electrical systems were created between 1895 and 1906, and many more populations were pushing for their own public systems. They were increasing at twice the rate of the private utilities. By 1912 a third of the power companies in the US were publicly owned, and most generated their own electricity.[10]

The private electricity companies also competed with each other. Some larger cities encouraged competition in order to keep prices low. In these cities a number of companies put up their wires and poles, making the busiest commercial areas a jungle of electrical connections, whilst other areas were not serviced at all. Competition in some areas was cut-throat, and led to underhand tactics such as the sabotage of equipment. The end results of such competition were mergers or takeovers of defeated competitors.[11]

Large companies that generated electricity for their own operations, particularly the railways, often sold their excess electricity. Apartment buildings and factories that had their own generator also supplied electricity to the immediate neighbourhood. At the end of the nineteenth century and in the first decade of the twentieth century, on-site generators supplied almost two-thirds of electricity in the US, and were major competitors for the electricity companies. Steam and electric co-generation firms also provided competition.[12]

> Smart money favored isolated plants over central power stations. Pushed by J. P. Morgan and other financiers, the new General Electric Company promoted small-scale systems that could be mass-produced and sold at a substantial profit to factories and office buildings.[13]

These early entrepreneurs sold power-generating equipment rather than electricity. "[Thomas] Edison was the first to conceive of selling electricity itself. He saw the growth of the business as dependent on construction of central power stations, each generating and transmitting electric current to hundreds of thousands of customers, all paying operating companies year after year all their lives for a supply of electricity."[14]

The Edison Electric Light Company was also one of the first companies to utilise public relations techniques in economic competition. It used direct current (DC) in the 1880s when Westinghouse Electric's alternating current (AC) systems were becoming popular. More than 130 towns had them installed. Edison tried to discredit the rival AC system, saying that "the first man who touches a wire in a wet place is a dead man. Just as certain as death, Westinghouse will kill a customer within six months after he puts in a system of any size."[15]

Edison, with the help of publicist/engineer Harold Brown, demonstrated the deadly effect of AC on various animals, particularly dogs, and successfully campaigned for electrocution with AC to be used by New York State as a means of execution. It then ran a publicity campaign asking, "Do you want the executioner's current in your home and running through your streets?"[16] They also lobbied state governments against installing AC.

However, DC was unable to transmit electricity over long distances, and AC was cheaper and increasingly favoured. AC companies were able to grow through coverage of larger and larger areas. This, combined with the steam turbine, which generated large amounts of electricity in one plant, facilitated the centralisation of electricity systems. (In 1892 Edison merged his company with an AC company to form the General Electric Company.[17])

It was the central power station with its associated transmission network that made electricity into a natural monopoly. The idea of natural monopolies is that some businesses require such high capital investment in infrastructure that monopolies are more efficient because they avoid duplication of expensive infrastructure and can take advantage of necessary economies of scale.

Political Strategies

In the nineteenth century, industry leaders got what they wanted by funding politicians. The railroad companies did it to get land grants, subsidies, and tax cuts. It was so common that one congressman complained in 1873 that the "House of Representatives was like an auction room where more valuable considerations were disposed of under the speaker's hammer than any other place on earth."[18]

The power companies also resorted to 'political donations', but their need to operate at the local level made the results more unpredictable. They also felt they were losing the battle against public utilities. The person who showed them the way out of these dilemmas was Samuel Insull, a master strategist who had started his electrical career as personal secretary to Thomas Edison.[19]

Insull was a firm believer in the value of monopolies. He recognised that competition was not good for business in the electricity industry because it meant duplication of lines and power plants, and this kept costs high. He bought out his competition in Chicago — some twenty other companies — creating a virtual monopoly for himself by 1907, which he named Commonwealth Edison. Insull built up his empire by offering cheap rates to large customers in areas covered by competitors. These rates were subsidised by other Insull customers. The rival utility would lose a large part of its rates base to the Insull company, and thereby become vulnerable to takeover. This tactic was common to many of the larger, predatory utilities.[20]

Insull argued that monopolies were more efficient and that, if companies were given exclusive control of a particular territory, they could provide a better, cheaper service. If power companies had a legal monopoly and were not subject to the whims of politicians who could withdraw franchises when they felt like it, the companies would be able to borrow money more cheaply because investors would be more assured of getting the money back. Also, they wouldn't have to compete with other power companies in the same region for capital.[21] However, the public was wary of private monopolies because of past abuses, particularly by the railway and oil companies.

By 1898 Insull was president of both major electric-utility trade associations — the Association of Edison Illuminating Companies (AEIC) and the National Electric Light Association (NELA) — when he told a NELA convention that the promotion of regulated monopolies was the way to hinder the formation of public utilities. There would be less need for public ownership if regulation ensured that the public got a fair deal. Regulation would also give legitimacy to private monopolies and head off the call for more competition in the industry to prevent excesses and overcharging.[22]

The executives of the private utilities were sceptical. To some, competition — or at least the appearance of it — was supposed to be the heart of capitalism. But Insull, who was building a vast utilities empire, was not someone to be dismissed easily as a socialist. He was a big-time capitalist, and he had demonstrated in Chicago that large private utilities had sufficient power and resources to get their own way with regulators when it came to rates and profits.[23]

The other utilities came to see the wisdom of Insull's strategy as the threat of increased regulation loomed. In 1907 NELA published a report admitting that some sort of regulation was inevitable, and that the issue was not whether there should be regulation but what form it should take. Regulation was preferable to public ownership of utilities, which some reformers were advocating.[24]

The regulation that NELA sought was really about protecting the future profits of private utilities and minimising competition with them. To achieve this end, the National Civic Federation (NCF) undertook a study. The NCF (formed in 1900) was made up of business leaders and government officials, journalists, academics, and union leaders who were opposed to socialism and too much government intervention. Its members included Insull, Andrew Carnegie, the president of Consolidated Gas, and several partners in J. P. Morgan, which now controlled General Electric.[25]

The NCF set up a Commission on Public Ownership to undertake the study, which took two years and was published in 1907. Whilst seeking to appear objective, the study had particular ends in mind. Participants were carefully selected from the utilities, banks, railroads, unions, manufacturers, and professions. The study was largely funded by private utilities and their allies, who were told that the contributions would be used "to combat municipal ownership".[26]

Not surprisingly the study's conclusions concurred with Insull's and NELA's prescriptions. It argued that a free market was not always the best way to achieve lowest cost and best service and that, in the case of electricity, state-regulated monopolies would be better. However, the participants were split over the question of ownership. The majority of the committee agreed that publicly owned utilities could be efficient. A strong minority refused to accept this conclusion, and wrote their own conclusion that public utilities were inefficient, "socialistic", and a "threat to democracy".[27]

Insull and other utility leaders argued that public monopolies were inferior because public officials were often corrupt and had little management experience. "And in attempts to maintain low prices, for political reasons, managers might neglect maintenance, refrain from necessary investment in capital equipment, and offer low salaries that would discourage hiring of superior engineers and staff."[28]

Because of these disputes, the report made no conclusions about the merits of public ownership. However, it was the minority, anti-public ownership view that was promoted in speeches by the NCF when it launched the study at a series of dinners that were widely reported in the media. Private power companies in the US and in Britain paid for advance copies of the report to be sent to "hundreds of technical and policy journals and newspapers in each state". They also identified hundreds of government officials, union leaders, and businessmen to whom the report was sent. In this way they were able to impose their own spin on the report before it was more widely published. "Thus, what the Report actually stated was less important than what the public, businessmen, investors, and public officials believed it to have said."[29]

Regulated Monopolies

The NCF drafted model legislation which was promoted by the private utilities in the states where they operated. It was adopted in thirteen states, including New York, Wisconsin, and Massachusetts in 1907.[30] The legislation included the elements favoured by the private utilities:

- State regulation by commission, taking control away from local officials and voters and competing businesses. (Utilities executives like Insull preferred to deal with a state commission than hundreds of local councils with just as many political agendas.)
- Long-term franchise with guaranteed returns based on capital valuation, ensuring that investors and bankers had secure, no-risk investments.
- Natural monopoly, ensuring utilities would not have to keep rates low because they didn't have to compete. Cities wanting public utilities could not set them up in competition with private utilities but would have to buy out the private utilities first.
- "Equal value" of all stocks, ensuring that private utilities that had

inflated the value of their stock to get a higher rate of return would be even more expensive to buy out by cities wanting to run public systems (see next section for more on inflated stock).[31]

In return for their protected monopolies, power companies were obliged to provide a reliable service at a reasonable price to all consumers in their service area, without discrimination. Private power companies were also given special privileges that are normally only available to governments, such as the right to acquire private property (eminent domain) in the course of providing their service, for example, to site generating plants and transmission towers.[32]

Regulators had a dual role. On the one hand, they were supposed to ensure that monopolies provided a good, affordable service and to prevent them from charging excessive rates. On the other hand, they had to ensure that the power companies received enough income from rates to remain financially solvent. The rates were calculated as a percentage return on the value of the utility's assets rather than a fair market value for the supply of electricity based on costs of production.

The institutionalisation of regulated private monopolies gained support from those whose ideology favoured private property rights, particularly from those who would gain from the new arrangements. These included investors who appreciated a secure investment, and large industrial firms which hoped to get cheaper electricity. The private utilities were promising lower per-unit electric rates for large users. Equipment manufacturers would gain because guaranteed returns on assets would give utilities an incentive to buy equipment to increase their capital value. Equipment manufactures often also owned stock in private utilities that had been given in partial payment for equipment. The proposed arrangements also suited leaders of the unions because guaranteed returns were calculated after operating expenses, including labour costs, had been deducted, which meant that there was no incentive for the private utilities to keep wages down, to minimise employee levels, or to push for greater productivity.[33]

The regulation and harnessing of large companies for community benefit also suited the progressive ideology of reformers of the time. And many consumers were optimistic that the new system would protect the public.[34] However, not everyone was fooled by the apparent public-interest nature of the legislation. Daniel Hoan, the mayor of Milwaukee, stated:

> No shrewder piece of political humbuggery and downright fraud has ever been placed upon the statute books. It's supposed to be legislation for the people. In fact, it's legislation for the power oligarchy.[35]

And, according to historian Gregg Jarrell, it was in the states where competition was most healthy and rates were lowest that regulation was first
adopted.[36]

By 1911 public opposition was gathering momentum in the face of high
rates and the obvious weakness of the state commissions with respect to regulating the private utilities. A further NCF study was initiated, aimed at creating "a model bill" that would prevent the mobilisation of support "for
government ownership and operation of public utilities". Lobbying by the
private utilities ensured that another seventeen states adopted state-regulated
monopolies over the next two years.[37] Others followed in the next decade: by
1922, 37 states had regulatory commissions to oversee private electric utilities.[38] Insull had, as he put it himself, helped to "shape the right kind of legislation before the wrong kind was forced upon him".[39]

The new regulations protected the private utilities from those seeking to
compete. They also blunted the call for public ownership, since regulation
was supposed to protect the interests of the public. And they caused a marked
shift from small, industry-based generating plant and municipal provision to
large, private, state-regulated monopolies. This was in contrast to countries in
Europe, where governments were giving up on trying to regulate utilities and
were turning to public ownership.[40]

State commissions, which also regulated other public utilities besides electricity, turned out to be easily influenced by utility demands for higher rates,
as Insull had predicted. The power companies employed "battalions of
lawyers to monitor state regulation and legislation" and deployed campaign
contributions, lobbyists, and public relations experts to influence it (see chapter 2).[41]

Hirsh notes in his history of the power industry that, "As the prestige of
the commissions declined, so did the quality of the people who served on
them".[42] They were poorly paid, and often received their appointments
because of their support for the governor and their acceptability to the utilities. The commissions increasingly became "dumping grounds for political
hacks and cronies of the governor."[43]

As a result, the regulators were easily 'captured' by those they regulated. It
was easy enough for the power companies to offer incentives, including jobs
with the utilities when terms of office expired. Former commissioners often
ended up as utility executives. The utilities invited commissioners to attend
their conventions as guests and speakers, and deliberately set about maintaining friendly relations with both the commissioners and their staffs. They also
funded campaigns to support the election or appointment of commissioners

they thought would be sympathetic. And when they had served their terms, the private companies sometimes provided funds to help them with their further political aspirations. For example, Insull admitted contributing $272,000 to the Senate campaign of Frank Smith, who was chair of the regulatory commission of Illinois in 1926.[44]

In this and other ways the power companies ensured that there was a close relationship between themselves and the commissions set up to regulate them. The effect of the regulation was therefore "to set a guaranteed floor under utility rates and profits", rather than providing a limit on rates in the public interest.[45] An article in *The American City* in 1921 stated:

> The public is dissatisfied with the creature it has created. It is not keeping rates for gas, water, electricity, trolleys, and telephones down, but constantly permitting them to mount higher and higher ... Thus, that which was the protection of the public a few years ago is now considered by the public to be its menace, and that which, in the mind of the utility operator, menaced the life of the utility and took away its individuality and independence is now its protector.[46]

When consumers complained about the utilities to the commissions, they not only had to deal with the frequent pro-utility bias of the commissioners, but they were up against the vast resources of the power companies. The companies could spend whatever they wanted making their case, and then pass the cost on to consumers. They had the best lawyers and the best technical experts; there were few electrical experts willing to testify against the companies who employed them or might give them work in the future. The companies could appeal decisions made by the state regulators in the courts, and tie up the case for years.[47]

Nevertheless, it was important to power companies, for public relations reasons, that the commissions appeared to be regulating effectively. They therefore frequently complained about the heavy burden that the commissions placed on them. And through outlets such as the magazine *Electrical World* they publicly exaggerated the role of the regulators in keeping them efficient, rates low, and services reliable.[48]

The power companies even defended the commissions when they came under attack. In 1923, for example, there were attempts in six states to abolish the state commissions and return control to local government. These were successfully opposed by the utilities and their allies. In Tennessee, both candidates for governor had made campaign promises that they would abolish the public utilities commission, and the bill passed the house with a vote of 72 to

fourteen. However, "only the concerted activity of every public utility industry in the state saved the Commission in the Senate, the repeal bill being
tabled by a vote of 18 to 11." In Missouri, the movement to abolish the state's
regulatory commission had the support of some newspapers; the bill was only
lost by one vote in the House of Representatives, and "that vote was a recon-
sidered one".[49]

The utilities had not forgotten the reason for having the state regulatory
commissions in the first place. This can be seen in the title of a 1926 report
by the Public Policy Committee of NELA, chaired by Martin J. Insull: "State
Regulation Through Commissions Urged as a Method of Combating Public
Ownership and Operation".[50] The strategy worked remarkably well, and the
electricity companies went on to expand and build power empires.

Holding Companies

With state-guaranteed monopolies, electric utility companies expanded, and
consolidated their power and influence. They remained vertically integrated
—that is, they incorporated generation, transmission, distribution, and retail
supply to customers within the one company. The improvement of transmission technologies allowed electricity to be carried for hundreds of miles.
Smaller companies could not compete and were swallowed up.[51] Because rates
were based on the value of assets, it made sense to continually increase those
assets; so growth became the goal of the electricity monopolies. Economies of
scale meant that additional customers could lower the cost of supplying electricity per customer.

Electricity companies grew through mergers and acquisitions, and by forming holding companies. The holding company incorporated several operating
companies within its structure, and issued stocks and bonds using the assets of
those operating companies as collateral.[52] The network of giant holding companies that dominated the electricity industry soon became known as the
Power Trust. As a result of their power and interstate range, holding companies
tended to be beyond the regulatory reach of the state utility commissions.

The holding companies became a means for a few people to increase their
wealth and power at the expense of the operating companies that provided
the electricity. As a result, electricity consumers paid much more than necessary for their electricity. The holding companies charged operating companies
inflated prices for financial, managerial, fuel, construction, and engineering
services, and these "inflated prices were then passed on to the ratepayer as
higher rates."[53] For example the Federal Trade Commission (FTC) found that
the American Gas and Electric Company had charged $2,228,000 up to the

end of 1928 for engineering and supervising fees for work that had cost them $586,000, giving them a profit of 279 per cent.[54]

Holding companies also charged extortionate fees for mergers and reorganisations of companies under them, and very large commissions for selling stock on their behalf. Such fees affected the rates electricity customers paid because the utilities' rate of return was calculated after operating expenses such as these were deducted.[55]

Since the profits of the utilities were limited to 8 per cent "by laws, court decisions, and the influence of public opinion", it was in the companies' interests to hide higher returns by artificially increasing the value of their investments. Holding companies did this through reappraisals and a variety of accounting strategies. Such 'write-ups' were referred to as stock watering. They concealed actual earnings on investment that could be as high as 40 per cent, and occasionally as high as 600 per cent.[56] If the public had known the real rates of return they would have demanded a reduction in their rates from the public commissions or the courts.

Stock watering was denied in all the power-company literature: "There is not enough water in the stock of all the power companies of the State of Missouri to wash a baby's face."[57] However, a federal inquiry uncovered stock watering as a regular feature of holding company operations. In 1932 Senator George W. Norris estimated that the value of the inflation that had been discovered by the FTC to that time was just under a billion dollars: "With investigations only partially finished, the Federal Trade Commission have disclosed write-ups in round numbers to the amount of $926,000,000.00, upon which the poor people, the common people, must pay a profit for all time ..."[58]

Power in the industry was concentrated through shared directorships and common ownership of stock. For example, in 1928 the Electric Bond and Share Company and its directors and officers owned 23 per cent of the voting stock of the American Power and Light Company, 19 per cent of the stock of the Electric Power and Light Corporation, 40 per cent of that of the National Power and Light Company, and 25 per cent of that of the American Gas and Electric Company, as well as stock in other companies.[59]

Concentration of control was further facilitated through interlocking and overlapping boards of directors. Power companies frequently shared common directors. For example, Sidney Z. Mitchell chaired the board of directors for the American Power and Light Company, the Electric Power and Light Corporation, and the National Power and Light Company; as well, he was a director of nineteen other companies, seven of which were not in the Electric

Bond and Share group. C.E. Groesbeck, vice-president of the Electric Bond and Share Company, was also a director of 31 companies.[60]

The Electric Bond and Share Company, owned by General Electric (GE), was formed by banker J. P. Morgan. According to historians Rudolph and Ridley, "Though the Morgan interests failed twice in attempts to take over the entire industry, his financial empire was to play a key role in its development …"[61] They note:

> In a larger sense most people have no idea of the role Wall Street firms and banks have played as silent partners in the power empire, the degree to which the money managers have shaped its course, and the stake they have in the industry's future … the course of the industry has been shaped as much by the need and interests of its main stockholders and financiers as by the demand created for electricity.[62]

The way the holding companies were structured meant that someone like Insull could control hundreds of electric companies, worth half a billion dollars in 1930, with an investment of only $27 million.[63] Other electricity holding companies, such as GE, were structured in the same way. Five hundred independent companies were swallowed up into Pacific Gas & Electric (PG&E). This put an end to financial competition between gas and electricity by combining them into one company that remained the largest private utility in the US into the 1990s.[64]

Figure 1 below shows how common stockholders in a holding company could collectively invest $12.5 million to control operating companies worth $1000 million and receive a return of $17.25 million in one year. Some holding companies had five layers of companies within them to maximise this process. In one case, an investment of $1 million was increased to $45 million over 24 years, and was able to control assets worth $375 million. In the most extreme case of this sort of concentration, the Electric Bond and Share Company made 3,102 per cent on its investments in the Southeastern Power and Light Company in 1927 when dividends of $148,800 were paid on stock that cost $4,795.95.[65]

By doing this sort of thing over and over, Insull built his empire to include 248 companies, selling electricity to more than 6 million people in 4,741 communities in 30 states, generating 9.5 per cent of the electricity in the US. His empire also included coal, railroad, and construction companies, and a radio station in Chicago. It was one of the largest conglomerations of power companies in the US. By 1929 Insull had a personal fortune of $150 million (at a time when a Ford motor car cost $700). He was president of eleven companies, chairman of 65, and a director of 85.[66]

Figure 1.1: Concentration of profits and voting power in holding companies

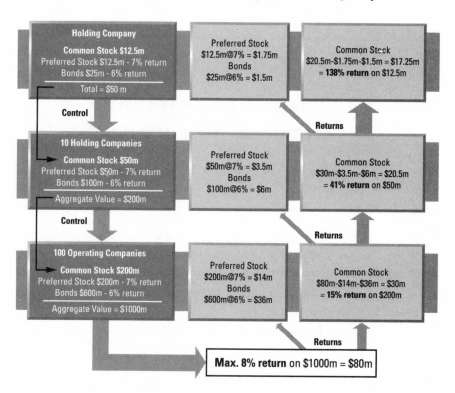

The figure shows how the 8 per cent return that each operating company earns is used to give non-voting stockholders (or preferred stock holders) a 7 per cent return and bond-holders a 6 per cent return. The remainder goes to common stockholders, and amounts to a 15 per cent return for them. However, this 15 per cent is again concentrated up the next level of companies. It is again divided with preferred stockholders and bondholders getting 7 and 6 per cent return respectively whilst the common stockholder gets the remaining money, which amounts to a 41 per cent return. The process is repeated at the top level and common stock holders end up with a 138 per cent return on their investment.[67]

CHAPTER TWO

Power Propaganda
Between The Wars

*[T]here has been in the past few years, as the Federal Trade Commission has
shown, a systematic, subtle, deliberate and unprincipled campaign of mis-
information, of propaganda, and, if I may use the words, of lies and falsehoods.*
Franklin D. Roosevelt, in 1932,
referring to a decade-long electricity industry propaganda campaign[1]

THE ELECTRIC POWER COMPANIES and their associations are masters of public relations, as has been demonstrated by their success in promoting deregulation in the 1990s. However, at no time have their public relations strategies
been so well documented and exposed as during the Federal Trade
Commission (FTC) inquiry of 1928-1934. It produced 95 volumes of
findings, mainly based on the testimony and documents of the private utilities, which give a unique and revealing insight into how the industry operates
with respect to shaping public opinion.

One of the key reasons for the survival and growth of private power companies in the twentieth century with very little government interference,
despite growing evidence of their extortionate practices, and popular movements for public control and ownership, was the effectiveness of their massive, coordinated, public relations campaigns. The scale and scope of these
campaigns were unprecedented anywhere in the world.

As we saw in the previous chapter, the private power companies had used
their full economic and political force to oppose public power in the first
decades of the twentieth century. They promoted the management of private
utilities as being superior and leading to lower costs and better service. They

portrayed their employees as public servants.[2] However, following the First World War, despite being regulated monopolies, the power companies were subject to increasing public criticism and revelations of holding company abuses. As a result, they were concerned that state or federal governments would move to introduce further regulation, or even nationalise the industry.

To head this off, the utilities "launched a nation-wide propaganda campaign to educate the American public about the dangers to the American Way of Life that would come if the utilities were ever allowed to slip from private enterprise to public control."[3] The private utilities sought to manufacture popular opposition to government ownership and to more effective regulation of power company activities.

The reasons for preferring a grassroots campaign aimed at the public and community leaders rather than a political lobbying campaign were outlined by J. B Mulaney, the director of the utilities' multi-million dollar campaign:

(T)o depend year after year on the usual political expedients for stopping hostile government legislation is short sightedness. In the long run, isn't it better and surer to lay the groundwork with the people back home who have the votes, so that proposals of this character are not popular with them, rather than depend upon stopping such proposals when they get to the legislature or commission.[4]

The work of the utilities' propaganda committees (as they were called) "laid the ground work" to such an extent that the FTC's investigation of the power companies revealed a nationwide propaganda operation that had been concealed from the public and reached into almost every avenue of American culture. Aimed at every group of people in every city across the country, the FTC concluded that "no campaign approaching it in magnitude has ever been conducted except possibly by governments in war time"[5] In the words of one of the industry's own representatives, they did "much to change and direct the economic thought and economic practice of the American people".[6]

The activities of the various utilities were coordinated by the National Electric Light Association (NELA), which had been formed in 1885 and covered private utilities throughout the US and Canada. NELA had an annual budget of one million dollars. In addition, it had funds for special purposes such as its advertising budget of $25-30 million per year. It employed 98 people, and included a public information department of fourteen people as well as an associated public relations national section with its own executive committee and geographic division representatives. This section had eight subcommittees on a variety of themes, including a Co-operation with Educational Institutions Committee, a Public Speaking Committee, a Woman's Committee, and an Industrial Relations Committee.[7]

Samuel Insull played a leading part in the propaganda drive as president of NELA. Insull had been impressed by publicist Phineas T. Barnum when Barnum had visited England in 1878, and when Insull came to the US to work for Edison he looked Barnum up and familiarised himself with Barnum's techniques.[8] Insull recognised the value of community good will early on. He was one of the first to institute annual corporate reports, and he created the industry's first advertising department in 1901. He promoted electricity use through a pamphlet he distributed to Chicago stores.[9]

During the First World War English-born Insull had utilised a state committee he headed, the Illinois State Council for Defense, as a propaganda outlet aimed at getting the Americans to support England in the war. It tailored press releases and speakers to rally patriotic feelings in citizens to get them to buy Liberty bonds. $1.3 billion worth of bonds were sold.[10]

After the war, Insull turned the Illinois State Council of Defense into a Committee on Public Utility Information. He used the same techniques and many of the same personnel to oppose public power, which was enjoying a renewed popularity after the war, and to regain public support for the private power companies, which were in bad odour because of rate rises at a time that other consumer prices were falling. "Insull borrowed the propaganda machinery he had used during the war and sought to equate patriotism with a favorable attitude toward utilities."[11]

Similar utility propaganda committees were set up in other states. NELA set up a committee to coordinate these state committees; and Insull's committee was taken over by NELA in 1921, when it created information committees for every state.[12] These 'public information' committees:

> distributed literature to newspapers, libraries, schools and fraternal orders. They dispatched speakers to clubs, forums, even to churches. They buttonholed legislators and public officials. College professors, students, editors, lecturers, were secretly placed on utilities payroll. Research was subsidized, and university funds replenished. Textbooks that told the truthful history of utilities finance were censored, and more agreeable writings procured in their place. A relentless campaign was conducted against the Bolshevik heresy of public ownership.[13]

NELA funded its activities with money raised through annual dues charged to member power companies, which in turn passed the cost on to ratepayers. Each state committee produced a barrage of literature, including leaflets, pamphlets, booklets, bulletins, and reports. The Illinois Committee on Public Utility Information alone, distributed more than five million pieces of literature within its first two years of operation.[14]

The campaign utilised smear tactics, and appealed to patriotic feeling rather than reason. Utility representatives were advised "not to argue with the advocates of public ownership but to arouse prejudice against them by pinning on them the bolshevik idea."[15] Henry Swift Ives summed up the campaign argument in a speech to NELA:

> The key issue in America today is whether the American people desire to preserve the institution of individual rights in property or substitute therefor community ownership supervised by a socialist oligarchy. This country can not exist half socialist and half free any more than it could have existed half slave and half free.[16]

The campaign was careful in its use of language. Public ownership became 'political ownership'; private utilities became 'public utilities' or 'public service companies'. Mergers were argued to be necessary because they were more economical and efficient. A holding company, according to Insull, was "more properly an investment company; even more accurately perhaps, a development company."[17]

Third Parties

NELA utilised the now-common technique of getting other third parties to convey their message so that it would not appear to be self-interested. Jack Levin, in *Power Ethics*, a book based on the 1928 FTC inquiry, observed how the utilities induced "the leading institutions and citizens to convey their message". These included "newspapers, schools, colleges, commercial, social, and civic clubs, insurance companies, churches, and other institutions, as well as 'engineers', 'experts,' civic heads, club leaders, educators, government officials, political leaders, bankers, editors, industrialists, and others."[18]

Public relations material was sent to every conceivable outlet. Thousands of lectures and talks were given to business, schools, and other groups. In this way, millions of people were reached each year. Employees were trained in public speaking and given courses in public relations. The recurring message was not only that municipal ownership had been a failure everywhere it had been tried, but also that it threatened American democracy.[19]

Female employees were also used by the utilities to influence the community. The women were trained to promote the utilities with "their friends and neighbours, their associates in business and professional women's organizations, social clubs and church societies."[20] They were taught how to casually bring the conversation round to the issue of utility ownership at social gatherings, so as to give the utility point of view. This view was not to be attributed to the utility, but rather to some other respected (but anonymous) community figure such as "my banker" or "my doctor". One company entertained 10,000 women in just two days at tea parties organised for this purpose.[21]

In some states the utilities managed to get their own women into every woman's club. In the Southwest they prepared playlets, and Oklahoma Gas and Electric Company even had a "girls' quartet" which "was singing its way into the hearts of the people".[22] An executive from that company, and chair of NELA's public relations section, James F. Owens, pointed out:

> We have been making a very great mistake in the past in employing stenographers solely because they could pound typewriters and not because they had the ability to go out and spread the gospel of the public utility business [by which he meant private utility business].
>
> It is about time we awoke to the fact that through women's clubs and through the cultivation of the women in the women's clubs we have one of the greatest avenues for the dissemination of correct information ...[23]

The willingness of utilities to provide real information was indicated by their response to the League of Women Voters, which sent out a questionnaire asking for detailed information about the utilities, such as rates charged and amount of securities owned by local customers. Utilities were advised by NELA neither to answer the questionnaire nor to provide the information sought. Instead the utilities made an effort to win the league over by contacting its leaders and establishing friendly relationships with them.[24]

Employees were encouraged to join clubs to have the opportunity to put utility views and to keep the utilities informed of club activities. The utilities paid for memberships of clubs such as Rotary Clubs, Lions Clubs, Young Men's Business Leagues and Junior Chambers of Commerce. Representatives of the utilities spoke regularly at Kiwanis clubs and they became active in the Boy Scouts and the Girl Scouts. The scouts were even paid to deliver *Utility News,* an outlet for utility propaganda.[25]

NELA and individual companies organised and paid for outings, such as deep-sea fishing, theatre parties, baseball games, and duck-shooting parties, and perks for influential people, including politicians, educators, business people and newspaper editors.[26] It got a range of organisations on side through "various forms of patronage similar to the use of advertising to win over the newspapers". In this way these seemingly independent organisations were persuaded to promote the utility viewpoint.[27]

The power companies and committees were active in various church organisations, gave speeches to church groups and Sunday Schools, and 'organised' church ministers including a "ministerial alliance" in Little Rock, Arkansas. Utility literature was sent to ministers as well as the YMCA and YWCA. One Easter NELA wrote a story about the development of the art of church lighting. According to a NELA director, George Oxley: "There is a lot of good will propaganda worked into the story and it is adaptable everywhere".[28]

Travelling salesmen were also utilised as "travelling evangelists".[29] J. B. Sheridan, director of the Missouri Public Information Committee, proposed in 1921: "We could get them to call upon the country newspapers, pass a little time with the editors, talk the facts of public utility operation, etc. then we could get them talking in the hotels and trains and every other place where they would go." By 1922 there were 30 men travelling "as unpaid, enthusiastic agents" of the Missouri committee. Sheridan then proposed providing these travelling salesmen with a small pamphlet to guide them in "a smoking car or hotel lobby discussion of the public utilities".[30]

The Media

The utility information committees spent an estimated $30 million annually in advertising, which served as a lever to ensure that the utilities could place news items for free when they wanted and to secure editorial loyalty in the general reporting of utility matters.[31] They consciously used their huge advertising budget to reward newspapers that gave them good news coverage, and withheld their advertising from those that were critical of the electric companies. Newspapers were told in advance when an advertising campaign was coming up, and their advertising became "a very large and dependable source of much-needed income" to the newspapers.[32]

Individual companies were also encouraged to advertise as much as possible in local newspapers to attain influence. The expenses were all passed on to the public in the form of prices for utility services.[33] According to a communication from one information committee to member companies: "Advertising done in the regular course of business can doubtless be utilized to engage the editor's interest in the facts of your case."[34]

Media support was also gained in various other ways. In the mid-1920s the Hearst papers ceased their populist front-page stories supporting public ownership of electricity systems after receiving a loan from Herbert Fleishhacker, president of the London and Paris National Bank in San Francisco and a leading advocate of the privatisation of water and electricity. Hearst instructed his employees to maintain "pleasant relations" with Fleishhacker and not criticise his activities.[35]

The utilities even tried to buy up many of the most influential newspapers around the nation so as to control press coverage. At the time newspapers were moving from individualised operations of particular editors to chain newspapers with syndicated content. For example, Ira C. Copley, who owned various utilities in Northern Illinois, also owned various newspapers in his area of operations. In 1928 he set out to buy a chain of fifteen newspapers in southern California, including the *Pasedena Evening Post* and the *San Diego Tribune*.[36] He achieved this by using public utility securities to finance the deal.[37]

When Copley bought the *Illinois State Journal* it was noted that the *Journal* gave minimal coverage to the controversy in which Copley's United Gas and Electric Company was entangled, whereas it was front-page news in the other Springfield paper. The general manager of the municipal utility in Springfield claimed that Copley's Illinois papers "were used to nurse along the people to keep them contented while Copley became immensely wealthy by collecting exorbitant rates for utility service." Copley also used his papers to get re-elected to Congress for six terms.[38]

Copley was not the only one, however, to purchase newspapers for the avenue of communication they offered. Henry L. Doherty, also the head of a large utility company, bought a controlling interest in the *Journal-Post* of Kansas City, Missouri. He wrote editorials in the paper promoting utility interests, and used the paper to defend gas rates.[39]

In 1929 the International Paper and Power Company attempted to buy dozens of newspapers nationwide. One of the men it sent on this mission told those he approached:

> The interests which I represent intend buying 50 or 60 newspapers in the United States from Maine to California. They will probably have five in the New England States, and in the other places they will purchase the key newspaper in these respective towns through the country.[40]

The company purchased a number of newspapers through its agents, including the *Chicago Daily News*, the *Chicago Journal*, *The Knickerbocker Press* and the *Albany Evening News*, the *Boston Herald-Traveler*, and the *Brooklyn Eagle*. It also attempted to buy many other papers; it was unsuccessful, not because of a lack of funds, but because the papers were not for sale.[41]

The utilities tried their hand at radio broadcasting as well. For example,

Edison Company built a radio station and studio on the roof of its office building. It broadcast entertainment and educational programs as well as political opinions, and was considered by the head of public relations for the company as "the greatest builder of good will which the company had ever developed."[42]

The power companies utilised press agencies that sent out news items, editorials, and features to newspapers around the country. Each state committee and the power companies kept the press agencies supplied with pro-utility news and other items. The Missouri committee, for example, claimed that the "Associated Press sends out practically everything we give them. They have 35 newspapers in Missouri. We get matter printed in from 1 to 25 newspapers on one story. Out of the 35 we will average about 13 newspapers printing stories sent out by the Associated Press." It also claimed that only one newspaper out of 600 in Missouri was critical of the electric industry.[43]

Often, information committee members would write an opinion piece and then get a prominent person—a governor, judge, attorney, or club president—to allow his name to be put on it as author. This ensured that newspapers printed them, and provided third-party endorsement for utility views.[44]

The power companies also gave financial support for private press services and paid to have their news items distributed. For example, The Darnall Newspaper Service was heavily supported by the Alabama Power Company. It supplied material to 600 newspapers nationally, and was very much against public ownership in many fields, including electricity. Another service financially supported by the electricity industry was Hofer & Sons Press Service, which supplied 13,000-14,000 newspapers around the nation. Its materials, mainly pre-written editorials, also opposed government participation in business, including electricity. The editorials were sent out free, and editors would print them as their own. Then NELA would clip them out and reproduce them as evidence of wide public support for its position.[45]

Education

Local managers were expected "to cultivate personal acquaintance with the school superintendents, teachers, to arrange for [private utility] lectures, offering prizes, making use of school papers."[46] The aim of propaganda in schools was, according to Insull, to "fix the truth about the utilities in the young person's mind before incorrect notions become fixed there."[47] One writer noted in 1951:

The impressively successful event of the public utility propaganda all over the country was such that many a schoolboy of that period still remembers that it was considered all but subversive even to intimate in a history or civics class that the utilities were not the greatest benefactors of mankind since history's dawn.[48]

However, the industry had to tone down its propaganda for the schools, as a public information committee chairman told a NELA meeting in 1924:

Some individual companies and various state committees on public utility information have profited by the opportunity of furnishing schools with textbooks on public utility problems. To be acceptable to school authorities and to be really effective, reading matter for schools should be free of *direct* propaganda. Plain instruction in fact about public utilities will be unobjectionable to school authorities and will accomplish the purpose of disseminating correct information and arousing the interest and friendliness of the students. Motion pictures also offer excellent opportunity for reaching school children ...[49] [my italics]

The utilities prepared many booklets for schools with thinly disguised propaganda. For example, one claimed: "in every case in which a community has attempted to operate a public service industry, it has been found that the costs of the service are higher than when the service is furnished by a private corporation".[50] This was clearly not the case, as will be discussed in the next chapter. The school literature frequently associated advocacy of public ownership with socialism and Bolshevism. And it repeatedly implied that private power companies were owned by the public because members of the public owned stock in the utilities, or had bank deposits and life insurance with banks and insurance companies that invested in utility securities.[51] For example:

The public service companies are owned in large part by the public generally, by persons of small means who own in small amounts bonds and stocks of the companies ... many of whom are widows and orphans.[52]

A series of four booklets on "Our Public Utilities" was distributed by the tens of thousands in schools in Illinois, Missouri, Pennsylvania, and Ohio, for example. More than three in every four schools in Illinois used utility materials in their classes.[53] Kindergarten children were not left out. A 32-page colour booklet, *The Ohm Queen*, was distributed to 400,000 kindergarten children to tell them about the wonders of electricity.[54]

The utilities also did their best to influence textbooks, which were a more permanent form of public relations. They did this by hiring or subsidising sympathetic authors from various universities and by pressuring publishers of other books to remove or change passages they didn't approve of, and to "update" texts using "practical men" whom the private utilities recommended. Some authors submitted the proofs of their books to NELA for approval, and NELA managed to get leading textbook publishers to do the same. Approved books which said that private ownership was the ideal were then promoted by NELA, which also helped to market them.[55]

NELA committees surveyed school textbooks all over the USA, particularly those on economics and civics, and "spent thousands of dollars criticizing university and high school texts that they considered unfavorable to private utilities".[56] Sheridan wrote:

> I have recently completed a survey of standard textbooks upon civics and economics used in the public schools in several states, and a survey of educational tendencies in the schools, and I am irresistibly driven to the conclusion that the chief effort of the public schools appears to be manufacture and production of socialists and communists.[57]

Textbooks were considered bad and socialist if they even reported that anyone held the view that the system of regulated private monopolies was anything but beneficial to the public, or that public ownership was more appropriate in a monopoly situation. In some cases, the utilities managed to get particular sentences removed from textbooks. For example, the following sentence was removed from *Community Life and Civic Problems*: "As late as 1926 a man then serving as the president of a number of electric light companies in the Middle West gave in a single primary election over $200,000 to the campaign funds of candidates of both parties." Mention of the success of public ownership in Europe or in some cities in the US was also targeted for deletion.[58]

The power companies used their influence to have undesirable texts removed altogether by lobbying local school boards.[59] Many of the state committees adopted this tactic successfully. The Iowa committee boasted: "after three years' work most of the really objectionable textbooks have been eliminated".[60]

Electric power and telephone utilities also commissioned their own textbooks: "By subsidizing a series of books—each citing prior ones—the utilities created a spurious body of authoritative works from which unsuspecting students would draw materials."[61] Such textbooks included statements such as "Public utilities [by which was meant private utilities] are properly and thoroughly regulated".[62] Textbooks were written for colleges and universities as well as schools.[63]

NELA funded the Institute of Research in Land Economics and Public Utilities, which prepared many textbooks on utilities. NELA also paid Professor James Mavor when he was writing a book discrediting the publicly owned Ontario Hydro-Electric Power System, and spent more distributing the book. In another case the utilities funded Professor E. A. Stewart of the University of Minnesota, who also did a study on the Ontario system that was hailed all over the country as an impartial study.[64]

Universities were offered financial assistance to gain their cooperation in ensuring that courses were conducive to private power company interests.[65] NELA also encouraged and subsidised courses on utilities. This was often not done directly, but by using people who appeared to be independent. Internal correspondence within the NELA demonstrates this:

> I feel that you will not get quite the results you wish if you go direct to the educa-
> tors yourself. In this state, while the idea originated in the committee, it reaches
> the colleges and universities through a man high in educational circles who
> broached the subject without mentioning the public utilities [ie private utilities] as
> being interested. Therefore, the colleges on their own volition developed the idea
> and the committee volunteered to render all possible assistance.[66]

Additionally, the utilities sponsored national educational conferences where university professors who received utility funding put their views (without revealing their interest). Such conferences were "designed primarily to establish utility courses and secure the adoption of texts that will teach that subject from the private-utility point of view".[67] The content of such courses was carefully monitored. For example, lecturers were advised not to use the word 'profit' in relation to utilities, as the power companies insisted that their guaranteed return on assets was not a profit.[68]

In Rocky Mountain, an educational committee was set up with a member of the faculty of each college in the state to help the utilities get subjects on utilities into courses and as topics for debating societies:

> I feel that we will make a three strike in this activity, as we will educate, to some
> extent, the members of the faculty who need such education, while at the same
> time assist in molding the opinions of the students and reaching a given part of
> the public through debates.[69]

The utilities ensured that people who supported the private utilities gained teaching positions in the universities. At the University of Colorado, some 24 power company executives became members of the faculty, and they prepared nine major subjects. The power companies gave grants and consultancies to professors, and sponsored their research, in order to get other faculty on side.[70]

The power companies also sponsored students and funded fellowships. This enabled the companies to get spokespeople who were able to speak with "all the dignity and prestige" that is normally attached to a university. For example, Hubert P. Wolfe received one such fellowship. The executive manager of the Rocky Mountain Division said of this fellowship: "This committee, of course, closely scrutinized his credentials, and intellectual leanings ... Thus far we have been engaged in imparting to Mr. Wolfe a practical utility viewpoint ..."[71]

One committee noted: "There ought to be some way in which they [under-paid teachers] could be better paid... with a view to changing their point of view on these economic subjects..."[72] The power companies often employed university professors to conduct surveys or give lectures and paid their expenses to attend utility meetings and conventions. In return they were expected to support the private utilities at regulatory commission and other hearings.[73]

In 1923 the managing director of NELA, M. H. Aylesworth, said:

> I would advise any manager here who lives in a community where there is a college to get the professor of economics ... interested in your problems. Have him lecture on your subject to his classes. Once in a while it will pay you to take such men and give them a retainer of one or two hundred dollars per year for the privilege of letting you study and consult with them.[74]

Similarly, the Rev Dr. Charles A. Eaton, member of Congress, president of the American Educational Association, and a manager of industrial relations at General Electric, told NELA in 1924:

> Here is a professor in a college who gets $2,500 a year and has to spend $3,000 to keep from starving to death, who walks up to his classroom in an old pair of shoes and some idiot of a boy drives up and parks a $5,000 automobile outside and comes in and gets plucked. Then because that professor teaches that boy that there is something wrong with the social system, we call him a Bolshevik and throw him out.
>
> What I would like to suggest to you intelligent gentlemen is that while you are dealing with the pupils, give a thought to the teachers and when their vacation comes, pay them a salary to come into your plants and into your factories and learn the public utility business at first hand, and then they will go back and you needn't fuss—they can teach better than you can.[75]

Lecturers who failed to fall into line with utility views were subject to attack. One such lecturer, Professor E.W. Bemis, who taught extension courses to the public, was targeted by NELA, which insisted that he be stopped:

> Above all else I think we have a right to insist that the mere charlatan who, infatu-ated with his own glibness of expression, goes out on extensive lecture trips, shall be curbed by his institution ... I think, no honest university man will claim that as a function of any university, and we can be charged with no interference of aca-demic control.[76]

Friends and Allies

A further part of the campaign was to encourage the public to buy shares in the utilities. In this way, more people would want to see the utilities do well as this would increase the value of their shares. This attitude could be rein-forced by public relations material that accompanied the dividend payments. Wide share ownership by the community could be promoted as a substitute for public ownership. "In the new language of utilities, 'real public owner-ship' meant customer ownership, not political ownership."[77] Any other form of public ownership was socialism.

'Customer ownership'—that is, selling power company bonds and securi-ties and shares to the public—was originally used as a way to raise money when banks were reluctant to lend. But it soon became a very useful public relations tool. NELA called it "an extraordinarily clever and astute flank attack upon the forces which advocate and fight for public ownership". Selling shares to consumers created, according to NELA's customer ownership committee, "A stalwart army of sound-thinking owners of private property" which was "the nation's greatest defense against socialism or communism—and every step toward public ownership is a step toward communism."[78] Customers who bought securities became "an army of friends for utilities":

> Once these plain people added their voices to the hue and cry of denunciation of the utility raised by the professional agitators, socialists, and public ownership advocates. Today they say with pride, 'This is my company; I'm one of its stock-holders!'.[79]

These ownership drives were successful, in part because of the success of the power companies in portraying themselves as trustworthy companies where investment would be safe. Insull increased the number of shareholders in Illinois utilities from 50,000 in 1919 to 500,000 in 1921, using advertisements that stressed their security. Previously, banks had sold bonds to large investors, and the idea of selling to the public was new: "a major innovation in corporate finance".[80]

NELA argued that 'customer ownership' provided real public ownership through direct investment, so public ownership through government was unnecessary. Of course, these 'customer owners' could not vote at general meetings, since it was mainly bonds, securities, or non-voting stock that they invested in. Nor were they otherwise able to exercise any ownership control over the companies.[81] In reality, all they were doing was lending money to the power companies; and, in the end, the companies turned out not to be the safe investment they portrayed.

The power companies even courted children as 'customer owners'. Not only did they encourage children to be future investors, but they also gave a sentimental value to the stock so that parents who bought some in their children's name were more likely to keep it. The chairman of one of NELA's customer ownership committees wrote to NELA's managing director in 1925:

I believe that you appreciate the great psychological value of having minors as stockholders ... I know that it has been your personal experience if you once buy something for your children, and place it in their names, it immediately takes on a sentimental aspect that the balance of your properties do not possess ... This is one field of investment that is of importance to us, for a new crop of investors is being born every day.[82]

One of the largest groupings of utility shareholders were the insurance companies which invested a large proportion of their funds in utilities, believing them to be a secure investment. In the mid-1920s life insurance companies alone had some $800 million invested in public utility securities. Insurance companies were therefore natural allies of the private power companies, "bound by the compulsion of economic and financial necessity" to support them.[83] For example, the president of the Metropolitan Life Insurance company wrote a letter that was distributed with premium notices to some 21 million policy holders that said, in part:

every policy holder is *ipso facto* a capitalist, and an attack upon capital investments is an attack upon the wage earners of the country ... Plans for municipal, state, or federal ownership of public utilities often sound well as presented by their advocates ... The late President Harding said truthfully: 'There should be less government in business and more business in government.'

The ownership of the electric light and power companies is now in the hands of more than two million direct investors in public utility stocks and indirectly in the hands of millions more of bank depositors and holders of life insurance polices through their ownership of public utility bonds. This is true people's ownership under proper public regulation, and the function of government is not to own and operate such utilities but to regulate them under the police powers of the state.[84]

Metropolitan Life Insurance also used the text of the letter in advertising in popular magazines and newspapers.[85] Similarly, the Casualty Information Clearing House distributed a message in support of private power companies via its 30,000 agents. The message was in support of the fight against the "public ownership menace", and argued:

> As a matter of fact the insurance investments industry represent a collective ownership of industry by insurance policy holders ... And it is these industries which must be saved from socialization if the insurance policy holder desires to protect his investments in insurance ... The foundation of our national prosperity rests upon private enterprise ... No class of people is more vitally concerned with maintaining the integrity of the private enterprise system than is the class composed of insurance-policy owners.[86]

NELA also had natural and powerful allies in the banking sector. Utilities were an attractive investment because of their very high returns (which were concealed from the public, as described in the previous chapter, by stock watering and inflation of accounts). On Wall Street, the power companies were known as the "dividend machines" because they required such large amounts of investment and produced regular and reliable dividends, as well as a rapid increase in the value of the investment.[87] About a third of all industrial financing went to power companies in the 1920s.[88]

Bankers sat on the boards of directors of the power companies, and in some cases owned them.[89] But, in addition to this, NELA made a special effort to nurture relationships with the banks. It had a special committee "to encourage understanding and establish cordial relations between the public utility industry and financial institutions" and particularly with local bankers.[90] The best way of doing this was through having deposits in local banks. The president of the Pacific Gas and Electric Company, A.F. Hockenbeamer, outlined the strategy in a letter:

> we have at this time accounts with 230 country banks scattered all over our territory, and while our policy keeps an average of around a million and a half dollars tied up in balances in these country depositaries, we believe it is well worth while: First, because the service they render to us as banker is worth something, and secondly, because it cements their friendship and co-operation. Incidentally, we require no interest on these deposits … My impression is that other power companies in California follow pretty much the same policies as I have above outlined … I would like you to treat this as a personal communication … We have already been suspected of undue connivance with bankers.[91]

The utilities also made sure that they maintained friendly relations with the managers and directors — "usually influential business and professional men" — and the personnel of the banks, and this was augmented by bank visits from head office executives. As a result, the bankers "became, and still are, boosters for our stock and an effective influence in spreading its sale".[92]

Bankers were helpful in supporting legislation that the power companies wanted passed. A NELA officer noted: "Personally, I have had the greatest success by using them as speakers before legislative committees regarding legislation." Similarly, James F. Owen, chairman of NELA's public relations section, urged utilities to make contact "with every banker in the country. No man outside of an editor has greater influence on the public opinion in the communities we serve than the local banker …"[93]

Other natural allies included electrical-equipment manufacturers and fuel companies that sold the coal and, in later times, oil and natural gas that ran the power plants. Together with the banks and investment houses "these companies made up the core of what was commonly recognized as an electric power empire bound together by a common belief that the prosperity of the nation, as well as their own success, was tied to maximum increase in the use of electricity" supplied by private companies. The American Gas Association, for example, worked with the public utility information committees to oppose government ownership of electric utilities.[94]

NELA joined with the American Gas Association and the American Electric Railway Association to form the Joint Committee of the National Utilities Associations. In addition, NELA enlisted the support of other utility companies that supplied water, telegraph and telephone services, and street car lines.[95]

NELA also had special committees "for the purpose of interesting and securing the support and co-operation of other forces and influences outside of the utility field". Cheap rates to key industrialists, subsidised by other ratepayers, ensured their political support, as did interlocking directorates and strategic investments in outside enterprises.[96] Carl D. Thompson, in his summary of the testimony given at the 1928 FTC inquiry, describes the "titanic power" of the electric companies as:

> concentric circles of power with the utilities at the center; their various committees reaching out over their radii to every circle in the mighty network of financial, industrial, economic, and cultural organizations of the country and tieing them into the web of their system by incorrigible bonds of economic, financial, and industrial necessity.[97]

CHAPTER THREE

Struggle For Control Before The Second World War

Nothing like this gigantic monopoly has ever appeared in the history of the world. Nothing has been imagined before that remotely approaches it in the thorough-going, intimate, unceasing control it may exercise over the daily life of every human being within the web of its wires.

Gifford Pinchot, Governor of Pennsylvania,
describing the US electricity industry in the 1920s[1]

DESPITE THE PROPAGANDA of the private power companies and their associations, there remained, in the 1920s, a popular movement for publicly owned systems. Repeated calls from farmers for electrical supply went unanswered by the private companies that did not believe serving rural areas would be profitable, partly because they did not think that farmers would use enough electricity. Rural politicians tried to disprove this assumption with various studies, but the private companies took no notice.[2]

In several states, movements grew for public control of electricity and its extension to rural areas. But whenever measures were taken to achieve this, the power companies organised to oppose them, and utilised the massive propaganda machinery at their disposal. A good example is the fight in California over statewide public ownership described below. However, California was not the only state to attempt reforms.

Some key struggles were staged by Republican senator George W. Norris, who was at the forefront of the public ownership movement, and Pennsylvanian governor Gifford Pinchot, who founded the National Popular Government League. This organisation was also concerned to prevent private power companies from getting control of the nation's rivers and using them for private hydroelectric projects. Another group campaigning for public ownership of electricity was the Public Ownership League of America formed in 1916, in which Pinchot also participated along with senator Robert LaFollette.[3]

Public Utilities

The private companies were not able to compete easily with the public systems because of the high levels of profits they were taking. Public systems continued to provide electricity at lower rates than private companies. J.B. Sheridan, a director of PR for the private utility companies, noted in a private letter in 1927:

> I believe in private initiative, but I don't believe in subsidizing it 3 to 6 cents per kilowatt hour. The privately owned industry should be ashamed of itself to permit a municipally owned plant, operated on the square to undersell it 4 to 6 to 7 cents per kilowatt hour. Don't say taxes? Taxes are less than $0.0023 per kilowatt hour in this state.[4]

The private utilities used average electricity rates to argue that their rates were cheaper. They were able to do this because many private power companies sold electricity to other utilities and to industry at low rates and even, on occasion, below cost. By offering low electricity rates to large industrial customers, private power companies were able to deter them from investing in self-generation facilities.[5] These rates, which sometimes applied to up to 90 per cent of the electricity they supplied, were subsidised by many residential or domestic customers, particularly those who used the lowest quantities of electricity. Municipal and publicly owned utilities tended to supply mainly residential customers. This meant they supplied smaller total volumes and so could not take advantage of the economies of scale available to the larger private companies. However, when comparing similar domestic services, the public utilities' prices were lower. What is more, Canadian householders who had access to a publicly owned system of electricity paid one-third the cost that American householders paid.[6]

Nevertheless, as Insull had hoped, the growth of publicly owned electricity systems dramatically slowed following the introduction of legislation for regulated monopolies. Proposals to establish municipal plants were defeated by private companies and their associations. Private companies in the region would reduce their rates, at least temporarily, to make the move seem unnecessary; and they would provide engineers' reports to discredit such proposals.[7]

Publicly owned municipal systems operating within city boundaries did not grow in the same way as private companies and where they sought to grow beyond those boundaries, power company-funded state politicians often wouldn't allow them to do so. Also the "private stranglehold over transmission lines" enabled private utilities to "surround and isolate public systems".[8] Many municipalities were limited, by law, in the amount of money they could borrow and this limited their ability to expand and acquire electric power plants. Insull, himself, continued to oppose public utilities by using his political power and financial resources to interfere with local efforts to raise money to establish new plants or upgrade old ones.[9]

The large private companies also pressured municipal undertakings to sell out, sometimes by offering cheap electricity to local industries, subsidised by ratepayers in other areas, to undermine the rate base of the public enterprise.[10] In California, the Unjust Competition Act was passed in 1913 in an effort to prevent private utilities from undercutting municipal electricity rates to put them out of business.[11]

Existing municipal plants were harassed with constant litigation. Councillors were paid off so that they would vote to sell up. For example, when the Foshay Company was seeking to buy the municipal plant in Camilla in Georgia, the company representative requested company permission to commit a percentage from the purchase price to paying people on the council a commission if they ensured the deal was approved. In Moultrie, Georgia, the Foshay Company sought to get candidates elected to the council who would vote for the sale of the city's utilities.[12]

The political 'donations' of private power companies were credited with "much of the political corruption in the municipal government".[13] In other cases it was a matter of getting key ratepayers to support the sale of the municipal plant:

> If you pick out two or three influential men in town who are big taxpayers, get personally acquainted with them and get them shouting from the housetops that taxes could be materially reduced if the city was free from its municipal utilities, know that you can put this deal across.[14]

Where municipal owners stood firm and refused to sell, the power companies offered them such good prices on wholesale electricity some found it wasn't worth building or upgrading their own generating facilities and instead bought the power from the private companies. In 1921 and 1922 twelve municipal light and power plants in Oklahoma were handed over to private companies and 50 electric light plants in Iowa stopped operation and bought their electricity from private companies. By 1923 more than one in three municipal systems purchased all their power from private companies compared to 7 per cent of them in 1907. Municipal utilities supplied less than 4 per cent of electricity, nationwide. Between 1923 and 1927 the number of public power systems further declined by more than 25 per cent.[15]

Californian Fight

In 1921 the League of Californian Municipalities sponsored a bill, The Water and Power Act, that would establish public ownership of electricity systems throughout the state. The bill did not survive the committee stage but the League then had the measure put to a public referendum in 1922, 1924 and 1926. Each time it was defeated.[16]

The defeats were largely due to the unlimited funds, personnel and other resources at the disposal of the six major private utilities in the state that opposed the proposal. A government inquiry later found: "That side won which spent the most money" referring to "vast expenditures for propaganda literature, advertising, and organized campaign workers". The utility campaign characterised the bill as socialistic and Bolshevistic: "Shall California be Sovietized?" They argued that public ownership of electricity supply would be hugely expensive forcing large tax increases, that it would create "a monster political machine" with too much power, and that it would be a failure in the end, as other public schemes had been.[17]

The two main players were the Pacific Gas and Electric Company (PG&E) in the north of the state, which spent over $660,000 on the campaign,[18] and the Southern California Edison Company (SoCalEd). Their campaign was described by Carl D. Thompson, secretary of the Public Ownership League, in a 1932 book based on evidence presented to the 1928 FTC inquiry. He claimed that the campaign was "unparalleled in the history of California politics".[19]

The private utilities formed a number of front groups to fight the measure on their behalf. The two main ones were the Greater California League, which based its opposition in the northern part of the state, and the People's Economic League, in the southern part. In addition there were a number of local organisations formed. These organisations purported to be independent of the utilities through "the use of high sounding, patriotic names under which the real identity of the interested parties and actual proponents or opponents is disguised".[20] A 1923 government report said of the Greater California League:

Such a name readily gives the impression of being a promotion organization which every citizen in California would feel free to join, and having nothing in its name to indicate that it was a political campaign organization.

The testimony before this committee showed that the Greater California League was in reality merely the name under which Mr. Eustace Cullinan, employed by the power companies, conducted the campaign against the water and power act in northern California.[21]

Cullinan appointed himself president, organised local branches, and employed various people, including a general manager, district organizers, speakers and house-to-house canvassers. The latter were often law students. Women were employed to go to entertainments and card parties in the evenings and talk to those gathered there and distribute literature. Millions of bulletins, leaflets and postcards were distributed. Advertisements were put in every major newspaper and on billboards. Cullinan also made good use of the Hofer Press Service (see previous chapter).[22]

Sometimes the influence was more subtle. For example, Cullinan paid for a tea party organised by a well-connected woman: "in the course of the party, or afternoon tea, she brought the conversation around to the subject of the state water and power act, and said, rather casually, in passing, that 'My banker tells me that is an iniquitous and dangerous measure,' and with a little comment of that kind passed on."[23] Those attending were completely unaware at the time that the tea party was part of a wider agenda.

Similarly, the People's Economy League was run by Herbert L. Cornish, employed by SoCalEd. Cornish, however, sought members and formed an executive committee. It grew to about 1000 members and fostered 60 local branches in Southern California.[24]

The campaign drew on allies in the banks, bonding houses, newspapers, and business and civic organizations. According to Thompson:

Bankers and bankers' associations, insurance agents, and insurance brokers, electrical contractors, business men's associations, Boards of Trade, women's organizations, organizations of the Farm Bureau and the Grange, engineers and ship owners' associations, real estate boards, irrigation districts, and innumerable other similar organizations of opposition sprung up all over the state. The suddenness with which the opposition arose, the thoroughness of its organization, and the effectiveness of its action were amazing. The sudden change of front in some quarters, the attitude of certain business elements, especially the bankers and the overwhelming defeat of the measure was puzzling at the time, to say the least.[25]

For example, the State Federation of Labor had been an early proponent of the act. However, someone was employed to visit all the union papers and persuade them to change their stance. A prominent labour man, a former president of the Building Trades Council of San Francisco, P. H. McCarthy, was also hired and paid a large sum of money to be used at his discretion to influence the unions. The federation changed its position.[26]

The utilities influenced many organisations by providing their most influential members, those "with standing and reputation as distinguished members commanding the confidence of their fellows", with expense accounts in return for getting their organisation to endorse the utility view-point.[27] A government committee reported in 1923:

> Another practice, shown by the testimony to have been extensively resorted to in the campaign and calculated to work deception on the voter, was that of employ-ing as campaign workers, persons prominent in commercial bodies, farm organi-zations, labor unions, social literary, and civic clubs, without these hired representatives disclosing their employment. In this way members of organizations were kept in the dark as to the real motive of fellow members who were apparently disinterested in their views.[28]

For example, the president of the Civic League of Improvement Clubs of San Francisco was employed by the campaign. The Civic League incorporated many of the professional, vocational and economic organizations in the city.[29]

Where organisations had voted to support the measure the campaign attempted to get it put to the vote again and stacked the new meeting by sending cars for people and persuading them individually of the case against it. In some cases, such as the North Beach Improvement Club, their strategy succeeded and groups reversed their position.[30]

The banks, insurance companies, and bond houses all sent out circulars and letters to their customers opposing the measure. The president of PG&E, A. F. Hockenbeamer, explained how the banks helped by sending "out hun-dreds of thousands of personal letters and pieces of literature to their deposi-tors and stockholders, as well as campaigning against it personally."[31]

The National Electric Light Association (NELA) also credited widespread 'customer ownership', which it had fostered for public relations purposes (see previous chapter), with the defeat of the ballot: "Obviously the extraordinary number of customer stockholders in proportion to the population of the state was not unconnected with the severe defeat of the proposal".[32]

Giant Power in Pennsylvania

Struggles for public power schemes occurred in other states and opposed just as ferociously by private companies and their allies. In Pennsylvania, governor Gifford Pinchot (elected in 1922) and consulting engineer Morris Llewellyn Cooke attempted to bypass the debate over public ownership by proposing a scheme that allowed private ownership but added more public control. Their Giant Power scheme was a statewide system of giant power stations that would pool electricity and increase the scale of generation to achieve greater efficiencies, enabling prices to be reduced and availability to be increased.[33]

The giant power stations (>300,000 kW), sited at the mouths of mines, would be integrated with coal-processing plants that would separate off various products such as gas and ammonium compounds before the coal was fed into the power stations. The electricity from them would be transmitted by a new network of high-voltage lines.[34] The giant power stations and the transmission system would be built and owned by private companies. The existing utilities, private and municipal, would buy and distribute the electricity from the high-voltage system to industrial and residential consumers, as well as continue to supply their own customers with power they themselves generated. They would also be free to sell any excess power they generated into the grid. New power plants would only be built by Giant Power generating companies; gradually, the other private companies would become merely distribution and supply companies, and would not be involved in generation or transmission.[35]

As both men were experienced publicists, the scheme received much attention, and "the presentation of Giant Power to the legislature—and to the people—was impressive in its persuasiveness."[36] Whilst the technical aspects of the scheme appealed to engineers in the private utilities who liked the large scale, economies, and efficiencies involved, they did not like its regulatory structure. It was clearly a government scheme, and so represented government interference in a business that was considered to be more properly the domain of private business. Despite Pinchot's assurances to the contrary,[37] it was perceived as a step towards government ownership.

This was in large part because of Pinchot's reputation as a reformer who favoured public ownership and criticised the private monopolies. Pinchot believed that electric monopolies needed to be "controlled in the public interest" or otherwise they would be all powerful and dominate all aspects of the national economy because of its reliance on electricity. One of the aims of Giant Power "was to prevent this huge monopoly from acquiring industrial, commercial, financial and political control of the country, and specifically to protect the general welfare of the people and to see that the public interest has, from start to finish, the first place".[38]

Pinchot realised that he could not achieve public ownership in Pennsylvania but sought instead to achieve a measure of public control. The whole system would be coordinated and regulated by a Giant Power Board. Pinchot also sought to avoid the system of state regulation that the holding companies so readily rorted. He noted that between 1920 and 1925 ten holding companies controlled electricity in Pennsylvania, and that their assets had increased in value by 296 per cent on average. Four of them had increased in value by 1000 per cent and one by 10,0000 per cent in that time.[39]

The generating and transmission companies involved in the scheme would receive a state-regulated profit that was not based on assets, which had been subject to abuse by regulated monopolies, but on investment at a rate sufficient to attract capital. After 50 years they could be taken over by the state, which would repay the investment that had been made in them in the meantime.[40]

The private utilities reacted predictably, labelling the scheme as dangerous, menacing, and communistic or socialistic:

Private initiative is to be driven out of the electric service companies and [to] be supplanted by a political plant based upon a socialistic theory and offering all the possibilities of the construction of a state-wide, all powerful, political machine.[41]

One of the aims of the Giant Power scheme was to get electricity to rural areas, which were poorly served by private companies. The scheme would require that these areas be served and that farmers could create their own voluntary mutual and district distribution companies to do this.[42] Another of the aims of the scheme was to end the discrimination in favour of industrial users of electricity that was evident in the way private companies charged rates: "the milking of the moderate and small users for the benefit of the few exceptional big users must stop".[43]

The utilities countered "that industries should not subsidize farmers and residential consumers by allowing them to be charged rates comparable to what the industries paid."[44] They also argued that the scheme's proponents preyed "upon ignorance or mass prejudice, arraying one class against another, seeking in the resultant discord to promote their own selfish political advancement."[45] Pinchot himself was accused of using the scheme to further his own political ambitions:

Governor Pinchot hit upon an idea to assist him ride upon a thunderbolt into the White House. He would take away ownership and operation of electric light and power from 2,500,000 Americans who own securities of light and power companies, deprive the states of their constitutional rights to exercise their police power in regulation of these public utility companies and turn over ownership of electric light and power to the politicians.[46]

The bill was considered by a joint hearing of House and Senate committees, which heard testimony from both sides. The private companies produced three well-known engineers to refute the proposal as being unrealistic and technologically radical. Their measured testimony was complemented by the colourful testimony of congressman James Francis Burke, who labelled the proposal as the most dangerous and destructive that had ever been presented to the legislature. "Is Pennsylvania to lead America in following Russia into the dismal swamp of commercial chaos and financial disaster?" he asked.[47]

The Pennsylvania Electric Association drafted a letter to be sent from utility companies to banks and trust companies. The letter argued that Pinchot's proposal was dangerously menacing. The association also paid people to testify at the hearings without disclosing their payment.[48]

The bill was rejected in 1926. "Pinchot blamed the power of a great and growing monopoly masterminded by giant financial interests; Cooke shared this view and also attributed the failure to the conservatism of the engineering establishment." In hindsight, historian Thomas Hughes argues that the opposition was based on the fear that "authority and responsibility of presiding over the growth of electric light and power systems" would shift "from the engineers, managers and owners of the existing utilities to the new men of the Giant Power system."[49]

Pinchot subsequently wrote a book, *The Power Monopoly—Its Makeup and Menace*, which attempted to detail the control and affiliations of the private power companies in the United States. He concluded that, in 1926, 80 per cent of power generated in the US was controlled by 41 holding companies and 35 of these were dominated by six interests: General Electric, Insull, Morgan, Mellon, Blyllesby, and Doherty. These few interests controlled two-thirds of US electricity.[50]

Senator George Norris's efforts were not any more successful than Pinchot's for many years. After a visit to Canada's Hydro-Electric Power Commission of Ontario, he showed that public power in Canada was cheaper than private power in the United States. The International Bridge at Niagara

Falls was half lit by the Canadian Power Commission at $8.43 a month and half by a private US power company for $43.10 per month.[51]

Such campaigning earned Norris public ridicule from the private utilities. Those who continued to champion public power were called "socialist" and "communist". The Alabama Power Company organised a public relations campaign against Norris, utilising advertisements that labelled him as a Marxist. Insull labelled him an "agitator", and NELA claimed his statements originated "with predatory politicians and demagogues". The utilities even paid a grocery clerk with the same name, George W. Norris, to stand against him when he stood for re-election to the Senate so as to confuse voters. Nevertheless, Norris was re-elected with a landslide.[52]

Twice, Norris won sufficient votes in Congress for legislation to develop public power systems; but both times, in 1928 and 1931, the legislation was vetoed by presidents Coolidge and Hoover, the latter a former engineer and a friend of the private utilities.[53]

The Rise and Stumble of the Holding Companies

In the 1920s fifteen giant interrelated holding companies or power trusts provided 85 per cent of the electricity in the US, and the growth of public power systems halted.[54] The General Electric Company alone controlled one-eighth of generating capacity in 1924. It had created nine holding companies covering some 200 utilities, and had minority holdings in other companies. This facilitated sales of GE equipment and ensured GE dominance over Westinghouse. Because of congressional concerns about holding companies, GE sold the giant Electric Bond and Share company in 1924 but continued to supply it with equipment.[55]

Between 1925 and 1929 there were almost 4000 mergers, including almost 700 municipal systems taken over by private companies, and 118 mergers with foreign companies. There were 228 mergers of holding companies with holding companies.[56] "By 1929 the House of Morgan alone controlled more than a third of the nation's electricity supply", and Insull controlled another 10 per cent.[57] In 1932 the number of giant electricity holding companies had been reduced to eight, and these "controlled almost three-quarters of the investor-owned utility business."[58]

Holding companies were not unique to the electricity industry. In 1929 200 corporations controlled about half of the corporate wealth of the United States. The country was also in the grip of speculation fever. With the share market soaring, people were investing their life savings, mortgaging their houses, and buying on margin (using loans from stock brokers) to make huge profits on the market. This frenzy drove share prices up beyond any rational assessment of the worth of companies. The Dow Jones Industrial Average went from 191 to 381 between early 1928 and September 1929.[59]

Share prices for the power companies soared before the crash of 1929. Commonwealth Edison went from $202 to $450 in seven months. In August 1929 Insull's securities were gaining value at the rate of $7000 a minute. His companies claimed $3 billion worth of assets. Then, in October 1929, the first of several stock market crashes occurred, fuelled by a panic that prices were falling. Many investors tried to sell their shares as confidence in the market disappeared. Banks that had speculated with deposits lost heavily, causing a run on many banks.[60]

In 1928 a Senate investigation was proposed into utility financing. Senator Thomas J. Walsh said:

> The purpose of the proposed investigation is to protect two classes of our citizens: First, the 17,000,000 of householders who pay for electric lighting; and, second, the great body of our people who are now putting their savings into the securities of these corporations.[61]

The proposed investigation was vigorously opposed by NELA, which was joined in its opposition by the American Electric Railway Association and the American Gas Association, as well as investment bankers and the National Association of Manufacturers. One senator observed: "There was assembled here the most formidable lobby ever brought together in this city"[62] The effect of this direct show of power was counterproductive in terms of preventing an investigation. However, the lobbies were able to have it transferred from the Senate to the Federal Trade Commission (FTC).[63] (The industry later learned to be more subtle in its show of power.)

Although it was a federal inquiry and the FTC had the power to subpoena witnesses and documents, utility executives stubbornly refused to answer some questions and hand over some documents, and the FTC had to go to court to compel them to comply. Even then, a number of important documents were "lost, strayed, or stolen".[64]

The FTC inquiry, whose findings were described in the previous chapter, ran till 1934, with damaging revelations being published along the way. It marked a low point for the fortunes of private power companies. With the collapse of some of the power holding companies in the first few years of the depression, the credibility of the power companies reached an all-time low.

Despite the crashes at the end of 1929, Insull continued to expand his empire as electricity demand continued to grow. He promoted his stock as safer than government bonds. However, money was much harder to raise after the crashes, and he had to borrow heavily from the banks to continue expanding his operations. In 1932, after a battle with JP Morgan's utility interests, Insull's holding company went bankrupt. He had borrowed $20 million from JP Morgan, using his company as collateral; and when the bank demanded the money back, it blocked other bankers from lending the money to him.[65]

"It was the largest bankruptcy in history up to that point".[66] Shares in Insull's Middle West Utilities Company, which had traded at $57 in 1929, were worth 25 cents at the time of the collapse. More than 100,000 stockholders lost about $4 billion. Hundreds of employees lost their jobs. Many employees had been prevailed upon to invest in securities, and lost their savings as well. Insull was forced to resign from his 85 directorships, 65 chairmanships, and eleven presidencies, and he fled to Europe. He was indicted for embezzlement, using the mails to defraud, and violation of the bankruptcy acts. The banks and insurance companies that had invested in Insull securities also suffered. Banks had to call in other loans, and other power companies went under as a result.[67]

The holding companies, and particularly the electricity holding companies, were credited with contributing to the Great Depression when their complex pyramid structures came crashing down, leaving bankruptcies behind them. "Millions of Americans lost their life savings to the Power Trusts in the 1920s".[68] By 1935 some 90 electric and gas companies had gone under. Nevertheless, the operating companies generally remained healthy and even profitable because of continuing electricity demand. Residential electricity demand increased 20 per cent between 1929 and 1933 because of sales of home appliances. Electrification of mass transit also increased demand.[69]

Nor did the Depression destroy the power of the electricity holding companies. The banks stepped in and gained control of many holding companies. Industry-wide, revenue for the power companies only declined by 6 per cent during the Depression because of government-regulated rates.[70]

Electric power was a major electoral issue for the first time in the 1932 presidential election, following the collapse of Insull's empire. Franklin D. Roosevelt stood against Herbert Hoover, the incumbent president. That same year Roosevelt, whilst he was governor of New York, referred to the propaganda that had been spread by the private utilities: "A false public policy has been spread throughout the land, through the use of every means, from the innocent school teacher down to a certainly less innocent former chairman of the Republican National Committee itself."[71] He wrote that holding companies were "a corporate invention which can give a few corporate insiders unwarranted and intolerable powers over other people's money." He also noted that the public service commissions that were supposed to look after the public interest were not doing so in many states, often because the commissions were made up of people whose "selection has been obtained by the public utility corporations themselves".[72]

The utilities were not going to allow, without a fight, the election of a president holding such views. In the lead-up to the election a group of 37 congressional leaders from the Democratic Party and the Republican Party published a statement which said, in part:

> The combined utility and banking interest, headed by the Power Trust, have the most powerful and widely organized political machine ever known in history. This machine cooperates with other reactionary economic, industrial and financial groups. It is strenuously working to control the nomination of candidates for the Presidency and the Congress of both dominant political parties.[73]

The power companies and their allies unsuccessfully campaigned against Roosevelt's nomination and then against his election. Had it not been for the discrediting the industry had suffered as a result of the FTC inquiry and the Depression, the result could have been very different, given the huge power the consolidated companies exercised. After he came to power Roosevelt introduced a number of reforms that directly affected the electricity industry, each of which was strenuously opposed by the industry's private sector.

In 1933, as president, Roosevelt established a public authority, called the Tennessee Valley Authority (TVA), to develop electricity. A group of nineteen private power companies went to court to challenge its establishment as unconstitutional; then, when they were unsuccessful in this action, they refused to allow it to use their transmission lines.[74] To overcome this problem, the TVA encouraged the establishment of rural cooperatives in the Tennessee Valley. Seventy-two cooperatives were set up within three years, each working closely with the TVA. Their success led to the establishment of the Rural Electrification Administration (REA) in 1935 to provide the same service nationally. The REA sought to help groups of farmers in rural areas to set up their own systems with the help of low-interest loans and technical expertise. By 1944 there were over 700 rural cooperatives, and almost half of the farms in the US had electricity.[75]

The Roosevelt administration, which lasted till 1945, set up large federal power agencies to develop electric power for the nation, particularly from the nation's rivers. As a result, four major hydroelectric projects were constructed.

> Besides electric power, these dams provided flood control, navigation, area development, and greatly needed work for the unemployed ... The Bonneville Project Act of 1937 pioneered the Federal power marketing administrations which marketed electricity generated by federal power projects. By 1940, Federal power pricing policy was set; all Federal power was marketed at the lowest possible price, while still covering costs. From 1933 to 1941, one-half of all new capacity was provided by Federal and other public power installations.[76]

In 1935 the Federal Public Utility Holding Company Act (PUHCA) was passed. Its aim was to break up the huge power trusts or holding companies that spanned the country. These companies had complicated structures and many levels of holding companies within holding companies, which enabled them to manipulate and hide financial transactions and escape state regulation (see chapter 1).[77]

The act prevented holding companies that owned at least 10 per cent of stock in an electric or gas utility from owning non-utility businesses, and prevented them from having more than one layer of holding company above the operating subsidiary. It forced holding companies that owned adjacent utilities to integrate their operations to ensure better economies of scale, greater reliability, and easier regulation. Utilities that could not be integrated in this way had to be sold. The act also provided for federal and state regulation of companies that covered more than one state. "Due to the enactment of PUHCA, ratepayers saw their electric bills drop by 14 per cent between 1938 and 1951."[78]

The Federal Power Act was also amended in 1935. It was originally introduced in 1920 to allow the federal government to regulate regional public electricity systems, such as hydroelectric schemes. The act had established a Federal Power Commission to oversee the siting and financing of dams. The amendments required the commission to oversee wholesale power contracts and to reduce the banks' and financial institutions' control over power companies. Utility executives and directors had to get commission approval before they could hold a position with another utility or in a banking firm.[79]

The Edison Electric Institute

These efforts to regulate utilities in the 1930s were also opposed, using public relations campaigns. Whilst that FTC inquiry had succeeded in documenting some of the propaganda efforts of the utilities, it did not stop them. NELA, whose activities had been so widely discredited, was dissolved in January 1933 and replaced with the Edison Electric Institute (EEI) on the same day. The industry was keen "to divest itself of all semblance of propaganda activities"; but the new organisation occupied the NELA offices, had the same executive committee, and continued with the same 'educational' materials.[80]

The financial sector and the power companies campaigned vigorously against the Public Utility Holding Company bill when it was proposed, claiming that it was unconstitutional and dangerous. The head of one of the industry's front groups told the press that the legislation "constitutes the most sinister peril to our Democratic form of Government that has ever threatened our people."[81] The new owners of the bankrupted holding companies, the banks, continued to utilise the industry's propaganda machinery "to flood Congress with more mail and telegrams than was received on any other legislation."[82]

The EEI coordinated the $1.5 million campaign, depicting the legislation in advertisements as contrary to the American Way. Ivy Lee's public relations company enlisted the support of the power industry's business allies against the bill.[83] Their strategy, masterminded by T. J. Ross, a partner in the firm, was to present the bill as the "thin end of the wedge", a first step in a move to destroy free enterprise:

Insurance executives, for example, were informed that company assets would be seized and used to fund holding company debts. Bankers were told banking institutions would be included in the definition of holding companies and become subject to its "destructive measures". And retailers, distributors, and manufacturers were given information that they would be classified as holding companies too, making their investments vulnerable to provisions of the bill.[84]

Investors were informed that their securities would lose value, and investment bankers were given kits on how to mobilise their clients to oppose the bill. Various front groups were formed, such as the American Federation of Utility Investors. It was funded by insurance companies, and brokerage and investment firms, but attempted to appear independent of Wall Street interests. It was also paid to produce pamphlets in support of the private power companies, which the companies then distributed to investors. Its supposed membership of 56,000 was gleaned from power company mailing lists.[85]

An artificial grassroots campaign (today referred to as 'Astroturf') was waged, generating tens of thousands of letters and telegrams to politicians, most not from genuine citizens. Senator Harry S. Truman received 30,000 of them. In another instance, a Western Union messenger boy was "sent out to solicit telegrams" that opposed the legislation. The boy got 3 cents per telegram, and they were sent for free to representatives such as congressman Driscoll in Washington, who received 816 of these telegrams in two days and became suspicious. Thousands of telegrams reached Washington in this way, "sometimes at the rate of 4000 an hour—signed with names taken at random and without authority from telephone books and directories."[86]

The EEI paid a public relations consultant $5000 a month "to bring to Washington friends of various congressmen who 'turned on the heat' in no uncertain terms." A whispering campaign, spread with the help of the EEI, suggested that Roosevelt was unnaturally obsessed with holding companies. His mental health was questioned.[87]

Nevertheless, the popularity of Roosevelt's reforms ensured that he won a third term of office in the 1940 election despite running against a utility mogul, Wendell Willkie.[88] Although the private power companies did not prevent Roosevelt's legislation from being enacted, they were able to use their influence to reduce its effectiveness. The bills, although passed, were watered down. The Federal Power Commission (later to become the Federal Energy Regulatory Commission) routinely approved some 800 applications after this legislation came into effect. A 1940 inquiry found that the financial community retained control of power companies despite the 1935 legislation.[89]

PUHCA failed to break up nine major holding companies and about 70 smaller ones.[90] A 1955 inquiry (Dixon-Yates) found that the "core of the old abuses and concentration of corporate dealing, though less direct, remained intact".[91] The power companies were resurgent once again during the Eisenhower presidency. A new set of holding companies was formed, and further centralisation took place.[92] PUHCA continues to be periodically challenged and campaigned against through to the present day (see part two).

CHAPTER FOUR

Continuing Propaganda After The War

By some variation of Parkinson's Law, the more the power companies spend on information, public relations, and advertising, the less the public knows about their operations.
Senator Lee Metcalf and Vic Reinemer[1]

THE PRIVATE POWER COMPANIES took over 103 municipal power systems and three rural electric cooperatives between 1949 and 1965 to supply 76 per cent of all power generation (see figure 4.1). The electricity industry had become the country's largest industry (apart from agriculture in aggregate).[2]

For several decades following the introduction of state-regulated monopolies, private electric utilities were able to provide reasonably priced electricity, despite their excesses and profligate waste. Their growth strategy, combined with aggressive promotion of electricity consumption, ensured that they were able to supply increasing amounts of electricity. Subsequent economies of scale combined with technological advances ensured that electricity prices did not rise during the 1950s and 1960s. And the cheap electricity promoted more consumption and further growth.[3]

Over time, other organisations spun off from the Edison Electric Institute (EEI): the Electric Companies Advertising Program to run national advertising for the industry; the National Association of Electric Companies to lobby for the industry; and the Public Information Program to mastermind the public relations for the industry. The message that these four organisations promoted was that private utilities were symbols of free enterprise offering cheap electricity but burdened by regulations and facing unfair competition from government-owned utilities. For public relations purposes the private utilities called themselves investor-owned utilities (IOU), and they campaigned furiously against public ownership. In advertisements, private utilities were sometimes depicted as the fullback being tackled by the referee or the track star leaping hurdles much higher than his opponent.[4]

> Through the use of pictures and text, the I.O.U.s identified themselves with the Statue of Liberty, the Star-Spangled Banner, Independence Day, Abraham Lincoln, Ben Franklin, Patrick Henry, and George Washington, as well as with the Bible and childhood.[5]

■ **Figure 4.1: Power generation in the US in 1965 by ownership**

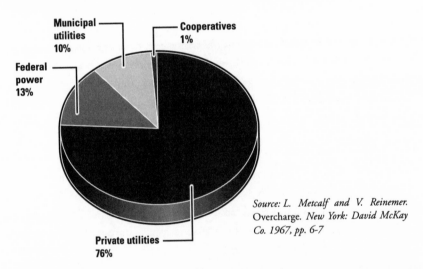

Source: L. Metcalf and V. Reinemer. Overcharge. *New York: David McKay Co. 1967, pp. 6-7*

These advertisements were generally paid for by ratepayers because the private utilities incorporated advertising costs in their accounts as an operating expense. In 1957 the Internal Revenue Service ruled that such ads were not a deductible business expense for taxation purposes because they were designed for "lobbying purposes, for the promotion or defeat of legislation or the development or exploitation of propaganda". The industry and its media allies were outraged. The *Standard* suggested it "could mean the end of free enterprise" if carried to an extreme, and the *Saturday Evening Post* suggested that the ruling meant that the federal government had "the right to censor advertising".[6]

Three years later, when the Federal Power Commission (FPC) ruled that such ads should be considered as a non-operating expense and should therefore be paid for by stockholders rather than ratepayers, the response was similar. "We are astounded that the Commission staff regards advertisements opposing communism and supporting the American system and containing basic concepts of economics as being 'political controversy'."[7] Despite these adverse rulings, utilities continued to charge advertisements to operating expenses and the advertising campaigns continued, except where state commissions were conscientious and well resourced.[8]

Utility Economics

As the cost of generating electricity went down during the 1950s and 1960s, utilities were able to collect higher returns than most industries without raising rates. In the mid-1960s they made 14 cents on every dollar of revenue, compared to an average of 6.1 cents in every sales dollar for leading manufacturing firms and 6.3 per cent for leading non-manufacturing firms.[9]

In theory, the public utility commissions (PUCs) allowed around 6 per cent as a reasonable rate of return on investment, enabling the utilities to borrow capital and satisfy investors. However, most power companies exceeded this return. It was the poorer customers who suffered most, as the price per kilowatt decreased with higher usage. Overcharging was evident when comparing the rates charged by private companies with those charged by municipal companies (see table 4.1). The municipal companies also contributed money to the city budget, enabling local taxes to be lower.[10]

■ **Table 4.1: Comparison between private and public electricity systems**

Ownership	Rates/kWh	Difference	Local Taxes	Federal Taxes
Private	2.51 cents		10.5%	13%
Public	1.57 cents	- 37%	10.5%	-
Rural Cooperatives	2.33 cents	-7%	10.5%	-

L. Metcalf and V. Reinemer. Overcharge. New York: David McKay Co. 1967, pp. 11-13.

However, there were few independent experts to scrutinise the situation. University courses on utility economics became fewer and fewer during the 1950s and 1960s, and "academic attention to public utility economics in the form of scholarly articles clearly has dwindled almost to the vanishing point". Those courses that remained were often taught by utility officials, editors of trade publications, or lecturers who focused on non-monopoly utilities such as transportation. In Texas, lecturer salaries were supplemented by the Texas Bureau of Economic Understanding, which received utility funds.[11] Such academics were unlikely to launch an investigation of utility operations.

> Power-company donations flow as steadily as electricity into many well-motivated organizations that would logically make such inquiries. Any organization whose name indicates it has to do with economics is a magnet for utility contributions—the Bureau of Economic Understanding, the Council for Economic Growth and Security, the Economic and Business Foundation, the Economists National Committee on Monetary Policy, and the Joint Council on Economic Education ...[12]

Senator Lee Metcalf and Vic Reinemer argued in their 1967 book, *Overcharge*, that academia never really recovered from the utilities' purge of texts and curricula in the 1920s, and that the gap was filled by the utilities themselves who, in the 1950s, were "perpetuating wondrous myths that electric utilities are taxpaying, locally owned, bargain-offering free enterprises beset by competition and bedeviled by socialists".[13]

The utilities continued to have a strong influence on school economics textbooks in the 1960s. One such textbook, *The American Economic System*, was written by Edwin Vennard, managing director of the EEI. Published in 1950 and updated in the 1960s, it argued that utilities competed in the marketplace, where "more new businesses fail than succeed"; it also argued against income taxes, claiming that "Distributing the income of wealthy people" was "one of the favorite arguments of the Communists".[14]

The utilities were supported by a number of think tanks and foundations which the utilities funded. For example, Fred G. Clark, who held that the Public Utilities Holding Company Act (PUHCA) and the Tennessee Valley Authority (TVA) were examples of socialism, founded the American Economic Foundation (AEF) in 1939. Before founding AEF, Clark was involved in broadcasting anti-socialist radio programs for the Crusaders, which he headed. He would use his radio programs to attack legislation that the utilities opposed, telling the utilities to listen to the upcoming program and then collecting contributions from them afterwards.[15]

The AEF was financially supported by a number of industry and conservative interests, including the founders of *Readers Digest* and the National Association of Manufacturers. Many utilities also contributed to it. From 1943 onwards, the AEF was heavily involved in providing economic training to millions of workers and thousands of teachers, as well as community groups. It produced films that were used by 7000 high schools in 41 states, as well as distributing editorials, promoting ideologically correct textbooks and organising a speakers' bureau. It compiled the "Ten Pillars of Economic Wisdom", which were promoted by other right-wing organizations, including the John Birch Society.[16]

Another foundation that the utilities used was the Foundation for Economic Education (FEE). Established in 1946, some 46 corporations contributed a million dollars to FEE by the end of 1949. It also raised money by selling literature promoting free enterprise. Its articles were used by hundreds of newspapers and magazines, and *Reader's Digest* was particularly keen on reprinting its articles. Its goals and leadership overlapped with that of the John Birch Society; whilst many of the funders of the FEE, including the power companies, would not want to be seen to be funding the John Birch Society, the FEE was a respectable target of their generosity. In 1964 alone, 31 power companies reported giving money to FEE.[17]

In 1954 FEE bought *The Freeman* and distributed it free, particularly to college students. *The Freeman* called for the abolition of income tax, the withdrawal of the US from the United Nations, and the withdrawal of the government from all public services—including post offices, education, roads, and electricity. A FEE pamphlet, "The T.V.A. Idea", argued that the power industry was "in great danger of complete nationalization", and that utilities were competitive because "the electric companies must compete with everyone else for the consumer's dollar."[18]

A FEE textbook, *Understanding Our Free Economy*, was published in several editions, and used the TVA as a case study of what was wrong with government being involved in business. It also argued that such things as minimum-wage laws, government control of interest rates and supervision of banks, and public ownership of land were all "encroachments on free enterprise".[19]

Cold War Politics

The anti-communist mood of the Cold War era suited the private power companies. The EEI campaigned for private control of nuclear power plants and also transmission systems, arguing that a federally owned national transmission system would be a step towards socialism.[20] The power industry equated its interests with those of the nation:

> Government ownership of utilities has always been the first goal of the socialists and communists. Because of this, the future of the American system of government

is dependent on the electric business continuing in the hands of investor-owned, tax-paying companies ... Our problem is not only to save our industry, but to save the American system of government.[21]

In 1949 industry studies showed that, while ads about socialism attracted readers, the public did not associate federal power with socialism. So the private utilities sought to make that association. Their PR firm, Bozell & Jacobs, came up with the slogan "Government in any business is socialism" to be put on stickers, posters, and in advertising, and to "rally other business and professional interests for a joint undertaking".[22]

One of these advertisements, entitled "The Story of Ten Little Free Workers", was awarded "ad of the year" by *Electrical World* in 1950. It was based on the song "Ten little, nine little, eight little Indians", and told how first the IOUs, then the doctor, then the railroader, the miner, the steelworker, the farmer, the lawyer, the grocer, the salesclerk, and the newspaper reporter all fell to socialism. It was used by 31 private utilities in the first year, as well as 20 other companies and organisations.[23]

From 1950 to 1952 the utilities advertised in the major US magazines, including *Time, Life, Look, Newsweek, The Saturday Evening Post, US News & World Report*, and various farm magazines and newspaper trade publications, with over half having the threat of socialism as their theme and publicly owned electricity systems identified as socialist.[24]

They also erroneously convinced many people that private utilities offered cheaper electricity rates than municipal utilities and federally owned systems. The polls showed that the number of people who believed that private utilities offered the cheapest rates went from 24 per cent to 34 per cent between 1949 and 1951. This was despite the fact that federal systems did not sell power to residential consumers and that publicly owned municipal utilities offered cheaper rates (see previous table).[25] In 1952 the *Saturday Evening Post* claimed that the campaign had shifted "the great weight of public opinion in favor of the electric companies."[26]

Readers Digest was a self-confessed supporter of the private utilities. Being by far the largest-circulation magazine in the US, with 25 million paying subscribers and an estimated 60 million readers, this was an enormous coup for the private utilities. The *Digest* told readers that the Rural Electrification Administration was "a many-headed monster that is eating into the entire electric power industry—and into the taxpayer's pocketbook."[27] *Digest* articles were further circulated through their reprint service and through utility mailouts of reprints to customers, shareholders, and selected community leaders.[28]

The electric companies were remarkably free of bad press from the 1940s through to the 1960s. One company "attributed its immunity from criticism" to participation by company personnel in community affairs (much of it financed by customers) and the expanded activity of its Speakers Bureau."[29] The latter had saturated the community with speakers in a strategic manner. In order to get speaking invitations:

> contacts were made with business and civic leaders upon whom we could count for help—always 'going through' employees where possible. From lists available through Chambers of Commerce, Presidents' Roundtables, county councils, etc., we found it a fairly simple matter to construct our own master list ... Carefully detailed records were kept of all maneuvers on both sides, locales pin-pointed on a system map—and with strategy and execution closely paralleling the recent 'Big Lift'.[30]

The electric companies also bought goodwill by contributing to local charities and, in many states, charged the gifts as an operating cost to the rate-payers.[31]

Moreover, electrical companies were seldom investigated by the media, partly because it was a 'neglected beat' and partly because of the self-interest of financial reporters and editors who often held shares in those companies or had accepted perks and gifts from them. *Harper's* magazine reported in 1963 that "A close-knit camaraderie has developed between the financial press and financial public relations men—a camaraderie that works to the disadvantage of the ordinary newspaper reader."[32]

The power companies also continued to use news services extensively to deliver prewritten editorials praising the private utilities to newspapers. One such news service was Industrial News Review (INR). It sent a couple of editorials in support of private utilities to 11,000 newspapers each week, portraying utilities as struggling to make small profits despite heavy taxation and unfair competition from rural electric cooperatives and the spread of socialism in the industry. They were often republished as independent editorials in the newspapers. The INR would then use the fact that these 'views' had been expressed in so many newspapers around the country to argue that they reflected "the viewpoints of a majority of the American people". Then Bozell & Jacobs, the utilities' PR firm, would combine the editorials and opinion surveys conducted by utility people to construct "their very own 'public opinion'."[33]

The INR had been transformed into an arm of utility propaganda in the 1920s by Samuel Insull, who pumped $84,000 a year into its running. As well as the INR, the National Association of Electric Companies and the Public Information Program paid the US Press Association to distribute editorials. The individual utilities also sent out their own barrage of press releases attacking the public electricity systems, congratulating themselves, or commenting on public statements by academics and others. These releases were often preformatted and ready to print. To ensure these press releases were used, the companies wined and dined publishers, and advertised heavily in their papers. They even helped get tie-in advertising from associated suppliers when an award-winning all-electric home was being publicised.[34]

The utilities also paid large amounts to local lawyers. For example, Arkansas Power & Light paid out $250,000 to 46 legal firms and individual lawyers in 1950 and 1951, and Mississippi Power & Light retained more than 21 law firms with a monthly fee, without requiring anything much from them except to keep them onside and prevent their being used against the company.[35]

In response to power company lobbying, the Kennedy administration softened its approach, allowing new mergers and consolidations, but it also encouraged public systems and facilitated federal transmission lines.[36] This prompted a new wave of anti-public ownership propaganda on the part of EEI. Advertisements were placed in popular magazines such as *The Saturday Evening Post* and *Readers Digest*, using Cold War themes. For example, an advertisement in *Atlantic Monthly* headlined "How is Freedom Lost?" said:

> Dangers that grow within our borders can string barbed wire around our freedoms as tightly as dangers that come from abroad. But they aren't as easy to see. Some of us are hardly aware of the threat that grows within — the expansion of government in business ... when government owns business, it has in its hands both political and economic power ... Isn't it time to call a halt to the expansion of government-in-business?[37]

The private power industry produced a Project Action Kit in 1963 that included a half-hour colour film entitled *The Power Within*, a 119-page manual on how to use the film, and various brochures.[38] After watching the emotionally manipulative and deceptive film featuring a rural family, people were given cards and materials for writing letters to their representative in Congress. The cards said:

> We the undersigned are becoming extremely concerned with increasing government encroachment into areas which by our American heritage have become free

enterprise endeavours ... We are particularly concerned with the unfair competition that exists from the R.E.A program against investor-owned power companies.[39]

They were also given sample letters and a list of legislative representatives, and asked to write their own letter, which those showing the film offered to post for them. The manual explained:

Sample letters should be on various colored and sized stationery and handwritten. This will give members of your audience an authentic guide, yet, because it looks as though it is an actual letter someone has written, avoids the chance of copying and standardized leters coming from your audience to any one Congressman.

This will allow the action to appear spontaneous to the recipient and not as though it were a planned concerted effort by any one interested group.[40]

The film was shown by 51 companies in 38 states, and even outside the USA. Some natural gas and telephone companies also showed the film, as did some banks and chambers of commerce. There were also efforts to get community leaders with no links to the electric utilities "to introduce the film at clubs and civic organization meetings".[41]

The Utilities in Trouble
The rise of the limits-to-growth movement in the early 1970s also prompted a wave of utility propaganda.

Merely to discuss 'zero energy growth' is to unleash a torrent of indignant advertising paid for by major industrial interests which benefit from growth in energy consumption. A typical utility company ad shows a bell-bottomed, well-heeled protestor carrying a sign: *Generate Less Energy.*

'Sure,' the ad replies. 'And generate galloping unemployment.'[42]

The utilities portrayed energy conservation as requiring people to give up electrical appliances such as refrigerators and washing machines. However, in California, where environmentalism was fairly strong, opposition to new electricity plants forced more emphasis on conservation, and the state adopted "the country's most stringent conservation program" at the behest of the California Public Utilities Commission (CPUC). It required utilities to implement conservation programs before it would approve new generating plants. The program included incentives for installation of insulation, and solar heating and energy-saving appliances in homes, as well as energy standards for buildings codes and appliance standards. [43]

The oil crisis in 1973 prompted hundreds of utilities to request rate increases, about half of which were granted, amounting to over $2 billion.[44] This further encouraged conservation nationwide. The utilities were not willing participants in conservation efforts, however. They preferred to build capital-intensive nuclear-power plants. Due to their guaranteed rate of return, the more money they invested, the more profits they made.[45]

Legislative efforts by the Carter administration to introduce conservation were opposed by the power industry, and when the Public Utility Regulatory Policy Act (PURPA) was passed in 1978 the power companies contested it in the courts for five years. The law was not specifically to do with conservation, but it required the utilities to purchase some of their power from independent sources, which included alternative energy suppliers such as wind and solar electricity generators, at a price that was less than what it would have cost to build a new power plant to generate the same quantity of electricity.[46] This law enabled non-regulated companies to produce electricity, and broke down the idea that electricity generation was a natural monopoly.[47]

For the first time since the Second World War, consumption levels began to fall. This was partly in response to rising prices and conservation measures, but also because of the increasing energy-efficiency of electrical appliances and motors, and heating and lighting systems. As demand fell, electric utilities constructed more generating plant than were necessary, further increasing prices.

In the late 1970s rates doubled, tripled, and quadrupled as the costs of building nuclear power plants similarly escalated and overran budgets by hundreds of millions — and even billions — of dollars. Safety became a public issue, especially after the accident at the Three Mile Island plant in 1979. Concerns over costs, safety, and need caused more and more cancellations of proposed nuclear plants, and construction programs were halted part-way through.[48]

> Between 1974 and 1986, 103 nuclear reactors had been cancelled ... By early 1984 half the forty-eight nuclear plants under construction were in danger of being abandoned because of soaring costs and a lack of need for their power ... *Forbes* magazine featured the failure of nuclear power on its cover, describing it as 'the largest managerial disaster in business history,' costing more than the nation's space program or the Vietnam War.[49]

Public Utility Commissioners started to question whether nuclear invest-ment costs should be passed onto consumers and shareholders who were, in some cases, left with the costs of unwise investments.[50]

Despite their soaring costs, or perhaps because of them, the financial sector loved nuclear power plants. Rudolph and Ridley, in their 1986 book *Power Struggle*, noted the key role that Wall Street still played in the power industry: "the influence of Wall Street has historically translated into bias in favor of high-cost, centralized power alternatives such as nuclear power plants, as opposed to decentralized solar and conservation."[51]

Banks were paid fees for every stage of a new power plant, "for advising a company on its financial plan, for selling its stock and placing its debt, and from dividends on power company securities the brokerage house or bank might own."[52] And these fees impacted on consumer bills: "As much as 40 percent of a consumer's bill goes to pay for financing charges … Half of the income of major investment bankers is estimated to come from financing pri-vate power companies." Merrill Lynch made its biggest profits up to that time on one project, and when citizens attempted to take control so as to contain costs, the contractors and Wall Street brokerage firms spent $1.3 million opposing them.[53]

Bankers also exerted influence through their membership of power company boards of directors. For example, three of the thirteen outside board members of PG&E, the largest utility in the US, were from banks or savings-and-loans associations in 1990. JP Morgan remained a dominant force in electricity. It "managed portfolios in 26 utilities and directors of companies associated with Morgan were on policy making-boards of 35 large electric companies."[54]

In fact, contrary to the intention of PUHCA, "as many as 1,000 bankers sat on the boards of power companies". This created conflicts of interest as well as the scope for distortion of electricity prices. Regulated rates of return to the utilities were based on the cost of capital, which depended on bank rates; if banks got together with utilities to put up those rates, both parties would benefit at the expense of the electricity consumer. Bankers supported utility interests at every opportunity—testifying at government hearings, lobbying politicians, and making appropriate donations and contributions.[55]

Other key players with heavy financial interests in the future of the power industry status quo included major engineering and construction firms such as Bechtel Corporation, equipment manufacturers such as GE and Westinghouse, and fuel suppliers such as Exxon and Peabody Coal. In earlier times (1961) GE and Westinghouse executives had confessed to conspiring to sell their equipment at inflated prices through secretly agreeing to bids in

advance and dividing up the contracts afterwards. The private power companies weren't bothered about this practice because they simply passed the costs
onto customers. It was the publicly owned TVA that blew the whistle. Forty-
two executives from 32 companies were indicted.[56]

Reagan's administration was sympathetic to the power empire. He himself
had been employed as a public relations person for GE for almost ten years,
and opposed public power as part of that job. Three other senior members of
his administration had been employed by the Bechtel Corporation. They
included George Shultz, Secretary of State, who had been president of
Bechtel; Caspar Weinberger, Secretary of Defense; and W. Kenneth Davis,
the deputy director of the Department of Energy (DOE), who had been a
vice-president of Bechtel. Reagan also appointed a veteran power industry
advocate, C. Michael Butler III, to the head of the Federal Energy Regulatory
Commission (FERC).[57]

The Coming of the Environmentalists

Just as the private power companies had used their public relations machinery
to persuade community leaders, bankers, teachers, and many others to support their point of view, they also targeted key environmentalists, enrolling
them to their cause, and attacking and discrediting those who were not so
easily persuaded.

During the 1970s environmentalists had attacked the expansionist mind-
set of the power companies and their allies, and the rating structure which
rewarded high electricity consumption and provided no incentives for conservation and efficiency. Consumer groups protested the increasing rates. In
addition, utilities had to deal with rising interest rates due to inflation and the
increased costs of meeting new environmental requirements, particularly with
regard to the Clean Air Act.[58]

Despite the declining rate of energy-consumption growth, the EEI ran a
series of ads warning the public of an impending energy shortage. They
argued that the refusal of the Public Utilities Commissions to allow private
utilities to increase rates put them in a terrible financial situation that forced
them to defer constructing new generating capacity. It argued that this might
"lead to serious reliability problems in some areas, including brown-outs and
black-outs", which in turn could "drive industry, jobs and taxes right out of
the country", as well as threaten national security.[59] Similar advertisements
were placed by individual power companies, including American Electric
Power (AEP),[60] and industry front groups, such as the US Committee for
Energy Awareness.[61]

The industry, which refused to accept the concept of overcapacity and blamed many of its woes on environmentalists, welcomed Arthur Hailey's novel *Overload* in 1979. Parts of *Overload* read like tracts from utility propaganda on the need for more power plants and the obstacles that environmentalists were putting up to prevent them. The hero, Nim Goldman, is vice-president of a utility called Golden State Power & Light (GSP&L). The story line involves radical activists, funded by a respectable mainstream environmental group, sabotaging utility facilities, causing blackouts and even deaths. The back cover screamed: "Switch off everything you don't need to survive!".[62] Goldman says in the novel:

Some of those who call themselves environmentalists have ceased to be reasonable believers in a reasonable cause and have become fanatics. They are a minority. But by noisy, rigid, uncompromising, often uninformed fanaticism, they are managing to impose their will on the majority … What they cannot defeat by reason and argument they obstruct by delay and legalistic guile. Such people do not even pretend to accept majority rule because they are convinced they know *better* than the majority … This breed of environmentalists opposes *everything*. There is nothing, absolutely nothing, we of the power industry can propose which does not arouse their ire, their condemnation, their fervent and self-righteous opposition.[63]

Whether or not Hailey got utility support for writing the novel, they were mighty pleased with it and helped to ensure it sold millions. San Diego Gas & Electric Co. (SDG&E) gave out copies to state officials as 'educational material'.[64] *Fortune* magazine noted:

We've been struck, though, by the raves the industry has given [Hailey's] efforts. Reddy Communications, Inc., which represents 150 investor-owned electric utilities, has given Overload a huge sendoff, mailing out prepublication copies to the public-relations departments of all its clients and suggesting to them that the book will do much to further public understanding of the industry's special problems.[65]

As demand for electricity went from an annual growth rate of 7 per cent in the early 1970s to 2 per cent, the surplus in 1982 reached almost 40 per cent.[66] Far from running out of electricity as predicted by the electric utilities and portrayed in *Overload*, California had excess electricity by 1983. Nuclear power plants, under construction or newly completed, simply added to rates without supplying any needed power.

Consumers rebelled against nuclear power plants, and attempted to gain some measure of public control over electricity industry decision-making in their states. Referendums were initiated in eight states by citizens for this purpose in 1982. They were opposed with well-funded power company campaigns. The power industry employed Winner-Wagner, a public relations firm that claimed to have defeated citizen initiatives seven times out of eight. Winner-Wagner utilised various PR techniques, including front groups incorporating bankers and business leaders, and "sophisticated tracking polls".[67]

In one case, a coalition of citizen groups and politicians proposed a bill to authorise the regulator to require utilities to get their electricity in the cheapest possible way, which in some cases might be by making it go further with conservation. The local utilities were supported in their fight against this by funding of $3 million from 28 companies in eighteen states. Their advertisements claimed that this measure would cost each household an extra $1800 each year because the bill would require the closure of a nuclear power plant whose electricity was not needed. The bill was defeated.[68]

Some citizens' initiatives won despite the weight of industry propaganda opposing them. As in earlier years, the cost of this propaganda was charged to consumers; as was the money paid by utilities to the EEI to lobby on their behalf, often against consumers' interests; as was, also, the money used by utilities to make their cases at PUC hearings for increased rates.[69]

The revolving door, which saw personnel changing jobs between the private power companies and public office, was, as always, supplemented by campaign contributions and political donations. These ensured that personnel appointed to PUCs were sympathetic to utilities and that governments did not pass legislation that threatened the utilities. Ralph Nader's Public Citizen found that politicians who always voted to protect utility interests received four times as much money as those who voted otherwise.

During the early 1980s, whilst government funding for solar energy and conservation was slashed, funding for nuclear research and construction was increased.[70] Also, utility conservation spending halved during the 1980s. Incentives for solar heating and other measures were dropped, and the utilities advertised to promote higher electricity usage.[71]

In the late 1980s sustainable development became the catchcry. Industry, with the help of the think tanks they funded, sought to promote market-based solutions to environmental problems.[72] In this vein, some mainstream environmental groups were swayed by the business-propagated promise of 'win-win' situations that enabled companies to make profits whilst supposedly helping the environment. They began working with industry to find these elusive 'win-win' solutions.

Ralph Cavanagh, a senior lawyer from the Natural Resources Defense Council (NRDC), set up the "California Collaborative Process" in 1989 whereby, according to the *San Francisco Bay Guardian*, "key environmentalists could meet behind closed doors with top executives from private utilities to smooth over their differences and hammer out energy-efficiency programs."[73] The Collaborative promoted the unlikely idea that energy efficiency could be achieved voluntarily through financial incentives to the utilities. They persuaded the CPUC to allow the utilities to earn a profit on energy claimed to be saved through conservation as well as energy capacity added.[74]

NRDC had been founded in 1970 by two Wall Street lawyers, to fight legal cases to protect the environment. It was funded by the Ford Foundation on the condition that it accepted a conservative board of trustees that included Laurence Rockefeller and other wealthy conservatives, and that its legal activities were cleared by a group of past presidents of the American Bar Association. One of the two founding lawyers, Stephen Duggan, was a partner in the New York law firm Simpson, Thatcher & Bartlett, which included utilities as a major part of their cliental. At the behest of the Ford Foundation, the NRDC also incorporated a similar group made up of Yale Law School graduates, which included John Bryson, who later became head of the CPUC and then chief executive of Southern California Edison.[75] According to author Harvey Wasserman, Cavanagh was a "disciple of Bryson".[76]

During the 1970s and 1980s the NRDC made a name for itself fighting legal battles to enforce clean air and water legislation, as well as cases to do with pesticides, arms testing, and a myriad of other issues. However, when it came to energy issues it moved from being a confrontational outsider to a significant player with a seat at the negotiation table, with the help of the San-Francisco-based Energy Foundation.[77]

NRDC received $3.1 million from the Energy Foundation between 1991 and 1997, and $1.13 million from the Pew Foundation between 1993 and 1995. Both foundations were set up with corporate money made in oil and other industries; these foundations dominated the funding for activist groups, ensuring that those lobbying on energy issues took a pro-business, pro-deregulation, and pro-private utility stance, or didn't receive funding. Nader claimed "the network of funders has become a network of enforcers. And these guys are all on a first-name basis with these corporate [utility] executives." The Energy Foundation ran conferences where environmentalists and consumer activists could hob nob with utility executives and get on their wavelength.[78]

The Energy Foundation promoted demand-side management (DSM) in a way that approached the problem of energy efficiency from a market-based, non-regulatory stance. The spin was that the utilities would voluntarily invest in energy-efficiency measures rather than new plants because this would improve their share value and financial position. Groups that did not support DSM were not funded by the foundation.

When The Utility Reform Network (TURN) was funded by the Energy Foundation for a two-year study into DSM, its economist concluded that private utilities were unlikely to promote energy efficiency because it went against their imperative to sell more electricity. This led to the termination of TURN's funding. Daniel Berman and John O'Connor argue in their book *Who Owns the Sun?* that DSM was little more than window-dressing from the utilities' perspective, and that they went along with it as long as it didn't significantly reduce energy demand and so long as alternatives such as wind and solar power were left out of the picture.[79]

PG&E's 'commitment' to DSM didn't stop it cutting industrial electricity rates and seeking to increase its share of that market by effectively subsidising wasteful industrial energy usage. However, the 'commitment' to DSM certainly earned them good PR, with the help of NRDC: "Suddenly, NRDC became an ardent public defender of PG&E, whether the issue was high electric rates or PG&E's environmental credentials." As a result of the Collaborative Process, PG&E was able to run television advertisements, paid for by ratepayers, of course, with titles such as "Conversations with the Earth" and "Smarter Energy for a Better World", that further greenwashed its image.[80]

In 1991 president Bush awarded PG&E the Environmental and Conservation Challenge Award, which was promptly advertised in a full-page newspaper advertisement in which Cavanagh praised PG&E for its conservation efforts.[81] Cavanagh also produced videos on behalf of PG&E, describing their conservation efforts, and coauthored an article on the same topic with PG&E personnel. He was appointed to a steering committee with Amory Lovins and others for a PG&E research project, and he generally received favourable media coverage for his 'positive' and collaborative stance.[82]

Between 1994 and 1998 Californian private utilities cut their budgets for achieving energy efficiency: PG&E by 38 per cent, San Diego Gas & Electric by 58 per cent, and SoCalEd by 23 per cent.[83]

PART TWO

The United States Deregulates and Markets Rule

THE CALIFORNIAN DISASTER OF 2000-1 — when wholesale electricity prices skyrocketed, blackouts were experienced, and the government had to bail out retail electricity suppliers — resulted from a failure to learn the hard-won lessons of past US experience and also the lessons of the British experience (see part 3). During the 1980s and 1990s various attempts were made to repeal the legislation implemented during the 1930s to regulate the excesses of the power holding companies. The disaster in California could have been foreseen, had it not been for the blinkers imposed by free-market ideology promoted by think tanks and front groups, and funded by corporate interests.

Attempts to repeal the Public Utility Holding Companies Act (PUHCA — see chapter 3) during the 1980s were defeated after campaigning by consumer and environmental groups. However, at least fifteen power companies and the Edison Electric Institute (EEI) opened up the issue again during the 1990s and lobbied for repeal of PUHCA.[1] Many significant exemptions from the act were granted. This enabled electricity companies to again grow into huge, profit-seeking, democracy-manipulating, price-gouging entities without any obligation to provide a reliable and affordable electricity supply. It was these self-interested companies that largely drove and shaped the new rules for the electricity industry. Enron is a prime example.

State-regulated utilities had been expected to meet established consumer standards, provide reliable and guaranteed service and, in some states, serve low-income consumers and use a certain percentage of renewable energy. In the 1990s, as market theology took over, planning and social objectives were discarded. Instead, the Public Utilities Commissions "increasingly emphasized competitive provision of power"; that is, "letting the market decide where and when to build new power plants and where and when to take energy efficiency measures".[2] The resulting havoc is being felt in many states, not just California.

CHAPTER FIVE

Driving Deregulation

Only after a long and determined propaganda campaign by conservatives to fetishize the market and denigrate the public sector did such notions as deregulating electricity become plausible. What could possibly be worse, they argued, than 'big government'?
Joe Conason[3]

AN ABUNDANT AND RELIABLE SUPPLY of cheap electricity, combined with a lavish supply of ratepayer-funded advertisements and public relations campaigns, meant that few challenged the system of state-regulated monopolies for several decades. However, the rate increases in the 1970s, caused by the costs of building nuclear power plants, rising interest rates, and the escalating costs of oil following the oil crisis, created discontent. This discontent was utilised and amplified by vested interests that saw profit opportunities or cost savings in the deregulation of electricity.

Their rhetoric was provided by a new brand of neoconservative think tanks proliferating in Washington and elsewhere. These think tanks, established in the 1970s as part of the conservative backlash against environmental and consumer movements, spent much time and energy attacking government intervention and regulation in most areas of business and the economy.[4]

This new conservative force began to assert itself with the election of Reagan, as it had with the election of Thatcher in Britain. The perception of effective regulation began breaking down. The Reagan administration did its best to undermine the Public Utility Regulatory Policy Act (PURPA—see chapter 4), arguing that the industry was already overregulated. Reagan cut conservation and solar energy programs and boosted funding for nuclear power, but insisted that "free market forces" would decide which was the better energy source.[5]

A series of deregulations during the 1980s in the airline industry, then natural gas, petroleum, financial services, telecommunications and railroad freight transportation, set the scene for electricity deregulation during the 1990s. The changes that followed transformed one of the largest industries in the US, valued at over $200 billion, into one with minimal public safeguards, wildly fluctuating prices, and multiple opportunities for profits and losses.

Vested Interests

Deregulation in the US was primarily driven by business interests; in particular, industries that used large amounts of electricity and wanted to be able to reduce costs by doing deals with competing suppliers, and private power companies that wanted an opportunity to make profits from the electricity business previously monopolised by the regulated utilities.

Even though regulators seemed to be powerless in the face of escalating rates, business interests and their allies blamed increasing electricity costs on too much regulation rather than a lack of regulation or democratic control. In fact, in many states electricity regulation was almost non-existent because it was so weak and afforded so little protection to consumers. Power companies seemed to be able to overcharge with impunity.[6] And it was this that had led to the overconstruction of expensive nuclear power plants during a time of waning electricity demand.

The administration of Bush senior developed an energy policy from 1989 that "sought to emphasize the use of free-market forces" to achieve economic and energy efficiency, and avoid government intervention. The foundation of the policy was to be open access to transmission lines to foster competition. Environmentalists also supported this, as they were convinced by deregulation's advocates that it would open the market to renewable energy sources. The utilities' reaction to the proposal was mixed. Some thought they could profit from selling their excess electricity or buying it from interstate. However, others opposed the move, creating the Electric Reliability Coalition to campaign against it.[7]

The opening of transmission lines to independent power producers was also advocated by large electricity users. It had become evident to them that some utilities charged much higher rates than others and they believed that wholesale electricity competition would reduce prices. As early as 1976 some of the large electricity-consuming corporations had come together to form the Electricity Consumers Resource Council (ELCON) to lobby state and federal governments for deregulation.[8]

Publicly owned utilities tended to provide cheaper electricity to householders, whilst private utilities garnered their profits and extra expenses by charging householders more. In this way, householders subsidised industrial consumers and enabled the private utilities to keep industry charges competitive with nearby publicly owned systems (see Table 5.1). However, the regional variation in charges was considerable, and those utilities that had invested in nuclear power tended to have the highest rates of all. Nuclear power plants made up almost half of the asset value of the US electricity industry in the mid-1990s, but only supplied 22 per cent of the electricity.[9]

New technologies created an impetus for change. They enabled power plants to be small and economical so that they didn't have to be a monopoly activity but could be built and bought by all sorts of companies, including large factories, and placed in locations much closer to users. This provided scope for the growth of new, independent, non-regulated generating companies. As the new technologies for generating power more cheaply became available, the older utilities were slow to adopt them.[10]

■ **Table 5.1: Electricity rates in 1994 in cents per kilowatt hour (kWh)**

	Residential	Commercial	Industrial
Public	6.7	6.7	4.9
Private	8.8	7.9	4.9

Source: D. M. Berman and J. T. O'Connor. Who Owns the Sun. *White River Junction, Vermont: Chelsea Green, 1996, p. 98.*

The big industrial users promoted deregulation because it would allow them to do deals directly with independent generating companies. Even if the regulated utilities built the new, cheaper, gas-turbine generation plants, the rates they charged would still reflect the mix of plants they owned; whereas if large consumers could buy their electricity directly from independent producers who owned only the new cheaper gas-fired plants, their rates would be much lower.[11]

■ **Table 5.2: Comparative Cost of Electricity Generation in 1992**

Nuclear	Non-Nuclear	Gas-Turbine Cogenerators
7.4 cents/kWh	4 cents/kWh	3 cents/kWh

Source: R. F. Hirsh. Power Loss. *Cambridge, Massachusetts: The MIT Press, 1999, p. 251.*

The independent generating companies (as opposed to the regulated monopoly utilities) were amongst the leading lobbyists for deregulation because of the profit opportunities it offered. For the same reason, aspiring electricity marketers (who buy power from generators and sell it to consumers and to electricity retailers) also lobbied vigorously for deregulation. The most prominent of them, Enron, will be described in chapter 8. The Center for Responsive Politics points out that "during the first six months of 1996 alone, energy interests spent at least $37 million to lobby Congress and federal agencies on deregulation". When Dan Schaefer became chair of the House Commerce Subcommittee on Energy and Power in 1995, donations to him from power companies, manufacturers, and lobbyists increased dramatically.[12] The *Washington Post* reported:

> An army of lobbyists, including former Capitol Hill lawmakers and staffers, have been hired by the companies and interest groups that want to shape the outcomes. "Every lobbyist in town is trying to get a piece of electricity", a House Commerce Committee staffer said.[13]

The Edison Electric Institute (EEI) devoted millions of dollars to its deregulation campaign — more than $11 million in 1996 alone. The EEI, as was seen in previous chapters, was a consummate lobbying organisation, and supplemented its eight in-house lobbyists with fifteen additional firms including the lobbying firms of three former congressmen, two Republican and one Democrat, and a former lobbyist for the AFL-CIO. It also funded various television and radio current affairs programs.[14]

Deregulation was pushed strongly by the Alliance of Energy Suppliers, a division of the EEI, which advanced "the commercial interests of power producers and marketers." It was dedicated to "shaping markets", "facilitiating business and networking opportunities", and "legislation and regulatory advocacy" in the interests of generators: "Through the combined efforts of member utilities, their affiliates, and other power producers and marketers, the Alliance, along with the vast resources [of] EEI, is working to define markets rules for a new competitive industry".[15]

The 1992 Energy Policy Act was the first milestone of all this lobbying. It required regulated utilities to let other companies use their transmission lines so that electricity could be traded across the country. It mandated wholesale electricity competition between states and "encouraged adoption of market-based principles as a way to increase the availability and efficient use of energy supplies." It exempted independent power producers from PUHCA rules, and allowed regulated utilities to own independent power companies in other states and even overseas, if they could show this did not disadvantage local consumers.[16] In 1994 "substantial regulatory authority" was shifted to the federal government, and in 1995 the risk of building new plants was shifted onto investors.[17] Little investment occurred after this because investors were waiting to see how deregulation would pan out.

The next battle was for deregulation at the state level. During the 1990s the large manufacturers and their allies argued that deregulation would dramatically reduce electricity bills for householders, farmers, retailers, and schools as well as manufacturers. They predicted a 15-50 per cent reduction. At first, they were opposed by some of the utilities who employed "an army of lobbyists and consultants, including several former members of Congress". It was estimated that they spent $50 million in 1997 alone on lobbying and advertising.[18] Campaign contributions also soared (see figure below).

The opposing utilities tended to be those with nuclear power debts who realised that nuclear plants were inefficient and unable to compete in a free market. Their lobbying was not so much against deregulation as for the right to recover those debts from ratepayers or taxpayers. Consequently, these utilities did deals in each state for the ratepayers to pay off those multi-billion dollar debts in return for utility support for deregulation. This occurred in California, Illinois, Massachusetts, New York, Ohio, Pennsylvania, Texas, and elsewhere. "Nationwide, the utility bailout could total over $200 billion, making it one of the largest corporate bailouts in history".[19]

Figure 5.1: Total electric utilities' contributions to federal candidates

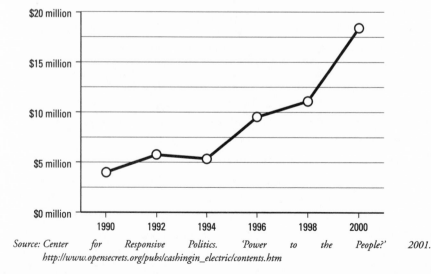

Source: Center   for   Responsive   Politics.   'Power   to   the   People?'   2001.
          http://www.opensecrets.org/pubs/cashingin_electric/contents.htm

Ideological Support

The case for deregulation had to be presented as being in the interests of the wider public. Groups such as the large industrial energy users utilised the language of free-market advocates to state their case in terms that were not too obviously self-interested.[20] The neo-conservative think tanks provided that language.

Conservative think tanks became especially influential during the Reagan years. For example, most of the policy recommendations of the Heritage Foundation were adopted by the Reagan administration and its president, Edwin Feulner, received a Presidential Citizen's Medal from Reagan for being "a leader of the conservative movement ... who has helped shape the policy of our Government." The foundation, set up in 1973, promoted deregulation of industry, an unrestrained free market, and privatisation. Its donors included corporations such as automobile manufacturers, coal, oil, chemical, and tobacco companies.[21]

In "Energizing America: A blueprint for deregulating the electricity market", Adam Thierer, a fellow of the Heritage Foundation, argued that regulation of monopolies had caused a "lack of price competition and consumer choices, limited innovations, and a lackluster environmental record", whereas "deregulation of the electricity marketplace" promised "rich rewards". These rewards included lower prices, lower operating costs for industry, more jobs, increased reliability of service, and a cleaner environment. Deregulation, he wrote, "means consumers, in free-market fashion, will call the shots in the electricity market, not regulators." Thierer argued that all federal regulation that involved rate-setting or price controls should end and that all legislation, such as PUCHA, should be repealed. Thierer also argued that there should be no mandatory use of renewable energy and that this, and energy efficiency, would be encouraged by competitive markets.[22]

The economic and ideological arguments against electricity conservation put together by think tank personnel and the academics associated with them provided ammunition to large industrial consumers of electricity who could now "attack regulatory initiatives without explicitly appearing to be opposed to publicly lauded goals of environmental improvement and energy conservation ... they instead tied their dissenting arguments to an increasingly popular framework that espoused less government intervention in the economy and the increased use of free-market principles."[23] Mandatory energy-efficiency programs were discontinued in the 1990s as market ideology demanded that energy efficiency should result from competition.[24]

Utilities also resisted conservation measures. Efforts to promote renewable energy sources were again cut back in the early 1990s, and state and federal tax credits for this purpose ended. In 1995 the Federal Energy Regulatory Commission (FERC) ruled that utilities could not be required to make long-term contracts with renewable energy producers that used sources such as wind and geothermal. This was in response to a utility petition. Spending on conservation halved from $1.6 billion in 1994 to $800 million in 1998, even though it is a more cost-effective and quicker way of ensuring demand is met than building new power plants.[25]

The Honorable Thomas DeLay set out his "free-market vision" for the electric power industry at a Heritage Foundation lecture: "Bringing electricity into the competitive world will unleash new products, greater efficiencies, business synergies, and entrepreneurial success stories. It will create new industries, new entrepreneurs, and new jobs ..."[26]

Even a more centrist think tank, the Brookings Institute, produced a report supporting electricity deregulation for its potential consumer savings. The report was financed by companies lobbying for deregulation, including Enron, Pennsylvania Power and Light, Wisconsin Electric Power, Cinergy, and the Electricity Consumers Resource Council, a coalition of large electricity users.[27]

A plethora of other corporate front groups and coalitions were also formed to promote deregulation, including the Alliance for Competitive Electricity, Citizens for State Power, Electric Utilities Shareholders' Alliances, the Alliance for Power Privatization, and the Coalition for Customer Choice in Electricity. Many used advertisements, as did individual companies, to promote deregulation.[28] Americans for Affordable Electricity coordinated the other coalitions in their campaign for deregulation. Its members included the Ford Motor Company, Enron, and various utilities, and it raised millions of dollars for lobbying and advertising. For example Enron contributed a $20 million ad campaign.[29]

> ... the energy deregulation lobbying only sounded like it was designed for consumers and end-users. In fact, almost all of the efforts were designed to sway a relatively small number of politicians, bureaucrats and other policy wonks. Even the TV and radio ads that were bandied about were intended more as a threat for what might run in the middle of the country than a plan for what actually would.[30]

Citizens for a Sound Economy (CSE), a front group with close Republican ties, spent tens of thousands on advertising in various states, and even used banners from airplanes to promote 'consumer choice'. CSE bills itself as "Americans working for free enterprise and limited government". It commissioned a study (which was funded in part by CSE patron, Enron) which found that deregulation would reduce the average electricity bill by 43 per cent.[31]

Politicians financed by business interests were eager to utilise think-tank and front-group data in their arguments for deregulation. When CSE's figure was cited by the Heritage Foundation, it was publicised as a confirmation of CSE's study. A press release from the House Commerce Committee claimed that "yet another *academic* study" (my italics) had concluded "that giving consumers the freedom to choose their own electric utility will result in lower rates, improved service and better reliability."[32] The committee also cited the Brookings Institute study.

Politicians tended to promote the concept of consumer choice as a primary benefit of deregulation because they wanted wide voter support, which is why bills for deregulation had names like the Electric Consumers' Power to Choose Act. When the chair of the Commerce Committee, Tom Bliley, appeared at a press conference promoting the reintroduction of the Electric Consumers' Power to Choose Act, he had with him representatives of what were supposed to be "690 consumer groups that support consumer choice in electricity", rather than corporate executives. This was to avoid the impression that the bill was being introduced for the benefit of big business. The press conference was to announce a "media outreach" initiative aimed at consumers to let them know that they would be able to save up to 43 per cent on their power bills with deregulation.[33]

Despite the effort to manufacture the appearance of grassroots support, deregulation was primarily driven not by popular demand, but by large industrial users, who thought they could save money; and by energy companies, who thought they could make money out of it. Most consumers weren't interested in the much-heralded consumer choice. Enron spent millions of dollars in California and offered two weeks of free electricity, in a failed attempt to persuade consumers to buy electricity from it. It only attracted 30,000 customers out of a potential 10 million, and promptly abandoned the efforts.[34]

At the end of 2000 less than 2 per cent of residents had switched providers, and most of those chose Green Mountain Energy, a company which "appeals to those willing to pay a premium to foster clean electricity generated by renewable resources". In contrast, 13 per cent of the electricity-intensive industrial companies switched.[35] David Morris, writing in *Alternet*, noted that "even the most fervent supporters of customer choice (i.e. retail competition) concede the lack of any grassroots demand". FERC commissioner James

Hoecker "called the public's general silence in terms of demanding customer choice 'positively deafening'."[36]

Nevertheless, the think tanks had done their job well, and there was now a widely acceptable rationale for deregulation. "Calls by large industries for utility deregulation found a ready chorus in academics, analysts, and politicians who believed that competition would produce lower prices, better service, and more innovation than government regulation". By the early 1990s "the tide of free-market hysteria reached a fever-pitch", and industry continued to lobby for deregulation so that many states decided to deregulate electricity.[37]

The business media also played an unquestioning part in promoting deregulation. "For years, the [*Wall Street*] *Journal's* editorial page argued strenuously for deregulation, and adopted a celebratory tone when that finally began to occur in energy markets in the mid-1990s."[38] One report read:

> Energy companies are trying all sorts of ways to compete in their new unregulated, anything-goes world. Some are acquiring, some are merging, many are charging into new markets with innovative products. New blood has infused much of the industry, raising bright, energetic newcomers into the top ranks of some of the most innovative energy companies.[39]

By the mid-1990s it was "taken for granted in the business press, and in the editorials, and to some extent in the halls of Congress, that deregulation is just the right and the natural thing to do".[40] Past lessons about the failings of markets in delivering public goods were conveniently forgotten.

Of course, the media was wise after the event, and conveniently ignored its own role in selling deregulation. The *Mercury News* wrote at the end of 2000, after a year of price gouging by out-of-state utilities: "while deregulation was sold to the public as a change that would benefit all electricity consumers — big and small — the basic elements of the plan were crafted primarily to benefit large industrial users and the utilities".[41]

California

In 1996 FERC issued rules that further deregulated the wholesale market, requiring companies with transmission facilities to allow other companies to use their lines for reasonable, non-discriminatory fees, and enabling states to unbundle their electricity industries into generation, transmission, distribution, and retail.[42] California was one of the first states to take advantage of the new rules.

The Californian Public Utility Commission (CPUC) had already held hearings on electricity restructuring in the state, and in 1994 issued a policy statement, referred to as the "Blue Book", which was replete with think-tank rhetoric and stated that it would "look principally, though not blindly, to markets and the private sector, rather than to *command-and-control* regulation, as the preferred means to achieve the goals established and benefits identified." In a news release, the commission stated its intention to rely on "*the discipline of markets* to replace often burdensome, administrative regulatory approaches" (my italics).[43]

To find the real reasons for deregulation in California, however, one has to look beyond the free-market rhetoric to the vested interests involved. Prices for the three major private utilities in California were higher than most other parts of the country, mainly because of cost overruns of billions of dollars on nuclear power plants. Industry groups threatened to move interstate because of high electricity rates, which was of concern to politicians whose re-election depended on the economic health of the state. They were persuaded by deregulation's advocates, as were industry groups themselves, and many others, that deregulation would lower electricity costs. In particular, manufacturing firms that used large amounts of electricity, such as the cement and steel industries, pushed for deregulation in the hope that it would bring costs down and enable them to buy electricity from the cheapest providers.[44]

Advocates of deregulation argued that the guaranteed return on investment for regulated utilities provided no incentive for the utilities to cut costs. One utility CEO joked in 1995 that "this is the only industry I've ever seen where you can increase your profits by redecorating your office".[45] Deregulation supporters said the utilities had become inefficient and expensive, but if they were exposed to the market that would change.

Big electricity users formed the lobby group Californians for Competitive Electricity to fight for deregulation. It encompassed a range of other coalitions, including the California League of Food Processors, the California Manufacturers Association, and the California Large Energy Consumers Association—a coalition of cement companies, steel manufacturers, and a gold mining company—and the California Independent Energy Producers Association.[46] The California Manufacturers Association spent $1.7 million on lobbying in 1995 and 1996. The California Large Energy Consumers Association and the Californians for Competitive Electricity also spent hundreds of thousands of dollars.[47]

The three major private utilities in California were very much in favour of deregulation. They are Southern California Edison (SoCalEd)—serving

eleven million people in Southern California, Pacific Gas & Electric (PG&E)
— the largest utility in the world serving twelve million people in northern
and central California, and San Diego Gas & Electric. Since the mid-1980s
these utilities had attempted to pander to the industry consumers' lobby by
reducing industrial rates by 16 per cent whilst residential rates increased by
36 per cent.[48] The utilities were concerned about losing big industrial customers "who were threatening to generate power on their own" because of the
high rates the utilities were charging.[49]

Wasserman, who wrote *The Last Energy War*, argued, "What they wanted
was to cash out those bad investments, keep their big customers and make
profits at will, without regulation."[50] They envisioned large profits rather than
the resulting losses. Donella Meadows agreed, saying that industries were
leaving the grid one by one, "leaving the utilities, with their huge, outmoded,
unpaid-for power plants, in a panic."[51]

So the utilities met with politicians. In return for giving up their monopoly status, the utilities negotiated a deal that would assure them a predicted
$28.5 billion of ratepayers' money to pay off past debts from capital invest-
ment ('stranded costs') incurred by the construction of nuclear power plants.
A rate freeze was imposed at an artificially high level, 50 per cent higher than
the national average electricity rate, to provide the utilities with additional
revenue before the rates were subject to market forces.[52]

The utilities had enormous influence because of the sort of activities that
power companies had engaged in for decades that were described in part one
of this book. The Center for Public Integrity estimates that three major
Californian utilities spent $69 million between 1994 and 2000 on lobbying
and political spending. Most of this was on the issue of deregulation, getting
legislation that suited them, including recovery of stranded costs, and fighting efforts to change the law afterwards.[53]

Apart from giving campaign contributions and other donations to local
politicians to ensure that the issue of public power was kept off the political
agenda, PG&E also donated money to a variety of community and civic
groups and charities. According to the *San Francisco Bay Guardian*, "PG&E
has infused itself into San Francisco politics, society, culture and business—
using its money to make connections that have insulated the company from
criticism or political challenge." It points out that whilst groups receiving
money do not admit that the money is conditional on their support for
PG&E, not one of them has openly supported public ownership of electricity, either.[54]

Ralph Nader is equally blunt: "the politicians and the community groups are all neutralized by the money, and there's no countervailing force to fight the utility." PG&E had insinuated itself into several influential business organisations as well, and onto the boards of large companies in the area. Even after prices for electricity soared and service became poor, business groups refused to publicly support a shift to publicly owned utilities. Nader also argues that PG&E spread large amounts of "money around to the big law firms, so there's no major firm that can take on PG&E. Then they enlist the political power of these law firms to press their agenda."[55]

The revolving door helped achieve bipartisan support for the deregulation bill. For example, a key advocate of deregulation was Democrat senator Steve Peace. David Takashima had been his chief of staff in the 1980s before working as a lobbyist for SoCalEd, and then returning to work for Peace, and helping to shape the deregulation bill. He then left to be director of government affairs for PG&E. Peace himself received $277,000 from the three large utilities.[56]

As well as campaign contributions, legislators also received personal benefits. Energy companies supported an organisation called the California Foundation on the Environment and Economy (CFEE), which had representatives of the three main utilities on its board of directors. CFEE paid for various overseas trips for CPUC members and politicians to "study deregulation".[57]

Many environmental groups were also enrolled in the battle for deregulation. They were persuaded that deregulation would remove incentives from the regulated monopolies to increase electricity sales, build large new power plants—particularly nuclear power plants—ignore environmental costs, and undermine alternative generation from renewable sources. This was despite the fact that CPUC energy-efficiency programs were discontinued in the 1990s as market ideology demanded that energy efficiency should result from competition. Environmental support was also bought with a small budget in the deregulation legislation for energy efficiency and the development of electricity generation from renewable resources.[58]

Wasserman claims that the pro-environmental measures in the bill were a "few eco-scraps" that enabled Ralph Cavanagh from Natural Resources Defense Council (NRDC—see chapter 4) to sell the deregulation bill behind the scenes to the media and in the mainstream environmental community. Cavanagh was utilised by the media as the voice of environmentalists on this issue, preventing those with more critical stances from being heard.[59] According to *The American Prospect*, John Bryson, former NRDC co-founder, and SoCalEd CEO, got NRDC support for deregulation by promising a commitment to various conservation programs, but he later "persuaded FERC to overturn the conservation mandate".[60]

Wasserman claims that the deregulation bill, AB1890, was drafted by SoCalEd lawyers in SoCalEd offices.[61] James Walsh in his book *$10 Billion Jolt* tells it a little differently. He claims that when the bill was being drafted by Peace, he would have lobbyists from the utilities and the big energy users in his office: "In the final weeks, Peace sometimes ordered lobbyists out of the room, telling them to return in 15 minutes when their issues were resolved. They would then tell the legislators what the 'deregulation' bill should say."[62]

Far from being of benefit to the environment, the legislation crippled the nascent solar and energy-efficiency industries because of the uncertain investment environment created and the surcharges necessary to bail out the utilities. It also preempted the adoption of wide-scale industrial natural gas co-generation by enabling the utilities to offer large industrial consumers cheap, subsidised electricity.[63]

However, most of the support for the bill came from the widespread belief, encouraged by the think tanks, that the introduction of 'free market' forces would lower prices.[64] When AB1890 passed with unanimous support in both houses in September 1996 within three weeks of being presented to the House, the president of SoCalEd exclaimed that it was "a great day for us", and that the legislation was an achievement that would assure "customers choice".[65] Governor Pete Wilson's statement showed more foresight: "We're doing more than signing a new law ... We are shifting the balance of power in California".[66]

According to reporters, Wilson had presidential aspirations, and thought that by making California the leading light of deregulation he would achieve his ambitions. He had been seen as "a difference-splitting, non-ideological moderate. This profile worked well in California; but it meant a lack of status among free-market conservatives in the national GOP ranks". Achieving deregulation in California ahead of all other states would gain him kudos in the right places.[67]

As elsewhere in the country, Californian politicians fulfilled the wishes of profit-seeking corporations because they believed in the beneficence of the market. "California's deregulation effort was based on an unquestioning faith in the power of the free market", a faith that led proponents to ignore expert advice about impending problems as well as evidence from Britain that 'market power' had been a problem after deregulation (see chapter 12). Even when disaster struck, proponents continued to believe that the market would prove itself in the long run, once the flaws had been sorted out.[68]

AB1890 involved the utilities selling off most of their fossil-fuel generating plant (mainly natural gas) to unregulated private power companies. The aim was to ensure there was plenty of competition between electricity-generating companies. More competition was supposed to mean lower prices and choice of suppliers for consumers. The rate freeze was to last until the end of 2001, or until the utilities had paid off their 'stranded costs', whichever came first. Then the owners of the utilities would have no constraints on the prices they could charge consumers.

Environmental and consumer groups attempted to repeal parts of the deregulation bill, including the ratepayer payout for nuclear debts, in a 1998 ballot — Proposition 9. In response, energy companies and their allies spent $40 million opposing the proposition, and it was lost by a substantial margin. As part of their campaign against Proposition 9 the utilities called in their favours from the charities and citizen groups they had been funding.[69]

The defeat of Proposition 9 was also facilitated by the active opposition of the NRDC. The NRDC supported the recovery of stranded costs through customer charges, and made a joint submission to the FERC with PG&E to this effect. SoCalEd employed its own front group, Concerned Stockholders of California, to the same end.[70] Senator Peace's production company produced a half-hour 'infomercial' opposing the proposition. In his role as senator, Peace had co-chaired a government hearing on the impact of the proposition.[71]

The major utilities spent huge amounts of money on advertising in preparation for the opening of markets and 'consumer choice'. Edison International, Enova Corp., and PG&E spent $90 million on advertising between October 1997 and May 1998. They also "stepped up marketing crusades to garner customers".[72] Enron spent about $10 million on a campaign in 1997 with the intention of setting up as a competitor before deciding to concentrate on large business customers. Southern Company spent $20 million on a campaign in 1998 to target decision-makers and large energy users.[73]

The state government also spent tens of millions on an 'education program' in preparation for deregulation. "Plug in, California" was an $89 million government advertising campaign aimed at householders and small businesses that emphasised the cost savings, reliability, consumer choice, and consumer rights that went with deregulation. It included television, radio, and newspaper advertising as well as direct-mail and trained speakers talking to 84 community groups.[74] A 10 per cent rate 'cut' along with the rate freeze, also helped win the public over. This was financed by a bond issue that would have ratepayers paying for their own rate cut for years to come.[75]

The generating plants divested by the utilities were bought by private companies, often based in other states, whose only interest was in making the highest profit they could. Even if state officials were blinded by their faith in the market and could not see the power they were handing over to the generators, energy companies could see the potential. As they scrambled for a piece of the action, trying to outbid each other, the generating plants sold for much higher prices than expected. The companies knew that they could get the price of the plant back from electricity buyers, with a healthy profit included.[76]

San Diego Gas and Electric made so much from the sale of its plant that it quickly recouped its stranded costs, and the rate freeze was lifted in July 1999. Ratepayers were then subject to market prices. However, instead of seeing rates fall as had been promised, they watched them climb. A kilowatt-hour of electricity at peak time increased from 2.7 cents to 52 cents. The average monthly bill of $50 at the time of the freeze became $120 by the end of August 2000, at which stage the government intervened. As a result, some $800 million was "transferred out of the local economy". Ratepayers were enraged, forcing the government to temporarily put a cap on rate increases. The money lost by the utility as a result of these price caps was repaid by ratepayers in 2002 with interest.[77]

As we will see in the next chapter, the independent generating companies made huge profits at the expense of Californian utilities and ratepayers.

CHAPTER SIX

Deregulation in California

For a decade the US has been selling the wonder of free markets to the rest of the world but it always exempted itself … In California, power companies and traders thought they could bring home to the US the free-market methods they used to huge profit in Brazil, Pakistan, Britain and other backwaters.
Gregory Palast[1]

DEREGULATION WAS SUPPOSED TO MAKE electricity cheaper by increasing competition and allowing markets to set prices. Instead, the cost of electricity to Californian residents and businesses increased by $US11 billion in one year, and billions of dollars were moved from the pockets of Californian consumers and utilities to energy companies and electricity brokers, many of them in other states. All this money did not buy a better service, however. California experienced its first major electricity blackouts since the Second World War. By February 2001 emergency alerts and pleas for people to use less energy were regular occurrences.[2]

Many features of deregulation in California were copied from the UK electricity restructuring process (see chapters 11 and 12). According to James Walsh in *$10 Billion Jolt*, the utility SoCalEd lobbied hard for adoption of the British power pool system, even utilising a front group — Consumers First.[3] The California Public Utilities Commissioners made several visits to the UK to study what was happening there.[4] However, they seemed unwilling to learn from the problems that restructuring had caused in the UK. As in the UK, the Californian power pool was subject to manipulation by the generating companies. "The most egregious example of price gouging, state officials

101

say, was when Duke Energy charged the state $3,880 for a single megawatt-hour that had cost about $30 one year earlier."[5] (The pre-deregulation cost was around $30.)

Mines, sawmills, and aluminium factories were shut down, and workers were laid off. Aluminium producers that had purchased relatively cheap electricity on long-term contracts found it more profitable to shut down their operations and sell their electricity to the Californian power pool. Three such producers are estimated to have earned $500 million in this way.[6] "Federal Reserve Chairman Alan Greenspan ... warned that California's energy crisis could plunge the entire country into a recession."[7] Rival states, including Nevada and Utah, used the opportunity to poach businesses that were suffering high energy prices and blackouts in California.[8] However, neighbouring states were not immune from the fallout of deregulation:

> As the impact of the California debacle cascaded through the western United States, workers have been laid off at smelters, paper mills and mines ... Washington State predicts that "43,000 jobs could be lost over the next three years." Kaiser Aluminum, at its Mead aluminum plant near Spokane, decided to sell electricity for $400 million rather than keep production going, idling 600 workers. Montana Resources closed its copper mine in Butte, displacing 325 workers. Georgia Pacific West shut down its paper mill in Bellingham, Washington last year, idling another 600 workers, all due to high energy prices ...[9]

In California the utilities, which had to pay soaring prices for wholesale electricity and were unable to pass those prices onto its retail customers, threatened to declare bankruptcy. The state government had to step in and buy electricity on their behalf.

The Power Exchange

Prices in the power pool were decided using a computerised market called the Power Exchange (PX), established in March 1998, which operated in a similar way to the UK power pool. Utilities wanting to buy electricity entered the amount of electricity they would need for each hour of the next day, and generators offered quantities of electricity at named prices. Each hour the computers set the price at which demand would be satisfied (see figures 6.1 and 6.2).

For example, the Independent System Operator (ISO) that ran the PX might receive offers of power for a range of prices from $20 up to $1000 per megawatt-hour (MWh). It filled the needs of the utilities from the lowest-priced offers first. Once the demand had been met, all generators whose electricity was used received the price of the highest offer accepted. If the demand was near the total supply, the electricity from the company with the highest bid of $1000 had to be used, and all companies received that price, even though most had bid far below it.[10]

■ **Figure 6.1: Setting the pool price for each time interval**

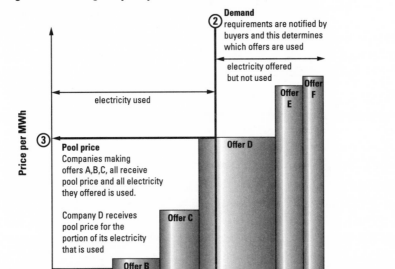

The idea behind the bidding system is that when supplies of power are adequate, generators will make bids close to their operating costs, because if they bid too high, their power plants may go untapped. In practice, when supplies are tight, generators can be certain almost any price will be accepted.[11]

If there was more demand (including a set reserve) than power being offered by the generators on the market, the ISO had to purchase the difference at premium prices—that is, at whatever price the generator cared to name.[12] A real-time spot market was set up for this purpose.

The Californian ISO was made up of stakeholders, including the utilities and the generators, and it had "no responsibility to California consumers".[13] The utilities supplying Californian residents were required to buy power on this daily market, and were unable to buy electricity through direct long-term contracts with generators. The utilities had lobbied to be able to negotiate

■ Figure 6.2: The power pool

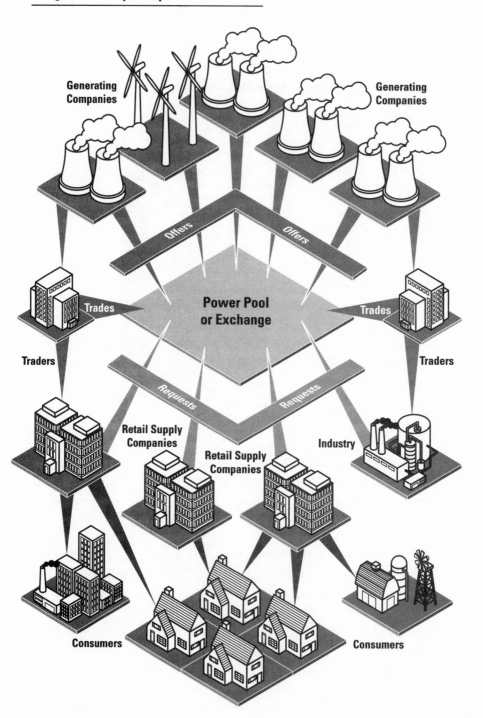

Generating
Companies

Generating
Companies

Offers

Offers

Trades

**Power Pool
or Exchange**

Trades

Traders

Traders

Requests

Requests

Retail Supply
Companies

Industry

Retail Supply
Companies

Consumers

Consumers

long-term contracts, but had been unsuccessful after the independent generating companies had opposed this. However, individual companies and marketers were able to buy power directly from other marketers and generators by private contract.[14]

For the first couple of years of deregulation the utilities bought electricity at much lower prices than they sold it to consumers. The two major utilities had made more than $5 billion each by the spring of 2000, according to consumer groups. However, in summer 2000 the price soared. In June, when demand peaked, electricity was cut to over a hundred thousand homes. In the following months, even though demand fell, electricity prices continued to rise.[15]

The price rises through 2000 and 2001 were explained by the power companies and the media as a result of demand outstripping supply because of a heat wave in 2000 and increased economic activity. However, California should have had enough generating capacity to cope with summer demand, which was not so different from the year before. On 29 June, for example, demand in 1999 and 2000 was comparable, as it had been the day before. Yet prices in the day-ahead market were more than ten times higher during peak hours. They were even more than four times higher in off-peak hours. What is more, the peak loads in 2000 were well below those in 1999, but in 1999 price hikes did not occur (see figure 6.3).[16]

■ **Figure 6.3: Average monthly prices compared to peak monthly demand in summers 1998–2000**

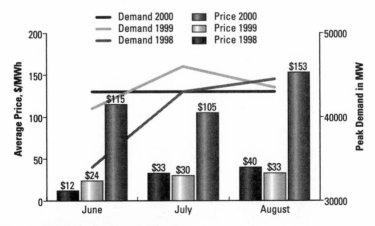

NB: Prices for Energy in Southern California
Source: W. Hauter and T. Slocum. 'It's Greed Stupid!', Public Citizen, 2001, p. 8; Southern California Edison, http://www.sce.com/005_regul_info/005c6g_generators.shtml

The prices remained high when the weather cooled and during weekends
when demand fell off (see figures 6.4 and 6.5). Even in the cool of November
2000 prices continued to be four times higher than November 1999. The
prices paid by the utilities on a corresponding Sunday in 2000 were seven
times more than prices on a Sunday in 1999, despite electricity consumption
being the same.[17] The California Public Utilities Commission (CPUC) compared similar days in 1999 and 2000, and found that "The price increase is
not explainable by increased costs, weather, volumes or even the existence of
a much higher wholesale price cap, in 2000."

■ **Figure 6.4: Average monthly wholesale electricity prices ($/MWh)**

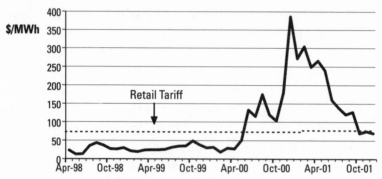

*Source: C. Blumstein et al., 'The History of Electricty Restructuring in California.' Berkeley, California: Centre
for the Study of Energy Markets. Aug. 2001, p. 20*

■ **Figure 6.5: Average PX prices by demand in 1999 and 2000**

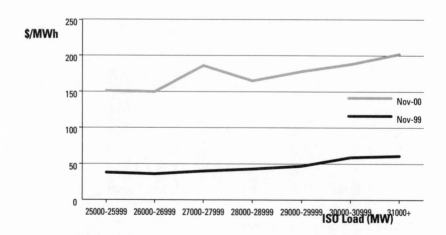

Source: Southern California Edison, http://www.sce.com/005_regul_info/images/pxprice.gif

Similarly a study by deregulation advocate Paul Joskow, a professor of economics and management at MIT, and Edward Kahn, of Analysis Group/Economics in San Francisco, demonstrated that the price hikes could not be explained by market conditions — such as rising natural gas prices, increased electricity demand, insufficient supply, or even increase in the price of pollution trading credits. They quantified the effects of each of these variables, and found that the wholesale electricity prices were still far more than they should have been in a truly competitive market.[18]

■ **Figure 6.6: Rolling blackouts vs peak demand, January 2001**

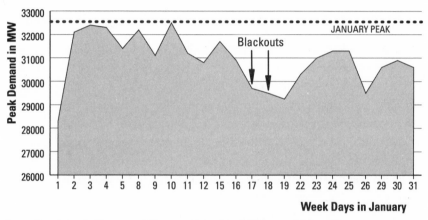

Source: *Foundation for Taxpayer and Consumer Rights, 'Hoax', 17 January 2002, p. 16*

In January 2001 rolling blackouts were ordered, affecting hundreds of thousands of people. But blackouts did not correlate with peak demand, either. For example, there was a blackout on a Sunday in January 2001 when demand was only 60 per cent of the peak demand in summer (see figure 6.6).[19] Public Citizen's Critical Mass Energy and Environment Program noted that blackouts had occurred in 2000 when demand was less than 30,000 MW, well below the peak demand in 1998 of over 45,000 MW.[20]

Withholding Supplies

What had happened was that the power suppliers had started exercising their market-power and manipulating the price. The main way they were doing this was by withholding some of their supply to create an artificial shortage to drive prices up (just as OPEC countries did with oil in the 1970s). Generators had an incentive to close some plants so as to get higher prices for the electricity from their remaining plants. Knowing that supply would be short, the generators could bid very high prices in the sure knowledge that all supplies would be needed.[21] Such bids had nothing to do with the cost of production. Joskow and Kahn concluded:

> there is considerable empirical evidence to support a presumption that the high prices experienced in the summer of 2000 were the product of deliberate actions on the part of generators or marketers controlling the dispatch of generating capacity to withhold supply and increase market prices.[22]

Suppliers were simultaneously shutting down generating capacity for maintenance just when the supply was most needed. The first blackout in the Bay area occurred on a hot summer day in June 2000 when nine power plants "were out of service, either for scheduled maintenance or repairs, or were operating at limited capacity". In August 2000 there was almost five times more electricity off line than in August 1999. On 28 January 2001, 49 power plants had been closed down.[23]

The existing plants were mostly old and needed a lot of maintenance. However, before deregulation the utilities would schedule maintenance for the winter months when demand was less. After deregulation this preventive maintenance in cooler months was down by 40 per cent.[24] Also before deregulation utilities would schedule maintenance so that different plants would not be shut for maintenance at the same time. The need for maintenance of so many plants at peak time in 2000 either indicated a lack of planning and an unlikely set of coincidences or an illegal coordination between suppliers to drive the price up.[25]

■ **Figure 6.7: Plant outages in California, 1999–2001**

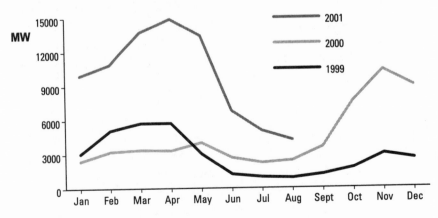

Source: Foundation for Taxpayer and Consumer Rights, 'Hoax', 17 January 2002, p. 24

Whilst it's illegal to collude, it doesn't hurt that when one of a generator's competitor's plants goes down, prices go up. And that if one of its own plants goes down, prices go up further. That's the beauty of the market system when power, literal and figurative, is concentrated into the hands of a few.[26]

Shutdowns for maintenance seemed to be suspiciously more frequent and of longer duration than previously required (see figure 6.7). Before deregulation, the utilities would do their best to get plants back online as soon as possible, and could usually manage it within two weeks. Now the generators took an average of four weeks to bring plants back on line.[27] However, "federal researchers noted that when prices climbed to more lucrative levels, some plants managed to come back to life".[28]

Maintenance in the previous five years had shut individual plants down from 5 to 10 per cent per year. In 2000 that rate was up to an average of 50 per cent of the year; as a result, there were days when up to a third of capacity was not available. Before deregulation, plants would have to advise the authorities of the reasons for a shutdown, whereas shutdowns now did not have to be explained.[29]

Because details about why these plants are off-line is confidential, the public is literally left in the dark ... suppliers are not even complying with the requirement to turn in an annual plan for when they will have plants off-line for maintenance, and there are no penalties for this lack of cooperation.[30]

In June 2000, power plant engineers working for Duke Energy accused their company of "virtually sabotaging one of their own plants by 'running it up and down like a yo-yo', shutting the plant on and off." Far from being part of maintenance, such a regime was definitely bad for the plant and would shorten its operating life. Duke Energy responded that it had to shut the plants off when their power was not required because of the bidding system. Either way, the market was not conducive to the efficient running of power plants.[31]

There was not enough excess generating capacity in the system to be able to stand so much inactivity, which is why some blamed the problems on a shortage of generating capacity in California. The introduction of electricity restructuring had meant that investors had stopped investing in generation whilst they waited to see how the new environment would pan out. "The most immediate and profound implication" of the publication of the master plan for electric restructuring in California "was the almost simultaneous withdrawal of investment capital from the power generation sector in the state and, to a lesser extent, the adjacent region."[32]

Before deregulation, it had been assumed the state had plenty of generating capacity. However, the last forecast, done in 1995, had assumed that 1500 MW of renewable and co-generation capacity would be bought. However, contracts for this extra capacity had been vetoed by the Federal Energy Regulatory Commission (FERC) after complaints by the utilities that the extra capacity wasn't needed. The 1995 forecast had also assumed that energy-efficiency measures would save a further 2000 MW, but these were never implemented.[33]

The market system provided little incentive for regular preventive maintenance, investment in new power plants, or for energy efficiency. When the Californian government set electricity rates and guaranteed the private utilities a set return on their investment, utilities had to serve all customers in their designated territories and ensure that there was enough power to meet those customers' needs for ten years into the future.[34] In the market, shortages are supposed to lead to high prices which, in theory, provide an incentive to build new plants. But, in fact, there was more financial reward in creating artificial shortages and avoiding risky investments that would lower the price by increasing supply.

In particular, deregulation positively deterred investment in conservation and energy efficiency: "the market competes for lowest up-front price, not lowest price over the lifetime of a product ... In the old electric system, it cost utilities less to subsidize our more efficient bulbs than to build another dinosaur plant." In the deregulated system, the incentive is to sell more electricity for premium prices.[35]

Natural gas prices also went up in California after the gas industry was deregulated because of withheld supply, which affected electricity prices. The Californian government blamed El Paso Corporation and Dynegy for deliberately restricting flow through their natural gas pipelines from Texas to California to increase prices. In 2002 El Paso was found guilty of this by a FERC judge. In one week the price of natural gas went up by ten times in California whilst the same natural gas was being sold on the other side of the border at a fraction of the cost.[36]

Normally, California relies on gas stored over the summer to meet its winter needs. However, because of the deregulation of the gas industry, large customers were no longer required to buy storage; they could make their own decisions about storage according to market forces. When the utilities sold off their gas-fired generating plants they also sold off their gas storage tanks that had been used to ensure plant reliability during winter. The new generators were not interested in keeping gas in storage because they had no obligation to the public.[37]

Other Strategies for Manipulating Prices

Just as it was in the interest of electricity generators to shut down plants to drive prices up, so it was in their interest to divert supplies elsewhere to drive up prices in California. Generators and marketers sold electricity out of the state; then, when prices soared in California because of the shortages, the electricity marketers would sell it back to California at much higher prices than they otherwise would have received. In fact, more electricity was exported from California in 2000 during the supposed shortages than had been exported the previous year. There was no regulation to stop generators doing this because that would have interfered with the free market.[38]

In a deregulated system, price manipulation could occur without scrutiny as the power companies did not have to show their account books. The CPUC called for the "bidding behavior of market participants that cannot be coincidental" to be investigated. But the ISO and PX refused to hand over data to the CPUC that might have enabled it to investigate.[39] The ISO did its own investigation, and reported that over ten months the generators had overcharged the utilities by more than $6 billion.[40] FERC also declined to identify those behind the price manipulations, although it had the data available to do so and was supposed, under the Federal Power Act, to ensure that prices were "just and reasonable".

In fact, no less than six investigations by state and federal authorities were underway by the end of 2000,[41] but it was not until Enron went bankrupt (see chapter 9) that documents came to light which proved that power companies had been manipulating Californian electricity prices and deceptively making money off utilities and consumers. Enron used a number of strategies for this as it sought to exploit each loophole and opportunity for profit in the system. To avoid Californian price caps imposed in 2000 in response to soaring prices, Enron sold electricity to another party outside the state, and then bought it back for a small additional fee and resold it back to California for prices far above the price caps. It was able to do this because the price caps only applied to electricity generated and bought within the state. Enron called this strategy "Ricochet"; others called it "megawatt-laundering".[42]

Sometimes Enron just sold electricity out of state to make a profit, buying it at the capped $250 per MWh in California, and selling it for up to $1200 in other states. This tactic was called "Fat Boy". Enron lawyers recognised that by doing this it could be contributing to power shortages in California, but argued in internal memos that "this strategy appears not to present any problems, other than a public relations risk".[43]

Using other tactics, which it named "Death Star" and "Load Shift", Enron artificially created the impression that power lines were congested: it overstated the power it was planning to deliver over them, so it would be paid to relieve non-existent congestion. Congestion payments could be as high as $750 per MWh, meaning that it was profitable for companies to offer to sell power at a loss if they could create congestion that they would be paid to relieve. In this way, Enron made more than $30 million in 2000. Enron lawyers described how "Enron gets paid for moving energy to relieve congestion without actually moving any energy or relieving any congestion."[44]

In another strategy, Enron engaged in phoney transactions, trading large volumes of electricity amongst its subsidiaries to drive the price up. The CPUC found that 30 per cent of Enron's transactions in the fourth quarter of 2000 were amongst Enron affliates and subsidiaries. During that time prices ranged from 5 cents to $3,322 per MWh. Commission president, Loretta Lynch, claimed: "Enron was selling the same megawatts back and forth to itself, causing the price to rise with each sale, all under the rules it helped create ... The selling back and forth also created the illusion of an active, volatile market." The rising price of Enron trades affected the price of other electricity trades.[45]

Enron made so much money by gaming the Californian market that it hid up to $1.5 billion of it in undisclosed reserves so it would not appear in its accounts. It made as much as $100 million in a single day, according to former managers and executives; and when accusations of market manipulation and price gouging started to be made, Enron felt it best not to reveal the extent of its profits.[46] In 2002 a senior Enron trader pleaded guilty to conspiring to manipulate the California electricity market and agreed to help federal authorities with their investigations.[47]

Enron was certainly not the only company to employ these strategies, as its lawyers noted in its internal memos.[48] Xcel Energy and Mirant Energy later admitted to using congestion and other schemes to get higher prices for their electricity.[49] Avista Corporation admitted to acting as a middleman between Enron and Portland General to allow transactions to take place that would otherwise have been illegal. El Paso Electric executives wrote in an internal memo that their deals with Enron, from which they made $7 million in one month from the Californian market, were "a great illustration of what is possible when teamwork, knowledge, initiative and accountability all come together".[50] A former energy trader from Goldman, Sachs told the *New York*

Times: "The whole reason for the existence of traders is to make as much money as possible, consistent with what's legal ... I lived through this: if you didn't manipulate the market and manipulation was accessible to you, that's when you were yelled at."[51]

The first corporation to pay damages after being accused of manipulating prices in California was the Williams companies. In 2002, without admitting guilt, it agreed to pay over $400 million to settle the case out of court. In return, the state government agreed not to seek refunds for customers. Williams also agreed to reduce by about $1 billion the cost of a ten-year power contract, signed by the state government when prices were high.[52]

Another company implicated in the gaming was Perot Systems Corporation, which designed the software for the power pool. Headed by Ross Perot, a former presidential candidate, the company was later accused of teaching energy companies how to manipulate the system. Documents in the possession of Reliant Energy, one of the companies accused of gaming the system, showed how Perot Systems explained strategies very similar to Enron's "Death Star" and "Fat Boy" strategies, including deliberately congesting the system to drive prices up.[53]

Phoney trades also occurred in the deregulated natural gas markets. El Paso was accused of engaging in wash trades—that is, buying and selling the same natural gas back and forth to the same party on the same day.[54] Gregory Palast reported in *The Observer* that internal documents from the El Paso Pipeline company seem to show:

> that when California "deregulated" the gas pipeline market, an El Paso executive speculated that if the company sold the pipeline capacity to its own subsidiary, it could squeeze California by the light bulbs anytime it reduced throughput. One corporate buyer calculates the scheme cost California $3.7 billion.[55]

The CPUC stated: "It appears that the FERC's assumption—that the market will discipline wholesale prices—is not a reasonable one at this time in California ... [We] have enough information to suggest that the system is operating in ways that are contrary to the public interest".[56]

The Power Companies

Electricity company profits soared in 2000 and 2001 as they exploited the Californian electricity market. Eleven companies sold power to the PX (see figure 6.8), including Reliant Energy, Dynegy, Duke Energy, and marketer Enron. Texas-based Dynegy increased its profits by 210 per cent in 2000, thanks to the new California market. North Carolina-based Duke Energy doubled its profits in 2000 and quadrupled them in the first quarter of 2001. Texas-based Reliant Energy had a 600 per cent increase in third-quarter earnings for 2000, and some $US100 million of that came from California. Electricity company profits continued increasing in the first half of 2001, despite a general recession in which average US corporate profits went down 12 per cent.[57]

■ **Figure 6.8: Source of electricity supply in California**

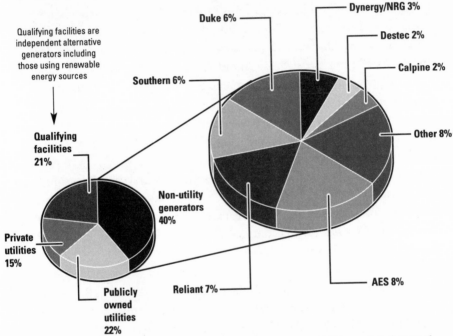

Source: Southern California Edison, http://www.sce.com/005_regul_info/005c6g_generators.shtml

When the prices started soaring and the energy crisis loomed, "an army of energy and utility official treated lawmakers, aides and commissioners to thousands of dollars worth of dinners, drinks, concerts, country-club greens fees and hard-to-get basketball tickets. The dining experiences ranged from food and beverages at a Hooters restaurant in Arizona to lunches in Barcelona, Spain and Dublin, Ireland."[58]

Most of the nation's leading power traders, including Reliant, Duke Energy, and Southern Company, were spin-off companies from the original, regulated utilities. Often they had acquired generating plant at big discounts from those same utility companies, since construction costs had been paid by ratepayers. The new unregulated power companies had gone on to make much larger profits than their regulated sister companies.[59]

Smaller firms with an entrepreneurial flair also made large amounts from California's situation. For example, New Energy Ventures was started by Michael Peevey, a former president of SoCalEd and Edison International, and spouse of Assemblywoman Carol Liu, who had "preached the virtues of deregulation, saying the country could save billions of dollars a year in power costs through increased competition". His company sought to cream off some of those savings by acting as a middleman between the wholesalers and the large consumers. The company grew in four years from three to 256 employees, with revenues of around $700 million per year. It was bought by AES Corp. in June 1999 for approximately $100 million. Peevey is now a commissioner in the CPUC.[60]

PG&E and SoCalEd were unable to pass the price rises on to consumers because of the rate freeze and built up large debts. At the end of 2000 they threatened that, unless they could raise rates by at least 30 per cent, they would become bankrupt. The claims of huge losses by the utilities need to be put into perspective, however. PG&E Corporation, the parent of PG&E Company, and Edison International, the parent company of SoCalEd, each made $3 billion from selling off their generating plant.[61]

The parent companies also made another $3 billion selling power from their remaining Californian generating plant at high prices. Their subsidiaries had also been making big profits out of high electricity prices, as did the utilities themselves because they still owned some generating plants in California. PG&E and SoCalEd sold power from these plants to the PX, then bought it back for distribution to their customers. The *LA Times* reported that of the $4.5 billion that SoCalEd says it spent on electricity that it was not reimbursed for through rates, $2 billion was "money it owes itself for power from its own generators and other gains".[62]

Both utilities continued to pay dividends to their parent companies, even after the problems in the wholesale market became apparent. PG&E paid $100 million in August 2000 to PG&E Corporation, and SoCalEd paid $97 million to Edison International. What is more, PG&E Corporation was expected to receive a tax refund of up to a billion dollars for PG&E's losses.[63]

Both parent companies and their other subsidiaries invested money that they received from PG&E and SoCalEd to buy power plants and other assets in other states and countries. Edison International owns power plants in seven countries, as well as thirteen states in the US; a telephone company in Switzerland; and a cable company in Mexico. Daniel Berman, author of *Who*

Owns the Sun, claims that Edison International "has siphoned off over $5 billion from its regulated utility's ratepayers to sate its imperial ambitions in Mexico, England, Australia, and Indonesia". Edison's International assets were worth about $38 billion in 2001.[64]

PG&E subsidiary US Generating Co. had 22 power stations by 1995; but PG&E, according to David Bacon, writing in *Corporate Watch*, ceased building plants in California, and "even bought up five plants belonging to independent producers and shut them down".[65] PG&E National Energy Group owns over 30 power plants in ten states. It earned $162 million in 2000, much of it in California, becoming the third-largest power trader in the US.[66]

■ **Figure 6.9: Cash flows from PG&E and SoCalEd, 1997–1999**

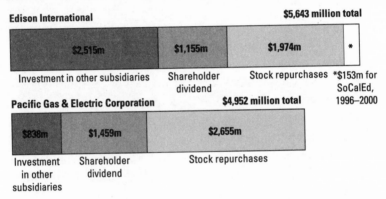

Source: *Associated Press. Interactive Guide: California Power Woes. 2002. http://wire.ap.org/APpackages/california_power/*

According to Ralph Nader's Public Citizen, the two corporations and their subsidiaries spent over $22 billion on power plants, stock buybacks, and other purchases between December 1998 and December 2000. This compares with the $12 billion debt that PG&E and SoCalEd were claiming. The bankruptcy of PG&E Company did not affect the PG&E Corporation or its other subsidiaries, which had already manoeuvred to protect their assets in such an event. PG&E Corporation which restructured itself in 1997, had $30 billion in assets and made profits of $753 million in the first three quarters of 2000, which was a 40 per cent increase on the first three quarters of the previous year.[67]

Executives of both utilities and suppliers have all benefited from deregulation. For example, the PG&E Corporation CEO (also chair of PG&E Co.) earned over $2 million in 1999, up 63 per cent from 1998. The PG&E Company CEO earned over $1 million in the same year, which was up 60 per cent on 1998.[68] Bryson, chair and CEO of Edison International and SoCalEd, earned over $1.86 million in 1999, up half a million dollars from 1996. And the chair and CEO of San Diego Gas & Electric's parent company – Sempra – received over $3 million in 1999, triple what he received in 1996.[69]

Ratepayers rightly asked why these companies could not bail themselves out by selling their assets rather than draw on taxpayers money. What is more, the $12 billion being demanded by the utilities as a bailout could buy all the power plants in California, according to consumer advocates.[70]

Bailout Blackmail

The CPUC granted a 10 per cent rate increase in early January 2001, but the utilities were still not happy: they demanded that they be bailed out. Their credit ratings were slashed, and SoCalEd and PG&E stopped paying their bills in mid-January 2001. Power sellers stayed away from the Power Exchange because they would not be paid and the utilities were suspended from it, effectively ending its operations.[71]

The utilities and their allies ran a public relations campaign to prompt the government to raise rates further and bail out the utilities. Having donated $600,000 to Governor Gray Davis before the power crisis, the utilities had reason to expect cooperation from him. Edison Electric Institute ran television advertisements; the utilities targeted journalists and met with editorial boards of newspapers to get editorial-page support; and the Los Angeles Business Advisors, a group of corporate CEOs, placed large advertisements in the newspapers supporting the utilities.[72] A group called the American Taxpayers Alliance was formed, headed by a Republican campaign manager and with secret funding sources, said to be energy interests. It spent some $2 million on television commercials blaming Davis for the crisis.[73]

There is some conjecture that the January 2001 blackouts which Northern California experienced were, in fact, a way of pressuring government officials to bail out the utilities. A leaked memo from Credit Suisse First Boston to clients suggested that the blackouts were "intended to soften up the Legislature and the voters to the need for rate increases".[74] And the president of the Californian-based Foundation for Taxpayer and Consumer Rights (FTCR), Harvey Rosenfield, pointed out:

> We didn't have blackouts until the utility companies, unable to win a $12 billion ratepayer bailout threatening bankruptcy, decided to stop paying their power bills ... The next day, blackouts began and the day after that, the legislature approved the governor's emergency request for an additional $400 million for the state to buy electricity. Then the blackouts stopped.[75]

In February the government took over the purchasing of electricity, spending around $50 million a day buying power for the utilities to distribute, which amounted to $8 billion in the first five months. However, some of the smaller independent electricity companies had not been paid by the utilities for months and had to shut down their plants, leading to further blackouts in March. Their bills were also paid by the government. The cost of electricity to the state's treasury was so significant that the credit-rating agencies downgraded California's rating.[76]

In April 2001, after negotiations with the state broke down, PG&E Company filed for bankruptcy protection, despite rate increases being approved which would have added billions to PG&E's revenues.[77] "The bankruptcy petition filed by Pacific Gas and Electric reported assets of $24 billion and debts of $18 billion", with ongoing expenses of $300 million per month that it could not recoup.[78] The utility also owned and maintained 140,000 acres of forest and prime environmental habitat around its hydroelectric plants. These were put at risk, under the company's plans to split itself into 26 limited liability corporations.[79]

In mid-2001 the Coalition for a Secure Energy Future launched a 'public information' campaign that included television and radio advertisements "designed to inform the state's consumers about the disastrous impact that an SCE bankruptcy could have on the California economy if the agreement between SCE and the state is not finalized soon." The coalition was a front group for SoCalEd (or SCE) and purported to represent "small and large businesses, taxpayers, consumers, educators, public safety, labor, and ethnic organizations". The advertisements urged citizens to "call your state legislators and ask them to support the agreement to prevent an Edison bankruptcy".[80] The state agreed to buy SoCalEd's transmission system for $2.76 billion, so as to prevent it from going into bankruptcy. It was valued in SoCalEd's books at $1.1 billion.[81]

The government negotiated long-term electricity contracts; but because prices were artificially high at the time, it was locked into paying excessive prices for electricity in the long term. It signed $43 billion worth of contracts for the following 20 years of electricity, committing taxpayers to paying $50 per MWh even after prices settled back to $20 per MWh. The contracts even contained a provision for the state to pay pollution penalties if the generating plants exceed regulatory pollution limits. Some estimate that this will cost consumers an extra $20 billion over the term of the contracts.[82]

In the lead-up to the summer of 2001 the energy industry and the academics they funded had predicted an energy shortage and a series of broad-scale blackouts. Independent assessments did not back up this prediction, however. Once the government stepped in to buy electricity: "Lo and behold, idle capacity came back on line, and the crisis was over."[83] The threatened energy shortage and subsequent blackouts never materialised, and FTCR notes: "For the energy industry, the sudden disappearance of the 'crisis' and the collapse of prices posed the same problem it faced when the crisis began: how to explain what looked to most people like a successful scam."[84]

The turnaround was explained by the industry and the government in terms of the success of conservation measures, mild weather conditions, and the construction of new generating capacity. The *New York Times* reported "Californians have led the nation in energy conservation. Instead of a scarcity of power, California now has too much, and the state has been selling electricity at a loss or even giving it away."[85] FTCR refutes these explanations as exaggerations to hide the truth:

> The alternative would have been to confirm what much of the public suspected: that the crisis was manufactured by the energy industry to boost its profits, that there was never any justification for blackouts in California, that blackouts were used to extort the state, and that the governor had been duped into signing long term contracts that obligated the state to pay excessive prices for up to two decades … Power prices began to decline and reliability concerns washed away for two basic reasons: the energy industry had already accomplished all the profiteering it could hope to do, and further profiteering risked not only a massive backlash in California but threatened the viability of deregulation throughout the nation.[86]

The government passed legislation in May 2001 that created a public power agency with the authority to raise $5 billion for new plants, retrofitting existing plants, and developing energy efficiency and conservation. The irony was not lost on the FTCR: "Nothing represented so great a negation of the ideology of deregulation than the fact that the first state to deregulate had been forced to become the state's sole electricity purchaser and to create a new public power agency."[87]

To ensure that the electricity purchased through expensive long-term contracts could be sold on to consumers, the government sought to prevent industry consumers from buying electricity directly from the generating or electricity-marketing companies. This prompted a new campaign fronted by Californians for Energy Action, a coalition of businesses formed "to voice the business community's perspective on energy issues. This coalition, led by the president of the California Manufacturers Association and the president of the Californian Chamber of Commerce, took out newspaper advertisements claiming that the proposal would 'effectively kill any hope of developing competitive electricity markets in California'," and would leave California "with a struggling economy and an investment climate that makes prosperity impossible". This would cause jobs to be lost, and therefore was bad for everyone.[88]

Yet it was business faith in electricity cost savings arising from competition that had led the government into deregulating electricity in the first place. It turned out to be an expensive mistake. In January 2002 the FTCR claimed: "In total, the deregulation law, enacted with the unanimous support of politicians in 1996, will cost Californians approximately $71 billion, or $2,100 for every man, woman and child in the state." This figure includes $23.6 billion in stranded costs, $10 billion in expected bailout costs for the utilities, $22 billion in inflated long-term contracts, and $16 billion in excessive prices paid during 2001.[89]

CHAPTER SEVEN

Federal Politics

If you believe in markets, you can't blanch at the sight of victims.
Bill Eastlake, Economist with Idaho Public Utilities Commission[1]

SINCE DEREGULATION IN CALIFORNIA, 42 other states have begun steps toward deregulation, and more than 23 have approved legislation or regulations to achieve it. In 1999 there were 25 bills being considered by the federal government related to electricity restructuring and the repeal of electricity-industry regulations. However, following the Californian experience, other states experienced similar problems, and seven states put their deregulation plans on hold. At the time of writing, only sixteen states have deregulated. Retail-competition legislation has been repealed in California, Nevada, and Oklahoma.[2]

Supporters of deregulation, including the federal government, have been keen to ensure that deregulation is not blamed for the Californian experience.[3] They attempted to depict the crisis as too little deregulation rather than too much. Despite the mounting evidence to the contrary, they continued to argue that deregulation would lower electricity prices. In a report commissioned by the Edison Electric Institute (EEI), Eric Hirst argued:

> Although a few states have decided, based on the California experience, not to restructure, I believe that is the wrong outcome. Instead, the primary lessons other states should learn from California are that competitive markets can work; competition is not to blame for California's problems; and basic economic principles of supply, demand, and prices affect market outcomes ...

In particular, letting private investors decide whether and when to build new power plants and retire, repower, or continue to operate existing units can, in the long run, lower the costs of electricity to consumers relative to the costs that would occur if regulators make those decisions ...

Today's wholesale power markets permit buyers and sellers to secure the best deals across large geographic areas. Such broad regional markets lower consumer prices and ensure that electricity is produced with the lowest-cost generating units, subject to transmission constraints.[4]

However, the experience in California has in no way been unique.

■ **Figure 7.1: Electricity deregulation in each state, July 2000**

Source: *Energy Information Agency. 'The Changing Structure of the Electric Power Industry 2000: An Update.' DOE/EIA-0562(00). October 2000, p. xi.*

Other States

Price manipulation and blackouts have been a feature in several states. Since federal deregulation of wholesale electricity prices in 1996, price spikes of many times the cost of production have occurred in New England, Illinois, Ohio, and New York.[5] Between 1997 and 1999 average wholesale prices in Chicago, the Upper Midwest, New York, and New England more than doubled; they tripled in some parts of the country, particularly the South; and they quadrupled in Texas. In New England, investigations found that generating companies manipulated prices by withholding power and shutting down capacity during the heat of the 2000 summer (see figure 7.2). Outages increased by 47 per cent.[6]

■ Figure 7.2: New England average monthly wholesale electricity price

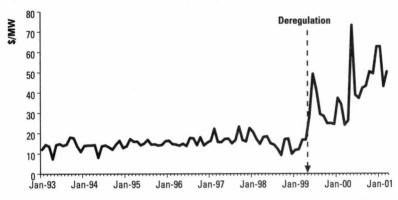

Source: J. Oppenheim. 'US Electric Utilities.' Brussels: European Federation of Public Service Unions. 2001. p. 10.

Charlie Higley, of Public Citizen, notes:

not one state has restructured their electric industry in a way that will truly benefit consumers or protect our natural environment. Instead, large industrial customers and utilities have used campaign contributions and strong-arm lobbying to get lawmakers to enact legislation that will benefit corporate interests at the expense of the consumer's interest.[7]

States where deregulation has not occurred have not experienced large increases in rates, and publicly owned utilities have kept rates 10 to 40 per cent below neighbouring, privately owned utilities.[8] However, western states that did not deregulate were affected by California's woes. Washington governor Gary Locke wrote:

In the State of Washington, we elected not to deregulate our retail electric power industry. We continue to expect utilities to serve their customers with low-cost power while earning a fair rate of return. But now, caught in the fallout of California's energy meltdown, we, too, are facing potential shortages, skyrocketing prices and escalating debt.[9]

This was because of the mutual dependence between California and Washington, whereby California bought Washington electricity in the summer to power its air conditioners, and Washington bought Californian electricity in the winter to power its heaters. The soaring prices in California caused the utilities to raise their rates in Washington, and also in Idaho, Utah, and Arizona, impacting on residents and local industries.[10]

The flaw in the Californian deregulation plan that was blamed for the problems was that rates to consumers were frozen. However, whilst this was a cause of the poor financial situation of the utilities, it was not a cause of the soaring wholesale prices. Ironically, the rates had been frozen for the benefit of the utilities, so they could recoup their stranded costs. Had the rates not been frozen, the soaring wholesale prices would have been passed on to consumers. This may have helped the utilities, but would have been much worse for ratepayers. In San Diego, where they were passed on, "the firestorm of public outrage forced the imposition of new controls".[11]

In New York there was no rate freeze when deregulation was introduced, and consumers there also suffered large increases in rates. As in California, they had been promised that the free market would bring lower rates and ensure businesses did not move state to get cheaper electricity. Instead, rates charged by Consolidated Edison, said to be the highest in the US before deregulation, went up 38 per cent within two years.[12] Gail Collins commented in the *New York Times*:

> Here in New York, deregulation is going great. Millions of residents can testify that our state government did not make California's mistake of putting a cap on retail prices. No sirree. Whatever the opposite of price controls are, we've got them, and if you call the local power company to complain about your bill, the consumer assistance person will ask whether you have a refrigerator — in a tone that suggests you've been manufacturing aluminium in the kitchen.[13]

There are many parallels between the New York and the Californian situation. In New York, too, faith in the free market caused authorities to ignore warnings about the need for surplus power to prevent price rises, and the need to deter the utilities from selling their generating plant to just a few companies that could then engage in price manipulation. As in California, the plant were sold for high prices as buyers expected to be able to charge high prices for electricity, and measures to foster energy conservation were dramatically cut. A 2 per cent surcharge on bills to promote conservation and conduct energy audits was eliminated. New York used the same method of price allocation as California, and there is evidence that prices were also manipulated in New York to artificially high levels. It is because of this price manipulation that regulators imposed a wholesale price cap in New York in 2000.[14]

One day, when a nuclear power plant was shut down, the price reached the wholesale price cap of $1000/MWh—and the energy companies instantly earned $70 million. Because supply was tight (private power companies had not built any new plants, as had been expected after deregulation), the government scrambled in 2001 to build ten small generators in New York City to avoid blackouts and price spikes the following summer. In their haste, government authorities avoided full environmental reviews, and placed the generators in poor neighbourhoods already suffering from poor air quality.[15]

By mid-2002 the system operator was asking large electricity users to reduce their consumption at times when significant generating capacity was offline. The Business Council of New York State Inc. was calling for more generating capacity to foster competition and drive prices down. It warned that, otherwise, "New York State risks serious economic damage". New York City is now considering public ownership of new and existing electricity-generation plants.[16]

A series of fires in electrical transformers caused power blackouts in New York City during the summer of 2002. These were the results of aging equipment being unable to keep up with demand because there was no incentive in the deregulated system to upgrade equipment, and no one being held responsible when it failed. A lack of maintenance also contributed to the blackouts in New York City, as it did in Chicago, Long Island, New Jersey, New England, and Texas.[17]

Nationwide, deregulation has led to a massive reduction of the utility workforce. As private, deregulated utilities shed staff so as to cut costs, 150,000 people have lost their jobs, including those who were responsible for the safety and reliability of electricity supplies. The Utility Workers Union of America (UWUA) and the US Department of Energy's Energy Information Administration (DOE EIA) have estimated that utilities now employ less than two-thirds of the workers they did in the early 1990s.[18] The UWUA claims that cost-cutting has led to the following problems, which threaten worker and public safety as well as system reliability:

- utilities perform inspections less frequently;
- necessary but non-emergency repairs are deferred, sometimes indefinitely;
- retiring workers are often not replaced; and
- some companies are cutting back on training programs for new employees.[19]

A 1999 DOE report found that: "The overall effect has been that the infrastructure for reliability assurance has been considerably eroded."[20] Jerrold Oppenheim, in a later report prepared for the European Federation of Public Service Unions, pointed out:

The industry infrastructure is aging and in need of continuous maintenance. Distribution system upgrades are needed not only to replace old and defective equipment but also to keep up with increasing loads on pole-top transformers, feeder circuits, and substations. Inspection cycles have doubled or tripled and critical equipment is often in poor condition when eventually inspected. There are neither sufficient numbers of workers nor adequate management systems to follow up on repairs identified through routine inspections. The problems range from poles that are condemned by workers but not replaced; to load tap changers that are inoperable, affecting proper voltage levels; to uninspected transformers that pose a serious risk of exploding. Field workers across the country observe that cables are tested less frequently; that substation and manhole inspection cycles are longer; and that condemned poles are often not replaced. Key system components will not perform as they were designed to perform due to age, lack of repair, or both.[21]

In Connecticut, where consumer prices are temporarily capped as part of a deregulation process, the state's largest utility, Connecticut Light and Power, demanded a rate increase to enable it to pay more for wholesale electricity so as to avoid the threatened shut down of three generating facilities owned by NRG Energy. However, the state attorney-general called the demand "almost a form of extortion ... holding a gun to our heads in threatening to shut down three key facilities unless their rates are raised contrary to the established process."[22]

In Nevada, the largest utility is facing the prospect of bankruptcy.[23] Texas, which passed deregulation legislation in 1999, also instituted a rate freeze when deregulation began at the start of 2002. A test run of its newly deregulated electricity market in 2001 quickly revealed market manipulation by six energy companies, including Reliant Energy, TXU, Enron, Mirant, and American Electric Power (AEP). Artificial congestion-creation, as occurred in California, was suspected after a fund of $20 million to pay generators to relieve congestion for eighteen months was used up in two weeks.[24]

In some states, governments were so keen to prove that deregulation was good for citizens that they enforced subsidies for an initial period, so that customers would be sure to see their rates fall. Companies such as Enron also shaved their profits in the initial period, in order to win customers.[25] However, as the widely acclaimed promise of deregulation, consumer choice turned out to be a shrug to most consumers. Many consumers could not see the point in changing suppliers. The electricity still came to their houses through the same wires, and in many cases the same utilities continued to bill them. In many states, consumer choice failed to materialise, except for industrial consumers, because of high wholesale prices that prevented new companies from being able to offer better prices than the existing utilities. But, of course, it had been industry that had demanded consumer choice, not citizens.[26]

In California, despite $89 million spent on getting consumers to choose, very few changed their suppliers, and most of those chose "green" energy. Few non-industrial consumers mourned the end of choice when it was revoked in September 2001. Californians who switched to Enron from Pacific Gas & Electric (PG&E) on promises of a 10 per cent cut in rates ended up with increases of more than 100 per cent after wholesale electricity costs went up and Enron abandoned its customers.[27]

Very few consumers in New York have bothered changing companies, either.[28] "States such as Massachusetts, where utilities were bailed out, have had no electricity suppliers willing to serve residential suppliers. The idea that there is competition in the market has become a joke."[29] The largest number of consumers, 10 per cent of them, changed utilities in Pennsylvania; but of these, a third switched back when the new utility, New Power (partly owned by Enron), decided it didn't want them. In Philadelphia, the original 24 companies that competed for retail business were reduced to two as wholesale prices approached the retail cap.[30]

Ownership Issues

Some cities, such as Los Angeles, were unaffected by price rises or blackouts because their electricity systems were publicly owned and were not subjected to deregulation — so their citizens and industries were not at the mercy of private suppliers. Figure 7.3 shows how, even with the 10 per cent rate cut in preparation for deregulation and the retail rate freeze, residential rates in California were much lower for those served by a publicly owned utility. Industrial rates charged by private utilities were kept just under those charged by publicly owned utilities during the 1990s (at the expense of residential rates), but these also soared following the crisis.

As the crisis unfolded in California, and in other states, continued support for public power grew. Nationwide, the rates charged by publicly owned utilities were 18 per cent lower on average than those charged by private utilities in 1999. Publicly owned utilities are able to keep rates low because they don't have to pay dividends, stock options, and large executive salaries, and they spend much less money on lobbying and winning influence in the community (see table 7.1).[31]

■ Figure 7.3: Average retail electricity prices in California, 1980–2001

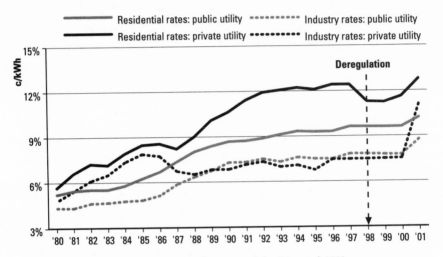

Source: *California Energy Commission, 'Weighted average retail electricity prices', 2002, http://www.energy.ca.gov/electricity/rates_iou_vs_muni_nominal/residential.html and http://www.energy.ca.gov/electricity/rates_iou_vs_muni_nominal/industrial.html*

Nebraska, the only state with all of its electricity supplied by publicly owned utilities, has some of the cheapest rates in the US.[32] What is more, the public utilities have led the way in conservation efforts. For example, the Sacramento Municipal Utility District distributed energy-efficient light bulbs, planted thousands of shade trees, offered ratepayers rebates for replacing old, energy-intensive refrigerators, and encouraged the use of solar energy, including household solar water heaters.[33]

In Montana, which deregulated in 1997, electricity prices soared and industries were forced to lay off workers. Before deregulation, rates in Montana were the sixth lowest in the country, due to the state having several hydroelectric dams and large coal reserves. However, local industries thought they could get cheaper electricity if Montana deregulated; so, despite widespread public opposition, the government deregulated, and state-based generating plants were sold off to a Pennsylvanian company. In 2001, seeing that something had to be done to redress escalating prices, the government set up a public power authority to construct new generating plant to deliver electricity at a regulated price. Electricity prices immediately dropped, and the power authority has not yet built or bought any new electricity plants. Many groups also lobbied to repeal the 1997 deregulation legislation, and in November 2002 a ballot for the state government to buy and operate the hydroelectric dams in the state was lost after the two utilities that owned the dams spent over $2 million campaigning against it. In the same ballot the 2001 legislation was rejected.[34]

■ **Table 7.1: Comparison between private and public utilities, 2000**

	PG&E	City of Palo Alto Utilities	LA Dept of Water and Power	Sacramento Municipal Utility District
Electricity customers	4,600,000	27,638	1,374,424	495,167
Monthly Rates	$94.06	$53.34	$72.92	$65.09
Employees getting over $250,000/yr	47	0	1	1
Lobbying expenses	$2,055,946	$0	$0	$126,894
Money transferred to parent company (1997-2000)	$5.1 billion	$0	$0	0
Money transferred for public services	0	$7.3 mil	$124 mil	0

Source: 'Public Power vs PG&E.' San Francisco Bay Guardian. *10 October 2001*

The latest ballot in San Francisco for the PUC to issue bonds to finance a public power plant and acquire PG&E's distribution system was also defeated after the supposedly bankrupt PG&E spent over $2 million campaigning against it. In contrast, despite a $3-million campaign by private company Nevada Power, 57 per cent of people voted in favour of a public power initiative in 2002 that provides support for the Southern Nevada Water Authority to buy Nevada Power.[35]

As prices soar in the wake of deregulation, various public relations campaigns have come into being to try to divert people all over the country from calling for public ownership. There has been a resurgence in anti-public ownership propaganda, and public ownership is again being labelled as "communism". The EEI still uses the argument that private utilities are virtually publicly owned, by pointing to the "millions of shareholders directly, or indirectly through other investments such as retirement funds, life insurance policies, or mutual funds".[36] A group of economics and business professors from Californian universities supported the anti-public ownership campaign, endorsing a manifesto calling for changes such as increases in retail electricity rates and various market fixes to ensure that the "benefits from deregulation" would be achieved. It argued that a state takeover of electricity would not be a solution as "taxpayers will be saddled with additional obligations for decades to come".[37]

Even though PG&E was going through bankruptcy proceedings, it instigated a mail campaign, under the auspices of a front group, Coalition for Affordable Public Services (CAPS), to oppose a ballot for a municipal utility in San Francisco. CAPS, funded solely by PG&E, spent over $280,000 opposing the public power initiative. PG&E's campaign against a municipal utility in San Francisco was aided by mail outs from telecommunications utilities SBC Pacific Bell and AT&T, in the interest of maintaining private utilities. The private utilities have also tried to enlist the support of other organisations. For example, the *San Francisco Bay Guardian* reported that the Police Officers Association was being pressured to oppose the proposal by a political consulting firm representing PG&E. The threat hanging over the police officers was that future Police Department initiatives such as pay rises might be opposed.[38]

Despite FERC regulations opening transmission lines, public power systems still have problems accessing those lines: the private companies that own them claim that the capacity is not available, or charge much higher rates than they had previously under regulation. In addition, FERC's 1996 ruling that the recovery of stranded costs should be allowed, and that "direct assignment of costs to departing customers" was the most appropriate method for this, has impacted badly on public power systems. Municipal systems may have to pay charges to cover stranded costs even where their contracts for power supply have come to an end and they no longer purchase power from the company with the stranded costs. In other cases, stranded costs deter municipalities from buying up local utilities.[39]

Deregulation has also encouraged many mergers and acquisitions (M/A).[40] The 1935 Public Utilities Holding Company Act (PUHCA) was amended in 1978, enabling the formation of 54 utility holding companies and 120 mergers of electric and gas utilities. "As deregulation fervor spread during the 1980s and 1990s, enforcement of PUHCA by the Securities & Exchange Commission (SEC) became weaker and weaker".[41] Currently, there are many more holding companies that are exempt from PUHCA (118) than are subject to its provisions (29).[42]

Despite the fiasco of deregulation in California and some other states, free-market proponents still called for the repeal of PUHCA so that mergers and acquisitions could go unregulated. In April 2001 the US Senate voted to repeal the Public Utility Holding Act of 1935, despite strong opposition from consumer groups and public power plants "that fear a return of the electricity behemoths that dominated the industry in its early days".[43] At the end of 2001 the chair of the House Energy and Commerce Committee, Joe Barton, proposed a bill to repeal PUHCA and end FERC's power to oversee mergers.[44]

Most recently, Senate majority leader Tom Daschle and Senator Bingaman have used environmental measures as a ruse to get an Energy Policy Act adopted which would repeal PUHCA. They have the support of the NRDC because of the environmental provisions, which include a "grab bag of favor-currying, but unrelated provisions concerning automobile fuel efficiency, energy policy on Native American lands, renewable energy sources", etc.[45] To date, PUHCA has not been repealed and it seems unlikely that it will be in 2003.

Between 1992 and 2001, 88 mergers and transactions were announced and 66 completed (see graph below).[46] By 2001, the top 20 power companies in the US supplied over half the electricity market nationwide. "Most of New England, once the domain of small local electric companies, is now powered by two giant corporations, one based in England and the other in Texas."[47]

■ **Figure 7.4: Mergers and acquisitions of investor-owned electric utilities**

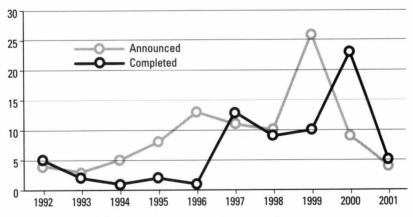

Source: M. Agnew, 'Mergers and Acquisitions', EEI, 29 Nov. 2001, p. 6.

A survey of chief executives of energy companies at the end of 2000 found that:

- 95 per cent of those surveyed thought they would go through a major M/A by the end of 2003
- 65 per cent believe that only one-half of the largest 50 electrics will remain independent by 2003
- Two-thirds think that approximately ten US electrics will be owned by non-US entities by 2003
- 54 per cent believe they are more likely to be acquired than to acquire[48]

■Table 7.2: Consolidation of private electric utilities

Ownership	1992	2000
Holding companies	70	53
Utilities that are subsidiaries of holding companies	113	112
Independent utilities	59	29
Generating capacity of holding companies	78%	86%

Source: Energy Information Agency. The Changing Structure of the Electric Power Industry 2000: An Update.' DOE/EIA-0562(00). October 2000, p. 97.

A similar trend is evident in the area of transmission, where concentration of ownership has grown in recent years. The top ten companies, including AEP, Southern Company, Edison International, and PG& E, own about 45 per cent of US transmission assets, up 20 per cent since 1995. *Public Utilities Fortnightly* predicted in early 2002 that this trend was likely to continue with further mergers and acquisitions.[49]

■ Figure 7.5: Concentration of ownership of private utility generating capacity

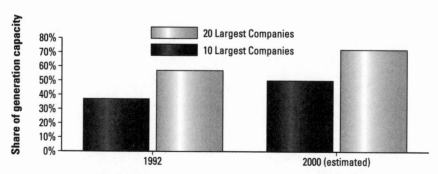

Source: Energy Information Agency. 'The Changing Structure of the Electric Power Industry 2000: An Update.' DOE/EIA-0562(00). October 2000, p. 98.

The utilities in deregulated states were asked to divest themselves of generating capacity and unbundle their transmission facilities so they would not dominate the market and have too much market power. However, mergers and acquisitions look set to achieve the same situation. The Department of Energy's Energy Information Agency notes: "Recent mergers have created large vertically integrated regional electric utilities, and more are expected as some of the pending mergers are completed."[50]

The Bush Adminstration

The Californian governor pleaded in vain for months for temporary federal price caps on wholesale electricity, as did seven other governors in the western states—four of them Republicans.[51] But the Bush administration refused to listen. Wholesale electricity price caps were opposed at the federal level because they were seen as a form of regulation that would interfere with the free market. It was said they would prevent the market from sending pricing signals to ensure new investment in generating plant when electricity was short. However, the unstated reason for opposing price caps was that they would stunt the huge profits being made by energy companies which had enormous political influence in Washington D.C.

Prior to the election of George W. Bush in 2000, president Clinton, although a strong advocate of deregulation, had tried to stop electricity price manipulation in California. The companies that were benefiting from price manipulation, El Paso, Reliant, Enron, and Dynegy, therefore gave generously to get George W. Bush elected: they donated $3.5 million to the Republican campaign. Within three days of being sworn in, Bush ended Clinton's anti-electricity price speculation measures, ensuring that those companies would profit in the following year. He also cancelled Clinton's emergency order of December 2000, which had required power suppliers from outside California to stop withholding power.[52]

Altogether, George W. Bush received about $50 million from energy companies based in his home state of Texas. These companies had benefited from his time as governor of Texas, and hoped to similarly profit from his presidency. The ten major power suppliers for California, together with the EEI, contributed $5.9 million to federal candidates in the 1999-2000 election, not including donations to the Bush-Cheney Inaugural Committee. This was more than twice the amount donated by these companies in the previous election. These ten power companies also contributed $1.6 million to House and Senate committees that might have influence when it came to imposing price caps. A special group of Bush friends formed a "Pioneers" group, and each personally pledged $100,000 towards helping Bush get the Republican nomination for president and getting his presidential campaign started. These included the chairman of Reliant; the CEO of Reliant; the president of the EEI, Thomas Kuhn; and the chairman of Enron, Kenneth Lay.[53]

In the end, Bush won the presidency by the narrowest of margins, and the contributions of the energy industry were clearly vital to his success. He formed an energy policy advisory panel whilst waiting to be inaugurated as president, and appointed to it Kuhn, Lay, and the chief attorney of the Southern Company, another heavy donor, but no consumer advocates or academics.[54]

Under the leadership of Curtis Hébert, who was appointed by George W. Bush, the Federal Energy Regulatory Commission (FERC) refused to introduce electricity price caps, despite the mandate of FERC to ensure "just and reasonable" rates. It argued that this would interfere with the free market.[55] Writing in the *New York Times*, Paul Krugman said, "Blame knee-jerk free-market ideology, or the political influence of the power companies (many of which are based in, yes, Texas). Whatever the reason, it is hard to imagine an administration less likely to be sympathetic to California's plight ..."[56]

Even FERC's own staff and one of its commissioners were concerned that enforcement was being made subservient to "free-market passions and the influence of industry insiders in its ranks".[57] It was accused of neglecting "its oversight responsibilities, while relentlessly pushing deregulation of electricity across the country".[58] When it did investigate complaints, FERC appointed Scott Miller to head the investigation. Miller was formerly employed by PG&E Energy Trading, a subsidiary of PG&E's parent company that was being investigated by the Justice Department for alleged price manipulations in New England. Miller had reported on his former employer's activities, but found the price spikes were not the fault of PG&E Energy Trading.[59]

In November 2000 FERC released a report, blaming the structure of the electricity markets for the problems in California. It proposed that the rules of the market be changed "to dampen extreme price volatility, provide a stable environment for generation investment, and ensure just and reasonable wholesale rates".[60] It proposed various measures that should be carried out within two years, including:

- the three private utilities should not have to buy or sell all their power from the PX but could make contracts with generators;
- all market participants should have to carry out 95 per cent of their transactions in the day ahead markets rather than leaving them to the real-time spot market;

- "temporary modification of the single price auction so that bids above $150/MWh cannot set the market clearing prices paid to all bidders". Those bidding over $150 would still be paid their price, however, but would have to report their bids to FERC; and
- changing the boards of the PX and ISO so that members would not be stake-holders.[61]

FERC would not allow the PX to set price caps, and argued that it did not have the authority to order refunds of unreasonable prices already paid by consumers or utilities under the 'flawed' market. Commissioner Hébert said he would have preferred to eliminate price controls altogether. He warned Californians not to let their focus on environmental issues prevent generation capacity from being increased. Commissioner Breathitt warned that FERC could not let the events in California slow market reforms elsewhere, and said that FERC's job was to help the market correct itself, not to engage in "command and control" type interventions.[62]

The Alliance of Energy Suppliers lobbied against the proposed rules "that would require generators and power marketers to file records of individual energy sales and other information about transactions".[63] They argued that "revealing certain information about prices, contracts, terms and conditions could be harmful to the development of robust electricity markets" and that such information was "competitively sensitive".[64]

Nevertheless, the rule went into effect in December 2000. Since the utilities were no longer required to buy their electricity in the Californian PX, the two major utilities were unable to pay for electricity anyway, and other traders took their business elsewhere, the PX declared bankruptcy and stopped operating shortly afterward. This left California with "no formal day- and hour-ahead energy markets".[65]

The EEI also opposed price caps, claiming that such caps would hinder new investment in generation. It did not recognise the existence of market power and price manipulation. And it argued that greater government regulation, although it might be popular, was akin to "turning back the clock", and that was near impossible. EEI pointed out the "need to 'act' in a manner that restores public confidence in the path towards restructuring":[66]

One needs to keep in mind that even the most robust of commodity markets are volatile by nature. Restructuring is not meant to produce stable prices, but is designed to increase competitive choices that customers have. This *eventually* will lead to innovation and lower costs that benefit customers.[67] [italics added]

Whilst some Republicans were calling for federal price caps on wholesale electricity in the wake of the Californian disaster, none was willing to blame deregulation: "don't expect Republicans in Washington or anywhere else to admit that deregulation is a disaster. Motivated by either ideology or greed or both, they continue to insist that there is no alternative to unrestrained corporate rapacity."[68]

Although four out of five American people supported federal price caps, the Bush administration continued to resist them. When price caps were finally introduced in the western states in June 2001, both the Democrats and the Republicans were keen to argue that they weren't really price controls but rather "a market-based mitigation plan".[69]

However, the share markets knew differently: shares for power generators and marketers dropped 30 per cent in the month after the news of the "mitigation plan" broke. Investors feared that, although the plan only applied to the west of the US, it would spread, limiting profits nationwide.[70] The marketers were also losing out in California as utilities turned to long-term contracts made directly with generators.

The Official Explanation

The crisis in California has been depicted in the US and the international media as resulting from a shortage of energy. The story, repeated in thousands of articles, is that a boom in industry and economic growth, as well as a sustained spell of unusually hot, dry weather, caused demand in energy to surge, but that power plants had not been built to meet this demand because of opposition from environmentalists and the onerous regulations they had insisted upon. Such claims were contradicted by the evidence, as outlined in the previous chapter, and by more independent studies, including figures from the Californian ISO. These showed that growth in demand was less dramatic than portrayed and not a primary cause of the crisis; but these were ignored by most media outlets.[71]

A coalition of groups, the 21st Century Energy Project, sought to ensure that the blame for the Californian crisis was placed on environmentalists who had impeded the construction of new electricity generation. It was put together by Ed Gillespie, a former George W. Bush campaign strategist, who concurrently did work for Enron.[72]

The surging-demand story—that demand had grown 25 per cent since 1995—was fed by the EEI. It argued that power blackouts in California were caused by a shortage of power with respect to demand, that the design of the power exchange was the cause of soaring prices, and that the regulated rates discouraged new competing power companies from wanting to supply consumers.[73]

The EEI also ran a campaign in 2001 "to position Edison as the voice of reason in the industry and to position the industry as a positive presence in America".[74] The ads promoted deregulation, stressed the importance of electricity to the economy and the need for a growth in supply, and explained events in California in this light. Advertisements ran in various newspapers and magazines, including "reaching out to Opinion and Business Leaders" through print advertising in selected magazines such as *American Heritage, Atlantic Monthly, New Republic, National Review*, and some leading business magazines. Public service announcements on energy use and in-flight audio programming were also used.[75] This was the message EEI put in its newspaper advertisements:

If you've been following the news lately, the power problem in California may seem to be about as messy as it can get. However, there are some lessons we can all learn from California, to avoid this happening in other places ... In the last decade alone, America's electricity usage has increased by over 21 per cent. And the U.S. Department of Energy forecasts that demand will continue growing for the next twenty years. To catch up, we simply need to build new power plants. However, to accomplish this, we must streamline the approval process and provide the proper incentives for companies to build the power plants America needs to keep growing.[76]

Even the utilities in California used their information channels to ensure that the crisis was not depicted as a failure of deregulation. PG&E inserted a letter into 4.6 million ratepayers' bills, saying that "the state's booming economy can be a mixed blessing", referring to rapidly growing population and the "multiple electronic devices" of the internet age: "new energy supplies have not kept pace with that growth ... Factors like that lead to shortages and shortages lead to higher prices."[77]

The mainstream media bought into the propaganda and helped to spread it. Deregulation, according to the media reports, was not to blame. Rather, the problem was too little deregulation: the rate freeze, typically depicted as regulation to protect consumers rather than a way for utilities to recover stranded costs, had prevented the free operation of the market.[78] For example, the *New York Times* stated:

Demand for electricity outpaced older power plants, while a botched experiment with partial price deregulation and longstanding environmental opposition combined to create disincentives to build new power plants or create cheaper wholesale prices through competition.[79]

The federal government used the Californian energy crisis to call for the easing of California's environmental rules, particularly its air-pollution regulations. California had already lowered its own air-quality standards in December 2000, allowing older plants that had been closed down to be brought back into operation. The EPA agreed not to prosecute violations of federal clean-air standards by electricity generators in California. However, a spokesman for Reliant Energy, which operated four plants in the state, claimed that the regulations made no difference to total electricity output.[80] It did, however, make a difference to total pollution output. In 2002, California experienced its worst air pollution for several years, "a sharp reversal after several years of improvements in air quality statewide."[81]

The energy industry also used the crisis as a rationale for a more general repeal of pollution regulations and withdrawal from the Kyoto agreement. In *Newsweek*, Robert Samuelson argued that pollution and global warming couldn't be curbed if consumers wanted cheap power. The Bush administration backed such sentiments. Vice President Dick Cheney suggested that Californian companies build power plants in Mexico to avoid Californian environmental regulations. The administration's antipathy to environmental regulations very much suited the large power companies whose goal, in helping Bush get to power, was to weaken air-pollution rules. Leading the lobbying on the issue was the Southern Company which, like other companies, was being sued to clean up its power plants.[82]

Each year, electricity plants cause thousands of premature deaths, and tens of thousands of asthma attacks and cases of acute bronchitis. A study by Abt Associates, funded by the Rockefeller Family Fund, found that 80 power plants owned by eight utilities, including Duke Power, Dynegy, and the Southern Company, would cause 6000 premature deaths, 140,000 asthma attacks, and 14,000 cases of acute bronchitis in 2007 — and that is assuming that air quality will improve! Such assumptions are becoming less likely as the Bush administration bows to power company pressure, despite protests from some states.[83]

In April 2001 Cheney, a former oil company chief, labelled energy conservation as 1970s-era thinking and reaffirmed the need for more fossil fuels to solve the energy crisis. In particular, he stressed the need to find new sources of oil and gas in the US, including the Arctic National Wildlife Refuge (ANWR), and to build more fossil-fuel power plants.[84] Economist Paul Krugman has suggested that "the general attitude in George W. Bush's Washington seems to be that real men don't conserve energy".[85]

The energy industry also used the depiction of an energy shortfall as the cause of the crisis to call for more nuclear energy and oil drilling in protected places such as ANWR. This was even though the utilities had admitted the uncompetitiveness of nuclear energy, which was the reason behind the rate freeze; even though most Californian generators used natural gas, not oil, to produce electricity; even though the blackouts were not caused by a shortage of gas or oil; and even though the curtailment of environmentally friendly sources of energy and conservation had contributed to the lack of surplus electricity in the first place.

The chair of the US House Energy and Commerce Committee, Billy Tauzin, warned in June that the whole of the US faced blackouts like those in California unless new power plants were built quickly. By 2001 many Californians had swallowed the propaganda, and a majority supported nuclear power plants—for the first time since the Three Mile Island nuclear power plant accident in 1979.[86]

An Alliance for Energy and Economic Growth was formed in early 2001 to influence the National Energy Policy being formulated by the federal government in response to the crisis. The alliance's 400 members included the American Gas Association, the National Mining Association, and the Nuclear Energy Institute (all big contributors to the Republicans in the 2000 election), as well as various energy companies, trade associations, and chambers of commerce.[87]

Documents obtained by NRDC showed that Cheney's energy taskforce had 714 direct contacts with industry representatives, including several with companies such as Enron (see next chapter) and the Southern Company, and trade organisations such as the EEI and the National Mining Association. Additional contacts occurred directly through the vice president's office. Only 29 non-industry contacts were made, and some of these were with energy industry-funded think tanks.[88]

The National Energy Policy, released in May 2001, recommended building "between 1,300 and 1,900 new electric plants", with an emphasis on natural gas and nuclear plants, and promoting "enhanced oil and gas recovery", which included drilling for oil in ANWR, as a way of dealing with the 'crisis'.[89] It blamed electricity shortages for rising electricity costs:

America in the year 2001 faces the most serious energy shortage since the oil embargoes of the 1970s. The effects are already being felt nationwide. Many families face energy bills two to three times higher than they were a year ago. Millions of Americans find themselves dealing with rolling blackouts or brownouts; some employers must lay off workers or curtail production to absorb the rising cost of energy.[90]

The energy policy, including the provision of $33 billion worth of tax breaks for energy companies, was approved in Congress in August. Republicans attempted to get it approved in the Senate through the remainder of 2001 by attaching it as an amendment to every piece of legislation being voted on, including emergency defence legislation following the September 11 terrorist attacks.[91] It was eventually passed, but without the provision for exploration in ANWR.

In 2002, after the release of documents proving Enron's market manipulation, a *New York Times* editorial stated: "It was obvious from the beginning that some of the explanations for the crisis that were being floated by

President Bush and Vice President Dick Cheney were nonsense. California's environmental laws posed no serious impediments to energy production, and there was no shortage of natural gas."[92] Krugman noted that "the truth is that California's deregulation probably was flawed, but the flaw was in trusting markets too much, not too little".[93] They had trusted that the market would not be manipulated.

The public, however, never really bought into the attempt to depict an energy-scarcity crisis. A *New York Times*/CBS News poll found that the public overwhelmingly favoured energy conservation over generation, and was willing to pay more for electricity and gas to protect the environment: "despite a huge White House public relations blitz, the public, by a nearly 2-to-1 margin, doubts whether an energy crisis even exists."[94] Similarly a Los Angeles *Times* survey found that 54 per cent of Californians didn't believe there was an energy shortage in their state and that two-thirds of them favoured reregulation of electricity.[95]

CHAPTER EIGHT

Enron On The Rise

The profits on the trades — of cubic feet of gas it didn't extract or burn, of kilo-watt-hours it didn't generate, and of fiber-optic lines it didn't light — sent Enron's revenues soaring.[1]

ENRON IS SIGNIFICANT, not because it became the largest corporate bank-ruptcy ever to happen worldwide when it collapsed in December 2001, but because it was a politically influential promoter of deregulation that made huge profits from exploiting the opportunities deregulation offered to specula-tors. In 2000 *Fortune* magazine labelled Enron "far and away the most vigor-ous agent of change in its industry, fundamentally altering how billions of dollars' worth of power ... is bought, moved and sold, everywhere in the nation."[2]

Deregulation transformed electricity into a tradeable commodity, and gave rise to a number of new companies and new divisions of older companies, and a new occupation of energy trader. "Aided by supercomputers, and oper-ating out of trading rooms as big as hockey rinks, the new breed of traders buy blocks of electricity anywhere along the nation's power grid, then borrow transmission lines to ship it to the highest bidder."[3] About a quarter of elec-tricity generated in the US is subject to this sort of wholesale electricity-trad-ing by unregulated companies.[4]

Following deregulation, Enron became one of the world's largest energy traders, and was given credit for creating the energy-trading market.[5] In its search for profits, Enron explored the lengths to which the commodification of energy could go. Whereas, before deregulation, a company needed generating capacity and transmission lines to be able to sell electricity, Enron demonstrated that a company could now sell electricity without owning a power station. It could become a broker, contracting to buy electricity from the generators and then selling it to consumers. "Enron's business model was built entirely on the premise that it could make more money speculating on electricity contracts than it could by actually producing electricity at a power plant."[6]

> In the traditional regulated market, utilities were monopolies with fixed prices: they hired engineers to build large reliable plants. In Enron's world, the engineers have been replaced by theoretical physicists trained in portfolio analysis: the reliability is engineered on the trading floor, where young traders price and strike deals with customers in something like 90 seconds.[7]

■ **Figure 8.1: Annual wholesale sales by energy traders**

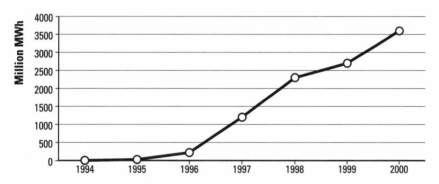

Source: E. Hirst. 'The California Electricity Crisis'. Edison Electric Institute. July 2000, p. 11.

Following Enron's example, other companies soon followed, and energy trading spread from the US to Europe and Britain. Enron was a key player in the spread of electricity privatisation around the world. Enron's website boasted: "Since 1996, Enron has become a leading participant in the liberalized U.K. and Nordic energy markets and is now one of the leading new entrants in the liberalizing Continental electricity and gas markets." It claimed to be "the first energy company to enter Central America". It also owned the "first private, independent power project in Poland".[8] The BBC noted: "Among its innovations, it has prised open the German power and gas markets, created a virtual gas storage facility in the UK, and pioneered the world's largest online commodity trading site."[9]

Enron became an icon of deregulation and the epitome of free markets. It said of itself:

We believe in the economic benefits of open, competitive wholesale markets, and we play a leading role in creating them. We initiated the wholesale natural gas and electricity markets in the United States, and we are helping to build similar markets in Europe and elsewhere.

Every day we strive to make markets in other industries ... such as metals, forest products, bandwidth capacity and steel.[10]

And for a long time markets were good to the Texas-based company. In 2000 Enron was the seventh-largest company in the US, based on reported revenue for the year of $101 billion. It was the leading energy broker in the US, involved in up to one-quarter of all energy trades, and the largest natural gas trader in North America and the UK. In 2001, before it went into liquidation, Enron had over 21,000 employees and claimed $47.3 billion in assets.[11]

Behind Enron was founder and chair Kenneth Lay, who passionately believed in markets and the opportunities that they offered for firms such as his. Lay combined an economics PhD with experience in the Washington bureaucracy, including work at the Federal Energy Regulatory Commission (FERC), where he made contacts in the arena of federal regulation. "When you join Ken, you believe you are going to change the shape of the industry — that you're on a mission", said one former employee. Enron's meetings with investors were described as being like "revival meetings".[12] The *Economist* referred to Lay as the "energetic messiah": "Spend long enough around top Enron people and you feel you are in the midst of some sort of evangelical cult. In a sense, you are. Mr Lay, with his 'passion for markets', is the cult's guru. His disciples are Enron's managers, an intelligent, aggressive group of youngish professionals ..."[13] Bonuses of up to a million dollars also helped earn the loyalty of top employees.[14]

Similarly, *Newsweek* described Enron executives as "deregulation's True Believers" and top executive Jeff Skilling as "like a religious zealot who couldn't stop repeating his favorite mantra as the solution to all the world's problems": deregulate.[15] Skilling told a PBS news crew: "We are looking to create open, competitive, fair markets. And in open, competitive, fair markets, prices are lower and customers get better service ... We are the good guys. We are on the side of the angels."[16] He referred to open, competitive markets as "the American way".[17] The irony is that Enron did its best to ensure that markets were neither competitive nor fair.

Skilling, who was CEO of Enron in 2001, was notorious for comments made to an industry conference, that electricity companies need to "cut costs ruthlessly by 50 or 60 per cent" and "get rid of people" because "they gum up the works".[18] Skilling also seemed to be making a laughing matter of California's plight, which Enron had contributed to. He had asked a business audience in 2001 what the difference was between the state of California and the Titanic, and answered: "At least when the Titanic went down, the lights were on".[19]

Enron described itself as "the world's greatest company".[20] The business media was ready to believe it, and the company won many accolades. In February 2001 *Fortune* magazine named Enron as the "Most Innovative Company in America" for the sixth year running, as well as one of the top five in terms of "Quality of Management" (see table below). These ratings were based on confidential surveys of 10,000 executives, directors, and securities analysts. In August 2001, four months before Enron's spectacular bankruptcy, *Fortune* magazine predicted it would be one of the top ten growth stocks to last the decade.[21]

■ **Table 8.1: Enron awards**

Awarded by:	Award	Year
Fortune Magazine	"America's Most Innovative Company"	1996–2001
	"Most Admired Pipeline Company"	1996–2000
	"Quality of Management"	2000
		2nd in 2001
Risk Magazine	"Energy/Commodity Derivatives House of the Year"	1999
Forbes Magazine	"World's Leading Power Company"	1999
Global Finance	"World's Best Global company in the energy sector"	1999
Financial Times	"Energy company of the year"	2000
	"Boldest successful investment decision"	2000
Business Week	"25 Top Managers" — Kenneth Lay	2000
Worth	"50 Best CEOs" — Lay and Skilling (no. 2 in 2001)	2000–01

Sources: Enron. 2002. 'Enron Australia.' Enron. http://www.enron.com.au/insideenron/; Rise and Fall of an Energy Giant.' BBC News Online, 28 November 2000.
http://news.bbc.co.uk/low/english/business/newsid_1681000/1681758.stm; Scott Sherman. 'Gimme an 'E;!' Columbia Journalism Review March/April 2002.

Enron Services

Enron was created in 1985 when Kenneth Lay merged two natural gas companies that were not doing very well. However, it was deregulation that launched Enron on its rapid ascent. Having lobbied for deregulation, Enron "beat rivals to new markets, turning debt-laden Enron into the nation's biggest, most profitable buyer and seller of gas". Lay hired former FERC commissioners and regulatory lawyers to make the most of the new deregulated environment.[22]

Enron then lobbied Congress to deregulate the wholesale electricity market, which occurred in 1992. Enron wanted to be able to sell electricity to large industrial consumers, and became an electricity trader in 1994. By 1995 Enron was the largest natural gas trader in North America, and by 1997 it was also the largest electricity wholesaler, selling mainly to privately owned utilities and municipalities. Rather than acting as a middleman between buyer and seller, and taking a commission, Enron entered into separate contracts with each party and took its profits from the difference, with neither side aware of the prices involved in the other transaction.[23]

Apart from marketing electricity and gas, and supplying energy and some other physical commodities, Enron provided financial and risk-management services to businesses. From as early as 1989, Enron helped its natural gas clients reduce the risks that arose from the price volatility that came with deregulation by establishing a commodities market trading in natural gas futures. Using the market, the customers could purchase natural gas in the future at a set price.[24]

Enron did not just trade in these commodities: it specialised in derivatives. Derivatives (derivative financial instruments) are contracts based on one party's promises to pay another party if a certain benchmark is reached or an event occurs. They are used to shift risk from one party to another, and were originally used to cushion the risk of fluctuations in currency, interest rates, and stock indexes.[25] A hedge contract is an example where the "hedger seeks to protect himself against loss resulting from price changes by transferring the risk to a speculator who relies upon his skill in forecasting price movements in the future."[26]

For example, if a utility is likely to lose large sums of money if wholesale electricity prices go above $100/MWh, it might buy a hedge contract, whereby another party contracts to pay the utility an agreed amount of money if the price does exceed $100/MWh. The other party is willing to enter into the contract because it takes the view —and the risk—that the price will not exceed $100/MWh often enough to outweigh the payment that the utility makes to have the contract. Increasingly, Enron itself got involved in derivatives, and before its demise it "employed a battalion of doctorates in mathematics, physics and economics to manage these complex contracts." Enron was described as "a giant hedge fund sitting on top of a pipeline".[27]

Enron also sold other services that, for a price, took the risk out of their clients' businesses. For example, Enron offered to hedge the risk of weather fluctuations for its clients. Companies such as electrical utilities could lose revenue if the weather was unusually mild—that is, if the winters were warm and the summers were cool—because people would use less electricity. Enron's hedge contracts provided a form of insurance against this, in return for a premium.[28]

Enron reasoned that, if it could make money out of trading electricity and gas, it could make money out of trading anything. So it widened its trading activities to include wood pulp, steel, television advertising time, broadband internet services, and insurance against credit defaults. It undertook much of its trading via the Internet, and became the largest e-commerce company in the world.[29] Enron also became a leading emissions-allowance trader in the US, specialising in SO_2 and NO_X allowances.[30]

Enron expanded its derivative products into overseas markets. For example, Enron Australia was established in July 1998 "to provide risk management, trading and financing solutions for a range of commodities, which include electricity, weather, renewables, coal and crude and liquids". It offered risk-management products to both distributors and consumers of electricity to deal with and "harness" price volatility arising from the operation of the national electricity market.[31]

This gradual shift from real production to virtual activity was labelled, in Texas-speak, as having "all hat and no cattle". Enron's share value was built on perceptions and market trust rather than on hard assets. Basically, Enron made much of its profits from gambling and speculating, particularly on the price of gas and electricity. During the Californian power crisis Enron made $7 billion, mainly, according to former Enron traders, from making large bets that the price of gas and electricity would go up.[32]

Enron operated under the belief that it could commoditize and monetize anything, from electrons to advertising space. By the end of the decade, Enron, which had once made its money from hard assets like pipelines, generated more than 80 per cent of its earnings from a vaguer business known as "wholesale energy operations and services." From 1998 to 2000, Enron's revenues shot from $31 billion to more than $100 billion...[33]

But Enron did not just leave it to the market to decide prices. It engaged in price manipulation, particularly in California (see chapter 6). However, when price caps were finally introduced in the western states of the USA, Enron was no longer able to reap huge profits, and it lost heavily on its speculation that prices would continue to soar in California.

The day after Enron filed for bankruptcy, the forward price of electricity dropped by 30 per cent—suggesting that Enron might also have been using its market power to push up long-term electricity prices. The drop occurred at a time when other energy markets were unaffected. Industry participants used forward price contracts to hedge against future price changes. Enron was the main trader amongst the few traders which dealt in such contracts, giving it dominance in this esoteric, unregulated market. Market manipulation by Enron clearly contributed to the high prices that the Californian government paid for its long-term electricity contracts, as well as the earlier pool prices that the utilities paid.[34]

■ **Figure 8.2: Enron revenues, $billions**

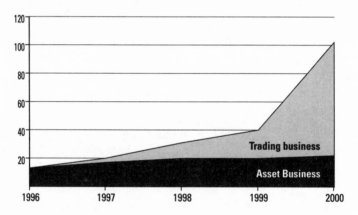

Source: 'Amazing Disintegrating Firm.' The Economist, 6 December 2001.

Political Ties

Enron was a key force for deregulation because of its substantial political influence. Deregulation required overturning a system that was supported by significant vested interests, as well as disinterested advocates. To combat these, "Enron bred and fed armies of politicians," "inundated these politicos with lobbyists and contributions, and ushered a steady stream of once and future public officials through its revolving doors".[35] All of this was reminiscent of the private power companies of the 1920s (see part 1).

Enron was one of George W. Bush's biggest backers, and Lay had had a close relationship with Bush since the days when he was governor of Texas. Even before that, Bush's oil firm, Spectrum 7, had worked with Enron. Lay had been a key fundraiser for Bush senior's presidential campaigns and one of the top contributors to George W.'s campaign for election as governor of Texas. Lay then headed George W.'s business council when he was elected governor. Lay became a personal friend of George W. Bush, accompanying him to baseball games in Houston. George W. referred to him as "Kenny Boy".[36]

Similarly, George W. aided Enron's business ventures. In 1997 he telephoned the Pennsylvania governor, Thomas J. Ridge, to vouch for Enron, which wanted to participate in the state's retail electricity market. Ridge was later made Secretary of Homeland Security in the Bush administration. Lay also made friends in the Clinton administration, including with its first chief of staff, and achieved a place in a Clinton golf foursome, along with Jack Nicklaus and former president Gerald Ford, on Clinton's first vacation.[37]

Enron donated over $2.4 million to federal candidates and politicians in the 2000 election, making it one of the top fifty donor organisations. Almost three-quarters of these donations went to Republicans, and $1.8 million went to George W.'s presidential campaign. During the campaign Bush made use of Enron jets to travel the country.[38] To hedge its bets, Enron also cultivated ties to the Gore camp. It hired a public relations expert for this purpose, who identified key Gore advisers that Enron officials should get to know and activities that it should participate in. Enron also hired an old friend and long-time supporter of Gore's.[39]

In total, Enron donated just under $6 million to election campaigns, beginning with the 1989-90 election cycle (see figure 8.3). It contributed to the campaigns of 71 current senators and 188 current members (43 per cent of the House). Those from Texas received the highest contributions.[40] These donations were a lucrative investment for Enron, enabling it to make many times more in profits from the deregulation that was achieved in this way.

Enron also spent millions lobbying Congress, the White House, and federal agencies (see figure 8.3). Its expenditure on these activities in 2001 was more than double that of 2000, and was mainly for lobbying on energy deregulation.[41] Additional money was spent in the states, especially Texas (see page 153).

Enron drew its lobbyists from both the Republican and Democrat Parties and administrations. In 1993 Lay hired as consultants former Bush cabinet members, secretary of state James Baker III and commerce secretary Robert Mosbacher, after Bush senior lost office. "After President Bush's 1993 Gulf War 'victory tour' of Kuwait, Baker and other members of his entourage stayed on to hustle Enron contracts."[42] Enron also had influence in the Clinton administration; even after its demise, Clinton's treasury secretary, Robert Rubin, lobbied the incoming Bush administration on Enron's behalf.[43]

■ **Figure 8.3: Enron's contributions to federal candidates and parties, and lobbying expenditure**

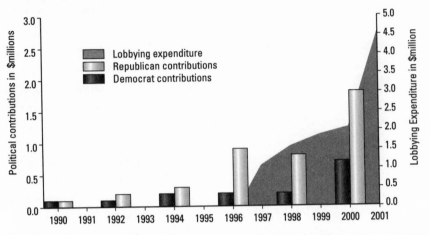

Source: Centre for Responsive Politics. 'Enron Total Contributions to Federal Candidates and Parties, 1989-2001'. 2002. http://www.opensecrets.org/alerts/v6/enron_totals.asp; Multinational Monitor January/February 2002, p. 43; B. Hightower and P. Spiegel. 'Documents Show Enron Spend $4.6m on Lobbying.' Financial Times. 13 March 2002.

The revolving door between Enron and the government continued after George W. was elected. A Bush campaign adviser, Edward Gillespie, made over $500,000 as a lobbyist for Enron in 2001. George W. hired various Enron employees, including Larry Lindsey as his economic adviser and Robert B. Zoellick as his trade representative. One of Lindsey's jobs was to assign staff to monitor energy markets, in which Enron was a major player.[44] White House documents admit that "Dr. Lindsey had a few communications with Ken Lay in the winter and spring of 2001, most likely about the California electricity shortage."[45] At the time, Enron was opposing price caps being imposed to solve the crisis.

Bush also hired Thomas E. White, head of Enron Energy Services when it was manipulating electricity prices in California, to become army secretary. White received a million dollars' severance pay from Enron and owned over $25 million in Enron stock, which he failed to divest himself of when he took up his government post. As army secretary, White set out to "move energy services at [military] bases to private companies, like Enron".[46]

Many members of the incoming Bush administration owned Enron shares. Apart from White, top political advisor Karl Rove "owned as much as $250,000 of Enron stock", according to the *Los Angeles Times*. Defense Secretary Donald Rumsfeld and his assistant; the assistant treasury secretary; the economic undersecretary; the vice president's chief of staff (Lewis Libby);

the education undersecretary; and various ambassadors and energy department officials owned Enron stock. Attorney General John Ashcroft received over $50,000 towards his 2000 campaign for the Senate from Enron.[47]

Texan Tom DeLay, majority whip in the House, was also closely connected to Enron, and a beneficiary of Enron donations. Enron also used two influential members of his "kitchen cabinet" as lobbyists. DeLay earned the name Dereg in Texas because of his efforts to promote deregulation. And he was one of those foremost in the push for deregulation of energy whilst in Congress. When a Japanese company won a bid to build a power plant in the Commonwealth of Northern Mariana Islands that Enron had also bid for, DeLay asked for the bidding to be reopened.[48]

An American Family Voices Report gives details of over 50 high-level Bush administration officials who had "meaningful ties" to Enron, and 35 members of the administration who held Enron stock. It assumed that there were more at lower levels of the administration. It claimed that "Enron embarked from its earliest days, upon a concerted, well-funded and startlingly successful effort to influence and compromise oversight and regulation of its operations at virtually every level of government."[49]

Enron's influence on Dr. Wendy Gramm and her husband, US senator Phil Gramm, give an insight into the way it created and used political ties. Enron was a key financial supporter of Senator Gramm {title rather than description} whilst Wendy Gramm was chair of the Commodity Futures Trading Commission (CFTC), appointed by the Reagan administration in 1988. When Clinton was elected in 1992, knowing that her term of office was about to end, she initiated changes to the rules — that Enron had requested — without consultation with her fellow commissioners. These changes "narrowed the definition of futures contracts, excluding Enron's energy future contracts and 'swaps' from regulatory oversight" by the commission. The changes were approved while the five-person commission was two people short, pending their appointment by Clinton. The regulation, or non-regulation, was passed 2-1 in January 1993 by the remaining Bush appointees. The dissenting commissioner labelled it "the most irresponsible decision" she had come across in her eighteen years in Congress.[50]

Six days later Gramm resigned, and a few weeks later she was appointed to Enron's board of directors. In the following nine years she received between $915,000 and $1.85 million in salary and attendance fees, from cashing-in stock options, and from dividends. Enron also contributed $260,000 to Phil Gramm's election campaigns, making it his largest contributor. Lay acted as regional chair when Gramm made a run for the presidential nomination in

1996. Enron could afford to be generous. In 1993 its revenues from the division that operated these deregulated futures contracts increased by 30 per cent to $6.1 billion, and Enron became a leader in futures trading.[51]

From then on, Enron devoted a relatively high proportion of its resources to lobbying and financial contributions. Enron became the sixth-highest contributor during the 1994 federal election cycle, and by 2000 the top contributor of all corporations in the energy/natural resources sector, which included much larger companies.[52] Apart from political donations, Enron spent millions on lobbying, creating "a formidable cadre of connected lobbyists, consultants and officials that make the White House resemble an Enron branch office."[53] By the late 1990s it employed over 150 people on state and federal government affairs in Washington.[54]

Enron's political influence was enhanced through the use of a computer programme called the "matrix" which facilitated the analysis of each proposed change in regulations so that it could quantify the effect on Enron and work out how much to spend opposing or supporting the change. Executives, who were paid high salaries by the company, were then expected to donate some of their **own** money towards political donations and campaigns to help the company.[55]

Following its successes in Congress, Enron spent money on lobbying at the state level for the introduction of deregulation. Enron lobbyists sought out consumer groups, schools, and other community groups that would benefit from cheaper electricity, and tried to persuade them that deregulation would be good for them. In preparation for the retail competition it was sure would come, Enron formed a 600-person unit, Enron Energy Services, in 1995.[56] In 1996 Enron supported DeLay's Electric Consumers' Power to Choose Act ("known as the 'Enron Bill' in DC circles,"[57]) saying: "Consumer choice is the equivalent of a $60 billion to $80 billion annual tax cut. It will reduce costs to all consumers large and small, spur economic development, and create new jobs."[58]

In 1997, in preparation for retail-electricity competition, Enron launched a new logo and advertising campaign in an effort to make the Enron brand as familiar to consumers as McDonalds and Coca-Cola. The ads were launched at a "star-studded Hollywood premier" in Houston, featuring celebrity look-a-likes and a "paparazzi of cameras".[59] Although it was the nation's largest wholesale marketer, Enron also wanted a piece of the retail market; it estimated that, for each 1 per cent share of the retail market it won, Enron would earn an additional $300 million a year in profits by 2000. It spent $25 million in the first six months of the campaign, and allocated $200 million a year for advertising to win customers and "to persuade Americans to demand faster deregulation".[60]

Business Week reported that Lay was becoming the "most visible and feared advocate of opening the nation's $215 billion retail electricity market to competition" with his "missionary zeal for electric deregulation". It stated:

> Lay is pulling out all stops to hasten deregulation. In April [1997], he launched a $25 million-a-year nationwide ad campaign and says he'll spend up to $200 million to argue the merits of free-market electricity. Behind the scenes, he has deployed legislative SWAT teams in front-line states such as New York, Massachusetts, and Texas.[61]

In Texas, Enron spent $5.8 million between 1998 and 2000 on funding state politicians and lobbying, including the use of 83 lobbyists, paid advertisements, and donations to Texan charities. As a result, according to Public Citizen, Enron was able to help craft the deregulation legislation. Enron had to wield enormous political influence to overcome the resistance of the incumbent, regulated utilities in Texas, which offered relatively cheap electricity, and to persuade a populace that was already getting lower prices through the 1990s that they would be better off with deregulation. As in California, the utilities were enrolled as supporters of deregulation with promises that they could recover their stranded costs. They were allowed to raise rates before deregulation to do this, hauling in billions of extra dollars.[62]

Enron's campaign included getting Patrick Wood III appointed by governor George W. Bush to the Public Utility Commission (PUC) in 1994. Within a few months he was chairing it. Wood understood that Bush wanted deregulation, and he set out to achieve it. Wood's efforts were supplemented by a major Enron campaign which included the usual political donations and lobbying, television and billboard advertisements, luncheons for politicians to explain the virtues of free markets, and Enron-funded front groups such as Texans for Affordable Energy, which gave the appearance of grassroots support for deregulation. In reality, the only voices calling for deregulation were corporate voices or corporate-funded voices.[63]

In California, Enron spent more than $345,000 lobbying for deregulation and another $438,155 on political contributions, including $97,500 to governor Gray Davis. It hired former legislators and Californian Public Utility Commission (CPUC) officials, and Jeff Skilling, who established Enron's trading operation, testified to the CPUC that deregulation would save

California almost $9 billion. The defective Californian electricity market became known as "the Enron model" amongst critics who claimed that Enron had helped to design it.[64]

Similarly, Enron lobbied in other states, spending $1.9 million on political donations in 28 states: "It's no secret we were very active," said Mark Palmer, an Enron spokesman. "We helped open markets that needed to be opened." In just four years, 1997-2000, 24 states passed deregulation legislation.[65] Phil Gramm tried to speed the deregulation process with a bill introduced in 2000, jointly sponsored with a Democrat senator, to require all states to deregulate electricity monopolies by 2002.[66]

Public Citizen estimates that Enron spent $3.45 million on lobbying Congress, and paid another $1.6 million to lobbyists during 1999 and 2000. One of its key aims was to have the trading of energy futures further deregulated. Phil Gramm helped to bury legislation deregulating energy futures trading in an appropriations bill shortly after Bush was elected. Enron also wooed individual government officials such as Linda Robertson, who was a senior treasury official in the Clinton administration at the time that Enron and Gramm were trying to get this legislation passed. Robertson was the liaison between treasury and Congress. Enron twice paid for Robertson to come to Houston to talk to Enron executives. Later, Robertson became head of Enron's Washington office.[67]

The legislation, the 2000 Futures Modernization Act, was passed without notice, committee hearings, or floor debate, and despite recommendations against such legislation by a high-level working group that warned it would lead to price manipulation and the withholding of supply. The legislation enabled Enron to run EnronOnline, an unregulated online auction for electricity and natural gas, and to avoid reporting on any of its activities to government authorities. This was in contrast to the Californian Power Exchange (PX), which had to report prices and volumes.[68]

Enron became "one of the biggest beneficiaries of the California power crisis".[69] A significant proportion of California's electricity and natural gas market operated through Enron's online auction. And Public Citizen argues that it "allowed Enron's unregulated energy trading subsidiary to manipulate supply in such a way as to threaten millions of California households and businesses with power outages for the sole purpose of increasing the company's profits". These profits were substantial. Enron's wholesale services revenues went from $12 billion in the first quarter of 2000 to $48.4 billion in the first quarter of 2001. It made a similar amount in the following quarter.[70]

Enron was given privileged access to Vice President Dick Cheney when he was formulating the National Energy Policy. Enron executives had at least six meetings with Cheney or his staff, and Lay himself had at least three meetings with Cheney, including a half-hour meeting to discuss the draft energy policy. At one meeting Lay gave Cheney a memo requesting that the federal government take no steps to keep the price of electricity in western states down.[71] The result of this was evident in the refusal of the Bush administration to introduce price caps until June (see previous chapter).

Enron's influence on the energy policy was aided by the participation of Rove, Lindsey, and Libby in its drafting, each of whom had Enron stock or earned fees from Enron. Republican Henry Waxman alleges that the final document included seventeen policies that Enron had advocated.[72]

Enron influenced various appointments, most particularly the membership and chair of the FERC. The *New York Times* reported that various candidates for membership of FERC had been "interviewed" by Enron officials, who had made it clear that their CEO had a close relationship with Bush. Lay met with the White House personnel chief, Clay Johnson, to discuss nominees, and sent him a list of preferred candidates. Johnson said that he had also listened to the views of the head of the Edison Electric Institute (EEI) with whom he and George W. had been to Yale. The two Republican vacancies were filled by candidates that Enron and other energy companies backed. One was Nora Brownell, who had been a member of the Pennsylvania PUC, when Pennsylvania deregulated. The other was Patrick Wood III (see page 152).[73]

The *Times* also reported that Lay had put pressure on Curtis Hébert Jr, the head of FERC, to "back a national push for retail competition in the energy business and a faster pace in opening up access to the electricity transmission grid to companies like Enron". Hébert told the *Times* that, in a telephone conversion, Lay said that if he did these things Enron would continue to support him as head of FERC. Hébert, who was himself "a fierce advocate of unfettered markets", was later replaced as chair by Patrick Wood, clearly Lay's preference. Wood's former position as chair of the Texas PUC was filled by Enron de Mexico president Max Yzaguirre. The governor who appointed him received a cheque for $25,000 the day after the appointment was announced.[74]

Enron and the Environmental Lobby

Enron was not only the darling of the business press and admired in financial circles; it was hailed as an ethical and environmentally responsible company. It won environmental awards (see table 8.2) and was on many of the socially responsible investment indexes, including the Domini 400 Social index, the Calvert Group, and the Pax World Balanced Fund.[75]

Enron claimed to be "an active participant" in organisations such as the World Business Council for Sustainable Development (WBCSD) and the Pew Center on Global Climate Change, which seeks to influence policymakers with respect to climate change and energy policy. Lay had also been a member of Clinton's Council of Sustainable Development.[76] Although these memberships are meant to be seen as indicators of corporate social responsibility, in reality they are another means of achieving corporate influence.

■ **Table 8.2: Enron environmental awards**

Awarded by:	Award	Year
Council on Economic Priorities	'Corporate Conscience'	1996
National Society of Fund Raising Executives, Houston chapter	'Outstanding Corporate Philanthropy'	1996
EPA	'Natural Gas Star Program Transmission Partner'	1997–9
	'Climate Protection'	1998

Sources: Enron. 2002. 'Enron Australia.' Enron. http://www.enron.com.au/insideenron

Whilst Lay and Enron believed in markets and deregulation, they were not averse to lobbying for more regulation where it suited Enron's likely profitability. So Enron lobbied for tougher regulation of air pollution because it traded emission credits. Similarly, Enron's stand on global warming had more to do with anticipated profit opportunities from greenhouse gas-emissions trading[77] than a desire to save the planet. One memo stated that the Kyoto treaty "would do more to promote Enron's business than will almost any other regulatory initiative outside of restructuring the energy and natural-gas industries in Europe and the United States."[78]

Enron donated money to Resources for the Future, a think tank promoting market instruments for environmental problems, including tradeable emission rights. Enron's donations of $45,000 a year and $2 million to enable the foundation to endow a research chair were followed by the appointment of Lay to the foundation's governing board in 2000. Enron also donated heavily to free market-oriented environmental groups. For example, the Enron Foundation gave the Nature Conservancy just under a million dollars between 1994 and 1996. Enron was on the board of the Nature Conservancy for fifteen years, and a member of its International Leadership Council.[79]

Enron's support of the Kyoto treaty had an additional benefit: it won the praise of environmentalists. An internal memo stated, "Enron now has excellent credentials with many 'green' interests including Greenpeace, World Wildlife Fund, Natural Resources Defense Council [NRDC], German Watch …" Ralph Cavanagh, from the NRDC, was particularly impressed with Lay's opposition to some anti-environmental measures in Congress: "he is part of the reason why the bad guys ultimately failed at most of what they attempted … on environmental stewardship, our experience is that you can trust Enron."[80] The NRDC promoted electricity deregulation in California (see chapter 5).

Although Enron gained praise from environmental groups for its stance on global warming and its investment in wind-powered turbines, its environmental credentials were dubious. It fought pollution restrictions in Texas, and was one of the companies that lobbied against new pollution rules for old power plants and factories, and achieved voluntary restrictions in their place. This enabled Enron's methanol facility to continue emitting over 3000 tons of air pollution each year. By 1999 smog levels around Houston were amongst the highest in the country because of the lack of regulation in Texas.[81]

Enron's pipelines in the developing world also caused significant environmental damage. However, even here, Enron's money bought influence. The US-based environmental groups World Wildlife Fund (WWF), the Wildlife Conservation Society (WCS), and the Missouri Botanical Gardens (MBG) agreed to support a controversial gas pipeline through the Chiquitano forest from Bolivia to Brazil, after initially opposing it. The pipeline was a joint venture between Enron and Shell, who agreed to donate $US20 million to a conservation program in the area that the environmental groups, together with a local Bolivian group, would administer.[82]

The environmental and social impact of the pipeline on the world's largest dry tropical forest was first highlighted by WWF. The World Bank declared the forest "one of the two most valuable forests in Latin America". It contained several endangered species including the jaguar and ocelot. The pipeline would bisect the forest, saving money for Enron, which would otherwise have to route the pipeline around the forest. Whilst WWF said it was satisfied that the benefits of the conservation project would outweigh the disadvantages of the pipeline project, others disagreed—particularly indigenous leaders and local environmental groups, such as the Bolivian Forum on Environment and Development.[83] At a public meeting, one person stated:

The signing of agreements such as that which occupies us, serves to grant a green stamp to a socially and environmentally questionable project, in exchange for

financing that no-one benefits more from than the organizations that have no
authority in the area, don't live in it, haven't conserved it and aren't responsible for
its administration.[84]

The support of environmentalists was important for attaining Overseas
Private Investment Corporation (OPIC) funding for the project. In 1997
Clinton had prohibited US lending agencies from funding "infrastructure
projects located in primary tropical forests and other ecologically fragile
areas". However, OPIC defined "primary forest" in such a way as to exclude
the Chiquitano forest (and every other forest in the world, according to a former chief biodiversity officer of the World Bank). The WWF later claimed
that it had been used and deceived by Enron, and that its position had been
misrepresented by Enron.[85]

Less than a month after OPIC voted to support the project, WWF backed
out of the conservation fund agreement because it claimed that indigenous
people had been left out, and Enron and Shell were demanding seats on the
fund board. And OPIC also backed out of its $200 million funding commit-
ment because it said Enron had failed to undertake the agreed environmental
measures.[86]

At the end of 2002 *The Washington Post* reported "The pipeline, completed
late last year, and its service roads have opened up the forest to the kind of
damage environmental groups had predicted: Poachers travel service roads to
log old-growth trees. Hunters prey on wild game and cattle graze illegally. An
abandoned gold mine reopened and its workers camp along the pipeline
right-of-way."[87]

Enron used donations and its good relationship with the NRDC to ensure
approval for its purchase of Portland General Electric (PGE), the largest electric utility in Oregon. There was much opposition to the purchase. Even the
state's PUC was opposed to the takeover, warning that prices would rise,
workers would lose their jobs, and the environment would not be protected.
Others went further, arguing that Enron planned to sell off PGE's assets and
to sell its cheap hydropower to California for large profits.[88]

NRDC's Cavanagh played a key role in pacifying some of this opposition.
He negotiated a memo of understanding between Enron and Oregon environmental groups, involving $500,000 worth of financial support from Enron to
the groups. To all and sundry, Cavanagh argued that Enron was a socially
responsible company that could be trusted. The takeover went ahead. And,
sure enough, in the following two years rates went up, assets were sold, and
PGE's electricity made its way to California. Enron then sold the utility.[89]

Globalisation Enron-Style

Enron also lobbied for broader policies, such as global free trade, that would facilitate its overseas operations. Whilst Clinton was in power Enron was able to participate in high-level US trade missions. It obtained cheap credit from the US export credit agencies (ECAs), particularly the Overseas Private Investment Corporation (OPIC) and the US Export-Import Bank, for its investments in developing countries.

OPIC alone approved $3 billion to finance and insure fourteen projects in which Enron was involved. In return, Enron led industry lobbying efforts to save OPIC from moves in Congress in 1997 and 1999 to terminate it as a way of reducing "corporate welfare". By the time Enron collapsed, OPIC's exposure to Enron amounted to over a billion dollars out of a total portfolio of $15 billion.[90]

After George W. Bush was elected, former Enron employee Robert B. Zoellick was appointed as US trade representative. He worked closely with the export credit agencies, which continued to fund Enron's ventures. In 2000 and 2001 Enron had its own employee on the Export-Import Bank board, which financed Enron projects to the tune of $825 million from 1992. Enron was even paid some $3.5 million by the US Trade and Development Agency to undertake fossil-fuel feasibility studies in Central Asia and Eastern Europe.[91]

Between 1992 and 2001 Enron received over $7 billion of public financing from 21 agencies (in the US, Europe, Canada, and Japan) and multilateral development banks, including over $4 billion from US taxpayers. This enabled it to take part in 38 projects in 29 countries (see table 8.3).[92]

Enron also exploited its political relationships to win contracts overseas. As far back as 1988, it is claimed that Bush Jr telephoned the minister of public works and services in Argentina to put in a good word for Enron. Enron was bidding for the construction of a natural gas pipeline across Argentina to Chile. According to the minister, Rodolfo Terragno, the caller said that he was the son of the vice president, and that awarding the contract to Enron "would be very favorable for Argentina and its relations with the United States". The telephone call, denied by George W., was followed up by several visits from the US ambassador to Argentina, who also pushed Enron's proposal and reiterated Bush Jr's support for it. However, Terragno was not inclined to award the contract to Enron, which had provided a "laughable" one-page outline with a ridiculous price tag. The project was not approved until the government changed. The new administration of Carlos Saul Menem, a friend of the Bush family, approved the project even before economic-feasiblity studies had been done. It awarded the contract to Enron, and included exemptions from tariffs and tax-breaks that enraged Argentines and caused a scandal.[93]

In 1994 Enron was awarded a part in a Mozambique gas field after heavy lobbying by US embassy officials. In 1995, when it looked like the deal was about to fall through, Clinton cabinet members threatened to cut aid to Mozambique, according to *The Texas Observer*, if it did not award the pipeline contract to Enron. Enron got the contract and Mozambique got its $13.5 million aid package.[94] Enron also obtained contracts for electricity plants in the Philippines and India, with the help of US ambassador Frank Wisner, who later joined Enron's board of directors (see chapter 18).

Enron had political influence in developed countries, also. Enron set up in Britain as soon as energy privatisation hit the agenda, and was the first company to begin work on a power plant once privatisation had occurred in 1989. John Wakeham, the UK energy secretary who was responsible for privatising electricity in the Thatcher government, approved Enron's bid for one of Britain's first gas-fired power plants. He was appointed to the Enron board two years after he retired in 1994. Enron also set up Enron Direct in the UK to sell retail electricity and natural gas to 100,000 businesses, such as restaurants and stores. It then set up similar services in Spain, the Netherlands, and the United States.[95]

■ **Table 8.3: Enron project financing and global assets**

Country	Financing* (US$millions)	Assets
Panama	>3.3 — WBG 60 — Ex.Im.	Bahia Las Minas (BLM) — 355 MW electric generation "largest thermal power plant in Central America"
Guatemala	124 — OPIC 98 — MARAD 0.7 — WBG	Puerto Quetzal Power Project — 110 MW power plant PQPLLC — 124 MW barge mounted power plant
Mexico	136 — IADB	
Nicaragua	50 — MARAD 30 — CDC	Margarita II — 35% interest in 70.5 MW barge mounted power plant
Puerto Rico		EcoElectrica — 507 MW gas-fired cogen. plant and LNG import terminal ProCaribe — LPG storage terminal San Juan Gas — gas distribution company
Dominican Republic	133.8 — WBG 84 — MARAD >74 — CDC 15 — other	Puerto Plata Power Project — 185 MW oil-fired, barge mounted power plant
Jamaica		Industrial Gases Limited — supplies all industrial gas and 40% LPG

■ Table 8.3: Enron project financing and global assets (cont.)

Country	Financing* (US$millions)	Assets
Colombia	65—WBG	Centragas pipeline—578 km natural gas pipeline Promigas—natural gas pipeline operator
Venezuela	400—OPIC 197—Ex.Im. 130—Other	CALIFE—electrical utility company INESLA—joint venture manufacturing valves/thermostats Vengas—leading distributor of LPG
Argentina	168—OPIC 375—IADB	TGS—largest natural gas pipeline system in S. America Modesto Maranzana Power Plant—70MW power plant
Brazil	390—OPIC	Elektro Electricidade e Servicos SA—electricity distributor Culaba Integrated Project—480 MW diesel/gas power plant CEG/CEGRio—share in natural gas distribution companies Gaspart—seven gas distribution companies
Bolivia	200—OPIC 365—IADB 366—WBG 734—other	Bolivia to Brazil pipeline TRANSREDES—hydrocarbon transportation assets
Nigeria	100—WBG 200—OPIC	
Poland		Nowa Sarzyna—116 MW natural gas power plant
Italy	493—OPIC	Sarlux Power Project—441 MW oil to gas power plant
Turkey	295—OPIC 251—Ex.Im.	Trakya Power Project—478 MW natural gas power plant
China	16.7—WBG >15—Ex.Im.	Chengu Cogen Project—284 MW coal-fired cogeneration plant in conjunction with Sichuan Electric Power Company
Guam		Northern Marianas Power Project—80 MW diesel plant
Indonesia	60—WBG	
Philippines	129—OPIC 26—ADB	Batangas Power Project—110 MW power plant Subic Bay Power Project—116 MW power plant
South Korea		SK-Enron—gas companies, gas distribution and LPG marketing
India	592—OPIC 302—Ex.Im. 524—other	Dabhol Power Project—2184 MW power plant

* Financing for projects that Enron participated in

ADB = Asia Development Bank; CDC = UK Commonwealth Development Corporation; Ex.Im. = US Export-Import Bank; IADB = Inter-American Development Bank; MARAD = US Maritime Administration; OPIC = Overseas Private Investment Corporation; WBG = World Bank Group

Sources: Enron. 'Enron Global Services.' Enron. Accessed on 2 January 2002. http://www.enron.com/corp/ pressroom/factsheets/egs/; Sustainable Energy and Economic Network. 'Enron's Pawns: How Public Institutions Bankrolled Enron's Globalization Game.' Washington, DC: Institute for Policy Studies. 2002. pp. 23-4.

Enron also entered the water business when water authorities were privatised around the world. In 1998 it formed a global water company, Azurix, aimed at "owning, operating and managing wastewater assets", providing related services, and "developing and managing water resources". Azurix bought Wessex Water in south-west England, and sought to participate in water privatisations in Rio, Berlin, and Panama.[96]

Enron was said to have close links to the Blair government as well. Enron Europe donated money to the Labour Party as part of a "Labour charm offensive", as did Enron's auditor, Arthur Andersen. Enron also donated money to the Prince of Wales Trust to facilitate good relations with Prince Charles. Enron had several meetings with UK government ministers between 1998 and 2000, leading to allegations of "cash for access". During this time the Blair government lifted a moratorium on the construction of gas-fired power stations, following lobbying by Enron, and it allowed Enron to purchase Wessex Water without referring the deal to the Monopolies Commission.[97]

Enron was one of the companies chosen to accompany the UK planning minister on a trade mission to Egypt. The head of Enron Europe, Ralph Hodge, was awarded the rank of Commander of the British Empire for "services to the power generation and gas industries" in the 2001 New Year's honours list. And in 2002 the director of Wessex Water, Gareth Jones, received an MBE in the New Year's honours list "for services to environmental quality".[98]

Enron was also accused of having an overly influential role in electricity privatisation and deregulation in Ontario, Canada. NDP leader Howard Hampton says that Enron gave political donations "to the Conservative Party and Energy Minister Jim Wilson while helping the government write the rules." He points out that it had representation on "handpicked advisory groups" with responsibility for designing the rules of privatisation of hydroelectric facilities, even though it was not a Canadian company.[99]

Enron was also influential in matters of international policy through its behind-the-scenes sway over US trade policy. According to Corporate Watch and the Polaris Institute, Enron was an active member of the US Coalition of Service Industries (USCSI), a group of large, multinational, for-profit service corporations, as was its auditor, Arthur Andersen. Enron heavily lobbied WTO negotiations, pushing an agenda of deregulation, privatisation, and free trade. It was also on the board of the National Trade Council and "a prime mover behind granting the President fast track authority over all trade negotiations", something that has been achieved post-Enron.[100]

Enron was particularly interested in negotiations on the General

Agreement on Trade in Services (GATS). The purpose of GATS is to allow corporations such as Enron easier access to buying up services, including energy services, in foreign nations (see chapter 17). Enron was "a leading player in the major big business lobby machines driving the GATS negotiations".[101] Enron's input was further facilitated by having Zoellick representing the US in the negotiations.

In each country, "Enron pursued a business strategy that exploited relationships with elected officials and regulators to pursue policies narrowly tailored to benefit Enron's immediate income needs."[102] It promoted free markets and deregulation, but was happy enough with regulation that gave it business. It was opposed to taxes and government intervention, but benefited handsomely from government funds. It extolled the benefits of open competition, but manipulated and dominated markets to avoid that competition. The ideology it sold to others was little more than a pragmatic recipe for Enron profitability.

Robert L. Borosage notes in *The Nation* that, although Enron clothed itself in the colours of the free market, it set out to rig the market and change the rules to maximise its profit opportunities. For several years, its shareholders benefited, with a return of 40 per cent in 1998, 58 per cent in 1999, and 89 per cent in 2000.[103] Enron's downfall is plotted in the next chapter.

CHAPTER NINE

Enron In Trouble

The history of unregulated markets in the United States is that they result in inflated, manipulated prices that create a balloon, and that eventually the balloon bursts ... The explosion not only wipes out the company, the investors, traders, creditors and consumer, it ultimately involves the taxpayers.
Michael Aguirre [1]

THE COLLAPSE OF ENRON is reminiscent of the collapse of Insull's empire in 1932 (see chapter 3). Like the power companies of the 1920s, Enron was an empire of partnerships and subsidiaries built up to benefit the few at the expense of the greater mass of shareholders and the wider public. Legislation brought in during the 1930s to stop such abuses of power had been whittled away through the persistent efforts of Enron and other corporations, enabling history to repeat itself. For example, in 1993 "Enron persuaded the SEC to grant it an exemption from the Public Utility Holding Company Act (PUHCA)",[2] which was put in place to prevent the sort of excesses that Enron engaged in.

When Enron filed for bankruptcy its stock stood at 26 cents, having plummeted from a high of $90, and 4,500 of its employees were laid off immediately. The majority of Enron shares were owned by institutional investors such as pension funds and mutual funds, so many other workers were also hurt, to the tune of some $25-50 billion. Banks were affected, too, having made loans of billions of dollars to Enron, much of it unsecured.[3]

Enron's collapse has been felt far from Washington as well. In Japan, the company's woes triggered billions of dollars of withdrawals from money market funds that had invested heavily in Enron stock. In India, a deal to sell a huge power plant that was built as part of the company's expanding overseas empire has fallen apart. Enron's energy customers in the United States have had to scramble to find new suppliers.[4]

Following Enron's bankruptcy, eleven congressional inquiries were set up to look into the collapse, as well as inquiries by the justice department and the Securities and Exchange Commission (SEC). The attorney general and his entire office had to excuse themselves from conducting inquiries because so many of them had past or present ties to Enron or Enron employees.[5] Many lawsuits were instigated against Enron and its auditor Arthur Andersen; more than 60 in Houston and Galveston courts alone in the first couple of months. For example, American National Insurance Co, which claimed to have lost over $15 million on its Enron investments, alleged that Andersen partners and Enron executives defrauded investors because they knew that the value of Enron securities had been artificially inflated.[6] The Amalgamated Bank of New York also sued. It had invested the pension money of union members in Enron shares, and alleged fraud and insider trading on the part of Enron executives. The US Congress had to sue the White House to get information about its relationship with Enron — the first time such a thing had ever happened.[7]

These lawsuits and investigations revealed information about how Enron operated that is not generally available about healthy operating companies; it gives an insight into how corporations involved in the electricity industry operate and the strategies they use to manipulate prices, raise their stated profits, and keep their share prices high.

Enron Accounting Tricks

Enron expanded during the early 1990s. Its investments soon came to over $10 billion, but they were failing to bring in the returns that Enron had hoped for.[8] In 1997 Enron's share price waned, and Wall Street stopped recommending the stock. Lay's bonus was cut by two-thirds to $450,000. Other companies were competing in the energy-trading business, rendering it more difficult to make profits. Enron had lost billions of dollars on its investments in India and Brazil, and its ventures in trading outside the energy sector — such as paper, steel, and bandwidth — were unsuccessful. For example, it lost about $2 billion on telecom capacity.[9]

In an effort to keep its share price up and hide its increasing debt, Enron used a number of accounting tricks to make the company appear to be more profitable and successful than it was. Enron's booming profits in the late 1990s were a mirage. For example, it counted as revenues (sales income) the total amount of every energy-trading transaction, rather than just the profits derived from them. This meant that the whole value for which it sold the energy was recorded as revenue, even if it had sold it at a loss.[10] This inflated revenue helped Enron's rise to become the seventh-largest company in the US.

The practice described in chapter 6 of trading electricity with its own subsidiaries in order to boost prices also meant that revenue increased with these 'internal' trades. Electricity and gas were also traded back and forth with other companies at the same price. These "wash trades" did not earn profits, but boosted claimed revenue. In other cases, Enron would book a profit as soon as it signed a contract, based on its expected profits over the term of the contract, which could be a period of up to 20 years. Expected profits from the contract were inflated by making overly optimistic assumptions about future energy prices, energy use, and the pace of deregulation in various states.[11]

By paying employees with stock options as part of their salary, reported profits were further exaggerated because the options were not recorded as an expense. This is a common corporate practice. The profits that executives make on stock options become a deduction on corporate tax, without having to appear on shareholder financial statements as a loss. The profits made by Enron executives in 2000, on cashing in their stock options, turned a tax bill of $112 million for the company into a refund of $278 million.[12]

Stock options, in turn, provide a powerful incentive for executives to ensure that the books look good enough to send the share price up; and if the real figures are not good enough, they can be manipulated until they appear to be. Enron executives were paid bonuses of $320 million in early 2001 because of the rising stock price.[13]

Inflated profits and hidden debts drove share prices up. This helped Enron to borrow even more money, to acquire other companies, and to attract employees. But, perhaps more importantly, it raised the personal wealth of the top executives who had been paid with stock options. In a rising market, the appearance of a prosperous company means that past investors benefit from each new generation of investors. The weakness of the company only becomes apparent when investors stop investing.[14]

Enron executives and the analysts employed by Wall Street firms that made money selling Enron shares and bonds did their best to talk up the stock and persuade investors that it was a good buy. "The bull market euphoria convinced analysts, investors, accountants and even regulators that as long as stock prices stayed high, there was no need to question company practices."[15]

The main way that Enron created its mirage of profitability was through its subsidiaries and partnerships. It had over 3000 of these, approximately one for every seven employees, many of them "off-balance sheet" companies. Offshore partnerships were used to borrow over $10 billion. The loans were guaranteed using Enron stock. The partnerships then traded with Enron, and the revenues from these trades were reported as revenues on Enron balance sheets. Some partnerships were created to sell assets to third parties in such a way that Enron's valuation of them would not be questioned.[16]

Generally, partnerships were created to keep losses off Enron's financial statements so that stock prices could be kept high. Companies are allowed to move debt-ridden financial assets off their balance sheets if they are owned by organisations that are not controlled in any way by the original company. Enron got around this rule of the Financial Accounting Standards Board by getting specially created partner organisations to "issue put options—obligations to buy something in the future at a specified price—on assets that were still on Enron's books". Douglas Carmichael, an accounting professor, told *Forbes* magazine: "It's like somebody sat down with the rules and said, 'How can we get around them?'" He claimed that Enron had structured its affairs "to comply to the letter of the law but totally violated the spirit."[17]

A report by Enron's board of directors after the collapse described some of the transactions with partnerships:

> They allowed Enron to conceal from the market very large losses resulting from Enron's merchant investments by creating an appearance that those investments were hedged—that is, that a third party was obligated to pay Enron the amount of those losses—when in fact that third party was simply an entity in which only Enron had a substantial economic stake.[18]

Not only did Enron executives make tens of millions of dollars out of these partnerships; so also did individual bankers from the large investment banks that Enron dealt with, who were given an opportunity to invest in them. Investors were lured to invest in partnerships with the promise of inside knowledge about Enron and its off-the-books holdings that was otherwise withheld from shareholders. The returns of over 100 per cent, in some cases, were another incentive to invest in the partnerships.[19]

The partnerships worked fine whilst Enron's shares were going up and the losses on assets by partner companies could be made up for by increases in the value of Enron shares. But when the shares fell below $68 in mid-March 2001, the partnerships began to go bankrupt and others had to be created to prop them up.[20]

Offshore partnerships were also useful in tax avoidance. Almost 900 of Enron's partners and subsidiaries were registered in offshore tax havens. "The partner, after taking its fee, then returns the profits in a form that is recognized as not taxable by American law."[21] These havens have weak bank-disclosure laws; Enron was able to hide money in accounts in these havens, and not only avoid taxes but creditors and regulatory scrutiny as well. (The Bush administration had intervened to weaken an OECD treaty on tax havens.)[22]

In four out of the last five years of its operation, Enron paid no taxes despite making millions in profits (see table below). Moreover, it achieved tax refunds of $382 million through the use of tax havens, stock options, and other tax-avoidance strategies. This was facilitated by retrospective legislation that Bush introduced, removing minimum tax requirements from corporations. Enron and other companies lobbied hard for him to do this. In California, Enron simply didn't pay the taxes it owed—almost half a million dollars in 2000.[23]

■ **Table 9.1: Enron federal US taxes, 1996–2000**

Year	US Profits	Tax Paid	Tax Refund
1996	$540 million	0	$3 million
1997	$87 million	$17 million	0
1998	$189 million	0	$13 million
1999	$351 million	0	$105 million
2000	$618 million	0	$278 million

Sources: D. Johnston. 'Enron Avoided Income Taxes in 4 of 5 Years.' New York Times. 17 January 2002. p. A1; Citizens for Tax Justice. 'Less Than Zero: Enron's Income Tax Payments, 1996-2000.' http://www.ctj.org/html/enron.htm.

Conflicts of Interest

The conflicts of interest started with Enron itself and its chief financial officer (CFO), Andrew Fastow: "Mr. Fastow was negotiating deals on behalf of the partnerships across the table from his own subordinates, who were representing Enron."[24] According to columnist Molly Ivins, Enron's board voted to suspend its ethics code twice so that they could create the shonky partnerships described above: "But how thoughtful of them to suspend the ethics code first! Otherwise, they might have violated it."[25]

Whilst "[b]ad investments became profits on the income statement",[26] Enron's auditors, Arthur Andersen, approved it all. Yet Andersen was no fly-by-night accounting firm. It employed 85,000 people in 84 countries, and was one of the world's Big Five accounting firms. (Most of the publicly traded US firms use one of the Big Five to audit their books.)[27]

Andersen had close links with Enron. Former employees of Andersen had been employed by Enron as top financial executives, including Enron's chief accounting officer. At the same time as it was auditing Enron's books Andersen earned more than $28 million in consultancy work for the company, with the prospect of more in the future, compromising its role as 'independent' auditor. Andersen was reported to have accepted millions of dollars for structuring these partnerships whilst not reporting on them to Enron's board. It then got paid to audit the books and say that everything was kosher.[28]

> It turns out that what's called consulting at Andersen is people inside the firm talking to Enron employees about how they can avoid financial disclosure. The right hand of Andersen is doing exactly the opposite of what the left hand of Andersen, the audit function, is supposed to be doing. And that sort of bold conflict pervades all of the gatekeepers, the banks and securities firms made hundreds of millions of dollars off of Enron over the years, not only from underwriting fees but from fees charged for various derivatives transactions.[29]

The conflict of interest, arising from accounting firms doing consultancy work for corporations and then acting as 'independent auditors', was recognised by the chair of the SEC, Arthur Levitt, who proposed in 2000 that the practice be banned. The proposal was opposed with heavy lobbying on the part of the accounting industry, coordinated by lobbyist Harvey Pitt, a lawyer for the American Institute of Certified Accountants, who had worked as a lawyer for Andersen in a case against the SEC. With the help of congressional pressure the proposal was not implemented. (Andersen and the other Big Five were big contributors to members of Congress.) Then, when Bush was elected, he appointed Pitt to be head of the SEC. Pitt, naturally, took a less 'confrontational' approach to the accounting profession, believing that they should be allowed to regulate themselves.[30]

The dozens of banks and financial firms promoting Enron stocks and bonds also had conflicts of interest. Wall Street bankers did not question Enron's partnership arrangements because they were involved in setting them up and made big fees from them. J.P. Morgan and Citigroup, which combined investment and commercial banking, were Enron's two major banks and also investors in Enron's partnerships. (Both lost heavily when Enron went down—at least $2.6 billion in the case of J.P. Morgan—showing that even long-term self-interest could not prevent their participation in Enron's schemes.)[31]

"The major houses of Wall Street play a double game with their customers —doing investment deals with companies in their private offices whilst their stock analysts are out front whipping up enthusiasm for the same companies' stocks." For example, Goldman Sachs earned $69 million from underwriting Enron, and was advising investors to buy Enron shares right to the end.[32] Merrill Lynch not only invested in Enron partnerships but "raised hundreds of millions of dollars from others to invest in the same. Dozens of investment banks received information about the true nature of Enron's financial situation, yet because they received it on a confidential basis, they could not share it with their brokerage clients."[33]

Analysts from many of the investment houses gave high ratings to Enron stock and bonds, right up till Enron's final collapse. This was not helped by the fact that the pay of analysts tends to be based on the investment banking business they generate, rather than on how reliable their recommendations are. Merrill Lynch's star analyst earned $12 million in 'compensation' in 2001.[34] "Of the security analysts following Enron, only one put a sell recommendation on the stock prior to the date of bankruptcy".[35]

Analysts who didn't play the game were likely to lose their jobs. In 1998 Merrill Lynch had lost a "lucrative stock underwriting deal" with Enron, which Merrill executives attributed to the poor relationship between Enron and one of their research analysts who had rated Enron stock "neutral". The analyst was replaced with one who rated the stock as a "buy"; Merrill consequently won Enron business, generating some $45 million in fees.[36] The dishonesty of Merrill analysts' public "buy" recommendations were disclosed in private Merrill emails that described Enron stock as "a piece of junk" and "a piece of crap".[37]

The banks were aware of Enron's shady accounting methods, often helping to set up partnerships for large fees and favours, and even participating in them.[38] "Together and individually, the banks and brokerages raised at least $6 billion for Enron through the debt or stock issues sold to unsuspecting investors from 1996 through 2001, when the Enron illusion finally expired. Another $4 billion or more was channelled into Enron's 'partnerships'."[39]

Investigations revealed that major investment banks also made multimillion-dollar loans that helped Enron hide its debts and inflate its profits. For example, the bank's insurers claim that J.P. Morgan's loans to Enron were made to look like oil and gas trading contracts, so as to keep them off the bank's balance sheets. And loans from banks such as Citigroup and J.P. Morgan Chase were recorded on Enron's books as advance payment for energy trades with offshore companies. The banks cooperated in various deals that seem to have been made solely for the purpose of making Enron's books look good. In return, they earned massive fees, commissions, and interest rates, as well as opportunities to invest in deals that promised huge returns.[40]

The banks also tried to sell such strategies to other companies, successfully in some cases. Investigator Robert Roach told a Senate hearing that: "The evidence indicates that Enron would not have been able to engage in the extent of the accounting deceptions it did, involving billions of dollars, were it not for the active participation of major financial institutions willing to go along with and even expand upon Enron's activities." Consequently, nine investment banks have been added to the list of defendants in the lawsuits brought by shareholders who claim that they were defrauded by Enron. These include Citigroup, J.P. Morgan Chase, Credit Suisse First Boston, Canadian Imperial Bank of Commerce, Merrill Lynch, Britain's Barclays Bank. and Germany's Deutsche Bank AG.[41]

Even the financial journalists were taken in, and "instead of digging for answers, collectively genuflected at the mere mention of the Enron miracle".[42] Enron had not left the media off its payroll. It paid at least four high-level journalists $50,000-$100,000 each to serve on an advisory panel that appeared to have no real function. Each journalist was writing about Enron at the time or editing magazines that were. Moreover, the major newspapers were hardly in a position to investigate Enron's accounting tricks when they were using some of the same accounting practices themselves. Some newspapers were even involved in Enron schemes. For example, *The New York Times* had a "newsprint swap agreement" with Enron that involved no physical trade.[43]

Enron on the Skids

Enron suffered further when price caps were finally introduced into the Californian energy market in June 2001. Enron was caught out with billions of dollars worth of contracts that it had assumed it would be able to sell for whatever price it asked.[44]

In August 2001, when Enron stock fell below $45 from $80 earlier in the year, Jeff Skilling resigned, after less than a year as the company's CEO. He cashed in his share options for over $60 million. Altogether 29 executives cashed in $1.1 billion of stock from 1999 to mid-2001. "This is the most massive insider bailout that we've ever seen and we've been prosecuting these cases for 30 years", said William Lerach, an attorney for one of the banks suing Enron.[45]

Following Skilling's resignation, Lay attempted to reassure employees. He emailed them: "I want to assure you that I have never felt better about the prospects for the company ... Our performance has never been stronger; our business model has never been more robust; our growth has never been more certain."[46] However, not all employees were so easily fooled. One executive, Sherron Watkins, vice president for corporate development, wrote anonymously to Lay, asking if Enron had become a risky place to work: "Skilling's abrupt departure will raise suspicions of accounting improprieties and valuation issues ... I am incredibly nervous that we will implode in a wave of accounting scandals."[47] Shortly after Watkins' memo, Lay stepped up the disposal of his Enron shares. He sold shares worth a total of $100 million in 2001.[48]

In September Andersen began shredding Enron documents, as well as destroying electronic records on advice from its lawyers. It was later found guilty by a federal jury of obstruction of justice, with respect to Enron investigations. (Enron also shredded documents and continued to do so after filing for bankruptcy.)[49] That month Lay again told employees that Enron was "continuing to have strong growth" and was "fundamentally sound", and encouraged them to "talk up the stock and talk positively about Enron to your family and friends".[50]

In October 2001 Enron announced a $618 million net loss in the third quarter, but claimed that a "26 per cent increase in recurring earnings per diluted share shows the very strong results of our core wholesale and retail energy businesses and our natural gas pipelines ... The continued excellent prospects in these businesses and Enron's leading market position make us very confident in our strong earnings outlook". [51]

This loss, and the revelation in the *Wall Street Journal* that Enron CFO Andrew Fastow had made over $30 million on a partnership, triggered an SEC investigation which revealed more Enron deceptions. Enron's share price, which was already down, plummeted 44 per cent to $20.56, making an aggregate fall of 75 per cent since the start of the year (see figure 9.1).[52]

In November, Enron had to restate its previous financial statements (1997-2001) to reveal a reduction of net income of more than half a billion dollars. Enron also announced a $1.2 billion reduction in shareholder equity (that is, the value of the company). Enron admitted that "certain off-balance sheet entities should have been included in its consolidated financial statements pursuant to generally accepted accounting principles".[53]

At the end of November, Standard & Poor's downgraded Enron's credit rating "below investment grade, triggering the immediate repayment of almost $4 billion in off-balance-sheet debt".[54] Enron was unable to pay, and filed for bankruptcy on 4 December. The wonder is that the three major credit agencies had not downgraded Enron's rating earlier. They had better access to Enron's books than most others, including Wall Street analysts.[55] This was another of the checks and balances that didn't work.

■ **Figure 9.1: Enron stock price, 1997–2001**

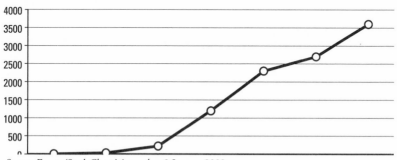

Source: Enron. 'Stock Chart.' Accessed on 2 January 2002
http://www.corporateir.net/ireye/ir_site.zhtml?ticker=ENE&script=300&layout=-6

Days before it filed for bankruptcy, Enron paid 500 senior employees $55 million in bonuses. The other 20,000 or so employees did not fare so well. Their retirement funds had been loaded up with Enron stock; when Enron stock plunged to less than a dollar it wiped out their pensions. Many employees also had their life savings tied up in Enron stock, and "Enron had many of them locked into rules that prohibited them from selling their stakes in the company" whilst Lay and his fellow executives sold theirs.[56]

Enron not Unique

Although many would like to think that Enron was unique and an aberration, many of its practices, including the use of aggressive accounting, were quite common. A study by Walter Cadette, a scholar and former vice president of J.P. Morgan, found that "corporate America appears to be overstating its earnings by at least 20 per cent".[57] This figure has been confirmed by Alan Brown, chief investment officer for the State Street group.[58] Similarly, John Coffee, professor of law at Columbia Law School, claims that "Many companies try to use off-balance sheet financing so that they don't have to show liabilities on their balance sheet".[59]

In fact, Enron was so proud of its "creative ways to manage its own cash flow and profits" that it "marketed that expertise to other corporations", including AT&T, Eli Lilly, and Lockheed Martin. At least six major corporations and many small businesses engaged in complex deals with Enron aimed at enhancing the balance sheets of both parties. This was a service that banks such as Merrill Lynch and J.P. Morgan Chase also offered its clients, using "a wide range of derivatives and other structured finance products to help big corporations reduce their taxes and deliver just the right amount of profits, quarter after quarter."[60]

Several companies restated their profits during the course of inquiries and investigations that followed Enron's collapse. Telecommunications giant WorldCom Inc., which went bankrupt in mid-2002, revealed that it had hidden nearly $4 billion in expenses through accounting tricks. Other companies with accounting irregularities included Xerox, Merc, and ABB.[61]

Yet there are those who believe, despite Enron's downfall, that what it stood for, in terms of deregulation and free markets, must be continued. For example, Mills and Huber wrote in the *Wall Street Journal*, "What serious deregulators must do now is allow a new generation of Enrons to build much larger markets ..."[62]

Various firms have emulated Enron's energy-trading strategies and are ready to step into the void it created. The business of derivatives has grown exponentially in recent times, and has been described as "essentially betting on a mass scale". In 1999 the derivative business amounted to $102 trillion worldwide, ten times the US GDP. It is now the largest financial market in the world.[63]

Dynegy, which attempted to take over Enron as it went down, is a smaller version of Enron. "Analysts say Dynegy is seen to have mirrored the fast, aggressive growth, policies and style of Enron", and it also has "a sophisticated electronic trading platform for oil, natural gas and other commodities".[64] But Dynegy is also being investigated by the SEC. One of the issues being looked into is the way a partnership was treated in Dynegy's accounts. Invidious comparisons were made to Enron, causing Dynegy's share price to plummet. Subsequently, Bradley P. Farnsworth, who was chief accounting officer at Dynegy from 1997 to 2000, claimed that he was fired after refusing to help manipulate the accounts to boost profits and hide energy-trading losses. (This was after the company lost a lot of money betting that gas prices would fall in Britain in 2000.) Not surprisingly, after disposing of Farnsworth, the company was able to claim it had met profit expectations for the quarter.[65]

The very companies that made so much money from California's crisis have since admitted to engaging in phoney trades that were made to increase trading revenue and volume rather than to buy and sell electricity. Included are Reliant, Duke Energy, and Dynegy. This increased their trading volume, making them seem to be doing more business than they were, and was a widespread practice in the industry. Some argue that it was also done to increase prices. Reliant was also investigated by the SEC after restating its earnings in the wake of the Enron crash. The SEC also investigated Mirant Corp., another energy trader, after it disclosed that it had misstated its assets by $253 million in 2001, and Duke Energy for accounting and trading practices.[66]

The revelations of energy company deception and accounting tricks caused a slump in investor confidence in them and across the stock market. This meant it became very difficult for them to raise money to build new generating plants. Some analysts warned that this would cause construction of plant to be stalled for a number of years, leading to a shortage of electricity and further hikes in prices.[67]

Enron is by no means the first energy company to be caught manipulating its accounts in modern times. Southern Company, which also profited from the Californian energy crisis, engaged in dubious accounting practices and political donations in the 1980s. A whistleblower executive on his way to confront the board of directors in 1989 was killed when a company jet he was travelling on exploded shortly after take-off. Nevertheless, "a grand jury voted to charge the company with criminal racketeering for manipulating its accounts", and the company admitted making illegal campaign contributions. Its auditor was Arthur Andersen. Southern was forced to pay back millions of dollars to customers. Having been caught breaking the rules, Southern campaigned hard for deregulation. Subsequently, industry lobbyists and lawyers helped get rid of rules which had made campaign contributions from power companies illegal, and also rules which required them to adhere to a standard system of accounting.[68]

Another energy group under investigation is the Williams Companies, which is also a major contributor to the Republican Party. In 2001 Williams refunded California $8 million, in settlement of a case in which the company was accused of withholding power to drive up electricity prices. (It did not admit to any wrongdoing, however.) Williams has also been accused of manipulating gas prices in California, loading up a spin-off company with excess debt, and inflating profits with overly optimistic estimates of the gains to be made on long-term contracts, credited to the current year's accounts. Ernst & Young, another of the big five accounting firms, signed off on Williams' accounts.[69]

Like the country's other major power traders, Williams has struggled to avoid the taint of malfeasance ever since Enron's problems began to become known late last year. But successive revelations about how many energy trading companies work —from the use of creative accounting to show increasing profits to their use of fictitious trades to fatten revenue—have peeled away the industry's denials to reveal uncomfortable similarities between some other energy companies and the bankrupt Enron.[70]

Nor was Enron the first example of Arthur Andersen being involved in a shady corporate bankruptcy. It has been associated with dubious accounting and corporate collapses at many companies, including Sunbeam and Waste Management, the Baptist Foundation of Arizona, and HIH in Australia. The other large accounting firms have been involved in similar scandals. According to author and journalist William Greider, "Andersen's behaviour is actually typical among the Big Five accounting firms that monopolize commercial/financial auditing worldwide."[71]

William T. Allen, the director of the Center for Law and Business at New York University, has pointed out that "Enron is a profound shock to the system because the fundamental causes are pervasive in the economy."[72] Similarly, Robert L. Borosage wrote in *The New York Times*:

Enron's bankruptcy, the largest in history, exposes the decay of corporate accountability in the new Gilded Age. No-account accountants, see-no-evil stock analysts, subservient 'independent' board members, gelded regulators, purchased politicians —every supposed check on executive plunder and piracy has been shredded. Enron transformed itself from a gas pipeline company to an unregulated financial investment house willing and able to buy and sell anything—energy futures, weather changes, bandwidth, state legislatures, regulators, senators, even Presidents.[73]

Many of Enron's activities could not have occurred without the deregulation that Enron and others pushed so hard for: deregulation of energy, banking, accounting, and commodity trading. First there was the exemption from PUHCA, which meant that Enron could expand across the country into other industries, build up a complicated corporate structure of partnerships and subsidiaries, and not have to publicly disclose data regarding its financial structure, assets, and contractual arrangements. PUHCA would have required the SEC to approve financial transactions between Enron and its partners, and the structure of Enron as a holding company.[74] And, as noted in previous chapters, moves are now afoot to repeal PUHCA so that other companies may follow in Enron's (and Insull's) footsteps.

In 1995, the Private Securities Litigation Reform Act gave immunity to accountants so that it would be harder to sue companies such as Andersen for endorsing accounts like Enron's. Companies like Andersen also helped defeat the SEC's efforts to prevent conflicts of interest by not allowing firms to audit companies that they consulted for.[75] And in 1997 Enron received a crucial legal exemption from the Investment Company Act of 1940 that enabled it to shift debt off the books of its foreign operations and allowed its executives to invest in Enron partnerships. Efforts to legislate for the disclosure of off-balance sheet deals in 2000 were opposed by Enron, Andersen, and many other companies. The banks' conflicts of interest were facilitated by the Gramm-Leach-Bliley Act of 1999 which repealed the Glass-Steagall Act of 1933, aimed at separating investment banking from commercial banking in the US because of perceived conflicts of interest.[76]

Recent efforts to institute rules concerning the way stock options are treated, in the wake of Enron, have met with stiff and concerted corporate opposition. A coalition of corporate executives, venture capitalists, and biotechnology and high-technology companies has formed under the name Stock Option Coalition. The coalition has hired "platoons of lobbyists", and has employed sophisticated email and Web-based campaigns aimed at both enrolling employees and prodding members of Congress who have received large political donations from the companies involved. Not surprisingly, the legislation that Congress passed to deal with accounting tricks did not deal with stock options and the way they provide incentives for executives to think up and exercise accounting strategies to increase their own wealth.[77]

Legislative efforts to do something about offshore tax havens have been greeted with similar resistance. According to *The New York Times*, they have been met with an "armada of former lawmakers", and lobbying has reached "fever pitch". The most aggressive firm in this lobbying effort is Accenture, previously Andersen Consulting (a spin-off of Arthur Andersen), which is incorporated in Bermuda.[78]

Similarly, efforts to re-regulate trades in energy derivatives and the energy futures market have met strong opposition from Republicans, including senator Phil Gramm, as well as Federal Reserve chair Alan Greenspan. The legislation being opposed would merely impose the same rules as those applying to the Chicago Mercantile Exchange, the New York Mercantile Exchange, and the Chicago Board of Trade.[79]

Deregulation of power companies, and those that audit and finance them, was facilitated by the promotion of a free market ideology that idealised the operation of free markets and demonised the role of government intervention. Marjorie Kelly, author of *The Divine Right of Capital*, describes this ideology:

> Left free to work its magic, self-interest (ie greed) ostensibly leads things to work out to the benefit of all, as though guided by an invisible hand. This myth is taught in Economics 101 as gospel truth, trumpeted routinely in the business press, and sold abroad as the cure for what ails all economies. The lie of it has been exposed many times.[80]

PART THREE

The British Experiment

IN THE EARLY 1990s Britain became one of the first nations to privatise its electricity industry. Its method of fragmenting integrated electricity systems into separate generation, transmission, distribution, and retail-supply companies became the *modus operandi* for both privatisation and deregulation all over the world. And its peculiarly one-sided power pool for deciding wholesale electricity prices, which has since been discarded in Britain as unworkable, has nevertheless been copied in various countries including Brazil, Gujarat (India), Australia, and California.[1]

The long-term politics of electricity in Britain have followed a very different course to that of the United States. Nationalisation—the government takeover of the electricity industry—was the result of a widely held belief, following the Second World War, that centralised government ownership would enhance social welfare and facilitate economic development. This contrasts with the situation in the US where private electricity companies have always been dominant.

The history of British electricity through the twentieth century demonstrates major swings in faith in the ability of government to deliver services efficiently. It shows how much the privatisation process of the 1990s was driven by ideology, in the absence of any continuity of experience with private ownership. The export of the British privatisation model to other countries means that the British zeal for market-driven service provision of the 1980s is shaping electricity supply around the world while few of the adoptee countries are learning from their mistakes.

CHAPTER TEN

Electricity Supply 1900–1980

[T]he issue of private enterprise versus collectivism was to dog the industry's future until it was finally resolved in 1948 by full nationalisation ...Perhaps even more serious than the technical diversity of systems was the division of ownership between company and municipal undertakings which was becoming firmly entrenched. The possibility of cooperation between the two sectors seemed to be receding with a growing mutual distrust.
Historian Leslie Hannah[2]

A STRUGGLE FOR PRIVATE CONTROL of electricity occurred in the early development of Britain's electricity system, as it did in the United States. However, whilst advocates of private control in the UK used similar arguments equating public ownership with socialism, they did not back these arguments up with massive propaganda campaigns, nor did they manipulate and undermine democratically elected municipal councils to the extent that American companies did. As a result, public sentiment continued to favour public ownership in the UK in the early twentieth century, and most municipalities owned their own electricity systems.

Nevertheless, the mixture of publicly and privately owned electricity systems caused problems of interconnection, and prevented economies of scale being achieved. These problems were not overcome until the British government nationalised the electricity industry after the Second World War, buying up all the private companies and taking over those owned by municipalities.

Municipal vs Private Control

Although private companies developed the early electricity systems, dozens of municipal systems were set up to supply electricity around the turn of the century, and local councils bought out private lighting systems. Municipalities entered the electricity business for pragmatic rather than ideological reasons.[3] In particular, councils could see the financial benefit of earning profits from the electricity business so as to reduce rates. By 1903, two-thirds of all electricity connections were to publicly owned systems, mainly in urban areas.[4]

The ability of municipal authorities to set up their own electricity systems and buy out private companies was facilitated by legislation enacted in 1882 in the light of experience with private gas and water companies that were widely thought to have provided unsatisfactory service. This experience ensured that the government did what it could to foster local government developments and protect the public from "exploitation by commercial monopolies".[5]

The legislation limited the tenure of private electricity companies. At the end of the period of tenure, local government could purchase the electricity plant and transmission system for the price of the individual components. The legislation also set maximum prices that private and public electricity systems could charge. At the time, private companies expected to be able to raise capital and make a profit despite their limited tenure.[6]

There was popular support for municipal control, not because of widespread socialism but rather because of "provincial civic pride".[7] What is more, electricity, like water and gas, was considered to be a special case where public and private interest might conflict. Joseph Chamberlain noted in 1881:

They involve the interference with the streets, and the rights and privileges of individuals. They cannot, therefore, be thrown open to free competition, but must be committed, under stringent conditions and regulations, to the fewest hands. As it is difficult, and, indeed, almost impossible, satisfactorily to reconcile the rights and interests of the public with the claims of an individual, or of a company seeking, as its natural and legitimate object, the largest attainable private gain, it is most desirable that, in all these cases, the municipality should control the supply, in order that the general interest of the whole population may be the only object pursued.[8]

The *Birmingham Daily Post* editorialised in 1882 that "a general feeling" existed that "the supply of electric light ought to be in the hands of the local governing authority" so as to prevent "the creation of a new monopoly in private hands, to ensure the control of the streets, and then to promote public convenience, and also to limit as far as possible injurious competition with Corporation gas lighting".[9]

As in the US, the success of municipal electricity undertakings caused consternation amongst business leaders, who believed that light and power were not essential services but luxuries that should be provided by private enterprise. In the late-nineteenth century they formed groups such as the Industrial Freedom League and the Liberty and Property Defence League to disseminate the idea that public ownership was a form of collectivism or socialism that threatened and unfairly competed with private enterprise. These groups were joined by the Chambers of Commerce, the Harmsworth press, and elements of the Conservative Party, who campaigned against public ownership.[10]

Supporters of private systems argued that the municipal supplier was too small and confined to take advantage of the development, over time, of electrical generation and distribution technology that favoured larger-scale operations with more widely distributed systems. However, councils fought hard against losing control of their power systems, and put pressure on local MPs to oppose government efforts to enable private companies to take over broader areas of supply and distribution.[11]

Private power companies were allowed to sell wholesale electricity to smaller electricity suppliers. Even so, they did not grow much. For this they blamed the municipal councils, which were not keen to negotiate for bulk electricity supplied by private companies.[12] Nor did councils allow the private companies to supply their larger industrial customers directly.

Municipalities were also often reluctant to cooperate with each other. Larger municipalities were not always keen to supply electricity outside their municipal boundaries, and the smaller municipalities were sometimes too proud to take electricity from a larger municipality. London was covered by a number of councils, many of which ran their own electricity supply, with private companies supplying the wealthier and more conservative districts. In the absence of any overall system of regulation, this led to a large variety in voltages, frequencies, and distribution systems.[13]

Londoners who could afford electricity toasted bread in the morning with one kind, lit their offices with another, visited associates in nearby office buildings using still another variety, and walked home along streets that were illuminated by yet another kind. This was a nightmare for the supplier of electric lamps and appliances; interesting problems arose when one moved one's home or business.[14]

In 1914 London was supplied by 70 generating stations owned by 65 electrical utilities. But in other major cities around the world a process of concentration had occurred, reducing the number of generating stations to a handful—for example, four in New York, and six in Chicago and Berlin. In the US, this concentration had been facilitated by the large power companies taking over smaller ones, and supplying wholesale electricity to municipal systems. In Germany, power companies gained the cooperation of local councils through generous incentives.[15]

London was thought to be backward because of this fragmentation. Its electricity was mainly used for lighting, it remained small-scale, and its cost was higher than in US and German cities. However, London had a smaller industrial base than the cities it was compared with, and used less electricity for traction for public transport, so it wasn't able to spread the load through the day as easily. Also, as gas, steam, oil, and coal were often more economical sources of energy in Britain, its low per-capita use of electricity did not indicate a failure to supply consumer demand. Nevertheless, widespread public ownership was the reason given by Americans, and some British industrialists, for London's lack of progress in electricity supply.[16]

Leslie Hannah argues in his history of British electricity, commissioned by the Electricity Council, that the question of ownership was less important than the problem of lack of interconnection; but the debate seldom got beyond the ownership question.[17] Proposals for a unified private supply for London were looked upon with suspicion: "any scheme for placing the electricity supply of so vast and important a district in the unfettered control of a private company arouses such opposition that it is hardly at present within the region of practical politics".[18] Much opposition was based on past experience with private monopolies in other areas such as railways.

Those in favour of private ownership believed in the superior management of private enterprise, where an owner who made a mistake "would have to pay for it out of his own pocket … In private enterprise there was some kind of a law which governed these things, and it was the law of the survival of the fittest."[19] The fact that publicly owned systems were able to provide electricity more cheaply didn't undermine this faith in the benefits of private management.

In the period 1910-1911 the average municipal price for electricity per kWh was 1.7d compared with 2.5d charged by private companies. When undertakings were of similar size and had equal access to cheap supplies of coal, the municipal schemes were able to provide cheaper power, with lower capital and working costs. This was partly because the councils were not profit-seeking organisations and were willing to lower the difference between the cost of supply and the prices charged. As a result, they attracted more customers and a higher load, which was also more economical to provide. Municipalities had an advantage in lending money because they could guarantee returns and therefore borrow at lower interest rates. However, private companies had no trouble raising capital and, as in the US, stockbrokers and bankers had close ties with the electricity-supply companies.[20]

During the First World War the electricity supply did not seem to be up to wartime requirements, and seemed to be inferior to German systems. The lack of large-scale central power plants and bulk supply was blamed for this.[21] The war also demonstrated the merits of cooperation over competition and the need for efficiency over ideology. By this time there were 600 or so electricity suppliers, and various wartime committees argued the need to rationalise them into a comprehensive and coordinated system. Even businessmen supported greater state intervention.

Legislative Reforms

After the war, the "failure to electrify industry and transportation in the age of electrification was seen as a root cause of the country's failing industrial strength". It caused widespread concern about Britain's national prestige, and a consensus grew that something had to be done to achieve large-scale electricity supply so as to improve efficiencies and lower costs. This meant large stations generating the power for large areas.[22] But that was as far as the consensus went.

Conservatives re-emphasised their push to reduce the role of the state, and they undermined government efforts to rationalise the electricity industry. Private enterprise champions such as George Balfour argued that interconnection and greater concentration would occur voluntarily and without state intervention because there were profitable reasons to do it.[23]

A bill to create district electricity boards that could take over generation and establish interconnections was met with strong opposition in parliament, particularly in the House of Lords. In the end, the Electricity (Supply) Act 1919 was considerably weakened, and all it achieved was the establishment of an Electricity Commission without any enforcement powers. As a result, reform was gradual and piecemeal. By the mid-1920s bulk supply accounted for less than 10 per cent of electricity sold, and the size of the power stations remained small.[24]

In 1924 a minority Labour government came to power. Many Labour MPs supported full nationalisation; but, as a minority party needing Liberal support, they could not expect to achieve this. It appointed Lord Weir, a wealthy industrialist, to chair a committee into the electricity supply situation. Weir, like many business leaders, was concerned about the inefficiency of the electricity-supply industry, and he and his committee felt that this was causing Britain to fall behind in its industrial development compared with other countries. The committee did not hold public hearings but did listen to expert witnesses, such as Samuel Insull from the United States.[25]

Weir's committee noted the lack of progress made by the electricity commissioners and sought a compromise. It recommended a Central Electricity Board (CEB) to coordinate planning, construction, and operation of power plants, with preference given to large, more thermally efficient plant, and to establish and run a national electricity grid of high-voltage transmission lines.[26] Ownership would not be interfered with.

> We propose not a change of ownership, but the partial subordination of vested interests in generation to that of a new authority for the benefit of all, and this only under proper safeguards and in a manner which will preserve the value of the incentive of private enterprise.[27]

The legislation for this board was introduced in 1926, and was immediately opposed by the Incorporated Municipal Electrical Association and the private companies.[28] Some Conservative MPs saw it as the thin edge of the wedge. For example, Sir Charles Wilson, MP, claimed that the bill "out-Herods Herod in its socialism … It is nationalisation of a very bad kind, and spoliation also". George Balfour exclaimed: "You may say that is only jumping the first fence of socialism, but, once you have got over a few fences, you will soon, no doubt take the rest of the course".[29]

Less ideologically driven Conservatives, including the majority of cabinet, saw this measure as a way of heading off nationalisation and, therefore, as a more effective counter to socialism in the face of obvious inefficiencies in the industry. Industry leaders supported the bill because they believed it would lead to lower prices for electricity, particularly given the failure of voluntary rationalisation. The bill also had strong support from the popular press and a good deal of popular opinion. The *Daily Mail* pointed out that a group of Conservative politicians who were opposing the bill had financial interests in the electricity industry. The backing of Lord Weir helped the bill through the House of Lords, and it was passed in 1926.[30]

To placate Conservatives suspicious of government interference, the CEB was established at arm's length from government, and its employees were not part of the civil service. It raised its own money by selling interest-paying non-voting stock to the public. It "had the status of an authorized electrical undertaking (utility) which owned and operated the Grid on behalf of the government."[31] It was supposed to be commercially minded but not concerned with the technical, planning, and regulatory functions of the Electricity Commission. Members were appointed by government for terms of five to ten years and could not be dismissed by the minister except after an absence of more than six months.[32]

The CEB bought electricity from selected generators for transmission on the grid, and resold it to retail suppliers without taking a profit for itself. It standardised the voltage, phase, and frequency of electricity in the grid. Although many power generators were privately owned, the CEB directed their operations and paid them their costs—including operating costs, capital costs, and management expenses—whether or not it called on their electricity. Participating generators with the lowest costs were chosen for base load. Others were only used at peak times. Utilities were then able to buy electricity from the grid, for distribution to customers, at a price guaranteed to be lower than the cost of them generating it.[33]

The CEB decided how much electricity each power plant would produce and what they would be paid for it. It also decided when and where new power plants would be built or extended, and how they would be designed. It guaranteed the repayment of all construction and operating costs. The companies themselves decided who they would employ, what duties they would perform, and where they would get their supplies. Those plants that were not selected by the CEB to feed into the national grid were able to continue to operate independently if they could provide electricity cheaper than that supplied by the grid.[34]

The CEB ensured that supply was reliable, secure, and adequate for the future. Hundreds of operators continued to exist, although under the CEB only some 200 of them supplied more than 90 per cent of the electricity and made over 90 per cent of the investment. Within a decade the CEB had reduced to 28 the number of companies providing base load, with fifteen providing more than half of the system's electricity requirements. This enabled the UK electricity system to compare favourably in terms of thermal efficiency with that of the US.[35]

In the space of fifteen years between 1925 and 1940 the national grid system enabled the British supply undertakings to overcome their previous lag in development and inaugurate a vigorous expansion of sales based on low prices for the consumer. By the late 1930's Britain's electricity consumption per head of population equalled that in countries with similar income levels.[36]

There was general satisfaction with the CEB's performance and "no significant public complaints about the economic organization of generation".[37] The CEB became, over time, a model of a public body that combined government authority with private investment power whilst remaining at a distance from direct ministerial interference. A professor of economics, William Ashworth, claimed:

The Central Electricity Board enhanced the prestige of the public corporation as a device for involving the state in business activity in ways that could be strategically and managerially effective, and which were not antipathetic to normal business usage.[38]

Distribution to customers remained dispersed amongst hundreds of companies and councils. "In 1934 over 400 undertakings accounted for less than 10 per cent of sales". Municipal boundaries often prevented larger, more economic distribution units from being formed, as each municipality defended its own undertakings for reasons of pride, profit, and political conflict. Because they often had different voltages inhibiting more efficient networking, and because areas of distribution were small, peak demand could not be spread. This also increased costs. In 1933-4 distribution accounted for 60 per cent of the cost of electricity.[39]

The municipal schemes continued to account for two-thirds of distribution and to provide cheaper electricity, despite paying higher wages and employing more workers than the private companies. By the end of the 1930s municipal prices were, on average, about three-quarters of the prices of private companies. The private companies were able to charge what they liked for electricity because price caps introduced in earlier years became irrelevant as technological changes made electricity cheaper to generate. The only constraint was public opinion and the incentive to increase sales by reducing prices. Smaller private companies tended not to pass on savings to customers, nor to expand their territories, "preferring instead to maintain high unit profit margins on a small input".[40]

Although supporters of private enterprise argued that private ownership was more flexible, innovative, and efficient, it was size that really made the difference in management styles. Consequently, there was little difference between the management performance of large companies and large municipalities.[41]

The private companies continued to do well through the Depression, able to raise money easily and keep their share prices high. As in the US, holding companies developed and dominated the private electricity sector. The holding companies made money off their subsidiaries, beyond the set rate of return prescribed in the 1926 Act (5.0-6.5 per cent for generation capital), by charging high rates for capital and excessive fees for services provided. In some cases, holding companies were controlled by equipment manufacturers, who charged the subsidiaries high prices for the equipment that they supplied to them. They also made sure that dividends paid by subsidiaries seemed to be reasonable by watering capital in bonus issues. The holding companies enabled insider groups to enrich themselves by lending capital to them at high rates.[42]

The largest holding company was owned by George Balfour, and accounted for 6 per cent of electricity sales. Another was the Edmonsons group, incorporating 29 supply companies, which became the target of American interest in the 1930s. US holding companies, including Insull's, were increasingly investing in foreign electricity businesses, and Britain was a favoured market.[43]

> The aim was to acquire financially weak undertakings whose prospects of being able to offer a supply of electricity economically had been improved by the Grid scheme, provided they could finance the expansion of their distribution systems. The holding company system of control also offered prospects, already realised in America, of achieving above-average profit levels through gearing and pyramiding.[44]

In 1928, a Chicago-based company set up the Greater London and Counties Trust (GLCT) and acquired 95 per cent of Edmonsons shares. It borrowed money using the existing company assets as collateral to acquire another 25 companies by the end of 1929.[45] This caused some consternation amongst MPs concerned about the foreign control of so many power suppliers.

GLCT used its public relations techniques to imply that Edmonsons was not controlled by Americans but "was rather cleverly using American money at low interest rates to electrify southern England". In 1929, to the same end, GLCT reorganised with Edmonsons as a sub-holding company; named Lord Birkenhead, a former lord chancellor, as chair of GLCT; and added some British former MPs to the board of directors. By 1932, however, the American holding company was experiencing serious financial difficulties and, although it tried to get as much money as it could from GLCT through charges and fees, it did not recover. GLCT was taken over in 1936 by British interests, who reinstated Edmonsons as the parent holding company and arranged, with the help of the British financial establishment, for shares to be bought back from Americans by locals.[46]

Other holding companies also milked their subsidiaries, but did not receive as much attention as GLCT, where it was being done by Americans. However, over time these other holding companies also came in for increasing criticism and calls for greater government scrutiny.[47]

Nationalisation

As with the previous wartime experience, the Second World War demonstrated the inadequacy of some infrastructure services and the benefits of cooperation and government intervention. When a Labour government was elected after the war it implemented a program of nationalisation. By this time, public ownership of essential services such as electricity had wide support outside the Labour Party, including support in the other political parties, professional societies, and investigating committees.[48]

The war had emphasised the strategic aspects of electricity supply and reinforced the perception that government needed to have control over the electricity supply for national strategic reasons. Britain faced shortages of electricity, and security of supply was not only necessary for the war effort but also for post-war reconstruction and economic growth. It was also believed that cheap, reliable, and universally available electricity was an essential public service necessary for industrial and public welfare, and that such goals should not be jeopardised by allowing electricity supply to be subject to the risks and vagaries of market forces or the local politics of municipalities.[49]

Nationalisation was thought to be the solution to various needs, including the promotion of larger-scale, more economic operations, increasing the efficiency and improving the safety of some industries, dealing with worker demands, and preventing large monopolies from developing whilst at the same time promoting large industrial concerns to compete internationally. Only government, it was widely accepted, could run a centrally planned, large-scale, national electricity system.[50]

Nationalisation was preferred to legislation because of the lack of success of regulation in various services and essential industries during the interwar period. There

> was a certain disillusionment, on behalf of what might be called 'middle opinion',
> with reliance on guidance or regulation or encouragement of the private companies

when they had proved so reluctant to recognize any of the alleged deficiencies in
their performance.[51]

However, vested interests were still represented in parliament, including
the municipalities and the private companies, and they fought against nationalisation. It was not until the election of a Labour government, committed to
public ownership, that the reforms could be introduced. Two of the larger
companies tried to oppose their takeover with a £70,000 advertising campaign that attempted to raise alarm about state ownership. State ownership,
the ads said, would cause a brain drain from the industry, increase costs to
taxpayers, and remove choice from consumers. It was an effort to "smash the
capitalist system". However, lacking the well-developed propaganda machinery of their US counterparts, the private companies were unable to provoke
public opposition to public ownership; for most voters, the nationalisation of
electricity was not a major issue. Belatedly, the companies offered to connect
95 per cent of premises in their franchise areas, introduce low standardised
rates, standardise voltages, and invest £150 million in the industry over the
following five years.[52]

Rather than have the nationalised enterprises run by government departments, which was the traditional way, public corporations controlled by
boards of directors were formed. This was an attempt to avoid the "bureaucratic rigidities and political interference" which were said to characterise government departments. The public boards, although appointed by
government, were to be autonomous; once appointed, they could not be dismissed during their term of office, even if there was a change of government.[53]

'Middle opinion' accepted the establishment of public boards that seemed
to offer a mixed-economy compromise that rose above the tired old debate of
capitalism versus socialism. In particular, the Central Electricity Board, a
forerunner of this sort of public board, had shown itself to be "business like
and effective" in its management of electric utilities.[54]

The public boards had a similar role to the boards of private companies,
but their objective was to serve the public interest rather than shareholder
interest, since there were no shareholders: "No one was to gain from any
profit earned". The board members were chosen for their broad backgrounds
and skills, rather than being chosen to represent interest groups.[55]

The legislation for electricity nationalisation in England, Wales, and
southern Scotland was passed in 1947 and came into effect in 1948. It established a British Electricity Authority (BEA) to organise and pool generating
capacity, and transmit it via the national grid and fourteen Area Electricity

Boards to distribute and sell the electricity. Northern Scotland was covered by a Hydro-electric Board that generated, transmitted, and distributed electricity.[56] (The BEA became the Central Electricity Authority in 1955 and then the Central Electricity Generating Board (CEGB) in 1957. An Electricity Council was established at this time to supervise the electricity supply industry.[57])

All 564 municipal and private electrical companies were taken over on 1 April 1948. The previous private owners and shareholders were compensated at market rates; the municipal owners were repaid the debts they had incurred in the electricity works and operations, but received no compensation.[58]

Similar moves were occurring elsewhere in Europe "under pressure of technical and economic logic as well as of political choice".[59] The governments of France, Italy, Ireland, Greece, and Portugal all took control of their electricity systems. Eastern European countries also adopted national systems under communist governments, and nations in Latin America, Asia, and Africa adopted nation-wide, government-planned and -directed electricity systems. Larger countries such as Canada, Brazil, India, and Australia adopted state or regional rather than national systems controlled by state or provincial governments. In contrast, Japan and Germany, which were under the influence of the US as part of post-war settlements, adopted private-ownership models.[60]

The aim of nationalisation was to ensure that the electricity industry was run in the public interest, in particular that of consumers and workers, rather than for profit. This entailed a concern for providing services at a price that was widely affordable. The Area Boards had various social obligations, including the supply of electricity without discrimination or undue preference to any group of consumers; the health, safety, welfare, and training of employees; the consideration of environmental impacts; and the stimulation of the economy.[61]

The Labour government sought to use nationalisation as a "means of achieving both justice and efficiency."[62] And indeed, following nationalisation, there were "dramatic improvements in efficiency", and electricity became more widely accessible and affordable.[63] Successive governments used the nationalised industries for political ends. The electricity industry, for example, was required by government to buy British coal and equipment, and to build nuclear power plants of British design.[64] Nationalised industries were often pressured to keep prices and wages low as an example to others, and as a contribution to preventing inflation.[65] Governments also intervened to reduce electricity tariffs to help large industrial consumers of electricity to be internationally competitive.[66]

Despite these diverse pressures, Professor John Chesshire claims:

> Without appearing too uncritical, the nationalized industry succeeded in expand-
> ing capacity and in providing a high quality standard for electricity supply. In
> international terms the ESI [electricity supply industry] achieved a deservedly high
> reputation for managerial and technical competence ... the electricity industry
> played a major role in supporting British coal production. It also provided major
> market opportunities for British heavy electrical industry. These were viewed as
> crucial when the balance of payments was seen as a dominant policy imperative.
> Its productivity performance, whether measured in terms of fuel efficiency or use
> of labour, was creditable if not outstanding in world terms.[67]

Although nationalised enterprises often had a good record of productivity,
financial objectives were often subservient to the goal of cheap service. As a
result, the public enterprises ran up debts and required government subsidies.
Financial losses "received much more public attention than the underlying
productivity record".[68] As time went by, the public enterprises were increasingly expected to be run along commercial lines and at least to break even,
rather than run up debts.[69] The priority given to public objectives came to be
seen as a failing rather than an advantage.

The CEGB placed a high priority on security of supply because of the
political cost of blackouts if supply was unable to meet peak demand, especially during very cold winters. For this reason, when the growth of demand
fell off in the 1970s, as it had in the US, the CEGB constructed more generation plant than was necessary—just as the regulated private monopolies in
the US had. Nevertheless, the oversupply in Britain led to criticism of the
state-owned system of electricity generation. It was felt in some quarters that,
because the CEGB was able to pass all generating and transmission costs onto
Areas Boards, it was "insulated from many cost disciplines" and therefore
there was no incentive to keep costs to a minimum.[70]

As we shall see in the next chapter, the Thatcher government reversed previous policies, giving priority to financial objectives above all others, including social objectives. It insisted that prices should cover costs, and provide
enough surplus to finance future investment. At the same time, costs should
be progressively reduced. The public interest now took a back seat.[71]

CHAPTER ELEVEN

The Ideology And Rhetoric Of Privatisation

Electricity privatization—more than any of the other privatizations—has been borne along on the intellectual and ideological trajectory of the New Right to the point at which privatization and competition appear to have achieved the near-total eclipse of the case for retaining public ownership.

Professor John Surrey[1]

IN THE 1980s the Thatcher government embarked on privatisation in a big way. It shifted from having the highest level of government ownership of industry of any OECD country in the early 1980s to becoming "the fountainhead of industrial privatization showering the alleged benefits over the rest of the world".[2] This was especially true of the energy sector. By the end of 2001 *Accountancy* magazine declared that "Privatisation in the UK has led to the most liberal energy market in the world—competition is fierce, with both gas and electricity being traded as commodities."[3]

Privatisation was not something that the public demanded. When the Conservative Party came to power in the UK in 1979 it made no mention of "privatisation" having been on its policy agenda.[4] Surveys in the following years consistently showed that most people opposed the privatisation of gas, telecommunications, electricity, and water.[5]

Business groups and associations, such as the Confederation of British Industry (CBI), played an active role in promoting privatisation. Support also came from individual corporations, consultants, and financial institutions that saw potential profit in such changes. The beneficiaries of privatisation were the banks, building societies, insurance companies, pension funds, and industrial and commercial companies that were able to invest in the newly privatised services and/or lend money to those who did.[6] Think tanks also played a major role in providing an intellectual rationale for privatisation in the UK, and in setting out the policy prescriptions for it.

Motivations

The rise of Thatcherism in Britain can be attributed in large part to the endeavours of two think tanks. The first was the Institute of Economic Affairs (IEA). The IEA set out from its inception to gain wide acceptance for the "philosophy of the market economy" through education directed at opinion leaders such as intellectuals, politicians, business people, and journalists. During the 1970s the IEA managed to enrol several academics and influential journalists—as well as some prominent MPs, most notably Margaret Thatcher—to promote economic liberalism. At its height in the 1980s it had a half-million-pound budget provided mainly by about 250 companies, including large multinationals.[7]

The Centre for Policy Studies (CPS) was to some extent an outgrowth of the IEA. It was founded in 1974 by Keith Joseph and Margaret Thatcher. The CPS was set up to convert the Conservative Party to economic liberalism and to formulate policies for the party that were in line with this philosophy.[8] It claims "a large share of the credit for initiating policies such as privatisation ..."[9] The chair of its working group on electricity, Alex Henney, wrote a book, *Privatize Power*, that was published by CPS in 1987. He accused the Central Electricity Generating Board of being inefficient, inflexible, and secretive. He recommended the separation of transmission to a separate company that would be mutually owned by the distribution companies.[10] This is, in fact, what happened (see below).

The IEA and the CPS were small compared to the average US think tank, but effective in the British environment because of the "extreme centralisation of British political and public life." This gave easy access to key people within government, the media, and the financial sphere: the think tanks needed only to concentrate their persuasion on "a strategic policy-making elite" to be effective. These two organisations played a major role in setting the policy agenda of the Thatcher government, providing it with most of its policy initiatives, including the privatisation of electricity.[11]

Another think tank that was considered to be a driving force behind privatisation was the Adam Smith Institute (ASI). It sought to make privatisation acceptable to the public by creating interests in favour of it through "encouraging management buy-outs, cheap or free shares to employees and widespread share ownership among the public".[12] It distributed pro-privatisation literature to councillors, civil servants, and the media.

The ASI had a budget of £200,000 in 1988, mainly from company donations. It worked closely with a group of Tory MPs calling themselves the No Turning Back group "devoted to renewing the energy of radical Tory ideas and keeping the Government up to the ideological mark."[13] The ASI attained a reputation for getting radical ideas turned into policy:

> It is a handy sort of body for the government to have around. It can trample on taboos, shout the unthinkable, sit back and take the flack. In time the hubbub subsides and in the still reflection that follows the idea no longer seems quite so outrageous. Whereupon along comes a minister and polishes off the job.[14]

Many businessmen were persuaded that government-supplied services were too expensive because of inefficiencies and because of the social goals that the electricity authority pursued. They believed that the lack of competitiveness of government providers made private industry uncompetitive, too.[15] Two business coalitions were formed to represent the interests of large electricity users. The Major Energy Users' Council was formed in 1987 and today portrays itself as a "powerful lobbying organisation" that helps members to "influence Government, regulators and suppliers". The Energy Intensive Users Group claims to have played a key role in "pressing for liberalisation of the UK's gas and electricity markets". Its members include trade associations such as the UK Steel Association and the Chemical Industries Association, as well as individual companies such as Alcan and Rio Tinto.[16]

The CBI agreed that prices paid by large industrial users of electricity in Britain were too high and increasingly more than those paid by their European competitors. However, it had concerns about the specific privatisation model being proposed by the government. It claimed its members were concerned that there would not be enough competition in the new system to lower prices, and that the inclusion of nuclear power in the privatised companies would lead to higher prices. Privatisation also threatened to increase costs because of pre-privatisation price increases aimed at making the assets more attractive for sale, proposed levies to protect nuclear power (see next section), and the elimination of the bulk-supply scheme that gave large users discounts.[17]

The Thatcher government initially justified privatisation on efficiency grounds, and this struck a chord with many who felt dissatisfied with the performance of the large, nationalised industries in Britain. However, this dissatisfaction stemmed in part from inadequate funding of public services, which created longer waiting lists for hospitals and housing.[18] However, the efficiency argument was rather weak when examined closely. As we have seen, experience in the US and the UK, where public and private enterprises supplied electricity contemporaneously, has consistently shown that public enterprises can provide the service more cheaply. There is little evidence that private or public ownership makes a difference in the technical efficiency of an organisation. Even advocates of privatisation admit that the evidence that private ownership, in itself, led to greater efficiency was ambiguous.[19]

The efficiency argument came from theoretical reasoning propagated by the think tanks, rather than from empirical evidence of the superiority of privatised organisations. Using deductive reasoning rather than evidence, the think tanks argued that, without the discipline of market forces, there was no incentive for publicly provided services to be efficient, and the needs of consumers of these services could not be transmitted properly.[20] Government departments were "characterised by their critics as bureaucratic, inflexible, inefficient and unresponsive to customer demands".[21] They were portrayed as hindering innovation and protecting outdated practices.[22] The CPS estimated that electricity in the UK was costing 20 per cent more than it should in 1987 because of bureaucratic inefficiencies.

On the basis of such arguments, the Thatcher government sought to "move decision-making for the productive sector of the economy from public to private hands".[23] It claimed that private ownership would ensure that there were better incentives to minimise costs, provide better management, and get employees to work harder. It argued that this would occur even without market competition. A major Conservative spokesperson on privatisation said that the government "would continue to return the state-controlled industries to the private sector. We will encourage competition where appropriate, but where it does not make business or economic sense, we will not hesitate to extend the benefits of privatization to natural monopolies".[24] And, indeed, the government privatised British Telecom and British Gas as monopolies.

Some privatised enterprises were already highly efficient years before they were sold off. For example, British Gas was studied by Heloitte, Haskins and Sells, and found to be performing at a level that "any commercial organisation could be proud of". It was nevertheless sold off in 1986.[25]

The goal of economic efficiency was a cover for more political and ideological goals. One such goal was to lower electricity costs by subordinating social objectives, including equity and environmental goals, to economic objectives—particularly prices to industry. Even the security of supply became a secondary goal, as a leaked draft speech of the managing director-designate of one of the newly formed generating companies demonstrated: "Our task will not be to keep the lights on whatever the cost. It will probably pay us never to over-stress our plant".[26]

Improvements in economic efficiency in public services were achieved prior to privatisation, by narrowing their goals to purely commercial ones and introducing tighter financial controls. This was done to ensure that the enterprises would be more attractive to buyers and would sell for higher prices. But it also showed that such enterprises could be good financial performers and "economically efficient" whilst still under government control, given a preparedness to subordinate social goals to commercial ones. For example, British Airways (BA) was prepared for privatisation by cutting the workforce from 58,000 to 35,000 and eliminating routes.[27]

> In fact efficiency improvements in state-owned network industries began under the stimulus of impending privatization and were largely attributable to the clarification and narrowing of enterprise objectives. Labour productivity in industries still nationalized at the end of the 1980s grew faster than manufacturing industry through that decade, at an average of 4.4 per cent per annum compared with 4.1 per cent.[28]

If government enterprises could be made more economically efficient without privatisation, economic efficiency could not have been the underlying reason for selling them off.

Political and Ideological Goals

A major ideological aim of the think tanks and the Thatcher government was to reduce the role of government. Government control of industries such as electricity was characterised by them as 'government interference'. Where the government protected industries for strategic reasons, this was characterised as insulating those industries from competitive pressures and allowing them to become inefficient and unable to adapt to changing circumstances.[29] "Socialism involved ownership of the means of production and control of the 'commanding heights' of the economy ... Mrs Thatcher saw privatisation as a means by which she could destroy Socialism."[30]

The Conservative Party, through the influence of neoliberal think tanks, was ideologically opposed to maintaining government deficits, and sought to reduce the public sector borrowing requirement (PSBR). This was reinforced by international organisations such as the International Monetary Fund, which imposed limits on domestic credit expansion in 1976, and called for tighter budgetary controls and monetary targets.[31] This meant that governments were less able to fund capital-intensive infrastructure development, upkeep, and renewal using government capital.

By 1983, when it was re-elected, the Conservative Thatcher government had also decided that raising money through privatisation was more politically acceptable than raising taxes or cutting public spending. Tax cuts before elections were particularly effective at ensuring re-election. Privatisation meant that infrastructure expenses would be financed privately, and Treasury could use money raised from privatisation to balance the budget. The Treasury hoped to gain £5 billion pounds from electricity privatisation.[32]

This was, of course, a short-term view, because privatisations also deprived the government of income streams. For example, in the financial year before preparations for privatisation (1987-88), the electricity industry provided £1164 million pounds to Treasury, as well as paying £304 million interest on loans.[33] "[S]ome privatisations actually worsened the long-run PSBR because the loss of the profit stream from the government's net revenue was not compensated by dividends and increased tax revenue."[34]

Another motive of the Thatcher government was to curb trade union power, particularly the power and political influence of the public sector unions that were "symbolic of the political strength of organised labour in the post-war years".[35] The nationalised industries were strongly unionised by powerful centralised unions, and because of this they had the power to disrupt a whole industry through strike activity. Employees of private companies, especially if they were in a competitive market, had to worry about strike activity affecting their job prospects, and this deterred strike action. Also, coordination in a fragmented industry would be more difficult.[36]

Privatisation was thought to be a way of breaking the hold of the National Union of Mineworkers (NUM) over electricity supply, which arose because 80 per cent of generation was from coal power stations supplied by British coal. Without the protection of guaranteed supply to the electricity industry, British coal would have to compete with coal imports in terms of price and reliability (as well as with alternative fuel sources), meaning that industrial action would damage the prospects of British coal and cost future jobs.[37]

Indeed, after the privatisation of electricity, the system of national wage bargaining disappeared; trade unions took on an advisory role, while managers were "put on individual contracts and formally excluded from collective agreements", and companies "communicated directly with employees, not through unions."[38] Privatisation also reduced union power through the downsizing of workforces and the contracting out of services in the privatised companies. Some 66,000 jobs were lost in the industry, and pay and conditions were undermined.[39] Privatisation also conveniently removed the government from the act of firing workers. The Thatcher government had no problem with a declining workforce in the private sector, since it espoused a "natural rate of unemployment" that the state could not directly influence.[40]

Privatisation was also justified on the grounds of widening share ownership in the community. This was supposed to establish, in the words of one Conservative minister, "a new breed of owners" and have "an important effect on attitudes", thereby breaking down "the divisions between owners and earners".[41] The Confederation of British Industry formed a wider share ownership taskforce, and the government formed the Wider Share Ownership Council. The float of shares in privatised companies was said to have "given a boost to popular capitalism unimaginable in the pre-Thatcher era", and the profits made by millions of small investors made it "difficult to question the logic underpinning privatisation".[42]

However, owning shares in a company does not give small shareholders any control in the company. They are not owners in any real sense, but merely investors. And many new shareholders treated their shareholdings that way, selling their shares in a short space of time after the price went up.[43]

Nevertheless, the rhetoric that privatisation would spread wealth more widely in the community and would create "real public ownership" of government enterprises so that more people benefited from capitalism was used by the Conservatives to sell privatisation to the electorate and to take away existing public ownership. And as more pension funds invested in privatised corporations, workers were "led to believe that action against these companies" would threaten their pensions.[44] Shares to British Telecom, for example, were sold through a massive advertising campaign to as many people as possible, to gain public support for the sale and to counteract union opposition.[45]

The aim of broadening share ownership in the newly privatised enterprises meant that the government sought to reduce the risk involved in public share flotations, so as to minimise political fallout. The lowest-risk companies were floated first, and were then subject to minimal competition to decrease the economic risk that they might fail. Even then, shares were sold below market value so that new shareholders could experience an immediate financial gain when the shares were floated and their price increased. This increased the popularity of privatisation amongst those who benefited or hoped to benefit from future share floats, and was seen by some as a deliberate bribe. There was an increase in Conservative voters amongst the new shareholders of the utilities.[46]

Privatisation, however, did not lead to wider share-ownership in the long-term because the new shareholders quickly realised their gains (made at the expense of taxpayers) by selling their shares. Although there was an increase in the percentage of the population owning shares in listed British companies, share ownership in fact became more concentrated in financial institutions such as banks, pension funds, insurance companies, and investment trusts so that more people own a declining proportion of the sharemarket (see tables below). In the electricity industry the number of individual shareholders dropped from seven million at privatisation to two million in 1997—and is still falling.[47]

■ Table 11.1: Share ownership in Britain

	1984	1992	1996		
Percentage of population owning shares	7%	21%	20%		

	Early 1940s	1957	1981	1992	1997	2001
Percentage of shares owned by individuals	80%	70%	28%	21%	16.5%	15%

Sources: C. Robinson. 'Pressure Groups and Political Forces in Britain's Privatisation Programme.' Paper presented at the Japan Public Choice Society International Conference. Chiba University of Commerce, 22-23 August 1997, p. 8; S. Thomas, Steve. 'The Privatization of the Electricity Supply Industry'. In The British Electricity Experiment. ed John Surrey. London: Earthscan Publications. 1996, p. 41; J. Flynn, 'Will Britain Ever Be a Nation of Stock-Keepers?' Business Week 19 August 1996, p. 42; National Statistics, Share Ownership: A report on Ownership of Shares as at 31st December 2001, 2002, p. 9.

The Privatisation of Electricity

Following an unsuccessful effort to introduce competition into electricity generation in 1983,[48] the Thatcher government announced in 1987 that it would privatise electricity. This was done with little forewarning, and it was largely accomplished by 1991. (For political reasons, the restructuring and privatisation had to be completed within one term of political office.)

Because of its size and importance, the privatisation of electricity was the largest and most radical of British privatisations. Unlike the other privatisations, it involved a major de-integration or unbundling of the industry and its restructure, with the aim of fostering competition at various stages in the electricity-supply chain. This was because of criticisms of previous privatisations that had merely transferred control from public to private hands whilst leaving monopolies intact. In particular, the privatisation of British Gas as a monopoly had led to an outcry because of price abuses and preferential treatment of industrial customers at the expense of residential customers.[49] (Scotland and Northern Ireland electricity systems were privatised as monopolies.)

The stated rationale for electricity privatisation was that competing private companies would provide a cheaper and better service and that this would be of benefit to all consumers, industrial and residential. Standards of service were already high before privatisation, so the main benefit that consumers looked forward to was cheaper prices. Post-privatisation price falls were facilitated by raising prices by 15 per cent in the two years prior to privatisation. This price increase was aimed at increasing rates of return so that the enterprises would be attractive to investors.[50]

The Central Electricity Generating Board (CEGB) was separated into two large generating companies, National Power and PowerGen. These were both sold in share floats that saw share prices rise steeply in early trading. Although more companies would have ensured greater competition, the government was keen to minimise the risk to new shareholders and investors, and to maximise the price gained from the sale. The government assumed that, as time went by, more companies would enter the electricity-generation market to increase competition.[51]

National Power, was purposely larger, incorporating two-thirds of the generating facilities, because the government planned that the nuclear plants would be included with it. It had to be large enough to be able to include the extra risks and costs of the nuclear plants and still be profitable. However, the nuclear power plants turned out to be too difficult to privatise. Some nuclear plants were nearing the end of their operating lives, and potential buyers faced huge decommission costs. Even the newer nuclear plants were expensive to operate.[52]

The CBI lobbied government backbenchers to support an amendment to the privatisation bill to leave the nuclear power plants out of the sale.[53] So the government was forced to separate the nuclear plants into a government-owned company, Nuclear Electric. The government was also advised that private investors were very unlikely to build new nuclear plants.[54] However, the Conservative government was committed to promoting nuclear-power development for strategic reasons. So it introduced a non-fossil fuel obligation (NFFO) that would require electricity retailers to buy some 20 per cent of their electricity from non-fossil fuel generators. Although this was designed specifically to promote nuclear power, the broadening of it to cover renewable energy sources had public relations advantages and gave it an environmental flavour. Its real aim, however, was to provide an incentive in the long term for the construction of nuclear power plants, and in the short term to force electricity retailers to buy the expensive nuclear power that already existed.[55]

In 1995 another attempt was made to sell the nuclear power plants. The older Magnox plants, that no private company would want, were moved to a state-owned company, Magnox Electric. The others were moved to a new company, British Energy, which was privatised in 1996, after the government agreed to underwrite the costs of plant decommissioning.[56]

Although keen to maintain a nuclear industry, the British government no longer believed there was a strategic need to maintain and protect the coal industry. Past UK governments had spent some $2 billion a year supporting the domestic coal and gas industry with subsidies, tax-breaks, and research, so as to be assured of an indigenous supply of energy and not to be dependent on foreign suppliers in times of conflict.[57] But this stopped with the Thatcher government, and has not been taken up by later governments. The strategic role of governments in deciding the fuel mix to be used in electricity has been abandoned.

In 2002 the Trade & Industry Committee affirmed this, and its report was welcomed by the Electricity Association: "We welcome the report's first conclusion, that it should not be the role of government to dictate the UK's fuel mix. We strongly believe that diversity of fuels, and diverse fuel sources, are central to achieving security of supply. Free trade and liberalised markets are the main means through which this security can be delivered."[58]

Additionally, the Thatcher government did not see the need to develop local technologies to suit local needs, and was content to leave technological progress to private firms developing technologies for the market. Previous governments had spent heavily on research and development (R&D) aimed at new electricity technologies, particularly nuclear technologies. It had been thought that such long-term R&D would benefit the nation and that private firms would not undertake it. The new faith in the market extended to the expectation that it alone would ensure appropriate R&D was undertaken. However, realistically, it was more likely that they would limit their research to that which achieved more immediate commercial ends.[59]

The aim of encouraging competition in the generating and retail sectors of the electricity industry was to be achieved through eliminating the vertical integration of the industry. The aim of unbundling was to ensure that the companies involved in the monopoly elements of the system, the transmission and distribution components, would not be able to cross-subsidise firms involved in the competitive parts of the system.[60] However, ownership of distribution was not separated from ownership of retail supply when the twelve distribution companies were privatised in 1990 (see table 11.2). The newly privatised companies were called Regional Electricity Companies (RECs): they were responsible for both distribution of electricity and selling electricity to consumers in specified regions. Over time, retail sales were to be opened to competition so that each REC and any other company could sell electricity anywhere in England or Wales.

To reduce risks to newly supportive shareholders, retail competition for electricity consumers was introduced gradually. The 5000 largest customers (with needs above 1MW) became contestable initially; more were to be contestable in 1994 (some 50,000 customers with needs above 100kW); and full competition was to be introduced by 1998. However, the introduction of the second phase of competition in 1994 produced chaos, as retailers were unable to keep up with billing requirements. The introduction of full competition in 1998 was therefore changed to a phased introduction of competition area by area. The gradual introduction of competition meant that retailers used their captive customers to subsidise prices for the customers they were competing for.[61]

The RECs were also initially given ownership of the National Grid Company (NGC), responsible for the transmission of high-voltage electricity, because of perceived difficulties with selling it. The standing requirement was that they would sell their shares in it in 1995 to ensure that it was independent of the original distribution companies, so that competing companies would not be disadvantaged.[62]

■Table 11.2: Structure of electricity industry in England and Wales, 1990-1991

Generation	Transmission	Distribution	Supply
National Power	National Grid Co. (NGC)	12 RECs	12 RECs
PowerGen	owned by 12 RECs		
Nuclear Electric			
First Hydro			
imports from Scotland and France			

Sources: Adapted from OFFER. 'Review of Electricity Trading Arrangements: Background Paper 1.' Office of Electricity Regulation. 1998. pp. 5, 44.

To retain the benefits of interconnection and scale, transmission and distribution remained monopoly activities in each region, so prices and access had to be regulated. Owners had to "publish standard, non-discriminatory tariffs for the use of the network", and prices were capped.[63] The method devised was that prices were allowed to rise according to a formula—the retail price index minus an incentive factor: RPI–X. The incentive factor was a way to pressure the monopolies to reduce costs by X per cent, and left them free to decide for themselves how they would do this. X would remain constant for a number of years to provide certainty and stability.[64]

The Director General of Electricity Supply (DGES) was to be the regulator, independent of ministerial control. The appointment of Stephen Littlechild caused some consternation because of his previous role as advisor to the government on electricity privatisation, and his alleged links with think tanks. Labour's energy spokesman, Tony Blair, accused Littlechild of having links to the CPS, and the IEA claimed him to be one of their supporters.[65] The Office of Electricity Regulation (OFFER) was to regulate the transmission and distribution systems using incentives rather than fines. However, OFFER received much criticism for allowing the privatised monopolies to make big profits at the expense of consumers. Also, the goal of replacing regulation with competition was illusive. Ironically, privatisation and restructuring ended up requiring more regulation, not less.[66]

Although the Labour Party opposed privatisation of electricity as well as other privatisations, it dropped its commitment to nationalisation in 1995. When it was elected it changed direction: far from reversing existing privatisations, it investigated the feasibility of further privatisations.[67]

In 2000, several years after the privatisation experiment had been embarked upon, the IEA published a paper by Irwin Stelzer that proclaimed it a success in terms of its ideological goals:

> Prime Minister Thatcher, as she then was, made no secret of her desire to alter the balance of political power by creating a "share-owning democracy", with more shareholders than there were trade union members. This goal, too, was achieved ... It was the pursuit of a the goal of creating a shareholder class that led to the underpricing of the shares of to-be-privatised companies ... The fact that huge values had been transferred from taxpayers to shareholders was not deemed troublesome ... To the ideologue—and I include myself in the group of those who think that taking away from government those things that can be done by the private sector is intrinsically a good thing—privatisation, then, was a success.[68]

CHAPTER TWELVE

Privatisation In Practice

In the pre-privatisation electricity industry in Britain, the telephones in the main company, the Central Electricity Generating Board (CEGB), were fitted with an "engineer's button", which an engineer could use to give his calls priority over all other calls. In the post-privatisation industry, if there had been an over-ride button, it would be for the commodity traders.

Steve Thomas[1]

THE SUCCESS OF THE BRITISH electricity-privatisation experiment was greatly exaggerated by proponents who sought to spread the gospel elsewhere. In the first years, the biggest beneficiaries were the private companies themselves, reaping huge profits and paying out large dividends and executive salaries. However, generators manipulated the prices of wholesale electricity in the artificial power market established to facilitate competition, and it had to be abandoned in 1997. Efforts to disaggregate the industry to promote competition were counteracted by a wave of mergers and acquisitions.

Electricity prices did fall following privatisation. But these reductions were because of reduced fuel costs, rather than because of privatisation. Prices would have fallen even if electricity had remained in public hands.[2] However, in the new world of private electricity the greatest gain from those fuel-cost reductions went to shareholders rather than consumers. What is more, although privatisation was supposed to reduce regulation, it has led to more complicated regulations than ever before.[3]

Big Profits

To promote the sale of Regional Electricity Companies (RECs), the government had offered discounts on electricity bills to shareholders. The lure was hardly necessary. When the RECs were sold the shares were in heavy demand. Prices went up 50 per cent in the first days of trading, indicating that their original price was much lower than they were worth.[4]

Within five years, shares in the RECs were worth more than three times the price they had originally been sold for, with very little additional investment Between 1991 and 1995 the value of shares in the two large private generators increased by 171 per cent. This compares with an 80 per cent increase in value in the wider share market. The reason for this dramatic rise in share value was a profit rise of 15 per cent per year in the competitive sector of the industry, and 16 per cent per year in the monopoly transmission and distribution sector (see figure 12.1).[5]

■ **Figure 12.1: Electricity company profits, 1990–1995**

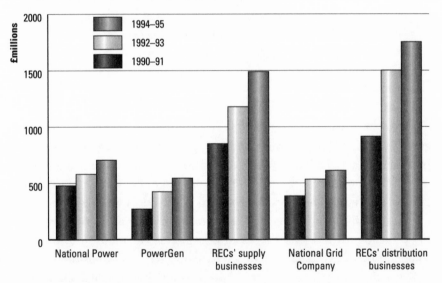

Source: G. MacKerron, and J. Watson. 'The Winners and Losers So Far'. In The British Electricity Experiment. ed John Surrey. London: Earthscan Publications, 1996, p. 199.

Theo MacGregor of MacGregor Energy Consultancy wrote in a professional engineering magazine:

Although world oil and natural gas prices plummeted, and electricity employment was reduced by 50 per cent, generating prices in the UK remained so far above the cost of production that the power companies literally did not know what to do with all their profits. In a single year, one of the two private power-generating companies that were created—National Power—paid dividends to stockholders that exceeded the entire value of the company's stock at privatization.[6]

At the same time, the benefits to ordinary household consumers were minimal, and the public saw clearly that privatisation had advantaged shareholders at the expense of consumers. The benefits had come from falling prices of coal rather than any improvements in management and efficiency that had been achieved by private ownership. The private generators had reduced their workforces dramatically, but their overall decrease in non-fuel costs of 2 per cent per year were similar to those achieved by the CEGB prior to privatisation. The RECs were able to keep increasing their charges, despite falling costs of electricity, because of ineffective price caps, ensuring excess profits at the expense of consumers.[7]

The profits to be made attracted foreign companies to the UK market. Companies, such as Southern Corporation in the US, discovered they could charge twice as much for electricity in England as they could at home, and they bought up the RECs.[8] In 1994 the regulator reduced the price cap, taking £2.5 billion off customer bills in the following four years. However, the market saw this as generous to the RECs, and REC shares continued to go up.[9]

The extent to which the RECs were ferreting money away became evident when one REC, Northern, promised shareholders £500m if they backed its fight against a takeover. Other RECs "rushed to secure public support with big customer rebates". The regulator made the RECs further reduce customer rates by £1.25m in 1995. Even this was criticised as "hopelessly inadequate".[10]

The other big winners were the executives of the electricity companies who had their pay increased significantly, as well as receiving packages of share options worth millions of pounds. Directors' fees in the RECs went from £60,000 in 1989-90 to over £200,000 in 1994-95. The chair of CEGB had been paid £100,000. The CEOs of the two companies formed from CEGB, National Power and PowerGen, received almost £850,000 between them in 1994-95.[11]

The Power Pool

The Power Pool established in Britain was supposed to be the "cornerstone" of wholesale electricity trading. All generators and suppliers had to trade their electricity via the pool.[12] It was a way of ensuring that competition would decide which generators would supply electricity and at what price. However, "the pool quickly became a playground for what the industry calls 'gaming'

—finding loop-holes in the rules; collusion, price gouging and all means of fleecing captive electricity consumers".[13]

Each generator would inform the pool the day before how much electricity it would have available for each half-hour slot the next day, and at what price it was willing to sell it. The system operator would draw on generators to fill their estimate of the next day's requirements on the basis of prices, the cheapest coming first. Those offering the most expensive electricity would only be called on if demand was high, and all bids had to be used (see figure 6.1 on page 103).

However, the price each generator would get did not depend solely on its own bid. First, each generator whose electricity was used would get the highest price bid by the generators which were used for any particular half hour. This was the System Marginal Price (SMP) or the Pool Price. Plants that could not operate for half an hour at a time, such as nuclear power plants, could bid zero, knowing that they would still be paid the pool price.

Ancillary service costs were added to the electricity price. There was an additional amount paid, a capacity payment, that was supposed to provide an incentive for generators to supply electricity to the market at peak times and to build additional capacity to be able to do this. The capacity payment was larger if supply only just met demand. This incentive was thought necessary because peak capacity would only be called on for a few hours a day. This turned out to be an incentive for creating shortages by withdrawing generating capacity and earning the capacity payment, rather than an incentive for new investment.[14]

This one-sided market, in which the buyer had to accept the prices at the margin, was partly a result of the time constraints on privatisation. Originally, the power pool was meant to be a place where generators *and* buyers could place bids, with the buyers bidding the highest price they were willing to pay, and the pool matching bids and balancing supply and demand. However, the complex software necessary to achieve this was not available in time.[15] Nevertheless, the one-sided system was adopted elsewhere, including Australia and California.

In the long run, the competition in the power pool was supposed to eliminate or greatly reduce the need for regulation and provide a benchmark price for those consumers who preferred to buy their electricity using contracts.[16] However, the large generators soon showed that they were willing and able to manipulate the pool price, which in turn affected the contract price.

The mandated use of nuclear energy (see previous chapter), and contracts between generators and distributors accounted for some 90 per cent of all electricity bought and sold. In these contracts, the distributor paid the contracted price rather than the pool price, even though the electricity supplied had to be sold via the pool. Those plants supplying electricity to fill contracts bid zero in the pool so that they were always included to supply demand.[17]

Several RECs and companies associated with them ordered combined cycle gas turbine (CCGT) plants, but it seems that this plant was constructed not to compete with the large generators on price but to reduce the dependence of the RECs on the large generators. (In contrast with privatisation advocates, the RECs expected the pool price would increase once initial contracts expired.) The gas for these new plants was bought on the basis of fifteen-year contracts with prices indexed to inflation. The electricity from the plants was contracted to supply various RECs for fifteen years, the price being based on the price of the gas.[18]

Critics argued that the power pool favoured the use of nuclear and gas plants over coal. This was because both types of plant tended to be operated at high load factors—nuclear plants because they were inflexible, and gas-fired plants because of the prearranged "take or pay" gas-supply contracts. As a result, both types of plants bid zero into the pool to ensure they were used. It was the bids at the margin that determined the price. This meant that the coal-fired plants could not also bid zero, or the pool price would be zero. So it was the coal plants owned by the large generators that tended to set the pool price, and their capacity was withdrawn strategically to keep prices high.[19]

The price of electricity in the pool was much higher at times of peak demand. National Power and PowerGen owned all the flexible plant that could be turned on and off to meet peak demand. With experience, they were able to predict reasonably well where the cut-off would be and therefore could force marginal prices up and make large profits on their peak operating plant.[20]

Potential competitors were fearful of trying to take on the large generators by building peak capacity that competed at the margins because the large companies sold a large part of their power via contracts and so could afford to undercut competitors in the pool and put them out of business. Similarly, RECs and large consumers were loath to buy electricity directly from the power pool because of the large price fluctuations.[21]

The rush to build gas-fired plants in the first two years after privatisation has been called the 'dash for gas', but it was short-lived as each REC could only legally supply to itself 15 per cent of the electricity it supplied to consumers. These plants did not really compete in the power pool because of the fifteen-year contracts. The two large generating companies also built new gas-fired plant. Although the extra capacity was not needed, the companies did not have to worry about getting their money back as they were virtually setting the prices between them for electricity. The new plants enabled them to reduce their dependence on British coal, to meet acid rain targets, and to buy up natural gas so that less would be available for competitors.

Thus, just as the nationalised system tended to oversupply electricity, the privatised system also oversupplied it. Ironically, it was this oversupply that had been one of the major criticisms of the nationalised system.[22] By 1999 coal had dropped to contributing only 38 per cent of electricity (from 70 per cent in 1990), whilst gas rose from zero to 25 per cent. The reliance on gas for electricity gave rise to concerns that any interruption to gas supply would lead to electricity shortages, especially during very cold winters.[23]

The strategy of withholding capacity to increase prices was first investigated in 1991. Complex bidding strategies leading to price spikes were first noted in 1992. In 1994 the director general of electricity supply (DGES) threatened to refer National Power and PowerGen to the Mergers and Monopolies Commission unless they agreed to divest themselves of some of their generating capacity and keep the average pool price below a set level for the next two financial years. The companies complied. They leased power plants to the Eastern company, which became a competitor. They also lowered average prices but hourly price fluctuations increased. The continued volatility of the pool served the interests of the large companies because it deterred competitors and drove consumers to favour contracts with them.[24]

By 1997 it had become evident that the power pool was still subject to price manipulation, despite there being more than five companies setting prices (see figure 12.2).[25] The power pool was still a major problem, and the regulator decided it was unworkable. It was temporarily replaced by the UK Power Exchange and the UK Automated Power Exchange, which provided voluntary spot markets. Other trading platforms later developed, including Enron Online.[26]

The Office of Electricity Regulation (OFFER) concluded in 1998 that:

> Capacity payments do not respond to short-term changes in capacity margin, are a poor signal for the long term, and are not working as intended. Bids into the Pool are not reflective of costs. Movements in Pool prices have not matched reductions in costs. Generators and suppliers are not faced with the full costs and risks of their actions.
>
> Market power has been a factor in maintaining or increasing Pool prices. But

present trading arrangements have facilitated the exercise of market power at the expense of customers by enabling all generators to receive a uniform price which in practice has been set by just a few of them; this market power has involved a lack of competition to run coal-fired (and oil-fired) plant.[27]

OFFER noted that since privatisation, costs had been falling because of reductions in fuel costs, reductions in capital costs for new plant, and increases in thermal efficiencies. However, these falling costs had not been reflected in pool prices, which had been falling much more slowly. In fact, over the previous winter all generators had increased their prices, and the DGES attributed this to the exercise of market power, particularly by National Power and PowerGen withdrawing coal-fired generators from production. OFFER also noted that the costs and risks of plant failure had been transferred from generators to retail suppliers and, ultimately, customers.[28]

■ **Figure 12.2 Generation of electricity in England and Wales**

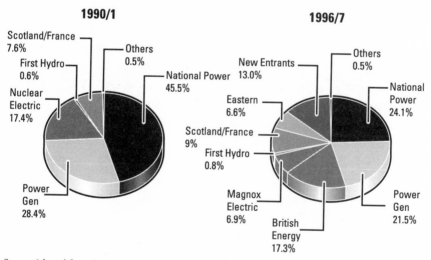

Source: Adapted from OFFER. 'Review of Electricity Trading Arrangements: Background Paper 1.' Office of Electricity Regulation. 1998. pp. 5, 44.

High pool prices pushed contract prices up and, therefore, the prices that consumers paid. The volatility of the pool price also pushed contract prices up because suppliers were willing to pay more for the security of a contract. Additionally, the prices did not vary with demand because they were being artificially manipulated, and industrial consumers who paid variable costs were not getting the price signals about when it was most efficient to reduce their usage. Moreover, high prices were not encouraging new investment and new entrants because they did not necessarily reflect a real shortage, and because extra capacity would reduce the capacity payments which were an important element in pushing prices up.[29]

In the transition period, whilst a replacement for the power pool was being devised, spot prices fell quickly and then, in early 2000, increased again as increasingly integrated companies began to exercise their market power. These companies were able to keep surplus power off the market so as to keep spot prices high.[30]

Callum McCarthy, director general of the newly merged Office of Gas and Electricity Markets (OFGEM), noted in 2000 that although all the main input costs had fallen significantly, "generating output prices have remained essentially unchanged. That is irreconcilable with effective competition. As a consequence of this absence of effective competition, generating output prices, which account for about half of final consumer electricity prices, are higher than they should be, for all consumers." The evidence of price manipulation was in the way the structure of bids from each company changed substantially without any underlying physical reason for it.[31]

Such problems continued to occur despite divestment of plant by the two large generating companies, and the abuses were not confined to those two companies. OFGEM argued that the special circumstances of electricity supply—the need for supply and demand to be balanced every minute, the non-storability of electricity, and the inflexibility of demand in response to price—meant that companies with relatively small shares could influence prices by their bidding strategies or by withholding capacity. McCarthy noted that OFGEM was investigating a withdrawal of only 500 MW by Edison First Power that was sufficient to affect prices.[32]

The power pool was replaced by New Electricity Trading Arrangements (NETA) in March 2001. The pool had cost the government £726 million to set up, modify, and run for the first five years. Each electricity company also had to spend money setting up its own computer systems and trading desks to be able to take part in the pool. It cost the government a further £100 million to change over to NETA.[33]

Prices are still set for every half hour. However, the price setting is more of a two-way process, with buyers and sellers placing bids on power exchanges a day in advance. "Now electricity is bought as a screen-traded commodity", so that buyers can seek out the cheapest prices available at the time or enter into longer-term contracts with individual generators.[34] Ninety per cent of electricity still bypasses the power exchange, and is traded by way of bilateral contracts.[35]

The system operator is informed four hours in advance of agreements made between buyers and sellers. It then makes sure that supply and demand is balanced: if more supply is needed, it calls for additional bids; or it asks generators to reduce output if less supply is needed. The operator buys and sells this electricity in what is called a "balancing market", and passes on the cost to the generators or retailers who misjudged their supply or demand.[36]

The bulk of transactions are outside the balancing market and are decentralised. However, prices in the balancing market have been very high, sometimes over £1000/MWh. This is particularly problematic for generators who are unable to accurately predict their supply, such as co-generators and those using renewables who are dependent on weather conditions.[37]

In order to prevent price manipulation, OFGEM inserted clauses, in April 2000, into the licences of various generators "prohibiting the abuse of substantial market power". OFGEM argued that market abuse could not be addressed in other ways, for example, by more competition or changing market rules, and that the new trading arrangements (NETA) would not prevent it. Five generators agreed to a "market abuse condition" in their licences; but two, British Energy and the American-based AES, objected, and the matter was referred to the Competition Commission. The Association of Electricity Producers argued that such a measure would just increase costs and deter new investment, and the commission ruled against the clause.[38]

Mergers and Acquisitions

The government retained a "golden share" of many of the privatised companies "which allowed it to block anyone from owning more than 15 per cent of a privatised company's voting share capital".[39] The "golden share" in the RECs expired in 1995, and they then experienced a wave of takeovers and mergers. By 1997, only five of the original twelve RECs remained independent. The RECs were also allowed to own a limited amount of generating plant.[40]

In 1999 National Power and Powergen were given permission to acquire REC supply businesses in return for selling off some of their generation capacity.[41] These arrangements meant that, in fact, the vertical de-integration or unbundling of electricity systems was not very thorough, and in many ways "the system became more fully integrated: the generation companies were able to enter the supply business to a significant extent and the RECs were able to integrate back into generation."[42] As early as 1995 it was observed that:

Market forces are pushing distributors to consider merging with one another, to ward off threats of takeover from outside the industry by taking advantage of economies of scale. Vertical reintegration is also occurring as distributors purchase their own generating capacity ... The take-over movement, inevitable in mature stock markets when large profits are visible ...[43]

Throughout the 1990s American companies bought up privatised UK electricity companies. By 1998 they owned 60 per cent of the distribution and supply companies.[44] John Cryer, MP, told parliament:

The reasons why American companies want to move into Britain are clear. First, British companies represent cash mountains—the money can be siphoned off for use in other, sometimes fairly dubious activities, usually in north America. Secondly, the American firms are fairly fond of our pretty lax regulatory regime. Thirdly, they see Britain as a springboard to the European electricity market at some point in the future.[45]

Cryer was concerned that it was more difficult to ensure foreign companies were accountable and acting in the public interest.

In 2001, after the Californian energy crisis, the number of US electricity companies involved in mergers and acquisitions internationally declined, and some US companies sold up in Britain. In their place European companies became very active, accounting for 77 per cent of international electricity deals in 2001. Included in these was the takeover of PowerGen by E.ON of Germany. This was followed in 2002 by the takeover of Innogy (previously National Energy) by RWE of Germany.[46] These foreign takeovers mean that only one of the original electricity suppliers in England and Wales, British Energy, is now British owned (see figure 12.3). And in September 2002 it had to be bailed out by the government.

Also, as the household retail market was opened to competition in 2000, economies of scale and integration became more important: "To be an effective player in this market, you need to have a foot in all parts of the chain", according to Derek Salter of London Electricity, which acquired SWEB, Yorkshire, and Northern Electric, and is owned itself by the French company Electricité de France (EdF). Salter also predicts, "There are going to be five or six players in the energy market, and they'll need a customer base of about 6m to be able to give their customers savings."[47] Similarly, Simon Skillings of Powergen predicted only four or five suppliers in Britain and perhaps across Europe.[48]

In contrast, an industry analyst told *The Sunday Times* that such large, integrated companies will mean that consumers "will probably pay more for their electricity over the longer term than they would otherwise have done." This is because integrated companies will be able to move costs and profits around and, without independent non-integrated RECs to use as a benchmark, it will be difficult for the regulator to know what is the real cost of supplying electricity when it comes to setting price caps.[49]

In April 2002 the National Grid company merged with Lattice, formerly part of British Gas. Lattice owned the gas pipeline network in England and Wales. The merged company, National Grid Transco, is a giant £30 billion electricity and gas transmission company with big international investment ambitions.[50] There have also been mergers between privatised electricity companies and privatised water companies operating in the same areas, supposedly to save overhead costs. The "multi-utilities" then have "distinct market power advantages relative to new entrants who cannot offer the range of services that a multi-utility might offer."[51]

■ Figure 12.3: Integration, foreign ownership and mergers: England, Scotland, and Wales, January 2003

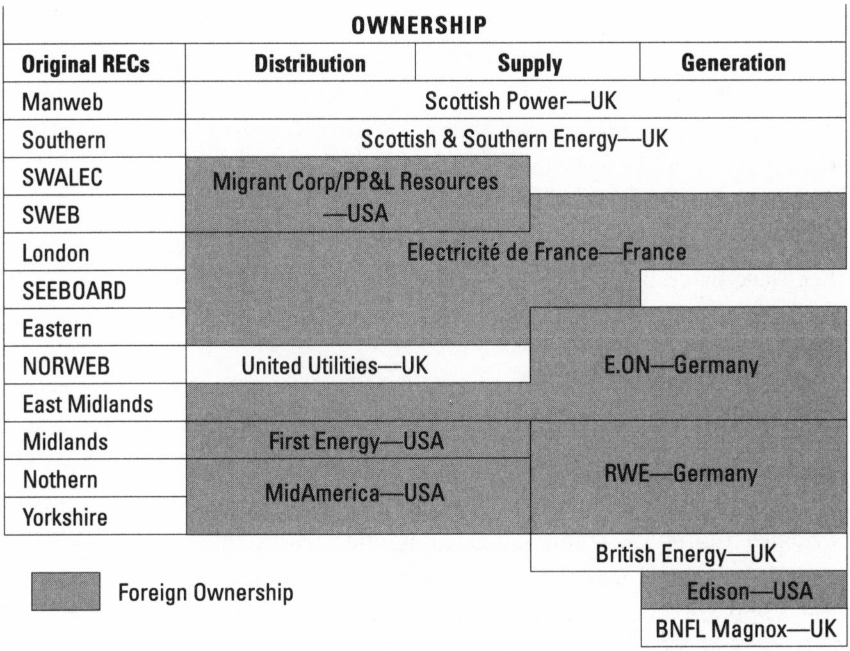

OWNERSHIP			
Original RECs	**Distribution**	**Supply**	**Generation**
Manweb	Scottish Power—UK		
Southern	Scottish & Southern Energy—UK		
SWALEC	Migrant Corp/PP&L Resources —USA	Electricité de France—France	
SWEB			
London			
SEEBOARD			
Eastern			
NORWEB	United Utilities—UK	E.ON—Germany	
East Midlands			
Midlands	First Energy—USA	RWE—Germany	
Nothern	MidAmerica—USA		
Yorkshire			
		British Energy—UK	
▨ Foreign Ownership		Edison—USA	
		BNFL Magnox—UK	

Source: Updated from Electricty Association, 'Who Owns Whom.', 18 January 2002.
http://www.electricity.org.uk/about_ea/bic_pub/who–owns–whom.pdf

Remaining Problems

In the mid-1990s the price of coal and gas declined significantly, leaving companies with fifteen-year natural gas contracts costing significantly more than the market price. Additionally, the cost of building gas-fired plants declined by 30 per cent whilst the amount of gas needed to run them decreased by 20 per cent: "Far from being the cheapest plants in the market, the new gas-fired plants had become the most expensive and their owners had to write-off billions of dollars in wasted investment costs and in buying out the uneconomic gas contracts".[52]

Following the introduction of the NETA in 2001, wholesale prices dropped dramatically because of the oversupply of generating capacity created by the dash for gas. The industry is now claiming that prices are too low. PriceWaterhouseCoopers, which took over Enron after it went into receivership, has argued that deregulation has led to too much competition, and that this could lead to disaster.[53]

As in the first years of privatisation, residential retail prices did not drop when wholesale prices did because the retail suppliers did not pass the savings on to customers, despite the introduction of competition between them; instead, they kept most of the gains from the price falls themselves. However, those generating companies that were not vertically integrated and did not have retail businesses suffered. The banks began to complain that the companies were failing to meet the interest payments on the £10 billion of loans they had made to purchase their power stations, and their credit ratings fell. A company in Wales went into receivership.[54]

British Energy was particularly hard hit. It claimed that wholesale prices were below its nuclear power plants' cost of generation. Its problems were further exacerbated by safety problems, which shut down some of its plants. It was losing millions of pounds each year, and in September 2002 threatened bankruptcy.[55]

A spokesperson for the regulator argued that it was expected that some companies would fail in a market system.[56] However, the British government was unable to stand by and watch British Energy—which supplied one fifth of Britain's electricity—go bankrupt, leaving its eight nuclear power plants sprinkled around the countryside, sitting idle with no-one to decommission them. The government therefore agreed to pay the company's liabilities of over £3 billion. (The government originally received £2.1 billion for the privatisation of British Energy in 1996). The bailout was criticised by the opposition, environmentalists, and competing companies with coal power, which argued that the financial aid would distort the market. The Belgium government also complained to the European Union that the bailout would distort the market.[57]

In October, American-owned TXU Europe sold its British assets because of the low wholesale prices in the British electricity market. The problem was that it had contracted to buy electricity at much higher prices than were now available on the spot market, and its parent company was refusing to give it financial support. A month later it called in the administrators and sought protection from creditors who were owed £2.9 billion, leaving generating companies that had contracted to provide TXU with electricity high and dry. Writing in *The New York Times*, Suzanne Kapner claimed that this "raised fresh questions about the health of Britain's privatized energy markets" and asked "How did Britain, the model of privatization for so many other countries, wind up with such a mess?"[58]

Powergen, owned by German company E.ON, announced that it would shut down a quarter of its generating capacity for the same reason, and might close more in future. It argued that the low prices did not encourage investment in renewable energy. Powergen/E.ON then bought TXU's British businesses, presumably to block other competitors from entering the market, making it Britain's largest supplier of electricity with six million customers.[59]

The original privatisation legislation provided no incentives to electricity suppliers to conserve energy or encourage efficiency. In their absence, the suppliers' only incentive was to sell as much electricity as possible.[60] The upside of the dash for gas was that, because gas generation causes lower greenhouse emissions than coal, for some years the greenhouse-gas emissions from power generation declined without government intervention. It seemed that this would significantly contribute to the greenhouse-reduction targets agreed to as part of the Kyoto protocol. Emissions of sulfur dioxide and nitrogen oxides, which contribute to acid rain, were also reduced. However, in early 2000, supplies of North Sea gas began to run out and natural gas prices again increased; generators switched back to coal, making it unlikely that Britain would meet its greenhouse targets. Between 1997 and 2002 carbon dioxide emissions in the UK began to rise again.[61]

The situation was exacerbated by the new trading rules that penalise forms of power that are dependent on the weather, such as wind and solar, and small plants such as combined heat and power (CHP), because of the high balancing charges for those who cannot accurately predict their output. Many CHP plants went out of business under the combined impact of balancing charges and rising gas prices, and the industry was described as being in a state of "meltdown". NETA has also encouraged less efficient, more polluting use of power stations because owners keep them running at less than full capacity so that their output can be increased suddenly to avoid having to pay for electricity on the balancing market.[62]

The free market was supposed to promote renewable energy sources through competition, where consumers chose green power even though it was often more expensive. In practice this did not happen. In an attempt to meet its targets, recognising that the commercial market would not do so without intervention, the government recently introduced a Renewables Obligation on energy suppliers, who now have to source 3 per cent of their power from renewables and this will increase to 10 per cent by 2012. Those companies unable to meet the obligation have to pay 3p for every KWh they are short to a pool to be shared amongst those companies that do meet the obligation.[63]

The Electricity Association, representing electricity companies, predicted that the obligation would cause a rise in retail electricity prices of 4.4 per cent. Other predictions were for a smaller rise and some noted that falling wholesale prices should mean no price rise at all. Nevertheless many companies raised prices to cover the cost of meeting this obligation. Some suppliers even charged business customers an additional charge for choosing 'green energy' whilst using this mandatory 3 per cent renewable component to supply them. Some companies are also charging extra for hydroelectric energy that they have always been using. A report by energy information provider Platts and environmental group Friends of the Earth found that only one company offered business a green tariff that actually created additional renewable energy beyond that which was mandated.[64]

In their comparative study of total factor productivity (TFP) rates in different countries, Mary O'Mahony and Michella Vecchi found that prior to privatisation productivity growth rates, at over 2 per cent, were similar to those achieved in the US and higher than those in Europe, apart from France, which had a strong state-owned electricity system. However, after privatisation productivity growth fell: "By 1997 productivity levels in the UK were some 20 per cent below those in the US and France."[65] Similarly, Steve Thomas from the Public Services International Research Unit (PSIRU) argues:

> there cannot be much doubt that if the old nationalised industry in Britain had been allowed to write-off about two thirds of its asset value, if it had been given reductions in fossil fuel prices of 30-40 per cent and it had been forced to abandon its uneconomic nuclear power programme, prices would have been lower than

they are now. On those grounds, and despite all the propaganda to the contrary, the reforms in Britain must, at best, be counted as not having succeeded so far, and much of this failure must be attributed to the problems in developing a competitive wholesale market.[66]

David M. Newbery and Michael G. Pollitt, from the University of Cambridge, did a cost-benefit analysis of privatisation to find out if the benefits such as efficiency gains from reduced labour outweighed the benefits that would have accrued without privatisation. They found in 1997 that they did, but that the benefits went disproportionately to the private companies at the expense of consumers. Benefits to government were marginal and outweighed by the costs to consumers (see table below).[67]

■ **Table 12.1: Distribution of benefits of privatisation**

£billions at 1995–96 prices

Electricity purchasers	-1.4 to-4.4
Government	0.4 to 1.2
Shareholders	8.1 to 9.7

Source: D. M. and M. G. Pollitt. 'The Restructuring and Privatisation of the UK Electricity Supply—Was It Worth It?' Public Policy for the Private Sector, No. 124. September 1997, p. 4.

Although British prices for electricity have fallen since privatisation, the decrease has been a fraction of the real reduction in costs involved in producing and supplying electricity. Retail prices for small households still remain high by European and US standards (see figure 12.4), and many countries that have not liberalised their electricity markets continue to offer cheaper electricity. Industrial users and affluent people, who use more electricity, have benefited from the largest price falls. Poor people and rural farmers have experienced price rises, as cross-subsidies put in place to protect them have been removed.[68]

The problem of "fuel poverty" affected about 16 per cent of households in the UK at the beginning of 2002. In other words, some four million households had to spend 10 per cent or more of their income to attain satisfactory levels of heating (using gas and/or electricity); in fact, there are over 30,000 extra deaths during winter each year in Britain because people cannot afford to heat themselves properly.[69] Dealing with fuel poverty is considered to be an objective outside the private company goals of economic efficiency and profit.

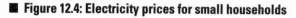

■ **Figure 12.4: Electricity prices for small households**

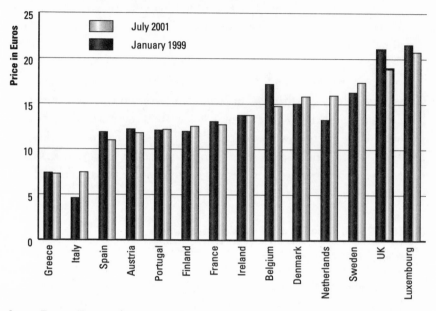

Sources: Eurostat, 'Energy and Environment', Statistics in Focus, 30 Nov. 2001; Eurostate, 'Electricity prices in the EU between 1998 and 2000', News Release, 18 July 2000.

In early 2002 consumer groups and the energy minister tried to prevent the lifting of price controls because of concerns about the impact on poor customers, particularly those on pre-payment meters.[70]

> The reality is that since privatisation, thousands of cash meters have been fitted in homes across the country. That means that the number of disconnections has dropped considerably—there are only a handful these days ... However, if some-one cannot afford to feed the meter, he effectively cuts himself off.[71]

Nevertheless, John Besant-Jones, from the European Bank for Reconstruction and Development, argued that the England and Wales model of electricity liberalisation was a good model for developing countries to follow, particularly:

> the pricing of electricity supply as a commercial service, rather than as a public obligation or a means of supporting low incomes. This policy not only gives users the correct price signals to use electricity efficiently; it also relieves hard-pressed government budgets of the burden of subsidizing the wealthy.[72]

However, he seems to miss the point that, in developing countries particularly, subsidies exist to help the poor, not the wealthy. And the UK model hardly offers a model for helping those on low incomes.

Similarly, the UK think tanks have turned their attention to the developing world. The Adam Smith Institute organised a conference in London in 1989, attended by delegates from all over the world. Peter Young, ASI policy adviser, pointed out that privatisation had become "a major British export", and that the ASI was now turning its attention to the developing world: "When we have done that we will sort out the communist world".[73]

PART FOUR

Australia: A Dedicated Follower of Fashion

DURING THE 1980S AND 1990S Australia had one of the largest privatisation programs of any OECD country—second only to the United Kingdom when calculated in dollar terms, and second only to New Zealand as a percentage of GDP. By 1999 Australia was the worldwide leader in both announced and completed privatisations. Investment banks were attracted to Australia to take advantage of the privatisation spree.[1] The International Energy Agency stated that "for most of the past decade, Australia has been at the forefront of energy market liberalisation".[2]

During the 1980s, as in the rest of the English-speaking world, Australian governments began to subscribe to a new economic paradigm: neoliberalism. This new paradigm was promoted by business groups, which saw government reform as a way of reducing their taxes, increasing investment opportunities and, in the case of the reform of government enterprises such as electricity, as a way of decreasing the cost of infrastructure provision to themselves.

The primary political motivation for privatisation in the states of Victoria and South Australia was debt reduction. But although state debt fell from $76 billion in 1993 to $47 billion in 1997,[3] taxpayers were often not any better off, particularly with respect to electricity privatisations. Electricity prices soared, blackouts became a regular fixture and, in South Australia, the government lost more in dividends than it saved in interest repayments. Elsewhere in Australia the national electricity market, based on the discredited UK power pool, has ensured that other states are also suffering from volatile wholesale electricity prices, caused by generating company manipulations. Far from reducing the amount of regulation, restructuring has caused a proliferation of regulatory agencies and regulations that are far more complex than ever before.

CHAPTER THIRTEEN

Privatisation In Victoria

Victoria was ... the state that, in its unseemly rush to privatise, committed
Australia to following the English approach to market reform that still bedevils the
emerging Australian national electricity market.
Robert Booth, energy consultant[4]

IN AUSTRALIA, electricity supply is the responsibility of the state governments. Each state developed its own electricity system in isolation because of
the distances between population centres. Transmission voltages varied from
state to state, providing a hurdle to interconnection. Private power companies
were established in the early twentieth century, but between 1930 and 1950
new development tended to be undertaken by state governments. By the
mid-1950s electricity was almost wholly a government enterprise.[5]

Some private power companies were nationalised by state governments:
"Private businesses were seen as unwilling to take the necessary risks to develop
public infrastructure and as demanding excessive returns when they did so."[6]
In South Australia there was a royal commission set up in 1945 to investigate
the privately owned Adelaide Electric Supply Company. Premier Tom Playford
believed it was too concerned with shareholders' interests at the expense of
service cost, reliability, and quality, and that it neglected the development of
energy self-sufficiency and industrialisation in South Australia. The royal commission recommended that the company be nationalised in the public interest
and, to the surprise of the conservative establishment, the Liberal Country
League Government did just that, forming the Electricity Trust of South
Australia (ETSA). Playford was labelled a "damned red" as a result.[7]

Each state was fairly well endowed with sources of electricity, which differed from state to state and accounted for differences in the price of electricity. The private sector tended to use oil and gas, whilst governments relied on coal reserves and hydro-electricity. In New South Wales (NSW) and Queensland there are plentiful supplies of black coal; and, in Victoria, of brown coal. South Australia uses lignite, whilst Tasmania relies mainly on hydro-electric dams. Because of these local sources of fuel, electricity prices in Australia have traditionally been low by world standards.[8]

Electricity supply in each state was undertaken by statutory authorities with varying degrees of vertical and horizontal integration. New infrastructure was financed through low-interest loans, available because of government guarantees. Statutory authorities were expected to provide a reliable and affordable supply of electricity to consumers, and to perform community-service obligations without additional payment. They tended to be dominated by engineers whose objective was meeting electricity requirements in a cost-effective way and charging uniform prices across the state to cover costs.[9]

Over-investment in electricity-generation facilities during the 1970s, in expectation of a minerals boom that did not happen, led to a price rise in the 1980s. In addition, various ideologically motivated studies carried out during the 1980s declared the industry to be inefficient and unproductive.[10]

Business Groups, Advisers, and Think Tanks

Businesses were aided in promoting privatisation and deregulation in Australia by "a network of well-funded research institutions, staffed mostly by market-oriented economists", including "the Industries Assistance Commission, the research arms of the Treasury and the Department of Finance, the Bureau of Agricultural Economics, Industry Economics and Labour Market Research", as well as university-based and private think tanks.[11]

The Industries Assistance Commission (later the Industry Commission and now the Productivity Commission) played a key role in influencing and supporting the reform process through its many reports on issues such as industry protection, microeconomic reform, and reform in the public sector. The recommendations of these reports were widely covered in the media and generated a fair amount of debate.[12]

In 1989 the commission produced a report that claimed a billion dollars could be saved if the performance of the electricity industry could be improved. It recommended increased private sector participation, open access to the transmission and distribution lines, and a national grid. In a 1991 report, *Energy Generation and Distribution*, the commission argued that efficiency improvements could save up to A\$2.4 billion per year. It pointed to poor investment decisions in the 1980s that had led to excess investment capacity which, together with overstaffing, meant that electricity was not being supplied at least cost.[13]

The commission recognised that the state authorities were improving their efficiency and productivity. The Electricity Commission of NSW had reduced staffing by 30 per cent in two years, and the State Electricity Commission of Victoria (SECV) had

- reduced staffing by 18 per cent in 18 months;
- cut operating costs per unit of output of 40 per cent in five years;
- reduced reserve plant margins from 45-50 per cent to 25-30 per cent;
- increased available capacity from 59 per cent to 69 per cent in four years; and
- cut average electricity prices by 3 per cent a year since 1985

However, despite these improvements in performance, the Industry Commission did not accept that full efficiency could be achieved without private ownership: "Private ownership brings with it the disciplines of the share and capital markets, the sanctions provided by the possibility of take-over and the risk of insolvency. It also significantly reduces the scope for interference by governments."[14]

The commission recommended that, in advance of privatisation, the public utilities should be corporatised—that is, organised as commercial organisations, having commercial aims such as maximising their rate of return, using similar accounting methods, and operating with minimal governmental intervention. It also argued that generation, transmission, and distribution sectors in each state ought to be separated in preparation for sale to the private sector. New investment ought to be subject to competitive tender in the private sector.[15] The commission proposed a power pool for trading electricity, and the division of generation capacity into separate, competing companies with open access for new, private generating facilities. These recommendations were subsequently adopted, first in Victoria and then in other states.

At the 1991 intergovernmental conference of state and federal government leaders, the Special Premier's Conference, it was decided that government enterprises should be corporatised and have to compete on equal terms with private companies offering similar services. Any community-service obligations would be explicitly purchased and paid for by the government.[16] In 1993 a federal inquiry into national competition policy, established "with the strong backing of business," reported that government business enterprises should be subjected to competition.[17] These reforms were strongly supported by the major international bureaucracies: the IMF, the World Bank, and the OECD.

Journalist and author Paul Kelly notes that there were three main institutional pillars of support for market-based infrastructure reforms in the Australian community: the financial markets, the "quality print media and its leading commentators", and the business community.[18] The financial markets and the business community were motivated by self-interest, and the media was influenced by business associations and corporate-funded think tanks. Businesses were concerned about the level of taxes they had to pay and the cost of infrastructure services.

For example, the Business Council of Australia (BCA) played a significant role in advocating infrastructure reforms. It was made up of the chief executives of the largest corporations operating in Australia, and therefore basically represented the multinationals. It was modelled on the US Business Roundtable, and sought to provide a strategy forum and voice for big business.[19] The BCA estimated in 1993 that government inputs accounted for "some 6.2 per cent of total industry costs" and that government enterprises absorbed "a substantial amount of the nation's capital and human resources", including 7 per cent of the labour force and 19 per cent of the nation's net capital stock. It stated:

> It is obvious that efficiency gains in these enterprises will mean that they will not only reduce their call on the nation's capital and human resources but also help to improve the international competitiveness of Australian business and industry.[20]

The BCA argued that government enterprises were inefficient and their services costly because they were often not subject to competition and seldom subject to commercial pressures. Many businesses also resented the commitment of government enterprises to social ends, particularly the principle of equity. And whilst they appreciated cross-subsidies that benefited business, they were opposed to those that helped disadvantaged and rural residents. They also resented the payment of dividends to government.[21]

In 1991 the BCA persuaded the government to direct the Bureau of Industry Economics (BIE) to undertake a series of studies identifying the costs of infrastructure services, such as electricity, comparing their performance with the best overseas, and publishing the comparisons regularly. This BIE/BCA benchmarking project was a high priority on the "Business Council's micro-economic reform agenda", and it committed "considerable financial and personnel resources" to it as well as to associated studies.[22]

Not surprisingly, the BCA-funded studies found some gaps between the performance of Australian services and the best around the world. Nor was it surprising that the BCA recommended that the government services be exposed to more competition from the private sector "by removing the monopoly powers of government business enterprises and other barriers to competition"[23], and that some of these enterprises should be divested to the private sector where they could be performed more efficiently.[24]

In 1993 the BCA formed an electricity task force, headed by the CEO of ICI Australia (now Orica), to "provide a leadership role to support and achieve reforms in the electricity industry, thereby assisting Australian enterprises in becoming internationally competitive." As a result, the BCA "played a prominent role" in electricity reform in Australia.[25]

Businessmen also played a central role in setting up, funding, and promoting think tanks and staffing their boards. These corporate-funded think tanks proliferated in Australia in the 1980s and 1990s. Most of them are pro-market and opposed to government intervention, and "their long-term aim is to re-define the terms of debate on political and social issues in ways favourable" to the corporations which fund them. They campaigned tirelessly to get privatisation and deregulation onto the political agenda.[26]

Their output has been massive, despite their limited funding compared with US think tanks. During the 1990s they published about 900 reports and discussion papers each year, and held some 600 conferences and symposia.[27] And they were "spectacularly successful" when it came to restructuring public services and reducing government intervention.[28] One of the most prominent corporate-funded think tanks, and the oldest, is the Institute of Public Affairs (IPA). It advocated "less regulation and smaller government generally", privatisation, free trade, and "rational economic policies".[29]

Another key Australasian think tank that promoted privatisation was the Tasman Institute. Michael Porter set it up in 1990, with the backing of businessmen, including mining magnate Hugh Morgan, media mogul Rupert Murdoch, and former New Zealand treasurer Roger Douglas, who was its deputy chair. It had 38 corporate members, including Arthur Andersen, the Australian Coal Association, the Australian Mining Industry Council, BHP, BP, Shell, CRA, Esso, Western Mining Corporation, ICI, News Limited, the New Zealand Business Roundtable, and the Electricity Corporation of New

Zealand. It played a key role in the early 1990s in bringing neoliberal free-market influences to bear on the Victorian government through Project Victoria (see below). In particular, Porter played a key role advising on the privatisation of electricity.[30]

Overseas think tanks have also played a role in promoting privatisation in Australia. *Privatisation: the facts and fallacies*, written by Madsen Pirie, president of the Adam Smith Institute, was published by Centre 2000 in Australia.[31] Pirie also toured Australia in the mid-1980s to promote the benefits of privatisation and to tell the good news about privatisation in Britain. In 1985 Edwin Feulner, president of the US Heritage Foundation, told an Australian audience that "privatisation is one of the few methods of cutting the budget which actually could develop a positive constituency".[32]

Project Victoria

The Australian state of Victoria is now the most privatised region in the world, and much of the groundwork for this was established by Project Victoria. Project Victoria "sought to develop new institutional reform structures for Victoria particularly for infrastructure".[33] It originated from the work of a consortium of private firms, employer organizations, and think tanks in Victoria, and is a prime illustration of the contribution to the privatisation drive made by the new breed of pro-market think tanks. At the behest of their sponsors, these think tanks have set the agenda, formed interlocking networks, and provided detailed advice on implementing privatisation.

In the early 1990s the Victorian state government had such a large government debt ($32 billion) that its credit rating was downgraded by international rating agencies.[34] Privatisation became more than just an ideology but also a way of reducing the government debt and therefore taxes and charges to business: in Porter's words, it would remove "the 'ball and chain' and the labour market practices that stop business ... from prospering". It was also seen as way of allowing private firms "to get a piece of the action".[35]

In 1990, more than a year before the neoliberal Kennett government was elected, thirteen business organisations commissioned the Tasman Institute and the IPA to establish *Project Victoria*. These organisations included the Australian Chamber of Manufacturers, the BCA, the State Chamber of Commerce and Industry, the Victorian Employers Federation, and the Victorian Farmers Federation. The Tasman Institute, as Porter pointed out, "provided most of the policy expertise, particularly for infrastructure issues, for Project Victoria."[36]

Project Victoria was far reaching. It covered water, ports, electricity, public transport, and workers compensation, and the Kennett government used it as a basis to extend variations of privatisation to roads, hospitals, prisons, and schools. Tasman and IPA prepared a number of reports and strategies between 1991 and 1993. "Project Victoria's reform agenda underlay many of the economic reforms of Victoria."[37] The Kennett government implemented most of Project Victoria recommendations after it was elected; in some cases it went further, as when it slashed the public service workforce by more than three times the level recommended in the 1991 report.[38]

A preliminary report, *Victoria: An Agenda for Change*, had been released in April 1991 while Kennett was still in opposition. It noted that the State Electricity Commission of Victoria (SECV) had been one of the least productive electricity providers in Australia, but admitted that one of the reasons had been its reliance on low-grade brown coal and that its performance had improved markedly during the late 1980s (see figure 13.1). But, like the Industries Commission, the preliminary report argued that more improvement would be possible under private ownership, which could provide the incentives of "profit motive, and the disciplines associated with the markets" to "eliminate waste and inefficiency".[39]

In contrast, an Electricity Supply Association study of 1000 utilities around the world found that the SECV was in the top ten for efficiency of resource use and that it was also highly efficient in terms of its technical efficiency of distribution. And a study by London Economics in 1994 found the SECV's resource efficiency compared favourably with best-practice utilities worldwide.[40]

Whilst still in opposition, the Kennett-led neoliberals set up a study group to examine the SECV. The group consisted of the shadow treasurer, Alan Stockdale, a fierce advocate of privatisation; the shadow minister for fuel and energy; and six individuals chosen for their expertise and their desire to see the SECV reformed. Stockdale had reportedly gained his ideology at the London School of Economics during the Thatcher era, and he was portrayed in the media as an "ideological warrior".[41] (After he had played a key role in Victorian privatisations as treasurer in the Kennett government, Stockdale joined the Macquarie Bank, one of the major beneficiaries of those privatisations.[42])

The study group met regularly for a year. It decided that the SECV had too much debt, was not performing at its best, and industrial relations problems loomed. It decided that the SECV should be split up and restructured, with its generation and retail sectors being opened up to competition.[43] This is what occurred when Kennett came to power.

■ Figure 13.1: Performance of the SECV, 1985-1990

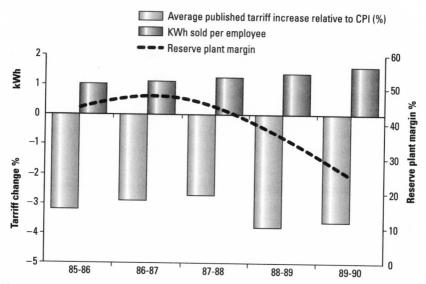

Source: D. Moore and M. Porter, eds. 1991. Victoria: An Agenda for Change. Melbourne: The Tasman Institute and the Institute of Public Affairs, pp. 4-5.

In fact, the SECV's debt was not a problem. In the year before it was broken up, 1992-3, "it paid $995 million in interest, a $191 million dividend to the State Government, and had a profit of $207 million."[44] Its debt-equity ratio was 342 per cent, compared with an average of 382 per cent for the top-20 Australian companies on the Australian stock exchange. In addition, a 1994 Bureau of Industry Economics study found that Victoria's electricity prices to industry were eighth cheapest out of 40 OECD countries.[45]

The authors of the Project Victoria report were also critical of community-service obligations, which raised the charges for most businesses. These included:

- uniform tariffs across the state to cross-subsidise remote customers;
- participation in the Victorian government's "Social Justice Strategy", which reduces the number of supply disconnections for non-payment of accounts and imposes no penalties for late payment;
- financing one-third of the capital cost of new major public-lighting schemes;
- financing under-grounding or relocation of power lines where a clear community benefit exists;
- providing the Home Energy Advisory Service free to people on low incomes;
- and satisfying non-statutory environmental obligations.[46]

According to Project Victoria, these obligations caused business users to be overcharged by 28 per cent (not including farmers, who were subsidised) and impeded "competitiveness by distorting service provision".[47] The Industry Commission had also been particularly scathing about cross-subsidies. The commission claimed they were penalising most industrial users, particularly those in the city. However, they also recognised that the heaviest industrial users of electricity were also being subsidised by some 11 per cent.[48]

In the second stage of Project Victoria, a report entitled *A Restructuring Strategy for Electricity in Victoria* detailed how the electricity industry should be broken up and sold off, and a national grid and power pool should be developed to facilitate competition.[49] It was written by Michael Porter and Wayne Gilbert, a former head of Mercury Energy in New Zealand. (Gilbert was head at the time Mercury was responsible for the extended blackouts in Auckland.) Gilbert had also been a member of the NZ Business Roundtable, and a member of the anti-union H. R. Nicholls Society, formed to oppose labour regulation in Australia. The plan devised by Porter and Gilbert was followed "closely by the Treasurer, Alan Stockdale".[50]

The undermining of union power was one of the unstated motives of privatisation of electricity in Victoria, as in the United Kingdom. Strikes were frequent in the industry; and demarcation disputes and overmanning had become a problem, with up to 24 unions covering each power station. However, these problems were addressed prior to privatisation when unions were rationalised with the help of the Australian Council of Trade Unions (ACTU): employee numbers were reduced from 20,000 to 12,000 and then to 8000 after the change of government in 1992, but prior to privatisation.[51]

Another driving force for privatisation, according to journalist David Walker, was the US private power companies:

> In the early 1990s, with their home market's power demands growing at snail's pace, these companies began expanding overseas. In China, India and South America, though, they ran into dysfunctional legal and social systems and governments that changed the rules at whim. Then they found clean, safe Victoria, which not only spoke English but offered leafy suburbs and schools, fine restaurants, theatre and other amenities for foreign managers.[52]

Electricity Privatisation

The first step towards privatisation was the unbundling of the SECV into three businesses in 1993: Generation Victoria, National Electricity (responsible for transmission), and Electricity Services Victoria (responsible for distribution and supply). An Electricity Supply Industry (ESI) Reform Unit was set up within Treasury to consider further restructuring, with a view to introducing competition and privatisation. It was headed by Dr. Peter Troughton, an Englishman who had prepared Telecom New Zealand for privatisation by shedding two-thirds of its staff and then becoming its first CEO.[53]

Robert Booth, who had been a commissioner of the State Energy Commission of Western Australia, as well as having worked for the SECV, described the nature of Troughton's reform unit:

> The determination of the ESI Reform Unit manifested itself early in the form of an intense distrust of anyone who had been involved in the previous SECV or of anyone who had special expertise in the industry, and who might therefore have a different view from that of the Unit. Individuals were identified and tagged, and gotten rid of very quickly ... The ESI Reform Unit never hired a consultant under this process whose views were at all uncertain, or may have been in conflict with the results which they were seeking .... General public consultation was never part of their technique—it was too uncertain and unpredictable. The entire process of change in Victoria proceeded without any degree of public consultation or exposure worth mentioning.[54]

Instead of consultation, the Victorian government spent $1.8 million on an advertising campaign to promote the sale of the electricity industry. Nevertheless, an AGB-McNair Age poll found that 60 per cent of those surveyed opposed privatisation. A coalition of many church, welfare, environmental groups, and unions—Public First—was formed to oppose privatisation of electricity, gas, and water. A spokesperson for the coalition, Jim Ritchie, argued that privatisation would merely be "shifting the debt from the public to the private sector" and would provide "no incentive for energy conservation or moving to sustainable sources."[55]

Booth argued that the members of the reform unit were selected to implement the UK model of privatisation and were blind to the flaws that were already evident in it, such as the unacceptably high pool prices and the manipulation of those prices by generators. The experts chosen to develop the trading system "all held an almost evangelistic fervour for the very unusual UK-style system of trading in electricity, and no contrary views".[56]

The reform unit used the same stringent control, according to Booth, in appointing personnel to the new businesses formed from the old SECV. Those with talent and ability were often overlooked because of their past positions. And the reform unit kept an eye on the new organisations by sending someone along to all board meetings "to make sure that they were not taking an independent line".[57]

The BCA had doubts about emulating the UK power pool model because of the problems of price manipulation there. It was promised that direct contracts between businesses and generators would be allowed and that the heavy-user industry tariff (Tariff H), which was subsidised by residential customers and lower than business tariffs in other states, would be maintained for five years so that business consumers represented by the council would not be subject to the vagaries of the power pool.[58]

As in Britain, the aim was to maximise the sale value of the SECV businesses in the hope of paying off state debt. To do this, the government sought to ensure "so-called 'revenue certainty' — for as long as possible. Customer interests were to become secondary." Cost savings made prior to privatisation were used "to bolster the commercial attractiveness of the entities being offered for sale" rather than to reduce rates.[59] The purchasers of government assets received tax subsidies from the Commonwealth government that "effectively subsidised" their purchases.[60]

The government had increased residential electricity prices by 10 per cent in 1992, prior to privatisation. It now announced that residential prices would be frozen till mid-1996, when the price could rise by 2 per cent; there would then be 1 per cent increases each following year till 2000, when full residential competition would begin. Five distribution/supply companies would take part in that competition.[61]

Generation Victoria fought to remain as one organisation, pointing to the significant improvements that had already been made in terms of productivity and efficiency. It reasoned that competition would come from other states with the introduction of the national energy market. Also an independent inquiry pointed out that the generating plants had been designed to operate in a coordinated way, and that forcing them to compete would result in inefficiencies, higher prices, and more frequent breakdowns.[62]

Dismissing these arguments, the government announced in 1995 that Generation Victoria would be split into five competing corporations. Despite its promises to the BCA, the government also announced a compulsory UK-style power pool.

Several of the same consultants who advised the Californian Public Utility Commission on the [power exchange] also advised the Victorian Government, and the same style of system as used in California was introduced in Victoria in early 1995. Once Victoria had decided to go this way, it was inevitable that the National Electricity Market, then under active development, would have to follow.[63]

All power had to be traded through the power pool. The pool price for each half-hour would be the highest bid by generators called on to fill demand (see figure 6.1 on page 103). Business customers with loads over 5MW (47 of them) could choose their supplier from December 1994; those with loads over 1MW (330 customers) could chose their supplier from July 1995. Eventually, suppliers would compete for all customers. The five distribution/supply businesses would be privatised from 1995.[64]

■ **Figure 13.2: How hedge contracts work**

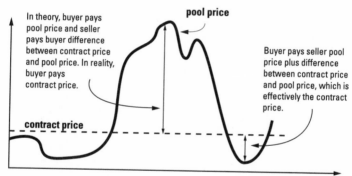

Source: adapted from NEMMCO. 'An Introduction to Australia's National Electricity Market.' March 2001, p. 26.

To help generators and retailers cope with the wildly fluctuating prices of the pool, vesting contracts were introduced, as in the UK, which allowed buyers and sellers to hedge the pool price. In other words, although electricity was traded in the power pool, those with contracts only paid the contracted price for the electricity. If the pool price was higher than the contracted price, the generator paid the difference; if it was lower, the buyer paid the difference (see graph above). These vesting contracts, or hedging contracts, or "contracts for difference" as they were called in the UK, initially covered 95 per cent of franchise customers (those not able to choose their supplier), and were supposed to gradually disappear over five years.[65]

As in the UK, a formula was devised to pay distribution companies based on CPI-X (Consumer Price Index minus an efficiency factor). And, as in the UK, the distribution companies made huge profits—30 or 40 per cent of their total revenue compared with the average for Australia's top-100 companies of 8-10 per cent. Foreseeing the profits to be made under this system, the five distribution companies that were privatised in 1995 fetched very high prices that amounted to just under twice the book value of the assets. Four were sold to US companies and the fifth to a US/Australian consortium.[66]

Privatisation in Practice

Pool prices were reasonably low at first because of the electricity overcapacity in the state, but prices started to climb in 1995. Whilst the generators were government-owned the government was able to exert some pressure on them to make their bids more reasonable. But the government began to sell the generating companies in 1996 to US and UK companies, with some participation of Australian companies. Again, the companies were sold for large amounts, indicating that the acquiring companies expected to be able to gain high electricity prices in the pool. The transmission grid was also sold to a US utility for a large amount.[67]

The high asset-sale prices, whilst a boon to the government, were of concern to industry analysts because of the large amounts of corporate debt they represented. This debt, which came at a higher price than government debt, was far more than the original SECV debt that the industry was not supposed to be able to support. The analysts claimed that the cost savings available to the private sector would not be enough for them to make a profit and service the debt, and therefore they would inevitably have to increase electricity prices or go out of business. Indeed, United Energy, one of the privatised companies, later admitted to the *Sydney Morning Herald* that it had been too optimistic in its estimates of the costs it could cut.[68]

Economies that could be achieved by slashing the work force had occurred prior to privatisation. Booth estimates that the cost savings from this could have led to price reductions of 30 per cent and could still have serviced the previous $9.5 billion debt. But because of the need to service the $23 billion spent by private companies buying the industry, there was pressure to increase prices rather than decrease them.[69]

For the first five years, however, because retail prices were controlled, it was shareholders who suffered, causing several of the distribution/supply companies to sell off their new acquisitions. When interstate competition began in 1998 there was hot competition between NSW and Victorian generators, and wholesale prices dropped well below the expectations of the privatised companies. The first casualty of this market was CMS Energy, which had to sell its 50 per cent ownership of the Loy Yang A power station and coal mine at a loss.[70] The business failures caused some consternation:

It is easy to say that this is simply the outworkings of the commercial world at work, but there is reason to worry when assets which form an important part of state and national infrastructure are being bought and sold like common chattels, with the attendant risk that they may not be there when really required.[71]

The other way that savings could be made was by cutting back on maintenance, something also necessitated by the much-reduced workforces. There were, therefore, a number of blackouts resulting from equipment breakdowns.[72] In 1997 a Coopers and Lybrand survey found a third of the privatised companies believed "previously experienced reliability levels would/may not be provided by the market". The Victorian government could not intervene to prevent blackouts, it argued, as that would result in "an unacceptable distortion of the market". Some companies took a cavalier approach to the difficulties blackouts caused consumers, one of them even going so far as to argue that "Customers need to experience some disruptions" so as to appropriately value their electricity supply.[73]

Prior to election in 1999 the Labor Party was very critical of the outcomes of privatisation:

Privatisation has seen the number of blackouts increase by 32 per cent. And compared with 1995—the year when the electricity companies were privatised—unplanned minutes off supply have increased 10 per cent. The most recent report on electricity prices by the Electricity Supply Association of Australia clearly shows that the electricity prices for Victorian households are the second highest in Australia, electricity prices for small business are the highest and electricity prices for rural Victorians are also the highest in Australia ... Victorians are now paying 79 per cent more than the national average for electricity services ... Businesses are seeing large volatility in their electricity costs (up to 70 per cent) and in some instances are having to pass these increased costs on to customers.[74]

In 2000-1 the price of electricity in the National Electricity Market increased by 60 per cent (see next chapter). In the first three months of 2001 the average price was triple the average price in 1999. However, most state governments did not allow retail prices to increase by anything like this because of the political backlash it would have caused amongst householders. Businesses in Victoria were not so fortunate. Small and medium-sized businesses, such as supermarkets, were able to choose to buy directly from the pool or from any of the retail suppliers in Victoria from December 2000.

However, whilst these businesses preferred to buy from suppliers rather than risk the vagaries of the pool, those suppliers were finding it harder to get long-term contracts with generators, who could refuse to sign contracts with consumers if they found it more profitable to sell via the pool.[75]

The scheduled introduction of deregulation for household electricity in Victoria, when domestic consumers would become contestable and price caps would be removed, was January 2001. However, this was postponed for a year because of the fear of huge price increases. When retail deregulation was introduced, price caps continued with 'safety net' prices being set by the government. The privatised retailers sought to increase these maximum prices by up to 19 per cent, but the government granted only 2.5-4.7 per cent increases to the city-based retailers; regional prices were increased by 13.5-15.5 per cent, with a $118 million government subsidy to protect rural consumers.[76]

Put in a similar position to Californian utilities—that is, unable to pass wildly fluctuating, deregulated wholesale prices onto consumers because of price caps on retail prices—the privatised Victorian retailer suppliers sought to sell up. Advocates of the market blamed the government's protection of consumers rather than the vagaries of market prices that had little to do with the cost of production.

Nevertheless, despite the complaints of suppliers, at least one supply company, Origin Energy, reported increased profits. Farmers pointed out that suppliers had got around government price caps by increasing off-peak electricity rates by 175 per cent and by decreasing peak rates to ensure that average increases met with the price caps. This particularly affected farmers, who take advantage of off-peak rates for many energy-intensive activities. As a result, many farmers saw their overall rates increase by up to 60 per cent. The president of United Dairyfarmers Victoria, Peter Owen, accused the power companies of "pillaging sections of rural Victoria with the Government's blessing".[77]

Part of the rhetoric of privatisation had been that it would create "new operators, nimble and competitive that would give consumers a new deal".[78] Instead, competition decreased as incumbent players consolidated their power throughout Australia. By 2002 some 30 per cent of the retail market was for sale. The prospect of "re-aggregation" in the industry increased as AGL (Australian Gas Light) bought Pulse, and Origin Energy bought Citipower (see table13.1).[79] Pulse, owned by United Energy, Shell, and Woodside, was "a classic creation of the new, private energy market ... seen as smart, fleet of foot and adept at the PR game". But United lost money trying to diversify into internet services, and lost millions in the electricity market by failing to have adequate hedge contracts.[80]

Analysts now expect the number of retail suppliers on the Australian east coast to fall from ten to only six by 2005.[81]

> Industry players are racing to create a new group of vertically and horizontally integrated structures (businesses owning generation or gas wells, and retailing in different state markets) in an effort to protect themselves from the wild gyrations of the energy markets and to gain economies of scale.[82]

AGL, a dominant supplier of electricity and/or gas in South Australia, New South Wales, and Victoria, with 31 per cent of the total eastern Australian retail energy market, says: "We want to be one of what we predict will be the three or four national energy players." It planned to expand into energy generation as well as supply.[83]

When retail competition was introduced in 2002, household consumers treated it with a shrug. Only 0.8 per cent of the market changed suppliers, and most of those were small businesses. The exercise of this choice was supposed to be one of the great advantages of electricity deregulation for consumers. However, the government never expected that choice would make any difference for household consumers in practice. Its own report, *Reforming Victoria's Electricity Industry*, admitted that metering and administration costs would result in limited choice for small customers; they expected there to be little advantage for retailers in chasing households outside their previous franchise area, and little advantage for household consumers in changing retailers.[84]

■ **Table 13.1: Electricity and gas retailers operating in Victoria, 2002**

Retail Supply Companies	*Customers*
{ AGL	2 million* }
{ Pulse (sold to AGL)	1.2 million }
{ Origin Energy	1.7 million }
{ CitiPower (sold to Origin)	0.24 million }
Energex (owned by Queensland govt.)	1.4 million*
TXU (for sale in 2001)	0.92 million
	* Australia wide

Sources: J. Durie 2002. 'Energy Heading for Consolidation Fast.' Australian Financial Review. 22 March 2002, p. 84; J. Thompson. 'High-Voltage Hard Ship.' Business Review Weekly. 28 February 2002, p. 32.

By January 2002 privatisation of electricity in Victoria had failed to deliver any increased generating capacity, and generator breakdowns were threatening blackouts. Despite the government's determination that it would learn from the UK's privatisation experience, the supposed efficiencies of privatisation did not eventuate; it did not lead to lower prices and better service for consumers. Even the Productivity Commission, which was keen to promote the success of electricity privatisation in Victoria, noted in 2002 that there had been price increases, and that low-income households had suffered most from them.[85] Ironically, even businesses, which had been prime drivers of privatisation, suffered from rising wholesale prices after 2000.

CHAPTER FOURTEEN

The National Electricity Market

*NEM currently operates too much like a highly speculative stockmarket, an
inappropriate model for the future of the electricity industry.*
John Spoehr, Centre for Labour Research at Adelaide University [1]

*I think this is a somewhat perverse way to develop a market that is supposed to be
for the public good.*
Lew Owens, SA Independent Industry Regulator

ALTHOUGH A NATIONAL GRID interconnecting most Australian states was
thought to be economically viable and good for competition, the South
Australian Independent Industry Regulator, Lew Owens, noted that it was
not necessarily the most efficient way of providing electricity—because the
transmission losses over the interconnectors could be 40-90 per cent. [2]
Nevertheless, a national grid was created which covered seven million customers in eastern and southern Australia by 2001. [3]

At first, a prototype market had been set up with only Victoria and New
South Wales participating. (NSW still had a government-owned electricity
system, as we shall see in the next chapter). Then, in December 1998, the
National Electricity Market (NEM) began operations, with South Australia
also taking part. The other states were not yet connected. At first, prices were
low because there was an oversupply of electricity in NSW. Even then, it was
only large industrial consumers of electricity which benefited, whilst household prices were not reduced. This was partly because only the large users
were contestable until the end of 2000 on the national market. So suppliers
competing for their business reduced prices for the large users. [4]

In mid-1998, whilst the earlier version of the market was still operating, NSW generators decided that prices were too low. They lifted the prices "quite suddenly" by withdrawing capacity and changing their bidding strategies. By 2001, when Queensland (also government-owned—see next chapter) was connected to the national grid, electricity prices had increased significantly "across most of South Australia, Victoria, and NSW".[5]

The national electricity market operated on the same principle as the Victorian market, which had been modelled on the now-defunct UK power pool. Cheapest bids would be accepted first, and more expensive ones next, until demand was met. For each five-minute period, the price for all electricity used would be that of the highest bid accepted. Because of the limited capacity of the interconnectors, and transmission losses, the price in each state could be different because not all spare capacity was available in all states.[6]

National Market Manipulation

Generators were able to withhold capacity on hot days until the price peaked, and then they could rebid their capacity at inflated prices. "This rebidding can see wholesale power prices jump from, say $12 per mega watt hour to $4,600/MWh within minutes."[7] Generators admitted that the reason for rebidding was "financial optimisation". Until 2001, electricity prices to households did not suffer much, "mainly through tight government controls". These were progressively removed after that date as retail markets were opened to competition, and the pain of skyrocketing rates began to be felt.[8]

Following the UK experience there had been plenty of warnings of the potential for price manipulation in the national market.[9] Also, a computer-simulation trial of the pool system had been carried out in 1993 and 1994. During this trial, the spot-market prices were much higher than the actual prices that participants were paying. The Business Council of Australia (BCA), Pacific Power (one of the NSW state-owned generating companies), and the Electricity Supply Association of Australia published a statement which argued that the proposed arrangements for the national market were "not suitable for implementation" because:

> the proposed market mechanisms are too complex; the trading system leads to volatile and unpredictable prices that are unrelated to the actual cost structure of the industry, and there is great difficulty in relating bid prices from generators to sensible (let alone optimal) unit commencement and dispatch.[10]

They argued that most electricity should be traded by contract rather than on the spot market. Their criticisms had been ignored by the National Grid Management Council (NGMC), which was strongly influenced by Victoria's Electricity Supply Industry (ESI) Reform Unit. The Victorians insisted that a national market had to be consistent with its market if it was to participate. And without Victoria the national market could hardly be credible.[11]

The Australian Consumer and Competition Commission (ACCC) also warned about the potential for "manipulation of pool prices arising from a concentrated market structure". It authorised the National Electricity Code Administrator (NECA) to impose some conditions, including a price cap, to be reviewed annually.[12] Until 2002, NEM prices were capped at a maximum of $5000/MWh compared to a normal electricity-generating price of $35/MWh (and a maximum pool price in California of $A1337[13]). It then increased to $10,000/MWh. Such a high price cap offered little protection to buyers.

After the market had been operating for a few years, price manipulation was confirmed by a study undertaken by the Australian Bureau of Agricultural and Resource Economics (ABARE), a supporter of deregulation and competition in electricity markets. ABARE argued that the primary objective of the NEM was to facilitate competition:

> This objective recognises that a truly competitive market results in the cost of con-
> suming the delivered electricity being as low as is economically feasible, but is still
> sufficient to induce investment in new capacity as is required … Indeed, one of
> the defining characteristics of any efficient market is that price is equal to the mar-
> ginal cost of producing the product.[14]

ABARE compared actual prices to marginal costs. Even though it estimated marginal costs from the generators' own bids, it found that NEM was not competitive:

> In the six months examined in 1999, prices were considered to have deviated sub-
> stantially from competitive outcomes for at least two-thirds of the period in all
> states except Queensland [which had not yet joined NEM]. The magnitude of the
> deviations is most pronounced in South Australia, with noncompetitive market
> outcomes being estimated to account for around half of the actual market value in
> every month in that state.[15]

ABARE found that the situation was even worse in 2000-1, noting that Queensland, which had now joined NEM, was also deviating from competitive pricing, and NSW was deviating in all months, more frequently, and with higher prices. Victoria also deviated across warm and cool months, and South Australia only appeared not to deviate because even the lowest bids, which were used as an indicator of marginal costs, were inflated by the generators. Such uncompetitive bidding was costing the Australian economy hundreds of millions of dollars.[16]

In late 2000 there were rumours of a generating company in Victoria buying up forward contracts on electricity (contracts to buy electricity for a set price in the following months). It was difficult to confirm this as the contracts were being bought through a broker "using complex arrangements that make them impossible to trace", although the ACCC did investigate. The concern was that this was a way of gaming the system. During periods of peak demand—for example, during hot weather, industrial disputes, or when another generator was offline—the generator would take one of its own generators offline, ensuring the price would peak at the maximum of $5000/MWh. Whilst it was offline it would be able to sell the electricity from its other generators at top price, and use the electricity bought on forward contracts to supply its own commitments.[17]

Although most electricity bought via the power pool was hedged by contracts (see previous chapter), the power-pool price affected the price of electricity in the contracts. In addition, there were allegations that market power was being exercised with respect to contracts, with generators only offering uncompetitive, highly priced contracts during the summer of 2000-2001.[18]

Whilst prices were initially manipulated by the physical withholding of capacity, generators moved to the practice of economic withholding in 2000 —that is, bidding large chunks of their capacity at very high prices. This practice began in Victoria, and spread to more companies and other states in 2001. Consulting firm Bardak Ventures conducted a study which concluded "that while in some high priced incidents examined, there is an initiating event, such as a loss of generator, interconnection limitations or exceptionally high load forecasts, the major factor contributing to the price spike is the bidding and rebidding practices of the generators." Rebidding, which happened about 800 times a day, enabled generators to offer capacity at very high prices at the last minute, so there was no opportunity for competing generators to put in a cheaper bid. In 2000 just 20 high-priced "events" cost an additional $912 million, and added 13 per cent to the average pool price.[19]

The rebidding process continued to be controversial, but generating companies insisted that it was necessary. A compromise solution put forward by the

BCA, that rebidding should only be allowed within three hours of electricity dispatch if the price was lower, was rejected by the ACCC. But "after criticism of price outcomes that arose during the summer of 2000-2001", generators were required to give reasons for their rebids that would be published.[20] This did not stop them from giving "financial optimisation" as a reason.

Stephen Kelly, the managing director of NECA, which had been set up to regulate the market, argued that there was no evidence of price manipulation. (He was formerly a Treasury official in the Thatcher government when it privatised electricity, but had no experience with the Australian electricity industry.)[21]

In contrast, independent industry regulator Owens argued that, since the 1998 reform of the national electricity market, prices had been soaring because the market had not prevented monopolies and price manipulation. Similarly, energy analyst Robert Booth pointed out:

Just as in California, there was a period of seductively low wholesale prices in the early years of the UK-style markets, followed by a steep increase as reserve margins declined and as market power could be exerted. The difference is that, whereas California has put into place measures which have a very good chance of preventing the kind of price exploitation which occurred in the latter part of 2000 and the early part of 2001, Australia continues on blithely assuming that the present system will not cause such effects here...

More generally, the decision of the United Kingdom to abandon the type of pool later adopted by California and Australia, and the effect of the FERC Order, means that Australia is the only country in the world continuing to try to make a compulsory, single-priced, energy-only pool system work. Even the New Zealand market, which is only partly compulsory, has experienced a price explosion in mid 2001, which is due to similar factors, including inadequate competitive forces and market rules capable of exploitation.[22]

However, Australian officials, business leaders, and media outlets resisted learning any lessons from the Californian experience. The media and privatisation proponents have repeatedly covered up the real cause of the problems with a "surging demand/obstructionist environmentalist" spin (see chapter 7), so that deregulation would not be blamed. The *Sydney Morning Herald* correspondent in Los Angeles reported:

Privatisation of California's electricity in 1996 coincided with an unforeseen surge of demand, mainly from technology companies in the booming San Joes area that exist cheek by jowl with conservationists who have blocked the construction and full running of environmentally unfriendly coal-fired power stations.[23]

The managing director of the Electricity Supply Association of Australia (ESAA), Keith Orchison, also citing surging demand and a failure to construct new generating capacity in California, warned that "we must be vigilant in Australia in ensuring that the news out of California does not undermine the community and political confidence in our own competitive energy markets".[24]

The chief economist of BCA argued that the only lesson Australia had to learn from California was that if deregulation in Australia was partial because of government interference, as in California, the market would not be competitive: "The Californian message for Australia is get on and finish reforms".[25]

As in California, it has become clear that NEM provides no incentive for generators to invest in new capacity, because undersupply keeps pool prices very high and the standby plant necessary to ensure system reliability "erodes generator profit … Generator profit is inversely proportional to the levels of reserve plant with no incentive for system reliability".[26] Also, existing generators can drop prices when potential competitors are seeking finance to build generation facilities. It would take a brave company indeed to risk investing in generating infrastructure that may be needed in three or four years' time— for that is how long it takes to get a plant up and operating.

Governments traditionally took responsibility for system reliability; but, with privatisation, that responsibility has been handed over to the market, which has other priorities. By mid-2002 there was a call for more generating capacity. ABARE forecast increasing electricity demand, and ESAA estimated that at least $20 billion had to be invested in fuel supply and generation to meet the demand. The problem was, who would make that investment? Rather than investing in new infrastructure, many of the private generators were selling up. There was $10 billion worth of existing electricity infrastructure up for sale in 2002. And that didn't include the $2.8 billion worth that US-based supplier TXU had unsuccessfully tried to sell the year before.[27]

Wholesale electricity prices increased again in winter 2002 as a result of concerted rebidding by generating companies, causing the NECA to complain about the lack of competitiveness in the market. From average prices of $20-$30 per MWh, the pool price began to sit at around $112 all day, peaking much higher in the evening when people turned their heaters on. Major companies in NSW and Victoria were offering limited amounts of electricity at thousands of dollars per MWh on cold evenings. NECA referred the matter to the ACCC, seeking to get permission to change bidding procedures.[28]

The ACCC noted:

> The Commission is concerned by the ability of generators to affect spot prices seemingly at will, and is troubled about the relative lack of competitive generator response that has been witnessed over this period ... The Commission is of the view that some generators in the NEM possess substantial market power. Further, the Commission recognises that under some circumstances, the current market rules enable such generators to take advantage of that power in their pursuit of profits. To date such behaviour has fallen within the market rules[29]

However, the ACCC refused to change the rules to the extent requested by NECA. It accepted generating-company arguments against the change, and said that "it did not accept that the benefits of the rejected changes would outweigh the anti-competitive detriment." It argued that price manipulation had to be dealt with in other ways, such as structural changes to the industry and the removal of barriers to encourage more competition.[30]

South Australia

South Australia (SA) imports about 30 per cent of its electricity from Victoria. This is because fuel costs in SA are high, and in the past it was often cheaper to buy electricity from Victoria than generate it locally. The state was reluctant to replace these convenient arrangements with Victoria with participation in a national market. Booth notes that it was only because of "intense pressure" and financial incentives from the Commonwealth government and other states that SA agreed to restructure its electricity industry and then join NEM.[31]

The Olsen Liberal government corporatised the Electricity Trust of South Australia (ETSA) in 1995 and allocated its generation assets to a new corporation, Optima Energy, in 1997. In 1998 ETSA was further separated into three companies to comply with the requirements of the national market: ElectraNet SA for transmission, ETSA Utilities for distribution, and ETSA Power for retail supply. Optima Energy was also split into three generating companies.[32]

It argued that privatisation was necessary to eliminate risks to taxpayers associated with NEM and to enable the SA government to pay off its debts. The business community and various think tanks also pressed for electricity privatisation, including the Institute of Public Affairs (IPA) and the SA

Centre for Economic Studies. Nevertheless polls showed that there was massive community opposition.[33]

The Olsen government had been re-elected in 1997 after promising not to privatise ETSA and Optima. However, within weeks it reneged and announced the sale. The SA Labor Party and the Democrats opposed the sale. Trade Unions, Friends of the Earth, the SA Council of Social Services, and various church and community groups took part in the Save ETSA Campaign. A candlelight vigil was held to oppose the privatisation and remind people of the blackouts that had been experienced in Auckland.[34] Privatisation was "one of the most unpopular decisions in recent South Australian political history". A 1999 television poll found 70 per cent of people in SA were strongly opposed to it, and the government lost office in the following election in 2002.[35]

The sale was promoted as a debt-reduction measure and the debt was portrayed as being out of control. In fact, the state debt was "at historically low levels". Opponents argued that ETSA brought hundreds of millions of dollars in dividends each year that would be lost by privatisation, and that the sale price would not adequately compensate for this loss of income. The Save ETSA Campaign commissioned an economic study which showed that ETSA would have to be sold for over $7 billion to make up for the loss of dividends over ten years, but the government expected to sell it for $4-6 billion.[36] The United Trades and Labor Council stated: "The Government's economic argument for the sale was always dubious and no one was convinced that it was anything other than a political and ideological decision."[37]

ETSA had contributed some $2 billion to state revenue over the previous decade, and its operating costs had decreased significantly.[38] Economist Richard Blandy later confirmed in 2002 that "revenues earned by ETSA for the South Australian government before it was privatised would match, if not exceed, the interest on South Australian debt retired as a result of ETSA's sale. Hence, South Australians now face historically high electricity prices compared with the rest of Australia for no net benefit to the state government finances."[39] Similarly, Australian National University economist John Quiggan agreed that "privatisation of the South Australian electricity industry has reduced the net worth of the public sector ... the interest savings on the sale price will fall consistently short of the earnings foregone through privatisation. This is consistent with most Australian experience of privatisation."[40]

The Labor opposition pointed out that the debt was like a house mortgage: whilst people could eliminate their mortgages by selling their house, there was no point in doing so if there were no problems in making repayments. ETSA claimed that the cost of splitting electricity generation into just two companies was up to $40 million per year because of duplicated services and loss of economies of scale. Splitting it further would cost even more.[41]

In an effort to gain public acceptance for the sale the government ran a major publicity campaign, referred to as "Project Crocodile" that included the Premier making appearances on prime-time television to persuade viewers. The government also threatened a $183 levy on electricity bills, increases in state taxes and budget cuts if the sale did not go ahead.[42] Business people and *The Advertiser* newspaper also campaigned for privatisation and a group of business leaders ran a full-page advertisement that presented the alarmist message that without the sale of ETSA "Taxes will rise. Business will leave. Jobs will go". Eventually two ALP MPs crossed the floor and enabled the government to have the numbers to pass the privatisation legislation.[43]

In 1999 the various parts of the former ETSA were leased for 200 years for $5.3 billion. Leasing, rather than outright sale, was a compromise necessary to win enough support in parliament, including the support of an independent member who had the balance of power in the upper house. The lessees were given operational control. ETSA Utilities and ETSA Power were leased to Hong Kong Electric, one of the two major utilities in Hong Kong, for $3.5 billion. (The same company has since bought generation and distribution facilities in Victoria.) The lease for the retailing company, ETSA Power, was then sold to AGL. The generating companies were leased for low prices compared with sale prices in Victoria.[44]

After privatisation the NEM pool prices for SA increased, and were much higher than for other participating states. In 2000 pool prices for SA were more than double those for Victoria and NSW.[45] The SA independent industry regulator, Lew Owens, claimed "Everyone assumed the market would drive prices down, but it is driving them up … This could have a serious negative effect on the South Australia economy."[46]

Prices spike during the heat of each summer. Between 1994 and 2002, residential rates increased by 40 per cent. Householders then paid more for their electricity than anywhere else in Australia, 30 per cent more than in non-privatised NSW (compared with 10 per cent more pre-privatisation and the opening of markets). Prices in SA have since increased even more with the start of retail 'competition'. AGL, which supplies households, complained in mid-April 2001 that it had been unable to secure long-term contracts with generators at anywhere near the wholesale prices in their previous contracts.[47]

When some 2800 middle-sized businesses became contestable and had their electricity prices deregulated in July 2001, they experienced price increases of between 30 and 80 per cent. Pool prices had begun to soar, and the privatised generators were reluctant to enter into new contracts at fixed prices. In early 2001 only 10 per cent of the state's major employers had been able to secure new electricity contracts to cover them when their old ones expired. Those with new contracts faced heavy price increases.[48]

Large businesses, which originally pushed for privatisation and deregulation, found that they were worse off. Although prices in South Australia were always high for households, big businesses in SA had some of the cheapest electricity rates in Australia before privatisation. However, by July 2001 their prices had increased by 25 per cent above inflation rates. Spot prices were so high that "a new summer pastime has grown in SA called 'curtailment', a term used to describe a situation where a business might find the cost of electricity so high they can make more money by shutting down their operation and on-selling the power they would have used".[49]

One of the key businesspeople behind the push for privatisation, Hugh Morgan (see previous chapter), complained that his company, WMC, which was SA's largest electricity user, was paying $10 million too much for power. Morgan had threatened to buy electricity from interstate sources unless ETSA was privatised, believing that privatisation would reduce prices. Journalists in *The Advertiser* reported: "Business, which originally was gung-ho in its support of the ETSA deal — even to the point of publicly attacking opponents — is now wary of the benefits of the national market and the effects on profitability and future employment prospects in SA."[50]

Some blamed NEM, pointing out that prices had also gone up in NSW for some businesses, despite continued state ownership of electricity. SA treasurer Rob Lucas argued: "If the State Government had retained ownership in SA the only way it would have been able to contain rising prices would have been to use taxpayer dollars to subsidise electricity prices". And he pointed out that when the NSW government had tried to do this it was investigated for possible anti-competitive practices.[51]

Some blamed undersupply for the severe problems in SA, but Booth notes that: "On any given day, large amounts of capacity are available, but not offered to be loaded ... NEMMCo [the National Electricity Market Management Company that operates NEM] issues 'low reserve' warnings for the South Australian region at an alarming rate, and many of them at times when demand is low and ample capacity obviously exists." He points out that capacity withdrawal is a particular problem in South Australia, where pool prices exceeded $4000/MWh 6.3 per cent of the time in 1999-

2000 at varying levels of demand. If a generating company has more than one generating unit, it can increase the price by withdrawing one unit.[52]

In fact, in the summer of 2000-1, when SA was suffering shortages and blackouts, SA power companies were selling power to Victoria under instruction by NEMMCO. Victoria's shortages were caused by union strike action over proposed worker redundancies. Prices on the market soared to the $5000 cap, and SA's privatised companies made millions selling electricity to Victoria whilst 35,000 SA households went without power.[53] "The US-owned Torrens Island B power station alone generated $8.4 million in revenue on Thursday [2 November 2000]—up from $75,000 the previous Thursday."[54] The Osborne power station made $3.8 million the same day. The publisher of *Electric Week* observed, "this is a business where you can make a fortune in just one day".[55]

That summer, electricity bills soared and blackouts were frequent.

Hardly a week goes by without a new revelation in the press about problems in the power industry. During the recent hot summer, SA had an unprecedented number of blackouts as the privatised local power generation plants and interstate connections failed to keep up with demand. The solution proposed by electricity retailer AGL was that the public should switch off air conditioners in hot weather![56]

Fuses and transformers across SA failed, and transmission across high-voltage lines was deliberately cut off to avoid potential fires on very hot days. There were 500 outages in January 2001 alone. In the face of rising community anger, state treasurer Rob Lucas was censured by a majority vote in parliament for "mishandling" the power crisis.[57]

Owens claimed that the network was outdated and neglected, and unions claimed that the 900 workers employed to check and repair powerlines in 1991 had been reduced to about 300, whilst maintenance crews were reduced from 270 to 90. According to SA auditor-general Ken McPherson, the leasing arrangements did not require companies leasing generating facilities to upgrade or even maintain those facilities. And certainly the market provided no incentive to do so.[58]

Before privatisation, ETSA had special-purpose maintenance teams which monitored transformers and replaced them before they failed, so that there was minimal interruption to the electrical supply. One theory for the increased failure of transformers after privatisation is that these teams were discontinued; instead, transformers were left in place till they failed, giving them a slightly longer life of a year or two. This would have saved money at the expense of reliability. Also, the life of a transformer can be increased by down-rating it so it does not run at full load and does not get so hot. This could be done by installing lower-rated fuses in the transformer boxes on suburban power poles that would blow before they reached full load. The power supply would be cut, but the fuse could be replaced rather than the transformer—a much cheaper option at $10 per fuse.[59]

Indeed, many of the interruptions to power supply in South Australia in 2000-1 were being caused by transformer fuses blowing. In just one night in February 2001, fuses blew on 45 transformers, cutting electricity to 750 homes—which wasn't restored for up to two hours. The previous summer, 270 fuses went in a couple of months, cutting power to 3000 homes. ETSA Utilities responded by blaming air conditioners, which put too much load on the fuses.[60]

Consequences in South Australia

The Australian Retailers Association's executive director, Stirling Griff, argued that shop-owners were having to shut up shop, losing substantial amounts in sales, because of low capacity and power failures caused by aging equipment that could not cope with the hot weather. This situation had been unheard of a few years before: "We might well have a lower state debt due to the sale of our power assets but at what long-term cost to business and the community?"[61]

Hospitals considered the possibility of switching to generator power during peak periods to be sure of a continuous electricity supply. There was "a mini-boom in generator sales to guarantee power supplies" in readiness for the following summer. ETSA Utilities replaced 2000 fuses and 475 transformers, and upgraded fourteen substations, in an effort to prevent some of the blackouts that had occurred the previous summer. Nevertheless, it underspent its predicted capital outlays for the financial year, a figure on which its regulated pricing levels were based.[62]

Additionally, it was reported that power supplies were not being kept at 240 volts and that, as a result, equipment—particularly that powered by induction motors—was being damaged. Industries at risk included primary industries, car manufacturers, and water supply. The low voltages were a result of deteriorating supply networks. In one area, Barossa, some 40 reports of equipment damage resulting from low voltage occurred in 2000.[63]

However, equipment failures were not the only reason for the blackouts. The inability or unwillingness of generators to meet peak demand was another reason. For this situation, many blamed the failure to open the Riverlink interconnector with NSW. In 1994, before it was privatised, ETSA predicted electricity shortages were imminent. One proposal for solving this problem was to have an electricity interconnection with NSW, which had excess capacity. In 1995 a memorandum of understanding was signed by NSW and SA ministers. However, Riverlink was knocked on the head once the SA government decided to privatise ETSA in 1998. Privatisation advisers told the government that the link would halve the value of the state's electricity assets because it would expose SA generators to competition from NSW.[64]

The SA election of 2002 was dominated by the issue of electricity prices and blackouts. The opposition Labor Party leader, Mike Rann, negotiated with the NSW premier in the lead-up to the election to fast-track Riverlink if he was elected. However, electricity companies with a vested interest in the link not going ahead embarked on legal action to oppose it.[65]

The Labor Party was elected on promises to do something about soaring electricity prices, including instituting large fines for failure to meet reliability and maintenance standards — to prevent breakdowns that lead to blackouts — and capped electricity prices. The incumbent Liberal Party premier, Kevin Foley, "accused Labor of being heavy-handed, saying its actions would only reduce competition.[66] But Rann claimed:

> The state of South Australia's electricity supply is the greatest crisis facing this state's economy. South Australian businesses now face massive electricity increases — averaging 30 per cent but in some cases leaping as high as 80 or 90 per cent, with contract offers locking those prices in for up to five years. Industry says it will cost jobs [and] from January 1, 2003, [when residential rates will be deregulated] every household in the state could face the same skyrocketing power bills.[67]

Following up on his election promises, Rann put in place an Essential Services Commission, chaired by Lew Owens, to determine whether electricity prices were justifiable. This commission was required to consider both fairness to consumers and adequate profit to suppliers.[68] In preparation for the lifting of price controls in 2003, when all households in SA would become contestable, Owens concluded that a maximum 30 per cent rate increase on prices could be justified. In his report he noted: "The Government has indicated it does not intend that this process should be used to set prices at a level below the costs being incurred, nor should it deny retailers the opportunity to make a profit commensurate with the risks."[69] He also noted that some people might think that his cost estimates were too high because of the need to rely on generators and retailers for the information, and that

> undue influence may have been had by retailers and generators who have an interest in the costs being high. However, if AGL SA adopts higher numbers than justified, it faces a real prospect of losing large numbers of customers to other retailers who will price below AGL SA—and it may never recover those customers.[70]

Such a prospect is not imminent since all households are supplied by one company, AGL, a decision that was made by the previous government to maximise the sale price of ETSA's retail division. The only other company that was showing any interest in becoming a competing electricity supplier was Origin Energy, which is the monopoly gas supplier in SA and a major electricity supplier in Victoria.[71]

Welfare groups immediately warned that such a large rate rise would drive some 100,000 households below the poverty line and further disadvantage people with chronic illnesses and disabilities. They called for the government to extend subsidies from pensioners and welfare recipients with dependents to all welfare recipients and low-income households. The new government, however, ruled out subsidies, which Victoria had introduced in January 2001, because SA could not afford them. It did attempt, however, to secure funds from the federal government for subsidies.[72]

AGL decided on a 25 per cent price rise for 2003 which was reduced to 23.7 per cent by the Essential Services Commission. The newly elected Rann government argued that there was little it could do about this. It claimed that the option of delaying deregulation of the retail market, and having price caps as in NSW and Queensland, was not open in SA's privatised system because of the contracts with the private companies.[73]

The energy minister, Patrick Conlon, said that if the government imposed a lower retail price AGL would not be able to afford its costs, including interest on its investment, dividends to shareholders, and wholesale electricity costs, and would be bankrupted. Conlon argued that AGL had a right to a reasonable return on its investment, and blamed the previous government for selling the government assets for such a high amount that a reasonable return meant high electricity prices.[74] However, he also suggested that: "New competition in retail is on track that should put downward pressure on price", which contradicted the claim that AGL was charging the lowest it possibly could.[75]

However, the promise that competition will bring prices down sounds eerily familiar to South Australians, who were told that prices would fall when they joined the national electricity market and found that they in fact increased dramatically.

When wholesale prices decreased in NEM, AGL was left with long-term contracts entered into whilst prices were high. It sought to pass on the cost of that mistake to consumers. Similarly, many businesses had signed up to long-term contracts with AGL only to see wholesale prices fall. They claimed that they had been pressured by AGL to sign the contracts if they wanted a guaranteed supply, but now many of them wanted to get out of them. Business SA chief executive Peter Vaughan argued: "There should be a legislative provision to retrospectively assess the contracts." Owens said he would look into the contracts, but that it was "very difficult for the Government to overturn commercial contracts freely entered into by two businesses."[76]

Businesses in regional SA are also finding that the cost of getting electricity connections or augmenting their electricity supply is often so expensive that it is "holding back development". Before privatisation the cost of extending the electricity infrastructure was paid for by the state-owned electricity authority. However, the Hong Kong-based owner of the transmission system is only willing to add to infrastructure if it is likely to get a large return. On the other hand, consumers across SA are unlikely to be willing to pay higher rates to "upgrade and expand a grid run by a private company." So the individual consumer has to pay the full cost.[77]

At the end of 2002 Flinders Osborne Trading, a subsidiary of US-based NRG Energy Inc., claimed it could not afford to pay the $4.5 million gas bill for the Osborne Power Station at Port Adelaide and that, unless the state government paid it within 24 hours, the company would go into voluntary liquidation. In the end, the parent company paid the bill; but it, too, is near bankruptcy. If it goes under, the SA government will be faced with some $140 million in liabilities. The irony is that another of the company's assets, Flinders power station at Port Augusta, is profitable, and energy expert Robert Booth had accused it of withholding power just the week before so as to make $2.17 million profits during a heatwave when the wholesale electricity price went from $59/MWh to $3102/MWh.[78]

CHAPTER FIFTEEN

Australia-Wide Deregulation

It takes a blackout to see the light.
Anonymous[1]

IN 1995, the state governments in Australia agreed to facilitate the private provision of public infrastructure, including electricity. The initial reluctance of the states had been overcome by incentive payments of $16 billion from the federal government. A National Competition Council was set up to oversee restructuring and deregulation.[2]

In each state the generation, transmission, distribution, and retail supply of electricity were separated and corporatised. Barriers to interstate trade were removed, and open access to electricity networks established. However, privatisation met with strong community opposition in most states. A 1994 Saulwick *Age* national poll had found that over two-thirds of those surveyed favoured public ownership, and an EPAC study the same year had also found that most Australians supported government provision of infrastructure.[3]

New South Wales

The Electricity Commission of NSW was created in 1950 to generate and transmit bulk electricity to existing electricity distributors. It became Pacific Power in 1992, after it was reorganised into separate business units with a commercial focus by the Greiner Liberal government. In 1995, under the newly elected Labor government, the transmission function was allocated to a separate organisation as required by the Competition Principles Agreement between the Commonwealth and the states. Distribution and supply, which had been undertaken by 25 local authorities, was amalgamated into six supply companies in 1995. The generation function was split into three in 1996 by allocating it to two state-owned corporatised companies—Macquarie Generation and Delta Electricity—while 20 per cent capacity remained with Pacific Power, which was still a statutory authority.[4]

Those opposed to the break-up of Pacific Power pointed out that three generators would be less efficient and have less investment power in the growing Asian electricity market: "electricity is increasingly a global industry, dominated by big American, British and European utilities which, for the most part, are so huge that they dwarf Pacific Power."[5] However, a break-up was necessary as a precursor to privatisation, to avoid Pacific Power becoming a private monopoly. Also, "the architects of Victoria's privatisation program were concerned that an intact Pacific Power might exert undue market power" in the National Electricity Market (NEM). They were supported in this by the Industries Commission.[6]

From 1996 electricity supply to large industrial consumers (which consumed over 750 MWh/year) was deregulated, and they were able to choose their supplier. Electricity was bought and sold via a power pool from 1996, and the three state-owned generating companies were expected to compete with each other. From July 1998 the supply to 15,000 medium-size business consumers, such as fast-food restaurants, was also deregulated.[7]

Privatisation of the generating and supply companies was and still is very unpopular. The chief executive of Pacific Power, Ross Bunyon, pointed out that Pacific Power supplied cheaper power than the privatised Victorian companies, and was still able to pay an annual dividend to the state government of $550 million.[8] A similar argument was put by researcher Christopher Sheil in 2001 who argued that state profits from the electricity industry would pay "for better schools, better hospitals, better public transport and roads, a cleaner environment …"[9]

However, the opening up of NEM exposed the government to commercial risks associated with wildly fluctuating prices that it was reluctant to take on. And it was these risks that were used as the main argument for privatisation: "taxpayers' funds shouldn't be put in jeopardy".[10]

Towards the end of 1996, the Labor government signalled that it was considering part-privatisation of Pacific Power as a way of raising capital "to survive interstate electricity competition". In August 1997 it released a report from a committee of inquiry headed by Bob Hogg, which called for immediate privatisation whilst acknowledging that privatisation would result in the loss of some 4000 jobs out of 13,500—already a dramatic reduction on the original 26,000 before restructuring. The government also used accounting firm Arthur Andersen to value NSW's electricity industry at $22 billion.[11]

Hogg's recommendations were accepted by the government. All that remained was to get party support at the October state Australian Labor Party (ALP) conference. However, to get agreement, the treasurer, Michael Egan, had to "tear down the last icon of the ALP Left—the party's adherence to the retention of public assets in public hands".[12] The opposition Liberal Party was in favour of privatisation, and premier Carr and his treasurer hoped that they could convince the unions that workers would get better protection if privatisation was undertaken by a Labor government.[13]

ALP polling showed that privatisation was so unpopular that the only thing that would prevent Labor from losing the following election if it went ahead with the policy was that the opposition was also pushing privatisation.

Egan, whom Carr had chosen for the Treasury portfolio precisely because of his tenacity and willingness to dig in against popular clamour, had identified the $25 billion sell-off of the NSW electricity industry as the greatest challenge to State Labor's orthodoxy in the postwar years.[14]

However, the left wing of the party, the left-wing unions, and the right-wing power industry unions formed a coalition to oppose privatisation. The unions were particularly angry because their acceptance of the restructuring of the electricity industry in 1995 had been dependant on a promise from the government that it would not lead to privatisation. Some 200 branches of the ALP in NSW sent delegates to the conference with instructions to vote against privatisation. This ensured that the conference deferred privatisation. In fact, the premier, Bob Carr, was slow-clapped, booed, and hissed for his stance on privatisation.[15]

This did not mark an end to the debate. Carr and Egan and the pro-privatisation forces treated the conference outcome as an obstacle on the way to an inevitable privatisation. They continued to meet with opponents in the following year in the hope of persuading them to change their stance. Hoping to bypass union leaders, they promised electricity workers job protection for three years, relocation, and retraining, and shares in the privatised utilities. However, they were unsuccessful, and by 1998 had withdrawn privatisation from their policy agenda, at least in the short term, because of the "overwhelming" opposition of the electorate.[16]

Unlike the Labor Party, the Liberal Party was able to commit to full privatisation in the 1999 election campaign. It made similar guarantees of three years of job protection to electricity workers, along with a payment of $1000 to every household, or $1100 worth of shares, after privatisation. What is more, it was able to make other election promises worth a billion dollars per year to be paid for by privatisation proceeds.[17] The incumbent government portrayed it as a crude election bribe; but the deputy leader of the Liberals, Ron Phillips, said that the reason that people were opposed to privatisation was that they didn't perceive there to be any "personal or tangible benefit", and that the promises were "aimed at winning the hearts of the [industry's] current owners, the NSW taxpayers".[18]

The Liberal Party's own pollster, Mark Textor, had warned them that privatisation of electricity would lose them the election. On radio talkback shows, privatisation of electricity was the number-one issue, with 70 per cent of callers being opposed to it. People were influenced by the power failure in Auckland and the stories of poor reliability and rising prices in post-privatisation Victoria. Even the majority of small businesses surveyed were opposed to it.[19] And indeed, despite the promised 'bribe', the Liberals lost the election resoundingly, indicating the strength of public feeling against privatisation.

In 2002 a new Liberal Party leader, John Brogden, promised not to privatise the state's electricity. And the Labor government also put its privatisation hopes on hold, with Treasury proposing that, instead, it would allow electricity traders to buy rights to the state's generating output. The price cap on wholesale electricity was to be doubled to $10,000 in April, which would increase the volatility of the market. The idea behind the proposal was to sell the electricity for a set amount for three to five years in advance, and let the traders make the profits and losses on the market.[20]

Because the generators were still state-owned, the NSW government benefited from NEM when prices soared, particularly at peak times. The state's three power-generating companies and six distributors made $764 million in just six months. In contrast, the state's businesses, whose supply had been deregulated, suffered, as businesses did in the other states. Those that had three-year contracts at set prices were finding that, when their contracts ended, the price they had to pay was increasing by 50 per cent.[21]

Nor were the risks confined to retailers and businesses. Pacific Power, one of the NSW generators, got badly burned by the market in 1997. At that time, the earlier version of NEM was operating, with spot prices averaging $10-$30 per MWh.[22] Powercor Australia, a US-owned distributor, had a franchise to supply electricity to consumers in a particular area of Melbourne, and to compete for large consumers in their own and other areas. To do this, it had to buy electricity on the spot market; but the prices for electricity on that market could go a lot higher than Powercor had contracted to sell it for. Prices to householders were regulated at the time, and business consumers demanded fixed-price contracts.

To hedge against the risk that spot prices would exceed regulated and contracted retail prices, Powercor engaged in commodity-derivative contracts or hedge contracts. Powercor had several of these contracts with Pacific Power. When the pool price was above the contract price, Pacific Power paid Powercor the difference; when it was below, Powercor paid Pacific Power the difference (see figure 13.2 on page 235).[23] In this way, Powercor was protected from high pool prices and Pacific Power was protected from low pool prices that were below its cost of production. If the spot price soared, Pacific Power could afford to pay the difference to Powercor because it would receive the higher price for the electricity it generated.

From June 1997, on the advice of people from its American parent company, Powercor also entered into derivative contracts for the purpose of making profits, treating them as a tradeable commodity in their own right that could be sold on to other companies. During 1997 it "made substantial money from its trading". Thirty-five contracts were made between Powercor and Pacific Power altogether.[24]

Unfortunately, in November, temperatures soared during a working day in Victoria. As individuals and businesses tried to cope by turning on their air conditioners, they caused a peak demand in the middle of the day—just when the interconnector between NSW and Victoria was out of action for servicing. This meant that the spike in demand in Victoria could not be met using NSW surplus power; as a result, the price peaked on the Victorian spot market at $4800 per MWh. This meant that Powercor was paying $4800/MWh whilst Pacific Power was unable to sell its power to Victoria and receive the high prices. Nevertheless, Pacific Power was contracted to pay the difference between the spot market price that Powercor had to pay Victorian generators and its own, much lower contracted price to Powercor. (Since it was a hedge contract it was not actually contracted to sell electricity to Powercor, but just to make up the difference in prices.) "By the end of that momentous day, Pacific had lost $9 million, a third of its total profit for that financial year."[25]

After this, Pacific Power attempted to get out of eleven of its contracts with Powercor, but the Supreme Court ruled that it could not. Powercor claimed $50 million for reneging on the contracts, and Pacific Power faced a potential payout of hundreds of millions of dollars in damages.[26]

Nevertheless, despite such instances, the NSW generators have been more profitable than their privatised Victorian counterparts. This has been partly because of the greater debt load of the privatised generators, meaning that NSW generators could make profits from much lower wholesale electricity prices. Because of continued state ownership, average electricity prices in NSW have fallen over the last ten years, in contrast to rising prices in Victoria and South Australia. Average business prices have decreased by 22 per cent and household prices by 11 per cent. This has been facilitated by NSW's equalisation fund: when wholesale prices are low enough for state-owned retailers to make a profit, they put money into an equalisation fund; when wholesale prices are too high to pass onto consumers, the equalisation fund makes up the difference. If there is not enough money in the fund, the state-owned generators make up the shortfall.[27]

In 2000, Pacific Power transferred its remaining generating facilities to a new organisation, Eraring Energy, as part of the "further evolution of the NSW Government's energy reform process". Pacific Power became essentially an engineering services and consultancy company.[28]

Towards the end of 2002 the Carr government proposed an overhaul of the state's electricity industry to protect it from surging prices in NEM. The plan involved vertical integration of generators with retail suppliers. Prices had been going from a normal level of $30 per MWh to over $1700 and up to $7000. The generators were caught out when equipment failures or non-availability prevented them from meeting commitments with their own electricity, and the retailers were caught out when surging demand forced them to buy extra electricity on the spot market. Integration would balance these risks and allow internal "equalisation". However, the ACCC was concerned that this would further concentrate the ownership of electricity in a state where it was already more concentrated than in other states.[29]

The NSW government is also keen to avoid having state companies trading in NEM, because of its attendant risks, and, according to *The Sydney Morning Herald*, is preparing to sell the rights to trade state-generated power as a substitute for privatisation. This was done by the Canadian state government of Alberta which earned over $C3billion in 2000 and 2001 by doing this but then saw electricity prices escalate.[30]

Other States
Queensland
In Queensland the electricity system was also broken up into various corporatised business units. The Liberal-National coalition government which was elected in 1996 committed Queensland to joining NEM, and formed a

Queensland Reform Unit to oversee the restructuring of electricity. These measures seemed unnecessary as the Queensland electricity industry was very efficient, had a surplus of low cost electricity, and "had become the standard that other states aspired to reach". However, a government-commissioned review found that restructuring was necessary for participation in NEM, that participation in NEM was necessary to increase competition, and that "the assets of the industry could be redirected to better use by the state through privatisation of the industry."[31]

Many of the reforms suggested by the Queensland Electricity Industry Structure Task Force and the Electricity Industry Reform Unit were adopted, apart from privatisation. In 1996 the government contracted with private companies to build gas-turbine stations to provide peak load.[32] In 1997 the government generating company Austa Electric was divided into three parts that would compete with each other in an internal market or pool modelled on NEM. Two retail organisations were formed, and large industrial consumers were able to choose their supplier from January 1998.

Early experience with the "Queensland Interim Market" in 1997 was indicative of future trends. Pool prices were so high in the first two months that it had to be stopped and prices imposed. When the pool was reinstated, prices remained high compared with prices in NSW and Victoria at the time. This was at a time when the reserve capacity exceeded peak loads by 25 per cent.[33]

Such bizarre outcomes have their roots in the insistence that government-owned entities behave like private companies and have commercial rather than public service goals. In fact, the high prices obtained in the Queensland interim market sent precisely the wrong commercial signals: they prompted a rush to build gas-turbine power plants and refurbish coal plants during 1998 and 1999 when the demand did not warrant them. The high prices were being caused by capacity withdrawal rather than undercapacity.[34] This has left Queensland with the worst of both worlds — overcapacity and high prices.

The wholesale market was opened to other public and private generators from any state in 2001, when Queensland joined NEM. Booth notes that various favourable aspects of the Queensland system were abandoned in the name of joining the market:

> Thus the state with the proud record of having the lowest electricity generation costs in the nation because of the exceptional performance of its generation sector, was transformed into the state with the highest charges imposed by the same sector — an extraordinary change of circumstances.

The government-owned generators made exceptional profits during that year [financial year 1997/98], and the government-owned retailers made exceptional losses. At the end of the year, State Treasury had to subsidise the retailers to the extent of over $400 million to avoid them reporting large losses.[35]

Privatisation has been politically difficult to achieve in Queensland, partly because of the subsidies to rural users that would be threatened by any selloff, and partly because the industry paid handsome dividends to the government — $850 million in 1997. Also, the Queensland government used electricity as a way of "shaping regional development" through offering cheap electricity to attract industry, such as the Korea Zinc smelter in Townsville. There was also a parochial motive. In 1997 opposition Labor leader Peter Beattie asked whether Queensland wanted to be run from Melbourne or even further afield: "What's to stop the whole Australian industry being owned from America or England and they don't give a stuff about what happens in Australia?"[36]

Since winning government and becoming Queensland premier, Beattie has ruled out privatisation of electricity. Queensland has also put off deregulating the retail electricity market. This is mainly because it would involve unravelling the cross-subsidies offered to rural residents. Government studies show that "customers in 10 out of 12 regions in Queensland would pay more if prices were deregulated, some as much as three times what they currently pay", and this would be politically unacceptable.[37] However, Energex, the state-owned retailer, sells electricity into other states that have been opened to competition, and retailers in other states say that this distorts the market.

Tasmania

Tasmania's electricity is generated by low cost hydro-electric power. However, the low cost of electricity is at the expense of wilderness areas in the state. Other states have not been able to take advantage of the cheap and plentiful electricity in Tasmania because there has been no interconnector between the island state and the mainland. However, a link, known as Basslink, has been given approval, and is expected to be commissioned in 2005.[38]

In 1998 the Liberal government made privatisation a major election issue in Tasmania when it proposed privatisation of the Hydroelectric Commission (HEC). Premier Tony Rundle proposed that the retail and transmission sections be sold and the generating assets leased for 99 years, arguing that HEC debt was weighing the state down. The government claimed that the $4.4 billion it would receive from the sale would not only erase government debt but would also leave it with a billion dollars cash.[39] As elsewhere, privatisation was supposed to bring prices down.

Employment in the HEC had already been cut by over 40 per cent, and productivity had been increased by a similar amount. Economist Clive Hamilton, head of the Australia Institute, pointed out that privatisation made little sense, because the efficiency gains had already been achieved, and splitting up the HEC would merely destroy economies of scale available to a centralised organisation.[40]

The Labor Party opposed the privatisation, arguing that the HEC was not only paying off its debt but was contributing revenue to the government which would amount to $2 billion over the next eleven years if it stayed in government hands. Although the public was concerned about debt, a newspaper survey found that only 22 per cent supported privatisation. As a result, Labor won the 1998 election, in which electricity privatisation was a key issue.[41]

Nevertheless, in preparation for joining the national electricity market, the government still went ahead and restructured the HEC by dividing it into three government-owned entities. Transmission was split off to Transend Networks, and Aurora Energy took over distribution and supply. The Hydro-Electric Corporation (HEC) retained responsibility for generation.[42]

Australian Capital Territory

In the Australian Capital Territory (ACT) the Carnell government attempted to privatise the ACT Electricity and Water Authority (ACTEW) by commissioning a report by consultants ABN AMRO, which found that privatisation would improve prices and service. However, the Australia Institute disputed the consultant's report, arguing that the report was based on "accounting errors" and inconsistent analysis that made the government's "current fiscal position look as bad as possible and the benefits of privatisation as large as possible".[43]

The campaign against privatisation of ACTEW was coordinated by the ACT Trades and Labour Council, and included a mass rally. Opinion polls showed that most people in the ACT opposed privatisation, and in 1999 the Legislative Assembly voted against it.[44] In 2002 the government came under pressure to deregulate its retail electricity market and open it up to competition. An Independent Competition and Regulation Commission report, which recommended the move, admitted that average household power bills would increase by 7 to 9 per cent, but argued that this would be offset by the lowering of business bills by 3 per cent and "future benefits such as more responsive and flexible prices, the possibility of more innovative products, a greater range of products, and consumer choice." The report suggested that the government would need to have a "public-education campaign" prior to deregulating the retail market but warned that, if it did not deregulate, millions of dollars in incentive payments from the federal government would be at risk. It also warned that introducing price caps into a deregulated market would produce a Californian situation.[45]

■ **Figure 15.1: Average retail prices by state, 2001–2002**

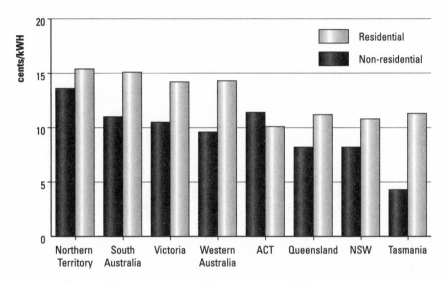

Source: Electricity Supply Association of Australia, 'Industry Data', 2002. http://www.esaa.com.au/store/page.pl?id=1281

Western Australia

In 2001 the newly elected WA Labor government decided to deregulate the electricity market and split Western Power's generation from distribution and retail supply. (It is uncertain at this stage whether deregulation will eventually lead to full privatisation.) The opposition Liberal leader expressed support for the restructuring in August 2002,[46] and it was endorsed by the Chamber of Commerce and Industry. The aim was to create "a market structure which is conducive to private-sector investment" because this would lower electricity prices and create jobs. Corporations such as Wesfarmers were pushing for privatisation, with the argument that public ownership meant higher prices: "I think the evidence of privatisation is that no matter how efficient a public [institution] believes it is, private ownership makes it more efficient."[47]

Consultants and Advisers

Whilst consumers, particularly residential ones, have gained little from privatisation and deregulation, a whole raft of advisers, consultants, merchant bankers, and stockbrokers have been enriched, as have some foreign companies and their executives. Consultants and advisers were paid about $160 million in the process of energy privatisation in Victoria alone, and the potential for lucrative consultancies ensured an active constituency for privatisation. The banks, including Macquarie Bank, Merrill Lynch, and Credit Suisse First Boston, were also major beneficiaries of privatisation, making millions from advice and consultancies.[48]

Consultants and advisers received tens of millions of dollars for advice on the privatisation of electricity in SA, as they had in Victoria. Investment Bank Morgan Stanley alone was expected to be paid some $20 million by 2000. The final estimate for consultants for the sale was over $110 million.[49]

Peter Troughton, who headed the Victorian Reform Unit, and his private consultancy firm Troughton Swier and Associates, were also primary consultants on the privatisation of the gas and aluminium industries. Troughton was said to be a trusted associate of premier Kennett and treasurer Stockdale. His firm earned millions for its advice on privatisation, $6 million in the first eighteen months of a contract to provide a project-management service that included "reform and restructuring of the energy sector", privatisation, and the introduction of competition. The contract was not put out to tender and so was not subject to competition itself.[50]

Project Victoria—the propaganda project for Victorian privatisation devised by Michael Porter's Tasman Institute—"continued to have an independent policy role, including high level annual meetings with business and community groups, the Premier, Treasurer and key sector Ministers."[51] Porter and his institute were commissioned by various international agencies, including the World Bank, APEC, the ADB, and AusAID to do work on infrastructure reform in developing countries. In 2000 Porter joined forces with Nick Morris of London Economics (Australia) to form Tasman Economics. Nick Morris was formerly in charge of research at the Institute for Fiscal Studies (IFS), where he had been involved with the privatisation of British Telecoms, British Gas, and rail privatisation. In 1986 he co-founded London Economics, which claims to have "played a key role in UK privatisation". For example, Morris advised the Electricity Area Boards and Scottish Hyro-electric during privatisation of electricity in the UK. He also helped develop independent power projects and helped with the design of the software for the power pool.[52]

London Economics was one of the leading consultants on the deregulation of Australia's government enterprises from 1989 to 1992. It worked with various state governments, and had "a strong influence on the utility reform process in Australia". It was a consultant for the restructuring of the State Electricity Commission of Victoria, Melbourne Water, and the Victorian Gas and Fuel Corporation. It advised the Queensland government on the sale of electricity generation, and led Queensland's electricity Industry Structure Task Force from 1996-98. It also advised the NSW government on privatisation of the electricity industry in 1997, and advised the Industry Commission on electricity-market reform in NSW in 1998.[53]

London Economics has also been involved in electricity and water industry restructuring in a number of other countries, including India (investigation for the World Bank), Malaysia, Thailand, Indonesia, and New Zealand. Morris has advised companies in France, Germany, Italy, and Spain on the impact of deregulation. Porter also advised Asian countries on privatisation. In 1997 he completed a report on the Southern Economic Focal Zone of the Socialist Republic of Vietnam, in which he recommended restructuring and privatisation of electricity, transport, and water.[54]

The newly formed Tasman Economics claims expertise in a number of areas, including corporatisation and privatisation, because of their experience in developing and implementing "models of private sector participation in the provision of infrastructure throughout Australia and Asia, including water and sewerage, electricity and transport". It has played a lead advisory role in "private sector participation in the Philippines, Indonesia and most recently Thailand." In particular, Tasman's claimed expertise included:

- Reforming public works and water and electricity sector entities;
- Unbundling existing institutions in the water and energy sectors; and
- Identifying areas where there could be private sector involvement.[55]

Its personnel, apart from Porter and Morris, include several people who once worked for the Industry Commission, including a former managing director John Zeitsch, who also held a senior position at the OECD. Its clients include the Asian Development Bank, the OECD, and the World Bank; business groups such as the Australian Industry Group and the NZ Business Roundtable; private companies including AGL, BHP, Shell Australia, and WMC; and electricity companies Citipower and Powercor. It has also worked for various electricity commissions and corporations in New Zealand, Australia, and Asia, as well as governments and government departments in

Australia and Asia, including Indonesia, the Philippines, Thailand, and Vietnam.[56]

Jan McMahon, secretary of the Public Service Association, argues that the main reason governments employ consultants to restructure public services, rather than doing it themselves, is to ensure that their work can be kept "commercial-in-confidence" to prevent it being made public through freedom of information requests and public inquiries.[57] The SA auditor general noted: "management arrangements for the disposal of ETSA Utilities and ETSA Power have significantly diluted the accountability obligations normally required of Advisers in a transaction of this nature".[58]

Consultants and advisers, particularly those from think tanks, have played a dual role: first, promoting privatisation as a scheme that will benefit everyone, and then reaping a good share of the benefits themselves in fees for advising on how to do it. Having been successful at this in Australia, some of them are now repeating their 'successes' in developing countries, as we will see in part 5.

Clinging to a Flawed System
Despite reams of consultants' advice to the contrary, prices went up after privatisation and deregulation. In general, the owners of the transmission and distribution networks have made very large profits, much higher than have been earned by most listed companies in Australia.[59] This has been at the expense of consumers.

The rush of new companies undercutting each other to acquire customers has not happened. Rather, as in the United States and the United Kingdom, the industry is consolidating amongst existing companies who are seeking to cushion themselves against market fluctuations and become big enough to avoid competition. "Very large amounts of money have been spent by NEMMCo and the retailers—reputed to exceed $200 million for New South Wales alone—for very little result. At the end of March [2002], the number of customers changing suppliers is less than 0.1 per cent of total customers in both New South Wales and Victoria."[60] In Victoria, the only householders changing suppliers seem to be those moving house. The others don't see any point.[61]

Apart from householders, the environment appears to be another loser. The amount of electricity generated by brown coal plants, the most polluting in terms of greenhouse gases and other emissions, has increased from about 23 per cent to 31 per cent of sources since 1992 (see figure 15.2). The increasing dependence on brown coal is because deregulation causes companies to seek the cheapest source of electricity with no consideration for environmental impacts. Brown coal is cheap, and dirty, old brown coal plants that have paid off their loans can produce electricity at low marginal costs.

■ **Figure 15.2: Source of electricity in the National Electricity Market**

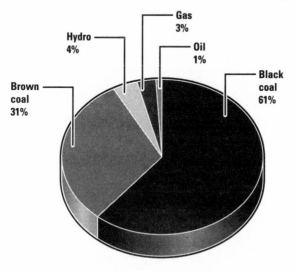

Source: NEMMCO. 'An Introduction to Australia's National Electricity Market.' March 2001. p. 4.

■ **Figure 15.3: Australian net carbon dioxide emissions in MT, 1990-1998**

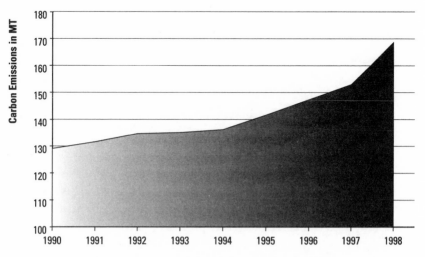

Source: The Australia Institute. 'Submission to the COAG Energy Market Review.' Canberra. 18 April 2002, p. 7.

A report commissioned by electricity distributor Origin Energy found that this meant that Victorian brown coal plants had, to a certain extent, displaced the cleaner NSW black coal plants and SA gas plants in electricity generation. Even outside Victoria baseload electricity tends to be generated by old coal plants rather than the newer gas-fired plants that emit less carbon dioxide. The latter tend to be used for peak loads because marginal costs are higher.[62] As a result, greenhouse emissions have increased in Australia (see figure 15.3). Additionally, Australia remains "one of the least energy efficient countries in the world", according to John Connor, from the Australian Conservation Foundation.[63]

As in Britain, financial incentives offered to power companies to use renewable energy are not working. A mandatory target for 2 per cent of electricity to be sourced from renewable energy by 2010 introduced in 2001. The Australian EcoGeneration Association claims that this Mandated Renewable Energy Target program is wasting more than a billion dollars paying incentives to existing generating facilities, such as hydroelectric power stations, which are neither using the money towards new investments nor pollution reduction.[64] At the end of 2002 a government inquiry recommended that the program be terminated.[65]

Yet consumer demand is insufficient to provide market incentives for increases in the use of renewable energy. At the end of 2002 the number of households in Australia willing to pay $1 a day extra for 'green' power was only 62,000 — less than 1 per cent. Even so, many were on a waiting list, as generating companies were failing to keep up with even this small demand.[66]

The federal government appears to have decided to put resources into cleaner coal technology rather than renewable energy sources. The government's chief scientist, Robin Batterham, who also works for mining giant Rio Tinto as their chief technologist, has been promoting this view, according to the *Sydney Morning Herald*. The government cut $10 million from the Co-operative Research Centre for Renewable Energy whilst providing $70 million to four research centres that Rio Tinto is involved with — including one researching the sustainability of brown coal — and $35 million directly to Rio Tinto to establish a Foundation for the Minerals Industry. [67]

The big users of electricity in Australia — aluminium, black coal, cement, paper, and glass — were the consumers that gained most from the reform process during the 1990s before NEM prices began to escalate.[68] The gains from competition in the 1990s were so "captured by the upstream sectors of the industry" that there were none left for residential consumers.[69] Additionally, aluminium smelters, which consume 16 per cent of all

Australian electricity, have been exempted from having to buy their electricity from NEM, according to Clive Hamilton from the Australia Institute. Because of their strong lobbying, they do not have to face the vagaries of the market; instead, they have been guaranteed fixed prices for their electricity which, in effect, are subsidised by other ratepayers.[70]

However, in more recent years wholesale and retail electricity prices have risen, wiping out even the gains to industrial consumers. The Energy Users Association of Australia (EUAA), whose members are businesses that spend more than $2 million per year on electricity and gas, including Alcoa, Boral, Caltex, Comalco, Exxon Mobil Oil, Foster's, Holden, Nestle, and Orica, complained that prices in 2002 were "now back at pre-reform levels".[71]

Another ad hoc group of large industrial energy users, including WMC, BHP Billiton, and Holden, outlined NEM's deficiencies in a 2002 submission, including:

- High wholesale electricity prices—which are well above competitive levels and have risen to pre-NEM levels whilst electricity production costs had fallen, including the cost of fuel, labour and capital;
- Volatile electricity prices;
- High retail prices—resulting from high wholesale prices and volatility;
- High cost of introducing retail competition;
- Reliability of supply—"deficient, compared with previous Australian standards" and tenuous in South Australia and Victoria
- Inadequate investment in generation—except in Queensland where artificially high prices have fostered over-investment. This lack of investment has been despite wholesale prices being "above those needed to support new power station investments";
- Lack of interconnections—because no-one takes responsibility for congestion;
- The exercise of market power—"Australia does not, and can never have, sufficient independent ownership and competition in the generation sector" to prevent this happening; and
- Absence of policy objectives—the electricity code "was written on the assumption that effective competitive market conditions would exist and that this would be sufficient for benefits to be achieved" and so it failed "to set out proper public policy objectives"[72]

Despite all this evidence that deregulation and privatisation had not delivered their promised benefits, the 'liberalisation mantra' continued to be espoused, even by those businesses that were suffering. They seemed to believe that their problems would be solved if only there were more competition in electricity markets. The EUAA had been formed to ensure that there was no backsliding on reforms and to be a voice for business users on issues such as environmental measures—ensuring that they "cause minimum economic damage".[73] In a press release at the end of 2001, the executive director of EUAA, Roman Domanski, said:

> There was a solid commitment to energy reform from both the Commonwealth and the States in the early and mid-1990s, but the job was left incomplete and the full benefits have never been delivered to energy-using industries ... As a result, their energy costs have never been reduced to genuinely competitive levels and, recently, market pressures and inefficiencies have taken their toll, reversing many of the earlier price reductions.[74]

In 2002 advocates of electricity 'liberalisation' were becoming increasingly concerned that there was some backsliding on the reforms.[75] Victoria was imposing price controls, South Australia was setting up a new regulator—the Essential Services Commission—while Queensland has decided to delay retail deregulation. Alan Mitchell noted in the *Australian Financial Review* in 2002 that the drift back to regulation was an easy path:

> First, they come under pressure to regulate to protect consumers, which increases the cost pressures on retailers. Then, to protect the retailers and consumers, they have to regulate the producers. And, before they know it, they are on the road back to the sort of inefficiency that provoked reform in the first place—the kind of inefficiency that gives states a bad name with investors.[76]

During 2002 the Council of Australian Governments (COAG) conducted a review of NEM, calling for submissions from interested parties with the aim of "identifying any impediments to the full realisation of the benefits of energy market reform" as well as "identifying strategic directions for further energy market reform". Whilst claiming that "Australia can be proud of its reforms so far", COAG's review identified some deficiencies in the energy market, including excessive regulation, perceptions of conflict of interest, excessive generator market power and power-pool volatility, fragmented transmission-network planning, and ad hoc responses to greenhouse-gas emissions. To remedy these deficiencies, it recommended that a national energy regulator be created in place of the various state regulatory bodies.[77] But it failed to recommend any significant changes to the structure of the market. (Three out of four people on the review panel had strong past or present ties to the fossil-fuel industry, including chair Warwick Parer, a director of two coal-mining companies and the Queensland Coal Mine Management company.[78])

COAG noted that generators exercising market power "can send power prices close to $10,000 MWh, and cause extreme pool price volatility. Even five hours a year at $10,000 can increase annual pool prices by over 15 per cent." It also noted that the hedge contracts that were supposed to protect market participants from the volatility of the pool were hard to come by, especially since intermediaries such as Enron had largely withdrawn from the Australian market. Nevertheless, it decided that the one-sided, compulsory, ex-UK-style power pool had "important advantages that should be kept". These supposed advantages included easy access for new market entrants and lower system costs.[79]

COAG argued that one of the reasons that hedge contracts were not available was the existence of the Electricity Tariff Equalisation Fund in NSW and the benchmark pricing scheme in Queensland, both put in place to protect consumers from market price fluctuations without resorting to financial derivatives. COAG therefore recommended that these schemes be abolished. COAG also admitted that generator market power increased contract risk, which discouraged intermediaries from entering the market. But its only solution to the problem of market power was to call for "NSW and possibly Queensland generators" to be "further disaggregated" and thereby create more competition.[80]

Advocates have long insisted that deregulation and privatisation would lead to electricity price reductions. However, COAG now claimed that government-imposed price caps were keeping retail electricity prices "artificially low" and that they should be removed. It argued that "full retail competition" be opened in all states so that prices could rise sufficiently to make investment in new generating facilities attractive.[81]

This was also an argument made by the Australian Chamber of Commerce and Industry (ACCI), the peak council of Australian business associations. It argued that "while prices suppressed by regulatory intervention may have short term political appeal" this would lead, in the long term, to "diminished investment in necessary generation capacity and delivery infrastructures."[82] In fact, COAG's recommendations were very much in line with those in ACCI's submission to the review. ACCI, like other business organizations, argued for a continuation of the 'reform' process:

> While some may be tempted to slow the reform process, even reverse toward the
> old central-planning model, commerce and industry believes the better, longer

term approach is to press ahead with the completion of an efficient, competitive NEM before 2005 … $A1 billion [is] available to be realised by pressing ahead with further reforms.[83]

ACCI pointed to "substantial reductions in employment" in the electricity sector as one of the beneficial "dividends" of privatisation and deregulation. However, contradictorily, it also argued that, in achieving greenhouse-gas reductions, the first priority should be that no Australian jobs should be lost.[84]

As things stand, a large number of jobs have already been shed from the electricity industry with little benefit flowing to the majority of consumers.

PART FIVE

Free Markets to
Far-Flung Corners

THE MAJOR INTERNATIONAL LENDING BANKS and development agencies have all promoted a policy prescription for developing countries that includes privatisation of state-owned enterprises and liberalisation of access to those enterprises for foreign investment. This policy prescription has benefited banks, multinational corporations, and international financial institutions, often at the expense of local business, and always at the expense of the poor. In Africa, such 'assistance' has caused a 23 per cent drop in incomes. In Russia, it has caused national production to be halved.[1]

International financiers are also helping to promote privatisation. Instead of lending money to third world governments, they now lend the money to foreign investors to construct and operate the infrastructure in developing countries. In this way, independent power producers (IPPs) are financed, and the electricity produced is then sold to existing state utilities who distribute it to customers. This is seen by advocates, including the World Bank, as a first step towards privatisation.

Privatisation is good for the banks because the money raised by the asset sales helps governments to pay the interest on their debts, at least in the short term. It is also good for multinational corporations because they are able to buy profitable government assets and tap more opportunities to sell their products and services into new markets, often with heavy, taxpayer-funded subsidies. However, the privatisation of services such as electricity has led to more unemployment and increasingly unaffordable prices, often without improving the quality, capacity, or reliability of the electricity system.

CHAPTER SIXTEEN

International Pressure To Privatise

The 1990s have started with a bang ... Privatization will, I am sure, be a continuing theme of the remaining years of the century, and the potential benefits to the countries concerned will, I have no doubt, continue well into the new century.
William Ryrie, executive vice president of the
International Finance Corporation (IFC), an affiliate of the World Bank[2]

FROM THE 1980S, under pressure from the Reagan administration,[3] the World Bank and the IMF used their growing influence over debt-laden developing nations to force them to open their public services, including electricity, to foreign investment. World Bank and IMF loans became dependent on conditions that included privatisation, outsourcing, downsizing of public service workforces, reducing barriers to foreign investors and redirecting government spending away from public services and publicly owned enterprises into debt servicing.

In April 2001, the former chief economist of the World Bank, Joseph Stiglitz, outlined the four steps that the World Bank and the International Monetary Fund (IMF) now apply to poor countries with debt problems. This formula, presented as a restructuring agreement, is applied to all these countries, despite their different cultures, political structures, and circumstances. The steps are as follows:[4]

Step 1: Privatisation—sell-off of government assets and government-run services and enterprises. This is often welcomed by politicians who can foresee kickbacks to themselves when these are sold for multi-million/billion dollar price tags. One or two countries are resisting. Malaysia, for example, has halted its plans for electricity privatisation in the wake of price volatility that has resulted from electricity markets in the US. Malaysia's deputy minister for energy claimed: "Price instability and unreliable supply are risks that we cannot afford in our quest to industrialize."[5]

Step 2: Capital market liberalisation—allowing free flow of investment in and out of the country. In practice, capital often flows out of the country more readily than into it. Investors tend to speculate in real estate and the local currency and then get out at the first sign of trouble causing a panic that sends capital out of the country and drains national reserves. To attract foreign investment after such a rout the IMF makes the countries raise their interest rates to ridiculously high levels—up to 80 per cent—which causes havoc with property values and industrial production.

Step 3: Market-based pricing—which involves removal of government subsidies on food, water, and services, and allowing prices to be subject to the market. This often leads to 'social unrest' and massive street protests by the very poorest, who are unable to afford to subsist any longer and have little to lose. Such 'riots' tend to be put down savagely, and that causes further capital flight from the country.

Step 4: Free Trade—which involves opening poor countries' markets to the goods of affluent countries whilst maintaining protection in the US and Europe against third world agricultural products.

In 1990 John Williamson, an economist with experience working for the World Bank, the IMF, and the UK Treasury compiled a list of policies that were being pressed onto Latin American nations "by the powers-that-be in Washington". He called this package of policies, which included the steps outlined above as well as tax reform and deregulation, the 'Washington Consensus'.[6]

The Washington Consensus was by no means limited to Latin America. It was the driving force behind the structural-adjustment packages being imposed on all developing nations who borrowed money from the World Bank or the IMF. The policies were also adopted voluntarily in affluent countries by governments of many different political persuasions during the 1980s, including the conservative governments of Margaret Thatcher in Britain and Ronald Reagan in the United States, and Labor governments in Australia and New Zealand.

The Washington Consensus placed an "exaggerated faith in market mechanisms" for solving economic problems and it gave economic goals priority over social goals, destroying socially beneficial traditions and desirable aspects of cultures in the process. Progressive taxation systems have been destroyed and government social services decimated. In the end, the responsibilities of governments are likely to be reduced to little more than law and order and national defence.[7]

The World Bank and the International Monetary Fund

Privatisation "is an ideological article of faith" at the International Monetary Fund (IMF) and the World Bank, and is routinely prescribed for countries seeking loans from these institutions. The IMF and the World Bank "have overseen wholesale privatizations in economies that were previously state-sector dominated" as well as "privatization of services that are regularly maintained in the public sector in rich countries".[8]

The World Bank took the lead role in advising on the design and implementation of public sector "reform" and privatisation. It is the largest international development bank. It finances projects, makes loans to member nations, and guarantees credit. It lends about $25 billion a year, 45 per cent of which goes to companies outside the target countries, mainly based in OECD countries. It is owned by 180 member nations, who provide the funds or guarantees for loans. When the World Bank makes loans it expects to get its money back with interest—as with any other bank.[9]

Voting power, or control of the bank, depends on the amount of money each country contributes. The USA, which contributes the largest amount of the bank's money, has the largest percentage of votes. The G7—USA, UK, Germany, France, Italy, Canada, and Japan—controls 43 per cent of the votes. (See figure 17.1)

The World Bank has been criticised as being a tool of US foreign policy. Although the USA now only has 16 to 17 per cent of the votes on the bank (compared with 42 per cent when the bank began), it has the right of veto over major lending decisions, and it appoints the bank's president. The bank is housed in Washington, D.C., and therefore employs a high proportion of US citizens, including those at senior management level. Walden Bello, executive director of the Institute for Food and Development Policy, argues that the USA uses the bank in three ways:[10]

• to punish dissident nations and reward allies;
• to integrate low-income nations into the international economy; and
• to protect US banking interests

Following the onset of the debt crisis in 1982, when the Mexican government threatened to default on its $US80 billion debt, the World Bank and the IMF focussed on ways to ensure that debt would and could be repaid by debtor nations. This meant a shift in emphasis at the World Bank from project lending to structural adjustment aimed at debt repayment.[11]

Structural-adjustment loans involved the imposition of conditions on countries wanting to reschedule their debts or get new loans. These required low-income countries to adopt austerity measures, such as cutting welfare spending and lowering wages. But they were also accompanied by a number of neoliberal policy prescriptions aimed at opening up third world economies to foreign investors. These included the removal of restrictions on foreign investment, lowering barriers to imports, devaluing the local currency, raising interest rates, cutting subsidies for local industries, and privatising state enterprises. "Privatization is a core element of the structural adjustment policy package".[12]

■ **Figure 16.1 World Bank voting power (selected countries, 2001)**

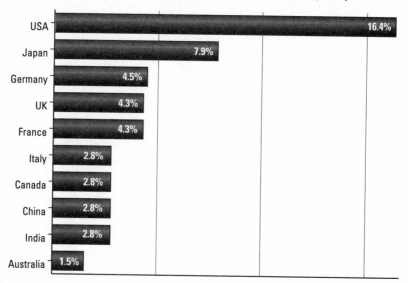

Source of data: World Bank. 'About Us.' 2002. http://www.worldbank.org/about/

In the 1970s the dominant economic consensus had been that government debt in poor countries was not a problem because it was necessary to invest in the infrastructure and services necessary for national economic growth. The new consensus of the 1980s was that governments should be discouraged from having balance-of-payment deficits. "Debt-service required immediate current account surpluses."[13]

Walden Bello and Shea Cunningham argue that economic growth in developing countries until the 1980s was facilitated by an "activist state or public sector" which assisted development in the absence of a strong private sector: "Contrary to doctrinaire conservative interpretations, the prominence of the state in post-colonial economic development did not stem from a usurpation of the role of private enterprise; rather it was a response to the weakness of private industrial interests."[14]

World Bank policies have ignored the positive role of state intervention and are not concerned by the lack of local private interests, as it sees this role being taken by foreign private companies. By the early 1990s structural-adjustment programs had been introduced into nearly 80 developing countries at the instigation of the World Bank.[15] "The proportion of World Bank structural adjustment loans made conditional on specific privatisation targets rose from only 13 per cent in 1986 to 59 per cent in 1992."[16] Privatisation was included in 70 per cent of the World Bank's structural-adjustment loans in 2000.[17]

As a result of these programs, the rate of privatisation quadrupled in Latin America and tripled in Asia. In the mid-1990s 42 African countries had undertaken some measure of privatisation because of pressure from the World Bank. Between 1988 and 1998 more than 10,000 companies were privatised.[18] The World Bank says of privatisation:

> Privatization is critical to reform in most developing countries; helping governments design and implement privatization programs has been a major activity of the World Bank for the past decade and a half ... Observing the immense difficulties of reforming public enterprises without changing ownership, the Bank emphasizes divestiture as a means of locking in the gains from reforms.[19]

World Bank pressure and deadlines forced privatisation to be carried out so quickly that in many countries it occurred even before any adequate regulatory frameworks had been put in place. This led to corruption and other undesirable outcomes.[20]

The IMF also lends money to low-income countries, and has become one of the few sources of such loans since Mexico threatened to default. The IMF is structured in a similar way to the World Bank: each member country contributes an amount to the pool to be loaned depending on the size of its economy, and this determines its voting power. As with the World Bank, the US has an effective veto because important decisions require an 85 per cent majority to pass.[21]

Like the World Bank, the IMF imposes conditions on countries borrowing money to ensure that they are able to repay the loans. Such conditions are justified by the IMF as encouraging countries to make their own efforts to solve external payment imbalances—that is, the imbalance between what they earn and their debt repayments:[22]

> IMF financing, however, can be provided only if the member country's authorities commit to necessary policy changes and reforms, and keep those policies and reforms on track, adjusting them if circumstances warrant. This is IMF conditionality … conditionality provides safeguards to the IMF that the money it has lent is being used for the intended purpose—to facilitate the adjustment process—and that the member country will be able to repay what it has borrowed from the IMF's pool of funds (to which all of its member countries have contributed).[23]

The initial conditions in IMF loans were that countries had to reduce government spending and increase exports. This resulted in less money being spent on social services, causing unemployment and cutting subsidies for food and essential commodities such as water. The rush to export caused commodity prices to decline, so that the incomes of many low-income countries went down even though they increased the quantities of their exports.[24]

> Structural adjustment may have failed on social grounds but it has succeeded famously for the private banks. The Third World has continued to ship out cheap resources to the industrialized nations even as their value on international markets has fallen. And they have continued to service their debts—even though the principal has hardly been touched.[25]

In 1987, because the earlier IMF conditions were not increasing the ability of debtor nations to repay their loans, "the complexity and scope of structural policy conditions attached to IMF loans" were increased significantly "to include structural measures—such as price and trade liberalization, privatization, and a range of policies touching on economic governance".[26] Privatisation was considered by the IMF to be "a key element of structural reform" and became "an important component of programs in a large number of countries". It was supposedly aimed at improving economic efficiency, but in reality it was intended to provide funds to pay interest on loans.[27]

The IMF conditions became a standard that other aid agencies used. Countries that satisfied IMF criteria were eligible for aid from these other agencies: "The Fund therefore serves as a gatekeeper to official loans and aid and has far more power than the funds it provides directly would suggest."[28] The acceptance of IMF policy prescriptions also gives "the green light" to foreign investment and loans from commercial banks.[29]

However, the nations following the IMF prescriptions did not prosper: "the majority of those nations that have followed the IMF's advice have experienced profound economic crises: low or even declining growth, much larger foreign debts and the stagnation that perpetuates systemic poverty." Many countries that had declined the IMF's "enhanced structural adjustment" loans were better off.[30]

The IMF had always argued that although the poor suffered in the short term from the austerity measures imposed by IMF structural-adjustment programs, they would ultimately benefit from the economic growth that these programs would achieve. Asian countries had been the economic-growth success stories. The Asian crisis in 1997 opened the IMF to more mainstream criticism. The IMF was unable to reverse the economic decline in countries such as Thailand, Indonesia, and South Korea. Structural adjustment is now carried out in the name of poverty reduction rather than economic growth, but the policy prescriptions remain unaltered.[31]

Privatisation was beyond the IMF's core areas of expertise, according to the IMF's Policy Development and Review Department, and so the IMF coordinated its programs with the World Bank and other international institutions. More recently, the IMF has decided to streamline its programs and leave the push for privatisation to the World Bank, with the IMF playing a support role.[32]

Development Banks and Foreign Aid

The World Bank has also increased its influence by "mobilizing other aid agencies", such as multilateral development banks, UN aid agencies, and national foreign aid agencies, "into country consortia or consultative groups, whose purpose is to coordinate and programme all foreign assistance to a given country".[33]

Like the World Bank and the IMF, other development banks have moved towards policy-based lending. The Asian Development Bank (ADB) is an example of how development banks have moved away from "their traditional emphasis on providing low cost finance for public sector projects to providing strategic policy advice, policy-based lending, support to the private sector and mobilizing private capital flows to developing countries".[34]

The ADB had previously adopted the Japanese model of development assistance, which stresses "project lending, investment in public infrastructure, protection of infant industries, a strong regulatory role for the state and mercantilist trade", but now it has aligned itself with the World Bank/IMF neoliberal model. ADB loan conditions have increased in recent years, and it is increasingly supporting private sector projects. The ADB argued

Utilities should not continue to depend on the government for incremental equity and debt, especially when governments have to cut budget deficits, control inflation, and meet requirements in the social sectors ... Also, the envisaged power subsector expansion program for the next 10 years is so large that it is beyond the implementation capacity ... of many utilities. It is, therefore, necessary and urgent that new participants and institutions come into the field.[35]

The ADB therefore advised, in 1995, that the electricity industries in various countries be restructured to introduce competition, reorganise utilities into corporate, commercial entities, and "allocate a greater role for the private sector", particularly foreign companies. "The overall medium-term goal will be to reach market structures which allow freedom of entry, remove restrictions on ownership and management, enable competition, and allow to the extent possible costs and prices to be determined by market forces." The ADB wanted to see thermal generators privatised, and in the larger, more developed countries, generation, transmission, and distribution separated and privatised.[36] The ADB stated:

The thrust of institutional work will be to identify government-owned utilities that cannot be privatized straight away and to prepare them for eventual privatization through a program of public enterprise reforms to restructure the utilities as corporate, commercial entities. Bank assistance to the power subsector from the public sector window will be in the context of demonstrated willingness by DMC [developing member country] governments to undertake meaningful subsector restructuring and institutional reforms. Simultaneously, the governments will be encouraged to create the legal framework and the necessary incentive and guarantee packages to allow and attract private sector entrepreneurs to build, own and operate the new power generating units supplying power to the grid at contracted prices.[37]

The bank offered to help governments "tackle" the expected "bureaucratic resistance and labor resistance" that were the "two key impediments to privatization". It stated that the majority of its assistance, technical and financial, would go to countries willing to restructure and privatise.[38]

Privatisation has also been pushed via bilateral aid programs, and many bilateral and regional trade agreements that incorporate some form of privatisation. For example, the Australian government has played an active role in pushing for privatisation in Papua New Guinea despite its unpopularity amongst PNG citizens.

PNG spends about 40 per cent of its annual budget ($400 million) on servicing its debt. The IMF and the World Bank require the PNG government to cut other government spending and to sell off public enterprises so that it will have enough money to service the debt. In 2000 prime minister Sir Mekere Morauta agreed to public sector reform and privatisation of state enterprises, including Elcom, in return for a promised $US200 million in additional loans from the World Bank. The promised funds were withheld in 2001 because of delays in the privatisation schedule.[39]

This program of public sector reform and privatisation is reinforced by the Australian government. As part of its aid program for PNG, which amounts to about $300 million each year, AusAID has a governance program which includes promoting private sector reform and privatisation. Privatisation in PNG offers many opportunities for Australian investors and consultants. In September 2000 a major summit was held in Sydney to outline these opportunities to fund managers, analysts, stockbrokers, government officials, potential investors, and consultants, including engineering consultants. According to the *Sydney Morning Herald*, all the privatisation project managers in PNG are Australian.[40]

However, public sector reform and privatisation are not welcome in PNG, as they will inevitably mean job losses. The World Bank loan includes money to pay for retrenchment packages for 7000 public servants, one quarter of the public service. Opponents argue that services will suffer following privatisation because many remote services are not profitable. They claim that prices will go up as foreign companies seek to make greater profits in the absence of competition, and safety will suffer.[41]

When thousands of people protested against the planned privatisations, and a number of students were killed and injured, Australian foreign minister Alexander Downer expressed concern that PNG might give in to the protests and abandon the program of "economic reform". He indicated that Australia might withdraw aid if the Morauta government were toppled.[42]

Who Benefits?

By the early 1990s, because of the debt crisis and structural adjustment programs, state participation in developing countries had been drastically reduced: privatisation was in full swing, and restrictions on foreign investment were reduced. However, the promised benefits of the policies have not eventuated—only the financial markets, banks, multinational corporations, and a few politicians have gained.

Throughout Latin America, despite the wide adoption of free-market reforms and widespread privatisation of government assets, GDP per person of working age has fallen by 5 per cent in four years. The gap between rich and poor has increased. Despite sell-offs worth billions of dollars, people are poorer now, on average, than they were in 1998. Forty-four per cent of them live in poverty, and unemployment has doubled in the last decade. For most people in these countries, privatisation means mass layoffs and high prices. In 1998, 46 per cent of people believed in the benefits of privatisation, in 2002 only 28 per cent of them did.[43]

A popular and political ground swell is building from the Andes to Argentina against the decade-old experiment with free-market capitalism. The reforms that have shrunk the state and opened markets to foreign competition, many believe, have enriched corrupt officials and faceless multinationals, and failed to better their lives.[44]

Michel Chossudovsky, professor of economics at the University of Ottawa, outlines how World Bank and IMF policies have transformed low-income countries into open economic territories and 'reserves' of cheap labour and natural resources available to multinational companies and consumers in high-income nations. In the process, governments in low-income countries have handed over economic control of their countries to these organisations, which act on behalf of powerful financial and political interests in the USA, Japan, and Europe. Having handed over this control, they are unable to generate the sort of local development that would improve the welfare of their own people.[45]

Western multinational corporations have sought investment in developing countries as a source of new markets because profit opportunities in affluent countries, especially in traditional areas such as primary industries and manufacturing, have declined. Privatisation in developing nations offers opportunities for such investment, and these corporations increased their push for privatisation policies in developing countries in the late 1980s. In particular, "trade-in-services is the fasting growing sector of the global economy".[46]

The United Nations Development Program claims that privatisation benefits multinational corporations (and some local firms) by allowing them to get access to industries in developing nations that had previously been closed to them and to buy up established enterprises, sometimes at cut rate prices: "In many countries the privatization process has been more of a 'garage sale' to favored individuals and groups than a part of a coherent strategy to encourage private investment."[47]

Similarly, Global Exchange points out:

Development projects undertaken with World Bank financing typically include money to pay for materials and consulting services provided by Northern countries. U.S. Treasury Department officials calculate that for every U.S.$1 the United States contributes to international development banks, U.S. exporters win more than U.S.$2 in bank-financed procurement contracts.[48]

Davison Budhoo, a former IMF economist who quit in disgust over IMF policies, argues that loan conditions were not imposed to meet the economic needs of the borrowing countries, but were rather aimed at increasing the economic and social needs of developed capitalist economies.[49]

Anti-privatisation movements are now growing in many Latin-American countries. An Inter-American Development Bank survey of 17 of these countries found that 63% of people thought that privatisation was not beneficial. In the early twenty-first century citizens began voting for left-wing candidates willing to protect the national interest against the World Bank's and the IMF's pro-market formulas. In Brazil, where incomes declined by 3 per cent despite (or because of) adherence to IMF policy prescriptions, Luiz Inacio Lula Da Silva, a candidate from the Workers Party who had not even got 25 per cent of the vote in three previous elections, was elected as president in 2002. In Venezuela, a leftist government led by Hugo Chavez was elected, which intended to scale back market reforms. In Bolivia, which had been among the earliest privatisers in Latin America in the 1980s, indigenous leader Evo Morales came in with the second-highest vote for election as president, after promising to nationalise industries. In Equador the sale of 17 electricity distributors was cancelled because of strong opposition.[50]

In Peru, there has been "a rising tide of citizen opposition to government efforts to sell assets to the private sector", with 70 per cent of those surveyed expressing opposition to privatisation. The sale of two electric utilities to a Brussels-based firm were shelved after six days of protests in Arequipa and six other cities left two dead, and protestors had to be dispersed by army troops with tear gas. The mayor of Arequipa, who led the protests, now has a national profile as one of Peru's most popular politicians. The people of Peru, as elsewhere in the developing world, were promised prosperity and modernisation as a result of privatisation; but after fifteen years of asset sales all they could see was massive job losses, higher rates, and poverty.[51]

In the Philippines, a grassroots organisation has formed, called Stop Privatization. It claims that state monopolies have been replaced by a few private companies which now dominate basic public services. The public, especially the poor, have not benefited, and services such as water and electricity "have been put even further out of reach by privatization".[52] In Guatemala, price increases following the sell-off of national electricity assets to Enron caused rioting. The president tried to dissolve congress, and declare martial law as a result.[53]

In South Africa, the ANC government has acceded to IMF policies, including privatisation, in the hope of attracting foreign investment. As a result, thousands have lost their jobs, increasing unemployment from 17 per cent in 1995 to 30 per cent in 2002, and deepening poverty. In preparation for a partial sell-off of Eskom, the national electricity provider, subsidies were eliminated and household bills in the poorest areas increased by up to four times, whilst bills for industry fell by 15 per cent.

In Soweto, 61 per cent of residents had their electricity cut off because they could no longer afford the rates. However, because municipalities in affluent white suburbs are able to buy electricity in bulk, they can supply it to residents at a third of what it costs in Soweto. Big industry pays 10 per cent of the rate per kWh paid in Soweto. A very small increase in business charges could subsidise the rates in areas such as Soweto, making it affordable to residents, but this would be to put social needs ahead of what is assumed to be economic efficiency.[54]

Blacks who managed to hold jobs during apartheid have found that privatisation has taken their jobs, increased their electricity bills, and then cut them off when they couldn't pay. The feeling against privatisation is growing to be the focus of the new struggle for poor blacks. At one protest march a banner read: "We did not fight for liberation so we could sell everything we won to the highest bidder."[55]

By 2002 even economists were growing disillusioned with the Washington Consensus because of its failure to deliver on its promises. The Asian crisis in 1997 was followed at the end of the 2001 with the economic collapse of Argentina, once the symbol of success of the Washington Consensus. Even the think tanks are having trouble justifying the consensus in the light of outcomes such as this. Brink Lindsey, a scholar at the neoconservative Cato Institute, said:

> In the early '90s, there was the sense that if you just opened your markets, and stabilized prices, and privatized industries, foreign investors would come to your door and you could enjoy rapid catch-up growth rates. And what has become painfully clear is that life is much more complicated than that.[56]

As in the case of Californian deregulation, those unwilling to admit to the failure of free-market reforms argue that the problem is that countries like

Argentina did not go far enough in opening up their economies to foreign markets.[57] The *Washington Post* editorialised: "The lesson here is that market reforms are easily undermined by failures of reformist energy .... In Argentina's case, the mistake was to postpone reform of the fiscal system ... Politicians who embark on reform often are tempted to feel that accomplishing three-quarters of their objectives is good enough. But failure to do the last quarter can sink the whole project."[58]

The World Bank was particularly keen to ensure that the Californian deregulation debacle didn't slow progress towards electricity privatisation in developing countries. In a paper published by the World Bank, Besant-Jones and Bernard W. Tenenbaum argued:

> In developing countries, the California power crisis may be creating the impression that power reform is too risky. **The power crisis in California does not justify this conclusion.** For many developing countries, the status quo in the power sector is the riskiest alternative of all. The status quo often creates a drag on economic growth through inadequate and poor quality power supply.[59]

They reiterated the false explanation for the crisis being touted by deregulation's advocates (see chapter 7) — escalating demand, siting and approval problems for new generating plant, and insufficient supply — which all led to increasing prices that could not be passed onto ratepayers. They concluded that what developing countries needed to avoid California's situation included:[60]

- market signals and incentives for new generating facilities;
- no barriers to investors in the wholesale power market;
- little political compromise to shield stakeholders from the consequences of reform;
- carefully designed spot markets introduced at more advanced stages of market development;
- rates aligned with wholesale prices and no rate freezes; and
- avoidance of wholesale price caps, as they introduce market distortions

This is clearly a prescription designed according to market ideology to suit vested interests, rather than a set of recommendations made in the light of experience to make life better for the majority of the people in developing countries.

CHAPTER SEVENTEEN

Independent Power Producers

The past decade has thrilled most electricity bosses in rich countries. Once they were considered mere bureaucrats, in charge of dull, often state-owned utilities. Now they have become more like oil executives, trotting the globe, signing deals in such places as Kazakhstan and Indonesia.

The Economist[1]

DURING THE 1980s, the expansion of electrical infrastructure in developing countries was financed by foreign borrowing because of a shortage of local capital. Debts built up because local consumers could not pay prices high enough to pay off those loans. In the 1990s, because of the high debt levels, the development banks stopped lending to developing countries to enable them to develop their own infrastructure, and encouraged them to rely instead on foreign investment. The trend towards private-sector financing and construction of electricity generation has increased around the world.[2]

During the 1990s almost US$187 billion of private money flowed into the energy sectors of 76 developing countries, as a result of World Bank and IMF liberalisation and privatisation policies. Over 600 private electricity projects were initiated, four-fifths of them for electricity generation. Investment boomed in Latin America and East Asia, in particular, until the crash of 1997 when it levelled off in Asia (see figure 17.1).[3]

Today, in developing countries, the private sector is "an important financier and long-term operator of infrastructure activities", including electricity. The projects of the ten largest investors accounted for over a third of all investment in this sector.[4] The top three in 1999 were American-based

AES, Enron,and Electricité de France (see figure 17.1 below).

A first step towards privatisation is to allow the new generation of electricity to be undertaken by independent power producers (IPPs). The electricity produced is then sold to the existing state utilities, who distribute it to customers. This is considered to be "particularly appropriate for countries that are just beginning to consider industry restructuring and have a need to attract additional capital to meet growing electricity needs."[5]

■ **Figure 17.1: Private electricity investment in developing countries, 1990-1997**

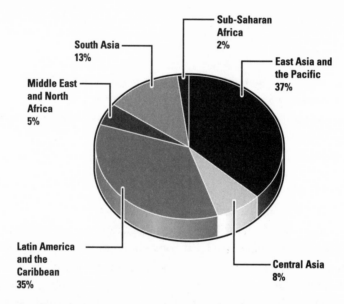

Source: A. K. Izaguirre. 'Private Participation in the Electricity Sector - Recent Trends.' The World Bank Group - Public Policy for the Private Sector. No. 154. September 1998, p. 3.

■ **Table 17.1: Largest private energy investors in developing countries, 1990-1999**

	Number of Projects	Total investment (billions of 1998 U.S. dollars)
AES Corporation	35	12.7
Enron Corp.	23	12.5
Electricité de France	22	11.5

Sources: A. K. Izaguirre, 'Private Participation in Energy.' The World Bank Group - Public Policy for the Private Sector. No. 208. May 2000, p. 2.

Whilst investment in Latin America has tended to be a result of full privatisation and mostly involved foreign acquisitions of government enterprises, investment in East and South Asia "focused on introducing independent power producers in markets dominated by vertically integrated, state-owned enterprises" (see figure 17.2 overpage).[6] IPPs are now a large market in Asia, particularly in China, Indonesia, the Philippines, India, Pakistan, Malaysia, and Thailand.[7]

In Asia, IPPs generally sell their electricity to a single state-owned utility, according to a contract that has been agreed before construction begins. The rationale for IPPs is that private investment will provide the capital and expertise needed to increase generating capacity quickly. In the Philippines, for example, in the early 1990s the Philippines experienced power shortages that were detrimental to the economy. As a result, the Aquino and Ramos governments fast-tracked 42 IPP projects between 1990 and 1994, and facilitated an investment of $6 billion by 1998. Forty five per cent of generating capacity is now provided by IPPs.[8]

In 1995 the Asian Development Bank (ADB) referred to the Philippines as an example of a country that was "moving in the right direction": "The Philippines has most of the distribution function in the private sector and has recently promulgated legislation to allow private sector participation in power generation through build-own-operate-transfer (BOOT) and build-own-operate (BOO) options."[9]

However, the fast-tracking of IPPs involved bypassing competitive bidding and agreeing to terms that were generous to foreign companied but turned out to be onerous to Philippinos. The World Bank notes that throughout Asia:

> The development of the IPP market has been accompanied by allegations of corruption and price padding. One reason for these allegations is that prices have varied widely across and within countries. Another is that rules for the solicitation, award, and close of contracts have been unclear and onerous, have allowed opportunities for graft, and have been perceived as unfair by sponsors losing out to competitors.[10]

In Indonesia, for example, the Suharto family and its friends are reported to have received "loan-financed" shares in the IPPs that were awarded contracts. They then paid back the loans with dividends from the shares. In Pakistan, allegations of corruption were investigated but not proven.[11]

■ Figure 17.2: International independent power projects (top 20 countries), 1999

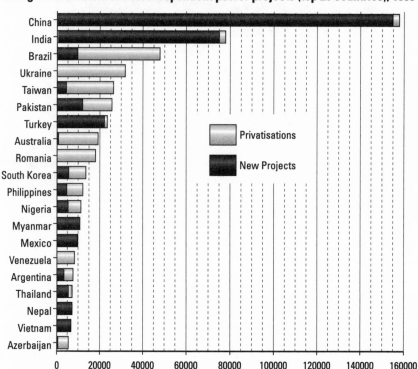

Source: 'Growth Slows in Independent Power Market.' Oil and Gas Journal 97(9) 1999: 36+.

Export Credit Agencies

Export Credit Agencies (ECAs) and Investment Insurance Agencies are "public agencies that provide government-backed loans, guarantees and insurance to corporations from their home country that seek to do business overseas in developing countries and emerging markets".[12] Most affluent nations have at least one ECA, and they compete with each other on behalf of the corporations based in their home countries. Together, ECAs provide the largest source of public support for private foreign investment in the developing world; more than twice as much as all the development aid supplied by bilateral and multilateral banks including the World Bank and the United Nations. In 1996 they accounted for "some 24 per cent of debt" in developing countries "and 56 per cent of debt owed to official agencies" by those countries.[13]

Unlike the development banks, ECAs do not pretend that they are there to facilitate development in poor countries. Rather, they are there to facilitate investment by their country's business people and to boost their sales of products and services. As a result, there is less pressure on them to consider the environmental and social consequences of the projects they help finance or insure, and they are much less subject to public scrutiny than development banks. In fact, ECAs often fund projects rejected by the World Bank and other multilateral banks because they are too risky or are likely to cause too much environmental and/or social damage. For example, the Three Gorges Dam project in China was refused support by the World Bank because of the environmental problems associated with it, but ECAs from Germany, Switzerland, Sweden, and Canada competed to finance it.[14] Another example, the Dabhol power project in India, is discussed in the next chapter.

Throughout Asia, the ECAs are supporting fossil-fuel burning power generation without the need to give any thought to global warming.[15] They are also keeping the nuclear industry alive at a time when nuclear power is recognised in the developed world as uneconomical and very unpopular:

> For example, ECAs have kept the Canadian, French, German, and U.S. nuclear power construction industry on life support through subsidizing reactor exports to developing and former communist countries. In contrast, the World Bank refuses … to support nuclear power on purely economic grounds — it is a bad investment.[16]

About half the $100 billion worth of long-term loans and guarantees ECAs make each year are on large infrastructure projects, such as power projects, in the developing world. They do not represent free market forces, as they are taxpayer funded. ECA activities mean that the taxpayer takes the risks of business investment whilst the private corporations take the profits. In so doing, the ECAs subsidise the activities of those private corporations.[17]

This type of funding is rapidly increasing whilst that of development banks is decreasing.[18] Thus the governments of affluent countries are giving their money to help wealthy corporations make more money in developing countries rather than lending money directly to developing countries to enable them to develop their own infrastructure. The role of these agencies in financing Enron's expansion in the developing world was described in chapter 8.

Risk

The generation of electricity in developing countries entails some risks. However, foreign investors make sure that their projects are not just insured by ECAs, but that much of the risk is shifted to the governments of developing nations. In this way, IPPs ensure "the socialization of loss and the privatization of profit".[19] The risk that the local currency might lose value against the IPP's home currency is avoided by requiring payments in foreign currency, particularly US dollars; otherwise, the payments are indexed to a hard currency such as the US dollar.[20]

The Asian crisis highlighted the way that currency risks have been borne by Asian governments rather than foreign investors. In the Philippines, the peso declined by about 35 per cent, whilst in Indonesia the rupiah went down 80 per cent. In both countries, payments to the IPPs were in terms of foreign currencies. Therefore the cost of locally produced electricity soared along with the price of imports. The World Bank estimated that electricity prices would rise by 70 per cent in India following the Asian crisis.[21]

Foreign investors eliminate the risk that there will not be sufficient demand for the output of a new plant by insisting that a power sales contract is in effect before construction begins. The Power Purchase Agreement (PPA) covers the first fifteen to 30 years of operation of the plant, and requires that the state utility buy the total output of the plant. Most IPPs in developing countries are built on the basis of a PPA.[22]

After the Asian crisis the demand for power dropped in many Asian countries, but the PPAs required governments to go on paying high prices for electricity that they no longer needed. In the Philippines, power demand dropped and the country was left with an excess electricity-generating capacity of over 40 per cent. In Indonesia, there is 50 per cent overcapacity in Bali and Java as a result of IPP contracts, forcing the state-owned power authority to stop using its own power plants in favour of those of the IPPs.[23]

Even the risks of technological obsolescence and poor management are shed by the PPAs. Long-term PPAs mean that developing nations are committed to paying for older, less efficient plants whilst technology advances and other cheaper fuels become available. The private investors don't have to worry about the risk that they will become inefficient, unreliable, or uncompetitive, because their income is assured, and there is little incentive for upgrading or ensuring that the plant will be available at times of peak demand. If the government tries to introduce competition in the generation sector, the private companies demand to be compensated for their stranded assets, as occurred in the US (see chapter 5).[24] And there is little incentive for new, more efficient generators to enter the market whilst the state utility is committed to purchasing power from the former IPPs for 20 or 30 years under a PPA. Far from being more efficient forms of generation, "the potential for inefficiencies is substantial if the IPPs meet a large share of the load".[25]

IPPs "rely overwhelmingly" on fossil fuels as the source of their electricity, and this fuel tends to account for 50-70 per cent of total operating costs. In the Philippines, for example, the IPPs favoured imported fossil fuels as a fuel over locally available hydro-power and geothermal power, and used oil and coal for 56 per cent of their generation. In Pakistan, which has its own source of gas as well as hydro resources, the IPPs used imported petroleum-based fuels for 74 per cent of generation.[26]

To insulate themselves from price fluctuations in the price of fuel, IPPs generally incorporate conditions in the PPA that compensate the investor should fuel prices rise. They may include the price of fuel in the final tariff, or index the tariff to the price of oil. In the Philippines and Thailand, where the IPPs mainly use imported fuel, the price of that fuel increased by 50 per cent between 1997 and 1998. In the Philippines, the National Power Corporation, Napocor, is responsible for supplying fuel to the IPPs.[27]

The risk that the state utility may default on its payment because of debts or inability to recoup enough from electricity consumers has also generally been transferred to the local government in the form of government guarantees. Sometimes such guarantees require money to be set aside in advance in special foreign exchange escrow accounts. Often the amount required in these accounts is in excess of PPA payments. For example, in Kenya 140 per cent of monthly payments has been demanded for a planned IPP at Kipevu, as well as a letter of credit for three months more. These tactics ensure that the IPPs have first priority in government budgeting, ahead of other needs such as health and education.[28] In other cases, governments are required to waive sovereignty and allow the PPAs to appropriate state assets in lieu of debts.

In theory, private entrepreneurs are willing to take on risks if the return is high enough, so that the greater the risks, the higher the price they charge. In reality, IPPs have often managed to ensure that the local government and credit export agencies take most of the risk; yet they have still charged exorbitant prices.[29] Even World Bank analysts admit "that IPPs have often inflated supply prices for utilities". In the Philippines, for example, the price of power from the IPPs, in 1996—before the Asian crisis—was US$76 per MWh, compared with US$57 for state-owned Napocor's power.[30] Electricity prices for consumers in the Philippines are now the highest in the ASEAN region.

The high prices for IPP-generated electricity, exacerbated by the Asian crisis, have sent many government electricity bodies into debt because consumers are unable to afford the high electricity prices and unused capacity has to be paid for under the terms of the PPAs. Many were in a poor financial condition to start with. For example, Napocor had liabilities of around $9 billion by 2000 that resulted from obligations to IPPs because of power purchase agreements.[31]

Capital Market Liberalisation

Foreign investment is supposed to provide developing countries with much-needed capital. However, the extent to which this foreign investment makes additional capital available for infrastructure development is questionable. Where full privatisation has taken place, such as in Brazil (see chapter 19), foreign direct investment (FDI) is increasingly going into mergers and acquisitions of existing enterprises, rather than into financing new investments and infrastructure. In fact, between half and two-thirds of FDI worldwide consists of such mergers and acquisitions.[32]

This has also occurred in Asia since the Asian crisis. "In 1998, for example, while total FDI flows to the five Asian countries affected by the crisis declined by $1.5 billion, cross-border M&A in those countries is estimated to have risen to more than $3 billion." Mergers and acquisitions enable foreign corporations to take advantage of a crisis situation when local share prices and market values are down. Much of this activity has occurred in the services sector, and is associated with privatisation programs.[33] "Similarly, new commercial bank lending—albeit on a much smaller scale—is being used to restructure existing external liabilities, rather than to invest in new plant and equipment."[34]

In the case of IPP projects, new infrastructure clearly results from foreign investment. However, the amount of money invested is small compared with the amount of money paid back by local utilities, often in foreign currency, that then leaves the country. Kate Bayliss and David Hall, from the Public Services International Research Unit at the University of Greenwich, claim that, because payments must be put in an escrow account or are subject to government guarantee, "using the private sector for power generation does not increase the funds available to pay for power generation" or other government activities. "Rather, an IPP will absorb large amounts of government finance through high prices and restrictive terms of a PPA. While IPPs are one way of financing power generation, they are far from the cheapest."[35]

The growth of IPPs have been facilitated by the 'liberalisation' of foreign investment rules, or capital market liberalisation, which is required by the IMF's loan conditions. Liberalisation prevents governments from being able to impose conditions on how money is invested.[36] This liberalisation has been blamed for the Asian crisis, when the unconstrained influx of foreign capital into Asian countries was quickly withdrawn at the first sign of falling stock markets, causing massive currency devaluations and escalating foreign debt. Chossudovsky claimed:

> The World's largest banks and brokerage houses are both creditors and institutional speculators. In the present context, they contribute (through their speculative assaults) to destabilising national currencies thereby boosting the volume of dollar denominated debts. They then reappear as creditors with a view to collecting these debts. Finally, they are called in as 'policy advisors' or consultants in the IMF-World Bank sponsored 'bankruptcy programmes' of which they are the ultimate beneficiaries. In Indonesia, for instance, amidst street rioting and in the wake of Suharto's resignation, the privatisation of key sectors of the Indonesian economy ordered by the IMF was entrusted to eight of the World's largest merchant banks including Lehman Brothers, Credit Suisse-First Boston, Goldman Sachs and UBS/SBC Warburg Dillon Read. The World's largest money managers set countries on fire and are then called in as firemen (under the IMF 'rescue plan') to extinguish the blaze. They ultimately decide which enterprises are to be closed down and which are to be auctioned off to foreign investors at bargain prices.[37]

One reason that governments are unable to borrow money is that they have low credit ratings; however, "if creditors might hesitate to lend directly to a government then they should be even more cautious about the government's ability to provide finance for the more restrictive terms of a PPA."[38] Bayliss and Hall point out:

> it is the eventual ability of developing country governments (tax-payers) and consumers to pay for infrastructure projects that determines the ability of private firms to raise finance for them. Yet this ability is precisely what the private finance option assumes not to be possible in the first place.[39]

The multilateral development banks won't lend money to governments if their existing foreign debt levels are too high, but these projects impose financial obligations that are little different from foreign debt, except that it cannot be refinanced. This makes their financial position even worse than it would have been with additional loans.[40]

For many IPP projects, foreign investors only put up, on average, 24 per cent of their own money. The rest is obtained through loans, mostly from foreign banks and agencies. This compares to the 25-40 per cent equity insisted on by the World Bank when it lent money for state investment.[41] Also, foreign investors have been advised to raise local money for their investments, particularly from pension funds: "Using local capital not only gives your neighbours a stake in success of your projects, but also reduces your exposure to currency risk ... "[42]

International trade and investment agreements are also smoothing the way for foreign companies to buy up public infrastructure in developing countries and invest in independent power projects. Multinational corporations have been lobbying at the international level to instigate international rules and agreements for this purpose. Negotiations for a multilateral agreement on investment (MAI) began in the OECD in 1995, but did not become public until 1997 when a draft was leaked. It aimed to strengthen the power of multinational companies and weaken the ability of governments to regulate foreign investment. The economic or trade ministry officials involved in the negotiations were lobbied extensively by industry at both a national and an international level by groups such as the International Chamber of Commerce and the OECD's Business and Industry Advisory Council.[43]

The MAI was designed to reduce the ability of national governments to restrict foreign investment in their countries, so a nation could not, for example, favor local companies for ownership of a privatised water or electricity company. Sanctions against companies on the basis of their environmental or human rights records would also not be allowed. The MAI sought to prevent environmental legislation that could be construed as imposing barriers to free investment. And countries that wanted to foster local development through conditions on investment, such as the use of local suppliers or materials, would be prohibited, as would restrictions on capital flows out of the country.[44]

The MAI was defeated at the OECD level, mainly as a result of concerted campaigning by non-governmental organisations. But the concept has now moved to the World Trade Organisation (WTO), where multinational corporations hope to have more success. Energy services were identified as a priority for the new round of WTO talks launched in November 2001. As part of the process, the US and the EU have been submitting requests for the removal of trade restrictions for specific energy services and the opening of access to markets in other countries.

Another mechanism for the pursuit of the corporate privatisation agenda at the WTO is the proposed General Agreement on Trade in Services (GATS). It was established in 1994 and is administered by the WTO. Negotiations are under way at present to extend it.

GATS covers all government services, as well as laws and regulations relating to those services. It aims to open up the provision of such services to international free trade, and prohibits governments from discriminating against foreign multinational companies that want to buy government services or compete to supply them. Under GATS, once a country decides to 'liberalise' its electricity industry it cannot put any limits on foreign ownership, nor limit how much of the electricity business one company can own. Also, a government is not allowed to favour local businesses: for example, if it subsidises green sources of electricity that are mainly local, this could be interpreted as discriminating against foreign service providers that use 'dirty' sources of power.[45]

GATS restrains government from imposing standards that might hinder free trade in these services. Existing GATS rules already contain provisions requiring governments "to eliminate regulations governing services and set conditions for the privatization of publicly delivered services". The new round of negotiations "are designed to not only strengthen these tools but also to expand the scope of the rules to include all public services".[46]

As was noted in Chapter 8, the US Coalition of Service Industries (USCSI), a group of large multinational for-profit service corporations, has been influential in shaping the GATS agenda. The UCSI includes General Electric, Citigroup, AT&T, J. P. Morgan Chase, American Express, United Parcel Service (UPS), Vivendi Universal and, before its demise, Enron.[47]

According to the World Development Movement, any developing country escaping privatisation of services under World Bank or IMF structural-adjustment packages "will feel a left hook coming in from the WTO". It notes that, if GATS negotiations are successful, "governments will be forced to privatise services and the sale will be irreversible".[48]

Stepping Stones to Privatisation

The stated goals of private foreign investment in developing countries' electricity systems include reducing costs to consumers; attracting private capital and thereby reducing government deficits; and increasing efficiency, presumably for the purpose of reducing costs. However, IPPs expand capacity at a very high cost that, in fact, increases government spending and foreign debt, inhibits competition, blunts technological innovation, and increases consumer costs.

What is the real reason for the development banks to push so hard for IPPs? Clearly, there are advantages to the foreign investors, who can achieve lucrative investments with little risk. Additionally, IPPs seem to open the way for electricity privatisation. When the IPP model of privatisation began to turn sour in the late 1990s, the World Bank and the other development banks began pushing for full privatisation as a solution.[49] The problems were blamed on a lack of market orientation, "such as subsidized tariffs, sector inefficiencies, and monopolistic market structures". To the applause of the World Bank, various countries—including China, Indonesia, the Republic of Korea, the Philippines, and Thailand—prepared to introduce power pools to foster competition in electricity prices. Korea, Thailand, and the Philippines also proposed to privatise state generating-facilities.[50]

It seems that, all along, the agenda was full privatisation. World Bank analysts Roseman and Malbotra argued that IPPs "plant the seeds for a top-to-bottom change in the structure and operation of the government-owned utility—seeds that are hard to stop from growing once they take root", and they can thereby "lay the groundwork for an upheaval ending in private ownership of much of the generation, transmission, and distribution sectors of utilities."[51] The ADB admitted that generating plants built by foreign companies, even when they were subject to competitive bidding, tended to be more expensive. Nevertheless, it argued that the "essential precondition to privatization is to free the power tariffs from direct government control".[52]

In June 2001 the Electric Power Industry Reform Act 2001 was passed in the Philippines, which aimed to deregulate the electricity industry and privatise Napocor. Deregulation is to involve the unbundling of generation, transmission, distribution, and supply (as in the UK), and the opening up of generation and distribution to competition. Transmission will remain a state responsibility. In order to privatise Napocor the government had to take on its stranded costs, including $9 billion worth of debts to the IPPs, and to "unconditionally and irrevocably" guarantee its debts.[53]

However, this course of action hasn't worked elsewhere. In the Dominican Republic, privatisation has not solved problems caused by IPPs; it has exacerbated them. "The effects have been disastrous with consumers facing massive tariff increases as well as lengthy blackouts."[54] The government sold its generating plants to a consortia of companies, including Enron and Seaboard of the US. The US-based Sustainable Energy and Economic Network reported:

> In the Dominican Republic, eight people were killed when police were brought in to quell riots after blackouts lasting up to 20 hours followed a power price hike that Enron and other private firms initiated. The local population was further enraged by allegations that a local affiliate of Arthur Andersen had undervalued the newly privatized utility by almost $1 billion, reaping enormous profits for Enron.[55]

By mid-2002 the country was suffering frequent and sustained blackouts and power shortages, because privately owned generators had been closed down as a form of blackmail (the companies called them "fiscal blackouts") to get the government to pay debts it owed the companies for electricity. Even though the plants were not operating, the government still had to pay them a monthly fee—in the case of one American plant, at the rate of $4 million per month. The electricity was restored a few months later, after violent protests and a government agreement to pay part of the debt.[56]

CHAPTER EIGHTEEN

Enron In India

Even granting that several states were bending over backwards to attract foreign investment in the early nineties, concessions which were extended to Enron were not merely extravagant but unconstitutional.
Darryl D'Monte, The Times of India[1]

INDIA HAS TRADITIONALLY USED its own technology and capital to build its infrastructure, and the government has played a "pivotal role" in these activities.[2] Its "electricity sector has been an entrenched symbol of the nation's state-led economic development approach". It was seen as a success, having an annual growth rate in generation capacity of 9.2 per cent to achieve a claimed 80 per cent electrification of the nation. However, many states required electricity boards to provide free electricity to farmers. Such subsidies were expensive for the boards, who often passed on the costs to industrial consumers.[3]

Like other nations, India was pressured by the World Bank and the IMF to undertake structural adjustments to make its economy more attractive to foreign investors. These included reducing the budget deficit, cutting spending on infrastructure, privatising government enterprises, liberalising trade, abolishing the wealth tax, and reducing the capital gains tax. In return for its compliance, India was offered $3.5 billion in loans. The World Bank and the IMF were also able to apply internal pressure, through having former employees in "key advisory positions in the central government ministries."[4]

In 1992 India announced it was opening up its state-run electricity industry to foreign investment as part of a wider economic-liberalisation effort. In preparation for this, legislation was amended in 1991 enabling generating plant to be 100 per cent foreign owned, and assuring investors of a very generous 16 per cent return on their investment and a five-year tax-free period. Not surprisingly, industry welcomed such moves, hoping that this would reduce their electricity costs.[5]

The government's first step towards 'liberalisation' was to sign a memorandum of agreement, in June 1992, with Enron to build a power plant in the western state of Maharashtra. The plant, to be sited 100 miles south of Bombay, was to cost $3 billion and be the largest in the world and the largest-ever foreign investment in India. The project was seen as a model for economic activity in India, and "the power giant's suave executives never tired of warning the government that how it handled the project would be a litmus test" for economic liberalisation in India.[6] Others also saw it as a model, a "poster child", of liberalisation and globalisation.[7]

■ **Figure 18.1: Providers of initial funding for the Dabhol Project**

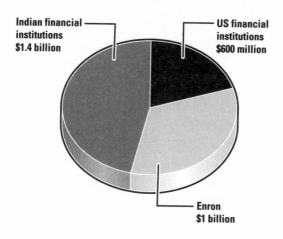

In 1995, as the ground was cleared for the plant, the Asian Development Bank referred to India as an example of a country that was "moving in the right direction": "India has opened its power subsector to local and foreign investors for setting up new power generation units and is offering a range of incentives and guarantees."[8]

The plant would be operated by the Dabhol Power Corporation (DPC), 80 per cent owned by Enron and 10 per cent each by American companies General Electric and Bechtel Corporation. Later, the Maharashtra State Electricity Board (MSEB) bought some of Enron's share, and it now owns 15 per cent. Indian financial institutions contributed $1.4 billion to the project.

Enron also received insurance coverage and direct loans worth hundreds of millions of dollars from about 40 international financial institutions, including US export credit agencies Overseas Private Investment Corporation (OPIC), which provided $160 million in loans and $180 million in risk insurance, and the Export-Import Bank, which provided $300 million in loans.[9]

However, the Dabhol project has been surrounded by accusations of bribery, corruption, and human rights abuses. It became a major public issue in India. Opponents correctly predicted that electricity prices would be too high and the effluent from the plant would pollute fisheries, and coconut and mango trees.[10] In June 2001 the plant was shut down after irreconcilable differences with the state electricity board over its unaffordable electricity prices.

Terms of Agreement

The memorandum of agreement was signed without the usual competitive bidding process as part of fast tracking to encourage foreign investment. Under the new legislation there was no requirement to have an Indian partner in the project, and this was unusual in India. At the time, Enron was essentially a gas-distribution company, with electricity generation only accounting for about 1 per cent of its revenue.[11]

From the beginning, the project was controversial: economists, academics, the Indian Press, trade unions, all the major opposition political parties, and NGOs opposed it on economic and environmental grounds. The Gandhian idea of self-reliance was popular in India, and many locals, including politicians, argued that the government could build its own power plants and generate power more cheaply than foreign multinationals. However, "the nation was presented with a fait accompli".[12]

When the World Bank was initially asked to review the project it argued that the memorandum of agreement was "one sided" in favour of Enron, and committed the electricity board to pay for electricity at a set rate without committing Enron to provide the electricity. The bank later declined to provide financing for the project as it was not economically viable, was too large to be justified by the power demands of the state, and would not provide power at least cost.[13]

The operating costs were high because, despite India's cheap coal reserves, the plant was to be fuelled by diesel oil and liquefied natural gas (LNG), to be imported from a planned Enron joint venture in Qatar in the Middle East. The gas was estimated to cost about four times the cost of coal; and yet the cost of construction, which is one of the economic reasons for favouring gas over coal, was also high — twice the cost of any comparable project world-wide, according to the *Times of India*, and twice the cost of a similar plant built by Enron in Teeside, England, according to *Multinational Monitor*.[14] A government sub-committee later noted:

> In fact the high capital cost wiped out the main advantage that the Dabhol power was supposed to bring. Because gas based technology was to be used, the capital cost of the Project should have been much cheaper than a coal based plant, whereas the running cost would have been much higher. In the instant case we have lost the advantage of a lower capital cost from a gas based plant while still retaining the disadvantages of a higher running cost.[15]

The subcommittee noted that "In a project like this where escalations have been built in and a guaranteed 90 per cent offtake of power is assured, the incentive to inflate costs could well be imagined."[16]

In fact, the Qatar project was cancelled in 1999 because of a global oil and gas glut, so Enron was left short of a supply of natural gas for its plant. In its efforts to get gas from elsewhere, Enron managed to get the US vice president's energy task force to change its National Energy Policy (see chapter 7) to include a provision to boost oil and natural gas production in India. "The amendment was so narrow that it apparently was targeted only to help Enron's Dabhol plant in India."[17]

Another option was to access natural gas from central Asia via a pipeline through Afghanistan. A contract to build a pipeline from Turkmenistan through Afghanistan to Pakistan, near the Indian border, was awarded to US company Unocal. However, the religious fundamentalists who ruled Afghanistan were uncooperative and, according to Brisard and Dasique, authors of *Bin Laden: the Forgotten Truth*, the US government and Unocal negotiated with the Taliban from 1997 till at least August 2001 in an effort to reach a deal concerning the proposed pipeline.[18]

India's Central Electricity Authority (CEA) also argued that the Dabhol agreement was too one-sided. There were no specific details about the costs of the project (required by Indian law), the price of power was high, and there was no provision to audit the project to ensure that prices were in line with costs. When the state government reminded Enron in 1992 that the law required them to submit accounts showing the project costs and return on equity, Enron wrote back: "we would advise you against auditing project costs and predetermining return on equity."[19] And they were not pressed further for this information.

Enron's lawyers lobbied for amendments to Indian regulations with respect to accounting procedures and scrutiny of the project. In response, the Maharashtra electricity board lobbied the state government not to apply provisions of the Companies Act that would require Dabhol to be subject "to public and judicial scrutiny" in the performance of its duties, such as "to operate and maintain in the most efficient and economical matter the generating stations." The board argued that such conditions "would not be acceptable to foreign promoters."[20]

Despite World Bank criticisms of the project and internal opposition, the state government went ahead and signed a Power Purchase Agreement (PPA) at the end of 1993. The agreement provided for the costs of construction and operation to be covered by charges for electricity. The agreed tariff amounted to $1.3-$1.4 billion per year for 20 years. The CEA argued that the resulting electricity tariff would be more than twice that which the CEA thought was acceptable.[21]

Despite the high prices, the risks—political, currency, demand, default—were all borne by the governments rather than the investors. The agreement required the power to be paid for in US dollars, highly unusual in India, so that the risk of currency devaluations was borne totally by the state. In 1993 a US dollar was worth 32 rupees. By 1999 it was worth 40 rupees, increasing the cost of electricity by more than 20 per cent. Also, the price of electricity was tied to the world price of oil, which happened to escalate after 1999. The unit price was higher the less electricity that the state bought.[22]

The agreement also committed the electricity board to paying for 90 per cent of the plant's generating capacity, night and day, whether or not it was needed or cheaper supplies were available, thereby further reducing risks to the private investors. To ensure that these payments were made, the electricity board was required to set up an escrow account, into which payment from electricity consumers would go, and to which Enron would have the first claim if the board defaulted or was late with its required payments. The amount in the account had to be at least 1.25 times the monthly capacity payment of the PPA.[23]

Additionally, the state government signed an agreement which guaranteed that if the electricity board defaulted on its payments the state government would pay up; and, as surety, the state government staked all its assets—past, present, and future.[24] The central government of India also signed a counter-guarantee in 1994 to the effect that if the state government defaulted the central government would pay the amount due. It also included a provision for Enron to seize central government assets—at home and abroad—if it failed to honour the agreement.[25]

So, although the foreign investment brought less than $2 billion in capital to the state, the state was going to be spending over $26 billion over 20 years, a good proportion of which was to become profits for the American companies and repatriated out of the state. Even that was without taking into account increases in fuel costs. Fuel, because it was to be imported would also represent a loss of foreign exchange of some $1.45 billion.[26] And although the power supplied by the plant was supposed to help the region's economic growth, the cost of the power was likely to be a severe burden on the very industries it was supposed to help. It would be even more of a burden on poor consumers and farmers who had been used to cheap, subsidised electricity.

A later state government subcommittee argued: "The conduct of the nego-tiations shows that the sole objective was to see that Enron was not displeased —it is as if Enron was doing a favour by this deal to India and to Maharashtra." Others argued that this, and the way the project was not subject to competitive tender and was decided so quickly and secretly, indicated cor-ruption and bribery. The documents leading up to the final PPA were not make public and were not even freely available to members of the legislature.[27]

Speculation of bribery was further fuelled by a mysterious $20 million that Enron spent on the project, described by Enron executive Rebecca Mark as an "education fund" for Indian politicians. Enron was also accused, by an Indian public interest group which filed charges against it, of bribing an Indian minister to secure the contract to sell oil and gas from local fields, in order to supply the plant.[28]

American Influence

The deal was challenged in nine court cases and two government reviews before it was finalised in February 1995. During this time the Clinton gov-ernment brought enormous pressure to bear on the Indian government to approve the project and provide government guarantees. This was the first of eight proposed large power projects in India worth some $8 billion[29] in all, and it was important to the US government that it was awarded to an American consortium. *The New York Times* reported how the Commerce Department had built what an undersecretary called an "economic war room" for promoting US business abroad:

> From that Washington war room, the negotiators for the Enron Corporation, the lead bidder in the American consortium, have been shadowed and assisted by a startling array of Government agencies. In a carefully planned assault, the State

and Energy Departments pressed the firms' case. The American ambassador to India, Frank G. Wisner, constantly cajoled Indian officials. The Secretary of Energy, Hazel O'Leary, brought in delegations of other executives ... And working behind the scenes, as it often does these days, was the Central Intelligence Agency, assessing the risks of the project and scoping out the competitive strategies of Britain and other countries that want a big chunk of the Indian market.[30]

The New York Times noted that the efforts to win business "often, as in the case of the Enron-led consortium's" project, require "arm-twisting in foreign capitals to change the way nations do business".[31] A few days after the deal was finalised, however, the Bharatiya Janata Party (BJP)-Shiv Sena (SS) nationalist coalition came to power in the state. During the election campaign, BJP-SS had demanded that the PPA with Dabhol be scrapped because it was too much in Enron's favour. It alleged corruption at the highest levels, including a $13 million bribe to the Congress Party, and referred to "loot through liberalisation".[32] These allegations were a deciding factor in the fall of the Congress Party.

The newly elected BJP-SS government set up a government review, which found that the deal with Enron "violates standard and well-tested norms of propriety for public organisations", that "several unseen factors and forces seem to have worked to get Enron what it wanted", that "the capital cost of the DPC project was inflated", that "the consumer will have to pay a much higher price for power than is justified", and that the high electricity tariffs would "adversely affect Maharashtra and the rapid industrialization of the State and its competitiveness". The state government therefore suspended the project, saying that it was stopping the multinational company from making huge profits "off the backs of India's poor".[33] A *Los Angeles Times* staff writer commented:

> In fact, Dabhol's travails may finally prove what India's critics have maintained all along—that the country's freewheeling, open system, querulous and opinionated press and highly stratified society make it an inherently risky place to do business.
> Riskier, some maintain, than a Communist dictatorship.[34]

In an effort to deal with all this democracy, Enron engaged in "an all-out campaign", placing advertisements in the India press, repainting a local health care centre, and donating $34,000 for a blood bank. Villagers were given access to water from the water main that Enron was laying for the project.[35]

Enron's efforts were again augmented by pressure from the US government, including ambassador Wisner and the US Department of Energy, which issued a statement: "Failure to honour the agreements between the project partners and the various Indian governments will jeopardize not only the Dabhol project but most, if not all, of the other private power projects being proposed for international financing."[36] According to the Transnational Institute, pressure was also applied by the US president and the British prime minister.[37]

Further allegations of bribery were made when construction suddenly recommenced after a visit by Rebecca Mark to the SS leader's home. No reasons were given for the reversal of the government's position on Dabhol, and the renegotiated PPA was even more favourable to Enron. The new contract committed the state to phase II of the Dabhol project and to a PPA worth $30-35 billion. Seventy per cent of imported gas delivered to the power plant would have to be paid for by the electricity board, even if it bought no power. The agreement was backed up by a central government counter-guarantee ratified by BJP prime minister Atal Bihari Vajpayee in 1996 on the day before his thirteen-day minority government came to an end.[38] Arundhati Roy wrote in *The Nation*:

> Indian experts who have studied the project have called it the most massive fraud in the country's history. The project's gross profits work out to between $12 billion and $14 billion. The official return on equity is more than 30 per cent. That's almost double what Indian law and statutes permit in power projects. In effect, for an 18 per cent increase in installed capacity, the MSEB has to set aside 70 per cent of its revenue to pay Enron.[39]

Allegations of bribery were investigated by an Indian commission in early 2002. It reported an "utter failure of governance", including lack of competitive bidding, by successive Indian governments with respect to the Dabhol plant.[40]

Enron continued to try to buy local support by donating money toward a hospital, a secondary school, and a vocational centre, but it failed to win over the villagers.[41] Several groups of affected villagers, activists, and lawyers were formed to oppose the project. Those who protested were subjected to police beatings and detention, and peaceful demonstrations were tear-gassed. Amnesty International was concerned by "the suppression by state authorities in Maharashtra of peaceful protests" against the plant. It accused the State Reserve Police — stationed at the plant at the expense of Enron, the local police, and Dabhol security guards, of being implicated. "Amnesty International is concerned at the collusion of the police with those supporting the construction of the project, which has increased the vulnerability of the protestors to human rights violations".[42]

The police did not investigate alleged attacks and harassment of project opponents by Dabhol contractors.[43] The international NGO, Human Rights Watch, pointed out that the Dabhol Power Corporation benefited from these attacks on protestors and failed to speak out against them when urged to do so by Amnesty International.

> Human Rights Watch believes that the state of Maharastra has engaged in a systematic pattern of suppression of freedom of expression and peaceful assembly coupled with arbitrary detentions, excessive use of force, and threats ….
>
> Human Rights Watch believes that the Dabhol Power Corporation and its parent company Enron are complicit in these human rights violations.[44]

When the human rights abuses were investigated by the US state department, Frank Wisner was in charge. Dabhol was cleared, and in 1997 Wisner joined the board of directors of Enron Oil and Gas.[45]

The plant began producing electricity in 1999. As a result of the PPA, power from the Dabhol plant was twice as expensive as any other power produced in the state and seven times more expensive than the cheapest power generated by the state electricity board. In fact, the prices were high even by world standards.[46]

The End of Dabhol?

When the Congress Party was returned to power in 1999 it declared that the PPA was financially unviable. It feared that the plant would bankrupt the electricity board and also the state (the richest and most industrialised state in India, with 79 million people). The second phase of the project was due to come on line in 2002. Analysts estimated that, although it would only add 20 per cent capacity, it would double payments owed by the board. In May 2000 the Maharashtra Electricity Regulatory Committee recommended that it would be cheaper to pay the plant's mandatory fixed charges ($220 million per year for 20 years, just for Phase I) and buy no electricity from it, because the electricity was so expensive. This was even though the state was short of electricity.[47]

Electricity shortages have been identified as a major factor holding up India's economic growth. However, expensive electricity is not the answer, because people cannot afford it. Channel 4 in the UK reported: "In a village just a few miles from the plant we came across a farmer and his family sitting through a power cut. The system breaks down so often that kerosene lamps are constantly to hand. Yet buying a regular supply from Enron would mean higher prices which these consumers refuse to pay ... 'Nobody around here is going to pay any more. As it is I cry when I have to pay my electricity bill. We don't have any money to eat properly, so how can we afford Enron's power?'"[48]

By the end of 2000 the electricity board was buying power from Dabhol at eight rupees per unit and selling it to consumers at two rupees. Then, in January 2001, the state government decided it could no longer afford to pay Dabhol the agreed amount under the PPA, and the electricity board stopped paying its bills. In return, Enron invoked the government counter-guarantee and threatened that, if the government did not pay up, it would sell off the government properties used as collateral in the contract. The central government paid the $61 million that was owing by taking it out of Maharashtra's budget allocation.[49]

In June 2001 the Maharashtra State Electricity Board officially ended the PPA. The power plant stopped operating and was put up for sale. Dabhol continued to charge the electricity board a fixed monthly capacity charge of $21 million, and Enron sought to recover some $3.5-5 billion in damages. The state electricity board, in turn, filed claims against Enron.[50]

Enron also appeared to threaten the Indian government with sanctions by the US government if Enron's investment was not repaid in full. In an interview with the *Financial Times*, Kenneth Lay stated: "There are US laws that could prevent the US government from providing any aid or assistance to India going forward if, in fact, they expropriate property of US companies ... If they try to squeeze us down to something less than cost then it basically becomes an expropriation by the Indian government."[51]

It seems that Enron was aided in recovering owed money by the US vice president, Treasury, and the state departments, and President Bush's National Security Council (NSC), according to emails between the NSC and OPIC obtained by the *Washington Post* and the *New York Daily News*. The NSC "is the president's nerve center for international crises and strategy and the US was now defining the national interest in terms of national economic interest" —a new version of "what's good for General Motors is good for America".[52]

The NSC apparently headed a working group on Dabhol with officials from various cabinet departments. In June 2001 Vice President Cheney brought the matter up in a meeting with Sonia Gandhi, then president of the opposition Congress Party. OPIC prepared talking points on the issue for the

VP's talks with the Indian foreign minister Jaswant Singh, and the US under-secretary of state for economic, business and agricultural Affairs raised the issue with Singh. Secretary of State Colin Powell also discussed Dabhol with Singh. OPIC prepared talking points in November on Dabhol for the president's meeting with Indian prime minister Vajpayee; but, as Enron's collapse became imminent, President Bush declined to discuss the issue.[53] According to Indian newspaper reports, various US officials threatened that "other investment projects would be jeopardized."[54]

In December 2001, despite its bankruptcy, Enron and its US partners in Dabhol claimed $200 million from OPIC for its Dabhol losses. A senior US official also threatened to cut off aid to India if government-backed lenders seized Enron's assets, thereby getting in before Enron's US creditors, whom the US government might have to compensate.[55]

In February 2002 Sandip Roy reported for the Pacific News Service: "Today in Dabhol, the power plant is considered polluting and undependable. Spring water has become undrinkable, the mango crop is blighted and the fish catch is dwindling. Often at nightfall, the electricity fails."[56]

As we saw in the previous chapter, there is nothing unusual in the PPA agreement between Enron and the Maharashtra State Electricity Board. Enron was typical of foreign IPP investors in many countries in Asia. Nor was the situation unique in India. In Gujarat, the state electricity board was making payments to three IPPs for their fixed costs, as agreed in PPAs, but was not using their electricity because the fuel they were using was too expensive.[57] A World Resources Institute (WRI) study has found that:

> The long-term impacts of the IPP policy were several and diverse, and are well illustrated by the high-profile case of the Enron project. First, key institutions responsible for long-term planning, and technical and economic clearance were weakened ... Second, the reckless focus on capacity expansion excluded consideration of a more rational least-cost planning approach to electricity development. Finally, in its conception and implementation, the IPP policy offered opportunities for graft and malfeasance.[58]

CHAPTER NINETEEN

Brazil

The electric Brazilian system is generous, it gives us a long time to correct eventual non senses. Nevertheless it doesn't admit five years of non senses. Then it turns cruel.
Brazilian electricity specialist[1]

BRAZIL WAS ONCE ADMIRED and envied for its plenitude of cheap electricity, made possible by the harnessing of its wild rivers. For this reason, it was referred to as the "Saudi Arabia" of electricity. By 2000 over 90 per cent of the country's electricity came from hydroelectric power, a higher proportion than in any other country.[2]

To deal with variations in rainfall, enough water to provide electricity for five years was stored, and the electricity network was interconnected to ensure that areas which experienced lower rainfall could be fed electricity from wetter regions. The system also incorporated a sophisticated planning system to enable increases in electricity demand to be forecast, and to trigger the construction of extra hydroelectric capacity whenever the simulation models showed a risk of future electricity scarcity of more than 5 per cent.[3] Brazilian author and publisher César Benjamin argued:

> The foreign specialists in hydroelectricity used to come to us, to learn, and they envied us. Which country would not like to have a clean, renewable, cheap energy system, capable to stock fuel for five years, capable to transfer great blocks of energy from South to the North, from the Northeast to the Southeast, controlling the hydrographic basins in an integrated way physically distant thousands of kilometers?[4]

However, in 2001 this system, which had worked reliably for decades, broke down. Brazil faced such a shortage of electricity that rationing had to be implemented, causing economic and social disruption. There were attempts to blame this breakdown on drought conditions and a lack of government investment, but it was really a consequence of moves to privatise the electricity sector—something which the World Bank had demanded as a condition of its loans. By 2001 Brazil's electricity system was owned by a complicated web of foreign private investors to an extent "unequalled elsewhere" in the world.[5]

Privatisation of electricity was not only mandated by the World Bank but also encouraged by the US: "The United States stands ready to work closely with Brazil in its efforts to make independent power production a reality ... It represents tremendous investment and export opportunities for U.S. business ..."[6] In 1998 the magazine *Business America* reported that, as a result of economic liberalisation, Brazil "offers a rich location for American exporters to explore for business". It breathlessly reported that "more than 1000 additional privatizations and projects are planned through 2002 ... In the last few months alone, 10 hydroelectric companies and five thermal power projects have been turned over to private sector control."[7]

The Brazil-US Business Council noted:

Prospects for investment in the electrical energy sector are extremely attractive. The proposed Ten Year Expansion Plan (1997/2006) for the sector, which proposes a 56.7 per cent increase in generating capacity, will require expanded infrastructure, especially for own-use producers ... In order to realize these goals annual investments of approximately US$7.7 billion will be required, the majority of which will be achieved through foreign and private financing.[8]

The British government has also seen the opportunities. In 2001 its energy minister, Brian Wilson, met with key officials, and told an audience of British and Brazilian business leaders in Rio de Janeiro that Britain was "well placed to capture a substantial share of the estimated £25 billion to be invested in the Brazilian energy sector over the next three years."[9]

However, such investment was only attractive if high returns could be assured, and the conditions necessary for this have been a focus of dispute in Brazil. A Washington, DC-based group, International Private Energy Association (IPEA), has been formed to promote private electricity investment in the developing world. Its executive director, Jay McCrensky, argued in 1996 that although Latin American nations need new generating capacity, "they won't get it unless the right policies and laws are in place to encourage inward investment."[10]

In 1995, when privatisation of electricity began, the Brazilian Constitution was amended to guarantee foreign enterprises operating in Brazil equal treatment with Brazilian enterprises. By 1998 Brazil led the world "in the number of companies that have been privatized in the areas of telecommunications and electrical energy."[11] By early 2000, 65 companies had been privatised and "58 public services turned over to the private sector". Privatisation occurred through auctions of assets rather than share floats aimed at involving the local population. Foreign investment made up 48 per cent of privatisations in Brazil from 1991-2001, with 16.5 per cent coming from the US-based companies and 14.9 per cent from Spanish companies.[12]

By 1998, as sale followed sale in quick succession, an increasing proportion of Brazil's electricity systems had new owners based in Chile, France, Portugal, Spain and the US, with active involvement also from Argentina, Bolivia and the UK.[13]

As a result of privatisation, electricity prices for householders soared, and many jobs were lost. "In Rio de Janeiro, Brazil, for example, prices following privatization shot up 400 per cent, 40 per cent of electricity workers lost their jobs, and the lights went out."[14] Brazil had become the most unequal economy in the southern hemisphere, according to the Inter-American Development Bank, with the top 10 per cent of families receiving almost half the nation's income.[15]

Privatisation

During the 1980s the Brazilian government, which had large foreign debts and was experiencing high inflation, used the thriving state-owned electricity companies to raise money to pay off its debt, whilst keeping electricity rates down so as not to fuel inflation. This effectively shifted some of the debt to the electricity companies, thereby providing a major justification for their privatisation in the 1990s. The government prepared these companies for privatisation by consolidating and annulling intra-sectorial debts, so that the companies would be attractive to investors.[16]

In 1990 the Brazilian government created the National Privatization Program, to be managed by the Brazilian Development Bank (BNDES). Its goal was "to redefine government participation in the economy, reduce public debt, eliminate bureaucratic bottlenecks which slow down economic growth, and increase the productivity and competitiveness of Brazilian business".[17] As elsewhere, the public was fed the erroneous idea that "state ownership is bloated and inefficient". However, some segments of the community, including unions, opposed privatisation.[18]

Privatisation of electricity began even before the regulatory agency, the National Electric Energy Agency (Agência Nacional de Energia Elétrica-ANEEL), was established in 1996.[19]

> The rationale for regulatory reform in Brazil is that such reform attracts foreign
> capital for privatizations and greenfield development and fosters the development
> of a competitive electricity market. The irony, of course, is that privatizations have
> largely occurred without reform having been implemented.[20]

The process of electricity restructuring and privatisation was designed by multinational accounting firm Coopers & Lybrand (C&L), which had experience with privatisation in the UK. C&L was hired by the Ministry of Mines and Energy to prepare a report recommending the way to establish a competitive electricity market in Brazil. Initially, C&L just offered the British model of restructuring in their 1995 report. The Brazilian government was concerned that the model had not been adapted to the Brazilian context, and asked them to revise it. The recommendations in the revised report, released in 1997, were then followed.[21] A writer in the *Observer* claimed:

> The terms of this Brazilian asset sell-off are dictated by a hefty document drafted
> by Coopers & Lybrand. While the term 'market' is sprinkled throughout, the
> blueprint is feudal, not capitalist. C&L divides the nation's saleable infrastructure
> into legally enforceable monopolies designed to guarantee new, principally foreign,
> owners super profits, unimpeded by real government control or by competition.[22]

As in the UK, the integrated system of power generation, transmission, and distribution was broken up. The regulatory oversight was also fragmented. ANEEL was set up as an autonomous independent agency to regulate the privatised energy companies, to promote and protect competition and private investment, and to set electricity rates. A private National System Operator was established to coordinate generation at all private and state plants. Its membership consisted of electricity generators, distributors, importers and exporters, and consumers, as well as the Ministry of Mines and Energy.[23]

A wholesale energy market, like the power pool in the UK, was to be used for setting spot market prices for electricity that had not been sold through contracts. However, the operation of the spot market has been delayed until 2003, and currently only short-term contracts are traded there. All the output of the existing generating companies was initially contracted to retail suppliers for eight years "to protect consumers from sudden price increases caused by deregulation". After 2002 these initial contracts would be gradually phased out, and generating companies would be free to compete to sell electricity to retailers by 2006. It was envisaged that, even then, only 15 per cent of wholesale electricity would be sold on the spot market, the rest being arranged through competitive contracts of at least a year.[24]

The retail and distribution sections of the system were privatised first. Light Servicos de Electricidade (Light) was auctioned in 1996 and purchased by a consortium composed of EdF of France, AES of the US, and CSN of Brazil. It is thought to have been the largest single privatisation in the world at the time. The terms of the contract meant that Light would buy hydro-electric electricity from the state at $23 per MWh and sell it to consumers for $120 (compared with $75 that EdF charged its more affluent French electricity consumers). This caused electricity rates for Brazilian consumers to rise by 108 per cent above the rate of inflation.[25] (Industrial electricity consumers are subsidised in Brazil by residential consumers, who pay more than twice the rates that industrial users pay.[26])

Light was under no obligation to pass on productivity gains to consumers nor to invest in new infrastructure. As a result, profits passed directly to shareholders, and AES made $300 million in the first two years. Light shed 40 per cent of its workforce, losing valuable knowledge of the electricity system in the process, and leading to a series of blackouts. The new owners were able to increase shareholder dividends by ten times. Similarly, when the Sao Paulo electricity company was sold to the same consortium, despite protests, a thousand workers lost their jobs, and blackouts became a feature of Sao Paulo's electricity system.[27]

By the end of 2001, 65 per cent of the electricity distribution was privately owned, often by multinationals such as Enron, Reliant Energy, and AES Corp.[28] "The electric Brazilian system began to be cannibalized financially ... and its slices went on being distributed throughout the whole world".[29]

Workers suffered because of the employment cutbacks and lowered working conditions introduced by foreign buyers. In fact, the World Bank, according to documents leaked to the *Observer* newspaper, advised a British Brazilian Council meeting that the following steps could be taken to "improve labour market efficiency":

- Reduce salary and benefits
- Cut pensions
- Increase working hours
- Reduce job stability and employment[30]

It was also proposed that all generation facilities would be privatised. After some of the hydroelectric plants were sold, further privatisations met with strong public opposition. Workers feared that they would lose their jobs, consumers feared that electricity prices would rise, and locals feared that they would lose their autonomy to foreigners. All these fears were well grounded in experience. The sale of hydroelectric plants was something that had not occurred in the US, even under Reagan, because of the national interest in controlling water reserves that are so essential to national wellbeing.[31] Benjamin argued:

> Nothing of that moved our technocrats. They understand about derivatives, future markets, hedges, postponing, bridge loans, financial flows in general, but they don't know anything about real economy, where the base is exactly the energy. They are employees of the financial capitalism. They wake up thinking [of] how to attract foreign investments to balance the external bills temporarily that they had themselves broke. They sleep thinking how to obtain, from the society, more resources to keep the terms in the payments of interests to banks and international institutions, that will give them later good jobs ... In their hands, the best hydro-electric system of the world, the engine of the Brazilian economy, turned into one more financial asset, available to do the cash flow. A wonderful patrimony to be consumed.[32]

Lack of New Generating Capacity

The ten-year plans that ensured reliability of electricity supply in Brazil had been made by experts working for Eletrobrás, the state-owned electricity company that was the holding company for all the state and federal electricity companies. However, when the government restructured its electricity system for privatisation, the unit that undertook this planning function was abolished and not replaced. The market was supposed to take care of planning: "the fundamental premise was the insane assumption that the companies operating in the market would invest in new projects whenever the price of energy, calculated on the basis of complex and questionable estimates of future deficits of the system, would project a profitable return on investment."[33]

However, whilst foreign investors were happy enough to buy existing plants that had no remaining debt so that they could make quick returns on their money, they were less interested in investing in new-generation capacity, despite the price incentives provided by the high electricity rates.

Prior to the privatisation of gas and electricity, natural gas has been a very minor part of Brazil's economy. There was little call for gas as a source of energy by industry whilst hydroelectricity provided cheap electricity.[34] Gas-powered plants were envisaged as a backup in years of low rainfall; when there were good rains there would be no need for them. And Brazil had not run out of potential hydroelectric capacity: "Even rejecting megalomaniac projects and accepting rigorous environmental restrictions, we can at least double that installed hydroelectric potential, expanding a system whose marginal cost (the cost of new units of construction)" is much less than those of gas.[35]

However, the market favoured the more expensive energy source. Foreign investors and international financiers preferred to invest in gas-powered power stations because they were much faster to build and their returns on investment occurred sooner. However, the cost of the electricity generated was also higher ($40-60 per kilowatt hour) because, of course, the gas had to be bought whereas the water was free. For banks, "a lower short-term investment is a more important advantage than the low fuel costs of a hydropower plant".[36] Investors were not concerned about the higher operating costs, as long as they could pass them on to consumers. Also, hydroelectric power needs to be planned because of the interconnections of rivers and the sharing of water resources. Gas plants, on the other hand, require less planning because they are more independent of each other.[37]

The push for gas as a primary source of electricity also came from companies, like Enron, that had combined gas and electricity in their business portfolios. The US NGO Project Underground noted in 1997 that Enron was "spreading the gospel of gas throughout the world as it builds new pipelines and power plants in countries ranging from Brazil to India, from Mozambique to the Philippines, but the service has proven to be neither just nor sustainable".[38]

There was, therefore, pressure on the Brazilian government to change the country's energy matrix so that it became more dependent on natural gas, which was also more polluting and added to greenhouse gases. This trend is occurring all over Latin America, where the structure of the power industry, once predominantly hydroelectric, is changing because of privatisation and deregulation.[39] Nevertheless, gas-powered plants only made sense in Brazil as a backup when the rains failed. As a backup, they enabled the electricity system to be optimised and reservoirs to be more intensively used.

In Brazil, natural gas is delivered via a pipeline from Bolivia. The 3000-kilometre-plus gas pipeline cost over $2 billion and is the largest private sector investment in Latin America. It caused major environmental and social damage as it cut a swathe through pristine forests in the Amazon, opening up areas inhabited by indigenous people to unsustainable development. It has been paid for by the Bolivian and Brazilian governments, several banks including the World Bank, the Inter-American Development Bank, the European Investment Bank, the Overseas Private Investment Corporation (OPIC), and a number of oil companies, including Enron, Shell, British Gas, BHP, and Tenneco Gas.[40]

The pipeline began delivering gas in 1999, but only 40 per cent of the gas it delivered was used in 2001. State-owned Petrobrás, which is the main investor on behalf of the Brazilian government, has contracted to buy the gas on very unfavourable terms. It is obliged to pay for all the gas that is delivered, whether or not it is used, and to pay in American dollars, at a price indexed to the price of oil.[41] Petrobrás therefore strongly supported gas-powered electricity plants.

In 2000 the government launched its Thermoelectric Priority Program, which involved the construction of 49 privately built natural gas plants. This would result in some 25 per cent of Brazil's electricity being dependent on gas.[42] Petrobrás would participate in some of these. However, private investors would not invest in gas-powered plants that would become superfluous in times of good rain when they wouldn't be able to compete with the cheap electricity supplied by the hydroelectric plants. So they demanded guaranteed sales in advance before they would invest. "Result: in the rainy months, Brazil will throw the water away (free energy) and will pay the gas (in dollars with indexation to the oil price)".[43]

Foreign investors had counted on a stable currency exchange-rate, guaranteed by the central bank, and a stable price for gas. The Brazilian government had counted on the foreign companies spending their profits on further investment in infrastructure in Brazil. Both sides were disappointed. In January 1999 the Brazilian real lost so much value that the government floated it. The price of gas also increased as it was indexed to the price of oil, which had tripled. As a result, the investors demanded that 70 per cent of any new project be financed by the Brazilian Development Bank; that the price for gas be established far into the future with long-term contracts; and that the Brazilian government take any losses resulting from a fall in the value of the real against the US dollar.[44]

Although Petrobrás offered to make up the foreign-exchange shortfall for companies buying gas for power stations, investors were unwilling to commit to gas-supply contracts that would require them to take 70 per cent of the contracted gas, because they wanted the flexibility to be able to reduce production when demand fell or maintenance was needed. What is more, they were unhappy with only being able to sell electricity on the lucrative spot market when demand exceeded what they initially contracted to supply. This could mean the difference between $2 per MWh and spot-market rates which, in mid-2001, were $300 per MWh.[45]

There was little incentive for new generating companies to enter the market, as they would not be able to compete to sell wholesale electricity to retailers that had already contracted to get their electricity from existing companies. Also, the retailers were not willing to sign new, long-term contracts whilst the price of gas was so high — specially since the privatisation process required that they would have to compete for customers from 2005. And ANEEL wouldn't allow the higher prices to be passed onto consumers before then because this would fuel inflation.[46] However, this meant that there was not much incentive for private investment in electricity generation because there were no long-term contracts to guarantee sales.

Some of the companies that had invested or were promising to invest in Brazilian assets threatened to withdraw. Enron suspended construction of two power plants worth $600 million. AES put $2 billion worth of investment on hold, and delayed the opening of another plant because these problems could not be resolved. FPL pulled out of Brazil. Entergy Corp's gas-fired power plant was also put on hold.[47]

Energy Crisis

By 1998 it had become clear that Brazil needed more generating capacity. Experts in the various regulatory authorities wrote reports warning of an impending crisis that would result from the dwindling water storage. However, the government was prevented from making any new investment in generating capacity because of IMF conditions that required it to achieve a primary budget surplus (over and above debt repayment). Investment in power generation would have been counted as a public deficit.[48]

Also, government investment would have been contrary to the privatisation program. Although some state-owned electric companies had sufficient financial reserves to undertake further investment, they were not authorised to do so. Other, cheaper measures, such as improving transmission efficiency and energy conservation, were not taken, either.[49]

The fragmentation of the regulatory function didn't help. The National System Operator was only responsible for coordinating and optimising the energy that was already available. The Ministry of Mines and Energy was unable to authorise investment by the state energy companies because all investment had to be approved by the National Council of Privatization. ANEEL was concerned to keep rates low to prevent inflation, so it prevented the retailers from raising rates to levels that might have encouraged private investment in generation. The Treasury didn't seem to take the threat of an electricity crisis seriously: it was primarily concerned with ensuring a fiscal surplus, keeping inflation down, and completing electricity privatisation.[50]

The government of Fernando Henrique Cardoso decided to take a gamble that there would be enough rain to prevent disaster before the next election: "Here, we are betting that this risk is a temporary one; you know that in economics, as in politics, you always bet on something, because politics is the kingdom of the unpredictable ..."[51]

At the end of 1999 the reservoirs feeding Brazil's industrial districts were at their lowest level for at least 70 years. Rains saved them in 2000, and when the predicted energy crisis emerged the following year, when rainfall was well below average, the government expressed surprise. Rationing was introduced in mid-2001, which affected three-quarters of the 170 million Brazilians, who had to cut their consumption by 20 per cent or face power cuts of up to six days. As a result, predictions of the country's GDP were revised downward by credit agencies.[52]

The start of the wholesale electricity market was put on hold till 2003 so that the government could set prices. Government price-fixing was unpopular with private investors. Enron South America's vice-president for government and regulatory affairs, Jose Bestard, stated that the question was whether Brazil would "move back toward price controls or forward" to a competitive market.[53]

In the end, however, price controls favoured the investors. Private generators and distributors, including AES, Enron, and Electricité de France, had been lobbying the government for electricity rate increases since August 2000, when thirteen of them joined forces for this purpose.[54] The government went "out of its way to make gas-fired electricity a profitable proposition. Hugely profitable, in fact," by raising the wholesale electricity price to $250/MWh throughout the country. This is about ten times more than electricity costs, on average, in Europe or in the US. As a result, "companies such as El Paso and Enron that already have capacity in Brazil get a very quick payback."[55] *Project Finance* magazine reported that Enron "made money hand over fist" during the electricity shortages in 2001.[56]

At the end of 2001 an energy crisis committee announced average rate increases of 6 per cent to cover the money that electric suppliers had lost in the previous year due to rationing. This increase was on top of annual rate increases granted by ANEEL. Brazil's central bank estimated that 2002 rates would be 30 per cent higher than in 2001. Further increases can also be expected, given the government's intention to install up to 4000 MW of emergency backup power in the form of land-based and barge-based mobile generators.[57]

Conclusion

Privatisation in Brazil resulted in massive job losses, unaffordable electricity price increases for many householders, and a major energy crisis with electricity rationing. In the long term, it will result in a partial shift from hydroelectricity to gas power stations that suit multinational investors, but will mean further increases in electricity prices and a loss to Brazil in terms of its comparative advantage.[58]

As in the Californian case, attempts have been made to blame the problems on a combination of extreme weather and a lack of generating capacity, together with too little privatisation rather than too much.[59] "Industry executives say a long history of over-reliance on hydropower and still-evolving regulatory thicket have conspired to stall the sector's development ... Only when Brazil's regulatory environment becomes more market friendly, they say, will more gas start flowing to the country's energy-starved consumers."[60]

One of the major reasons for privatisation was to provide foreign capital for Brazil to reduce its debts. But Brazil's debt continued to climb, as did its dependence on foreign capital: "In July, the deficit reached $260 billion, an increase of over 800 per cent from the $32 billion deficit registered in December of 1994."[61] To prevent capital flight, the government spent billions of dollars trying to prop up the exchange rate of the real, after floating the currency, and is paying interest rates of the order of 40 per cent internally.[62]

Economist Roberto Macedo concludes in a paper published by the Carnegie Endowment for International Peace that inequality in income distribution was aggravated by Brazil's privatisation programme:

> the poorest groups did not have access to the assets and the gains of privatization, and will in the end share in the payment of an increased public debt and of a larger interest bill. The better off, on the contrary, reaped the benefits of privatization, and of the larger interest rates practiced by the government.[63]

However, privatisation was always intended by outside agencies to provide opportunities for wealth creation for a small number of international energy companies, and to undermine the previously established ideal of providing an essential service for the Brazilian public. The Transnational Institute argues: "The evolution of the power crisis in Brazil showed that the liberalisation of the energy sector was technically and financially unjustified. It was based on pure ideology and in concordance with concrete business interests of foreign corporations."[64]

The Great Electric Confidence Trick

confidence trick *persuading victim to entrust valuables to one as sign of confidence*
The Concise Oxford Dictionary

THERE ARE TWO BASIC WAYS to view deregulation and privatisation. The first way is to see it as the logical outcome of one hundred years of experience; as something that has been undertaken to improve electricity provision at a time when old-fashioned governance structures are causing inefficiency and waste, and development of infrastructure is becoming too expensive for governments. Alternatively, it can be seen as a confidence trick, undertaken to swindle the public out of their rightful control of an essential public service; a trick conceived and perpetrated by vested interests that seek to gain from private control.

From where I stand, it looks more like a confidence trick than a rational evolution of electricity systems. Consider the massive public relations and lobbying campaigns involved; the efforts of think tanks to construct and peddle an economic rationale for it; the coordination of disparate companies, financial institutions, think tanks, and front groups; the haste to introduce privatisation all over the world before the results of the British experiment could be properly assessed; the unwillingness to learn the lessons of market manipulation that were evident in the early years of the British power pool; the continued insistence that electricity prices would go down when almost everywhere they have gone up; the idealistic portrayal of how the market works; the demonisation of government intervention; and the distorted portrayal of the performance of government power authorities. To me, these are all good reasons to suspect the motivations of those pushing behind the scenes for deregulation and privatisation.

Take the promised rate cuts—the most widely promoted benefit of both privatisation and deregulation. Did the private power companies and their allies really believe that electricity bills would be reduced for the former owners and controllers, the general public? The huge prices paid by investors for generating, transmission, and distribution assets in many countries attests to the fact that they expected large profits. Where were those profits to come from, if not from price increases or service cuts?

The claim was, of course, that publicly owned and state-regulated electricity monopolies were so wasteful and inefficient that private companies competing in a free market could save enough money to both cut prices and make a profit. But the supposed inefficiency of publicly owned electricity providers has been shown to be unfounded rhetoric used to gain and maintain private control. It is belied by the cumulative evidence of one hundred years of electricity provision all over the world. Publicly owned electricity enterprises have consistently provided electricity at no greater cost than privately owned enterprises, and often for prices far lower than those charged by private companies. What is more, in the United Kingdom and Australia savings that might have been available to a new management regime were made before the sale of the companies so as to maximise their sale prices.

Did the private companies that snapped up public electricity assets really think that they would be able to cut prices and maintain the same level of service whilst paying more for their loans than the previous owners; paying huge salaries to executives; paying dividends to shareholders; funding PR, advertising, and lobbying activities; and, at the same time, making big profits as well? Did they believe in the gross inefficiency of state-owned or state-regulated monopolies? I don't think so. I think it is much more likely that they thought that, once they owned an essential public service, and prices were deregulated, they could charge what they wanted for electricity. They were willing to pay a premium for the ability to exploit this opportunity.

Sure, the big industrial users of electricity believed that they would get price cuts. But, again, they were under no illusion as to the source of those cuts. They were to come from the removal of cross-subsidies to rural consumers and the poor. Industrial electricity cost-savings were to be made by shifting the burden of payment from industry to householders. The truth is, deregulation does not end subsidies; it merely shifts them to favoured customers.

Price cuts for industrial consumers were also to come from shifting the burden of paying for the non-commercial objectives associated with the provision of electricity—including equity and environmental goals—from electricity ratepayers to general taxpayers. Since most corporations have strategies for keeping their taxes to a minimum, this would reduce industry costs. For these large, electricity-intensive corporations, 'economic efficiency' is a euphemism for keeping electricity costs low by removing these non-commercial goals from public services, which have traditionally aimed to do more than make money. The shifting of costs to taxpayers is called making non-commercial expenditure "transparent".

The large, energy-intensive industrial consumers also believed in their ability to negotiate better pricing deals with electricity suppliers. But such deals had to be at the expense of other consumers. Deregulation was in large part "driven by large, commercial users who had the means to negotiate aggressively and purchase power from the lowest bidder. That's why they were so sure 'deregulation' would result in lower prices—for them—because they had the manpower and buying leverage to assure good deals."[1] It was they, not householders, who wanted 'consumer choice'. But the slogan of consumer choice was useful in persuading household consumers that there would be benefits for them in the deregulation of the retail supply market.

The worldwide post-privatisation declines in service and reliability were also sacrifices that were consciously made in the name of 'efficiency'. The claims that deregulation would ensure better service, because competing electricity companies would be more responsive to customers' needs, contrasted with the criticism meted out to 'inefficient' state-run facilities for the spare capacity and 'excess' maintenance staff that they employed to ensure reliability. Proponents of privatisation and deregulation clearly viewed this reliability as an unnecessary expense: "The heavy government regulations meant that reliability was more important than efficiency. In any business, complete reliability is expensive; it usually requires some overproduction or excess inventory. In the electricity business, this was doubly true".[2]

And the private companies had no intention of creating spare capacity when they could manipulate prices so much better, with more justification, if reserves were kept to a minimum. In this context, rising prices should have been no surprise to anyone. As business writer James Walsh says so succinctly: "Charges of price gouging are often a sign that the person making the accusation is an economic idiot. Prices are supposed to go up when supplies are scarce—whether the market is for electricity or for taxi-cab service in a rainstorm".[3] And how easy it was going to be to create scarcity by scheduling maintenance at peak times or in concert with other generators.

Nor, as it turns out, did the private power companies believe in competition—although it is from competition that so many of the benefits of deregulation and privatisation are supposed to flow, particularly where utilities were already privately owned. In the real world, competition is what every large corporation does its best to avoid. It is the main reason for the mergers and acquisitions that are causing ownership and control to be concentrated in fewer and fewer hands.

Proponents of deregulation portrayed an industry teeming with small, nimble, innovative electricity companies competing with each other to bring prices down. They argued that new technologies had made economies of scale unnecessary—and therefore the need for publicly owned or regulated monopolies obsolete. Now, after privatisation, the argument has been reversed. The power companies argue that they need to be large to be competitive: "By combining resources and eliminating redundant or overlapping activities, larger companies hope to benefit from increased efficiencies in procurement, production, marketing, administration, and other functional areas that smaller companies may not be able to achieve."[4] However, it is fast becoming apparent that the merged companies are seldom more efficient.[5]

In reality, mergers and acquisitions are usually undertaken for strategic reasons that include reducing competition and increasing market power. The CEO of Edison International has predicted that by 2011 there will be only ten energy conglomerates worldwide.[6] Such conglomerates will have even more ability to manipulate prices and avoid competition, further negating the supposed benefits of deregulation.

Private power companies promoted the idea that competition amongst themselves would keep electricity prices down. They then acted in concert to raise them, manipulating the artificial markets that have been created as a way of turning an essential service into a tradeable commodity. Market power has not been limited to power pools of the type used in the UK, California, and Australia. It is a problem in markets of various design, "suggesting that there are other underlying reasons for the existence of market power in electricity markets other than market design".[7] That underlying reason is the fact that electricity supply is an essential service, and competition to supply that service is little more than rhetoric advanced as part of a confidence trick to deliver market power to private companies.

The Confidence Trick

A confidence trick has three elements. First, it involves deception (the *trick*); second, it involves gaining the *trust* or confidence of the victim; and third, if successful, it results in the *transfer* of assets or property from the victim to the con artist. Electricity privatisation and deregulation have all the elements of a successful confidence trick.

The deception or *trick* has involved persuading the public, and the politicians who represent them, that a dramatic alteration in the governance of their electricity systems would be in the public interest. Electricity consumers were promised electricity rate cuts, better service, and 'consumer choice' as a result of the competition that deregulation would foster. The existing utilities were offered the chance to quickly recover past, unwise, nuclear investments — their stranded costs. And environmentalists were assured that deregulation would provide opportunities for small eco-companies. Energy efficiency budgets were also promised (see figure C.1).

■ **Figure C.1: Deregulation promises**

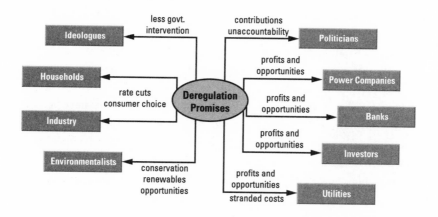

Where electricity systems were privatised, the promises were similar because privatisation was generally accompanied by restructuring of the industry and deregulation. In addition, governments were promised reduced budget deficits and less responsibility for an increasingly complex and capital-intensive service sector. In developing countries, privatisation and private foreign investment in the electricity sector was presented as the only way to finance the growth of the electricity sector. In developed countries, such as the UK and Australia, privatisation promised reduced union power as well (see figure C.2 below).

As explained above, such promises were scarcely credible, and would not have stood up to any independent scrutiny or analysis. For the confidence trick to succeed, the private electricity companies and their allies have had to foster public *trust* in themselves. More importantly, they have had to enlist trusted social institutions to shore up faith in these flimsy promises and allow people to put aside their critical faculties.

■ **Figure C.2: The promises of privatisation**

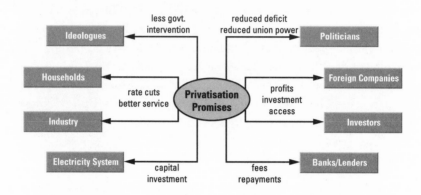

Since early in the twentieth century the private power companies in the US have learned to utilise some of the most sophisticated and deceitful public relations techniques ever devised, and have had enormous financial resources at their disposal to supplement these techniques with every conceivable inducement to buy allies, politicians, and credible spokespeople. They have been able to enrol community leaders, educational institutions, the media, the churches, clubs, women's groups, environmental groups, charities, and experts and professionals to help make the case for the private control of electricity.

In particular, governments, entrusted with carrying out the will of the people and protecting public assets, have been coopted by all manner of devices, ranging from the sophisticated persuasion of well-funded think tanks to the less-than-subtle pressures exerted by international lending organizations. All this has been combined with frequent and generous financial contributions to the campaign funds of political parties, and offers of future career opportunities for retired politicians and bureaucrats.

As a result, there has been a massive *transfer* of ownership and control of electricity assets worldwide from the public to private companies. The companies that have taken over electricity provision in most countries are multinationals with little interest in the welfare of local citizens. Increasingly, these companies are concentrating—through mergers and acquisitions—into a small group of very large conglomerates that dominate national and international electricity provision. Californian governor Gray Davis belatedly moaned, in a state-of-the-state speech in 2000: "We have surrendered the decisions about where electricity is sold, and for how much, to private companies with only one objective: maximizing unheard-of profits …"[8]

If privatisation and deregulation are taken to their logical end, which is the aim of their advocates, the public will be unable to influence the development of electricity systems, the terms of electricity provision, the reliability of its supply, its accessibility, or its price. These will all be decisions made by a cartel of electricity producers whose primary motivation is profit and power. This cartel will be able to exercise power over national, state, and local governments. It will decide how much electricity is available, when it is available, how much it will cost, and who will have access to it. And because electricity is so essential to modern societies, where it holds the power of life and death as well as the key to economic development, these corporations will also have gained enormous social and political power.

Broken Promises
Price Cuts

As we have seen, retail electricity prices increased, often dramatically, for households and small businesses in most places where electricity was privatised or deregulated. Where wholesale prices declined, it was usually as a result of external cost-reductions, particularly in the cost of fuel, as in the United Kingdom. Had the government owned system remained in place, consumers and/or taxpayers would have reaped the benefits; however, in an unregulated private system, private electricity companies along the electricity-supply chain have largely retained the savings from lower fuel costs. Large industrial consumers may have reaped benefits from lower wholesale prices, but rarely have residential consumers gained more than a tiny trickle of the cost savings.

A World Bank study of 61 privatised electricity companies in eighteen countries found that their profitability rose an average of 45 per cent. However, this profitability was often achieved at the expense of workers and consumers, rather than through the managerial expertise and increased efficiency of operations under private ownership.[9]

It has been more usual for wholesale prices to go up rather than down, because of market manipulation. In places such as California, where government-imposed price caps are in place, retail suppliers have not been able to pass these high wholesale prices on to consumers, causing them to experience financial difficulties that have led to blackouts and government bailouts. These problems are then blamed on a failure to complete the deregulation process by fully deregulating the retail market. However, had the retail suppliers not been forced to bear the burden of extortionate wholesale prices, they would simply have been passed on to residential consumers.

Service and Reliability

Service and reliability have also declined in privatised electricity systems because the service obligations of government-owned electricity companies are replaced by short-term commercial goals. In the public service it was not uncommon for employees to have a strong public service ethos, particularly in the utilities, where they "traditionally took pride in their safety record, in the quality and impartiality of advice offered to consumers, and in a number of socially responsible activities such as free servicing of old age pensioners' appliances".[10] This public-spiritedness was lost as employees were forced to take a more commercial view of their work.

The supposed efficiency gains to be made by private, competitive companies have been achieved through short-term cost savings, which include cutting the quality or level of service, rather than offering the same level of service for less money. Sometimes, return on investment has been increased by charging more for the service. Often, cost savings have been made by lowering rates of pay and conditions for workers, and by making thousands of public sector workers redundant. Full-time, permanent employment has been increasingly replaced by part-time and temporary work.[11] In this way, private enterprises may seem to be more efficient; but the gains to shareholders are at the expense of workers and consumers, who suffer a decline in service levels.

Another easy way to lower costs, although a short-sighted one, is to cut safety, maintenance, training, and research budgets. Old equipment is neither regularly serviced nor replaced in advance of its likely failure. As a result, accidents and equipment-related blackouts increase, as do blackouts related to network congestion, because planning and responsibility for network maintenance and development is not a market priority.

Blackouts also increase as a result of lower reserve levels of generation capacity. This is caused by the perverse incentives of the market system, which offer greater profits to private generating companies during times of electricity shortages. These perverse incentives not only discourage investment in new generation capacity, but also encourage the withholding of electricity during times of peak demand in order to send prices higher.

What is more, it was the unwillingness of private companies to take on the risks associated with constructing capital-intensive electricity infrastructure that led to the government provision of electricity in many countries in the first place. The biggest risk for private companies in building new generation facilities is that they might cause wholesale electricity prices to fall. In a public system, the risk of lower returns to taxpayers who pay for the infrastructure is balanced by the lower prices to electricity ratepayers, who are usually the same people.[12]

A study by the Federal Bank of New York found that consumers can expect more volatility in prices with frequent price spikes, and less reliability of supply: "Market forces may be *inadequate* to guarantee that providers can always deliver a sufficient quantity of electricity to maintain the grid's stability during peak-load periods." [my italics][13]

Even in developed countries, access to electricity for rural and disadvantaged people has required concerted government action. In the US, for example, federal legislation was necessary to create the Rural Electricity Administration to give rural people access to electricity. Without regulation, profit-seeking companies do not willingly widen access to those who might not always be able to pay their bills or to those who are more expensive to reach. A World Bank study of Bolivia concluded: "the necessary expansion of the grid to connect the poor will not take place as a consequence of privatization and restructuring".[14]

Reducing Government Deficits

Government debt has been stigmatised by the propaganda aimed at promoting government asset sell-offs. However, there is nothing inherently wrong with debt. Indeed, the privately owned electric companies will continue to have debts—higher debts, in many cases, than when the electricity supply was publicly owned. Debt is financially advantageous if the nett income from the assets it supports is greater than the debt repayments. It enables the costs of building long-term capital infrastructure to be spread over the lifetime of the asset, which can cover several generations of taxpayers.

In most cases, the benefits that were supposed to follow from reduced government budget deficits have also turned out to be a mirage. The money raised from electricity asset sales is often presented as if all of it is bonus revenue for a government. However, governments only gain in the long term if the savings they make in interest repayments from reduced budget deficits and the fresh tax income they receive from the new private companies—less the additional costs resulting from mopping-up after market failures and abuses of power by the private companies—exceed the lost dividends. This is a dodgy assumption at best.

Private companies, freed from social obligations, are able to undertake profitable activities whilst the government continues to pay for unprofitable aspects of electricity supply, such as environmental protection and equitable access. Previously, governments were able to subsidise unprofitable activities with profitable ones. The inability to spread costs across a whole service means more expense to taxpayers and savings to industry.

When bankruptcies are threatened, governments have to be prepared to step in and bail out private companies so as to secure the electricity supply. Taxpayers have been caught having to bail out companies when wholesale prices went up, as in California, and when they went down, as in the UK. Taxpayers clearly get the worst of both worlds. They no longer reap dividends from electricity production when it is profitable, but they still have to pick up the bill when it is not. The reason for this is simple to understand: electricity is not a commodity that consumers can choose to take or leave depending on price and supply; it is an essential service that is central to the maintenance of modern life-styles.

The confidence of private companies that governments will come to their rescue encourages them to take risks they otherwise would not dare to undertake. This sort of risk-taking has been termed 'moral hazard'. However, 'moral hazard' is often applied to government enterprises, and is then used as an argument *for* privatisation. Bayliss and Hall of the Public Services International Research Unit note:

> One of the reasons put forward for privatisation is that government bureaucracies can suffer from 'moral hazard'. This is the inefficiency that arises from economic actors being insulated from the real risks of their actions. In the private sector, where profits are at stake, the argument is that managers will use resources more efficiently.[15]

However, moral hazard does not disappear with private ownership. It remains in the case of essential services, because governments cannot afford to allow them to collapse. Moral hazard works against the 'disciplines of the market' that are supposed to ensure that private companies are efficient and well managed. The *Financial Times* noted after the failure of Railtrack, but before the government bailout of British Energy, that "where governments feel they would genuinely have no choice but to preserve the company, perhaps because there is no other way of keeping the service in continuous operation, they should reconsider whether this is really a suitable candidate for privatisation."[16]

Bayliss and Hall argue that another kind of moral hazard is involved with Independent Power Producers (IPPs) because of their government-guaranteed power purchase agreements: "Managers have no incentive to respond to market changes or to improve technological practices."[17] Such agreements have forced governments to bear most of the burden of risk associated with electricity projects, and thereby "undermined the very reason for introducing private power in the first place — to cap public debt and force private power producers to take the financial risks instead of governments".[18]

In poorer countries, where lack of capital combined with subsidised electricity for the very poor ensured that government-owned electricity authorities were debt laden, the new flood of foreign investment has often not provided the much-needed capital for extra generating capacity. Foreign companies have bought up existing government facilities — often at bargain-basement prices — put up prices, and then sent their profits home rather than invest in new generating facilities. Power purchase agreements with IPPs have ended up costing governments far more foreign capital than that originally invested in the electricity projects.

Environment

The environment has been another victim of the con trick. Environmentalists, trusted by the community, were enrolled as agents of the power companies with promises that deregulation would be good for the environment. In retrospect, it is difficult to avoid the conclusion that most of these environmental leaders were either naïve or worse. A study by the World Resources Institute of electricity reform around the world found that:

> Financial concerns and donor conditions have driven electricity reform. Managed by closed political processes and dominated by technocrats and donor consultants, environmental considerations play almost no role in a re-envisioned electricity sector. Social concerns are given more importance, but only to the extent that reforms affect politically powerful groups.[19]

Deregulation allows, and in many instances encourages, the maintenance of old, polluting, coal-fired power plants that contribute smog, mercury, and particulate matter to the atmosphere, causing thousands of deaths annually.[20] In Australia, deregulation and privatisation have led to the increased use of the most polluting type of coal, brown coal. Even the Electricity Supply Association of Australia (ESAA) has admitted that there has been a 31 per cent increase in greenhouse gases as a result of energy deregulation.[21] In the US, the Bush administration has used the problems created by deregulation as an excuse to relax air-pollution controls on power plants. The Commission for Environmental Cooperation, a NAFTA (North American Free Trade Agreement) agency, has found that electricity deregulation caused the energy-efficiency budgets of North American power companies to be cut by 42 per cent between 1995 and 1999.[22]

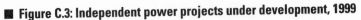

■ **Figure C.3: Independent power projects under development, 1999**

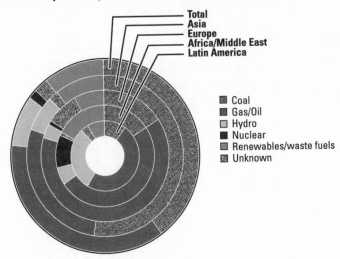

Source: 'Growth Slows in Independent Power Market.' Oil and Gas Journal 97(9) 1999: 36+.

IPPs "skew incentives towards new generation and against meeting electricity needs through greater efficiency. In addition, the purchase contracts have forced use of high-cost power over lower-cost power already available".[23] There is not much likelihood that electricity suppliers will encourage their customers to use electricity efficiently if they are committed to purchasing more electricity than they need from an IPP. Moreover, the export credit agencies that often fund them are usually not subject to even the minimal environmental requirements that governments and other funding agencies, such as the World Bank, are. As a result, IPPs have tended to favour oversized, outdated, polluting, fossil fuel-based power projects.[24]

The folly of relying on markets for fostering renewable energy has been recognised in many countries with 'liberalised' electricity systems. As a result, governments are again resorting to regulations to increase the use of renewable energy. In California, utilities are now required by the government to meet 20 per cent of their supply from renewable sources.[25] As we have seen, when the market decides on the fuel source there is no incentive to take account of its environmental costs. As a result, new generating capacity around the world continues to be dominated by fossil fuels. For instance, more than three-quarters of projects under development in 1999 were based on fossil fuels (see figure C.3).[26] In the US, consumption of electricity produced from renewable sources fell by 12 per cent to reach a twelve-year low. It now only accounts for 6 per cent of US energy consumption. The current growth source worldwide is gas, which is expected to account for 40 per cent of Europe's electricity within a decade, largely as a result of deregulation.[27] Although cleaner than coal, it still contributes to global warming and is not renewable.

Winners and Losers

It is clear that the vast majority of people in each country where the great electric confidence trick has been played are its victims rather than its beneficiaries. Jobs have been lost, electricity prices have risen, service and reliability has fallen, pollution has increased, and taxpayers have had to bail out private electricity companies in bad times without receiving any dividends in good times (see figure C.4).

Apart from the private electricity companies themselves, the real beneficiaries of privatisation and deregulation have been the banks, building societies, insurance companies, and other commercial companies that have been able to invest in the newly privatised or emergent companies, and/or provide loans to those who did.[28]

In particular, the banks have continued to play a major role in the shape and direction of the electricity industry, as they have done since the early twentieth century when J.P. Morgan controlled General Electric. Banks are major investors in power companies, and their executives populate the boards of electricity companies. They have advised on privatisation schemes and helped draw up deregulation legislation around the world. In California, they also advised politicians on how to deal with the mess that deregulation had created, and organised the bonds that would pay for the state's purchase of electricity. They have collected fees from brokering the purchase of independent power companies worldwide, and have been involved in energy trading themselves. In Australia, banks are also becoming involved in electricity trading. Westpac has bought Enron's Australian trading team, and the Commonwealth Bank is deciding whether it too should participate in the volatile electricity market.[29]

Big industry has also generally benefited, as their greater bargaining power in the market place has enabled them to shift the burden of electricity costs further onto the shoulders of small consumers. Of course, the biggest winners have been the power companies themselves. But any confidence trick carries risks, and even amongst the tricksters there have been losers. Enron, which was a major player in the deregulation con trick, has become one of its most spectacular losers; yet, even there, the executives ensured that they personally reaped large fortunes before the company went under.

■ **Figure C.4: Outcomes: winners and losers**

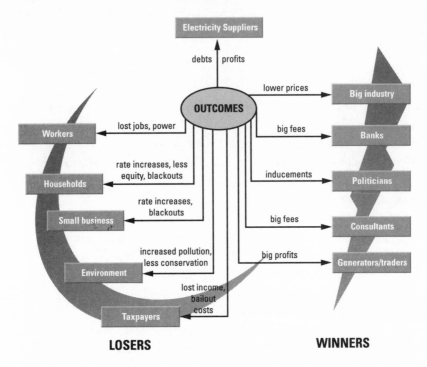

The failure of deregulation and privatisation to deliver on its promises has not been fully exposed yet. Electricity 'liberalisation' remains a continuing confidence trick, where the benefits are always on the horizon. As with all good cons, the failure of the benefits to materialise is explained by a lack of confidence, an inability to fully embrace the deregulatory prescription. These days, electricity privatisation and deregulation are presented as 'historically inevitable' and part of a worldwide trend that individual countries can't go against.[30]

However, as time passes, the deception is becoming more difficult to sustain, and the opposition more outspoken and determined. The excuses for the resulting fiascos are wearing thin. In California, a majority of people do not believe that their crisis was caused by a shortage of electricity; most believe that deregulation was a mistake, and they favour re-regulation.[31] It is becoming increasingly difficult to privatise electricity in developed countries such as Australia, France, and Canada because of voter opposition. In many developing countries, privatisation proposals are being greeted with mass protests, and leftist candidates are being elected to office. It is unlikely that the trend towards electricity 'liberalisation' can be sustained much longer.

Notes

Introduction

1 Daniel Chavez. 'Lights Off! Debunking the Myths of Power Liberalisation.' Amsterdam: Transnational Institute (TNI). May 2002, p. 3.

2 Ibid., p. 4.

3 Navroz K. Dubash, ed. *Power Politics: Equity and Environment in Electricity Reform.* Washington D.C.: World Resources Institute. 2002, p. xiii; Richard Lapper. 'Piling on the Pressure.' *Financial Times.* 5 October 2002, p. 1; Juan Forero. 'Still Poor, Latin Americans Protest Push for Open Markets.' *The New York Times.* 19 July 2002, p. A-1; Canute James. 'Leader Acts to Tackle Power Shortage.' *Financial Times.* 18 June 2002, p. 9; Rachel L. Swarns. 'In South Africa, Leaders Face Blacks' Ire.' *New York Times.* 2 October 2002, p. A10

4 Andrew Ward. 'S Korean Electricity Workers End Strike.' *Financial Times.* 3 April 2002, p. 10; Mark Forbes. 'The Day the Students Died.' *The Age.* 4 August 2001, p. 1; 'France Inches Nearer Energy Reforms.' *BBC News.* 4 October 2002; Mark O'Neill. 'Power Plant Sale Agreement Sparks Outcry from Workers.' *South China Morning Post.* 20 August 2001, p. 3.

5 'The Lessons of Privatisation.' *Business Review Weekly.* 1 March 1999, p. 48.

6 Glenn English. 'Putting Consumers First.' *IEEE Spectrum* June, 2001, p. 19.

7 Richard Rudolph and Scott Ridley. *Power Struggle: The Hundred-Year War over Electricity.* New York: Harper & Row. 1986, p. 19.

8 EIA. 'Privatization and the Globalization of Energy Markets.' US Dept of Energy. October, 1996. http://www.eia.doe.gov/emeu/pgem/, p. v.

9 Christopher Sheil. *Water's Fall: Running the Risks with Economic Rationalism.* Annandale, NSW: Pluto Press. 2000, pp. 26-7

10 EIA. 'Privatization and the Globalization of Energy Markets.' p. 3.

11 Sheil. *Water's Fall.*, p. 23

12 Ibid., p. 26; Frank Stilwell. 'Economic Rationalism: Sound Foundations for Policy?' In *Beyond the Market: Alternatives to Economic Rationalism.* ed. Stuart Rees, Gordon Rodley and Frank Stilwell. Leichhardt, NSW: Pluto Press. 1993, p. 34.

13 José Piñera. 'Chile'. In *The Political Economy of Policy Reform.* ed. John Williamson. Washington, DC: Institute for International Economics. 1994, p. 225; Chavez. 'Lights Off!', p. 4.

14 Walt Patterson. *Transforming Electricity: The Coming Generation of Change.* London: Royal Institute of International Affairs and Earthscan. 1999, p. 10.

15 Access Economics. 'Impact on Victoria of the Privatisation of the State's Electricity and Gas Assets.' Canberra: Access Economics. June 2001, p. 8.

16 European Commission. 'Opening up to Choice: The Single Electricity Market.' EU 1999?

17 Ibid., pp. 5-6, 12.

18 Victor Mallet. 'France Goes on Sale.' *Financial Times.* 18 June 2002, p. 22; Victor Mallet. 'For Five Decades, EdF Has Been a Bastion of French State Industry.' *Financial Times.* 2 October 2002

19 EIA. 'Privatization and the Globalization of Energy Markets.', pp. 3-4.

20 Ibid., p. 4.

21 Consumers Union. 'Deregulated.' *Consumer Reports* July, 2002, p. 30.

22 Ibid., p. 31.

23 Ibid., p. 31.

24 Dexter Whitfield. *Making It Public: Evidence and Action against Privatisation.* London: Pluto Press. 1983, p. 52.

25 Ibid., p. 44.

26 Navroz K. Dubash. 'The Changing Global Context for Electricity Reform'. In *Power Politics: Equity and Environment in Electricity Reform.* ed. Navroz K. Dubash. Washington D.C.: World Resources Institute. 2002, p. 13.

27 Patterson. *Transforming Electricity.*, pp. 130, 131.

28 Ibid., p. 128.

29 John Quiggin. 'Market-Oriented Reform in the Australian Electricity Industry.' Canberra: School of Economics, ANU. 15 March 2001, p. 7.

30 Ibid., p. 7.

31 F. T. McCarthy. 'The Slumbering Giants

Awake: Energy Companies Will Never Be the Same Again.' *The Economist.* 10 February 2002

32 Sarah Disbrow. 'Sitting on an Electric Fence: The Looming Threat to Nebraska Public Power.' Nebraskans for Peace. 2000. http://www.nebraskansforpeace.org/2000/o00 .electricfence.html

33 Michael Harrison. 'London Electricity Handed £2m Fine.' *The Independent.* 10 October 2002.

34 Steve Thomas. 'The Development of Competition'. In *The British Electricity Experiment.* ed. John Surrey. London: Earthscan Publications. 1996, p. 75.

35 Steve Thomas. 'The Wholesale Electricity Market in Britain — 1990-2001.' London: PSIRU, University of Greenwich. August, 2001, p. 3.

36 Chavez. 'Lights Off!', p. 11.

37 Dubash. 'The Changing Global Context for Electricity Reform'., p. 16.

38 Patterson. *Transforming Electricity.*, p. 15.

39 Dubash. 'The Changing Global Context for Electricity Reform'., p. 11.

40 Charlie Higley. 'Disastrous Deregulation.' Public Citizen. December, 2000, p. 1.

41 Richard F. Hirsh. *Power Loss: The Origins of Deregulation and Restructuring in the American Electric Utility System.* Cambridge, Massachusetts: The MIT Press. 1999, pp. 1, 46; Daniel M. Berman and John T. O'Connor. *Who Owns the Sun: People, Politics, and the Struggle for a Solar Economy.* White River Junction, Vermont: Chelsea Green Publishing Company. 1996, p. 84.

42 Steve Thomas. 'Strategic Government and Corporate Issues'. In *The British Electricity Experiment.* ed. Surrey, p. 260.

43 Steven Pearlstein. 'On California Stage, a Cautionary Tale.' *The Washington Post.* 21 August 2001

44 Patterson. *Transforming Electricity.*, p. 16; Thomas. 'Strategic Government and Corporate Issues'., p. 261.

45 Pearlstein. 'On California Stage, a Cautionary Tale.'

46 Patterson. *Transforming Electricity.*, p. 16.

47 Edward B. Flowers. *U.S. Utility Mergers and the Restructuring of the New Global Power Industry.* Westport, Connecticut: Quorum Books. 1998, p. 200.

48 Patterson. *Transforming Electricity.*, p. 84.

49 Flowers. *U.S. Utility Mergers.*, pp. 1, 175; Patterson. *Transforming Electricity.*, p. 84.

50 Flowers. *U.S. Utility Mergers.*, pp.1, 202.

51 Chavez. 'Lights Off!', p. 3.

52 Ibid., p. 11.

53 Flowers. *U.S. Utility Mergers.*, p. 200.

54 'Energy, the New Convergence.' *The Economist.* 29 May 1999; Patterson. *Transforming Electricity.*, p. 84.

55 Patterson. *Transforming Electricity.*, p. 84.

56 Public Services Privatisation Research Unit. 'Public Services Privatisation Research Unit.' The Privatisation Network. January 1996. http://www.psiru.org/reports/96-01-TPN.doc

57 Patterson. *Transforming Electricity.*, p. 120.

58 Ibid., p. 121.

59 Ibid.

60 Ibid., p. 121, 129-30.

Chapter One

1 Quoted in Daniel Berman. 'The Birth of the Public Power Movement.' Public Power Now. Accessed on 19 December 2001. http://www.publicpowernow.org/story/2001/6 /21/0114/78378

2 Patrick McGuire and Mark Granovetter. 'Business and Bias in Public Policy Formation: The National Civic Federation and Social Construction of Electric Utility Regulation, 1905-1907.' Public Power Now. August, 1998. http://www.publicpowernow.org/story/2001/7 /26/161517/294; Richard Hirsh. 'Emergence of Electrical Utilities in America.' Smithsonian Museum. December 2001. http://american-history.si.edu/csr/powering/hirsh1/history.htm; Richard Rudolph and Scott Ridley. *Power Struggle: The Hundred -Year War over Electricity.* New York: Harper & Row. 1986, pp. 32, 34.

3 Harvey Wasserman. *The Last Energy War: The Battle over Utility Regulation,* ed. Stuart Sahulka, *Open Media Pamphlet Series.* New York: Seven Stories Press. 1999, p. 17; McGuire and Granovetter. 'Business and Bias in Public Policy Formation.'; Rudolph and Ridley. *Power Struggle.*, pp. 32, 35;

4 Quoted in Rudolph and Ridley. *Power Struggle.*, p. 33.

5 Quoted in Berman. 'The Birth of the Public Power Movement.'

6 Rudolph and Ridley. *Power Struggle.*, p. 22.

7 Ibid., p. 22.

8 Ibid., pp. 23, 34.

9 McGuire and Granovetter. 'Business and Bias in Public Policy Formation.'

10 Richard Munson. *Power Makers: The Inside Story of America's Biggest Business ... And Its Struggle to Control Tomorrow's Electricity.*

Emmaus, Pennsylvania: Rodale Press. 1985, p. 60; Berman. 'The Birth of the Public Power Movement.'

11 Rudolph and Ridley. *Power Struggle.*, p. 31.

12 Munson. *Power Makers.*, p. 55; McGuire and Granovetter. 'Business and Bias in Public Policy Formation.' .

13 Munson. *Power Makers.*, p. 55.

14 Rudolph and Ridley. *Power Struggle.*, p. 28.

15 Quoted in Munson. *Power Makers.*, p. 51.

16 Thomas Hughes. *Networks of Power: Electrification in Western Society, 1880-1930.* Baltimore and London: John Hopkins University Press. 1983

17 Richard F. Hirsh. *Power Loss: The Origins of Deregulation and Restructuring in the American Electric Utility System.* Cambridge, Massachusetts: The MIT Press. 1999, p. 13.

18 Quoted in Rudolph and Ridley. *Power Struggle.*, p. 31.

19 Hirsh. *Power Loss.*, p. 13.

20 Ibid., pp. 13-14; Berman. 'The Birth of the Public Power Movement.'

21 Rudolph and Ridley. *Power Struggle.*, pp. 38-9; Hirsh. *Power Loss.*, pp. 23-4.

22 McGuire and Granovetter. 'Business and Bias in Public Policy Formation.'; Rudolph and Ridley. *Power Struggle.*, p. 40; Hirsh. 'Emergence of Electrical Utilities in America.'

23 Rudolph and Ridley. *Power Struggle.*, p. 39.

24 Hirsh. *Power Loss.*, p. 24.

25 McGuire and Granovetter. 'Business and Bias in Public Policy Formation.'; Rudolph and Ridley. *Power Struggle.*, p. 39.

26 McGuire and Granovetter. 'Business and Bias in Public Policy Formation.'

27 Hirsh. *Power Loss.*, p. 25; Hirsh. 'Emergence of Electrical Utilities in America.'

28 Hirsh. 'Emergence of Electrical Utilities in America.'

29 McGuire and Granovetter. 'Business and Bias in Public Policy Formation.'

30 Hughes. *Networks of Power.*, p. 207; McGuire and Granovetter. 'Business and Bias in Public Policy Formation.'

31 Franklin D. Roosevelt. 'FDR's 1932 Speech on Public Power.' Public Power Now. Accessed on 19 December 2001. http://www.publicpower-now.org/story/2001/6/21/03041/3752

32 Hirsh. *Power Loss.*, pp. 26-7.

33 McGuire and Granovetter. 'Business and Bias in Public Policy Formation.'; Carl D. Thompson. *Confessions of the Power Trust.* New York: E. P. Dutton & Co. 1932, p. 155.

34 Hirsh. *Power Loss.*, p. 23; Rudolph and Ridley.

Power Struggle., p. 41.

35 Quoted in Rudolph and Ridley. *Power Struggle.*, p. 40.

36 Cited in Adam Thierer. 'Energizing America: A Blueprint for Deregulating the Electricity Market.' *The Heritage Foundation Backgrounder.* 23 January 1997

37 NCF quoted in McGuire and Granovetter. 'Business and Bias in Public Policy Formation.'

38 Richard F. Hirsh. 'Revamping and Repowering.' *Forum for Applied Research and Public Policy* 15(2). 2000

39 Easley, Ralph M. to George Perkins, N.Y. 9 June 1909, Box 38, National Civic Council Federation Papers, Library of Congress, Washington DC

40 McGuire and Granovetter. 'Business and Bias in Public Policy Formation.'

41 Munson. *Power Makers.*, p. 69.

42 Hirsh. *Power Loss.*, p. 42.

43 Thomas McCraw quoted in Ibid., p. 43; Rudolph and Ridley. *Power Struggle.*, p. 189.

44 Thompson. *Confessions of the Power Trust.*, pp. 599-601, 605; Hirsh. *Power Loss.*, p. 45.

45 Daniel M. Berman and John T. O'Connor. *Who Owns the Sun: People, Politics, and the Struggle for a Solar Economy.* White River Junction, Vermont: Chelsea Green Publishing Company. 1996, p. 71.

46 Quoted in Thompson. *Confessions of the Power Trust.*, p. 608.

47 Rudolph and Ridley. *Power Struggle.*, p. 41.

48 Hirsh. *Power Loss.*, pp. 44, 46.

49 Thompson. *Confessions of the Power Trust.*, pp. 597-8, 628.

50 Ibid., p. 612.

51 Rudolph and Ridley. *Power Struggle.*, p. 41.

52 Hirsh. 'Emergence of Electrical Utilities in America.'

53 Public Citizen. 'The PUHCA Primer.' Public Citizen. 29 January 1998. http://www.citizen.org/print_article.cfm?ID=4245

54 Thompson. *Confessions of the Power Trust.*, p. 141.

55 Ibid., pp. 95, 155.

56 Ibid., pp. 62, 5, 118-9.

57 Quoted in Ibid., p. 116.

58 Quoted in Ibid., pp. 119, 137.

59 Ibid., p. 73.

60 Ibid., pp. 69-70.

61 Rudolph and Ridley. *Power Struggle.*, p. 210.

62 Ibid., p;. 211.

63 Hirsh. 'Emergence of Electrical Utilities in America.'

64 Rudolph and Ridley. *Power Struggle.*, p. 42; Berman and O'Connor. *Who Owns the Sun.*, p. 69.

65 Thompson. *Confessions of the Power Trust.*, pp. 96, 102, 185.

66 Ibid., p. 232; Wasserman. *The Last Energy War.*, p. 24.

67 Thompson. *Confessions of the Power Trust.*, p. 232; Wasserman. *The Last Energy War.*, p. 24.

Chapter Two

1 Franklin D. Roosevelt. 'FDR's 1932 Speech on Public Power.' Public Power Now. Accessed on 19 December 2001. http://www.publicpowernow.org/story/2001/6/21/03041/3752

2 Richard F. Hirsh. *Power Loss: The Origins of Deregulation and Restructuring in the American Electric Utility System.* Cambridge, Massachusetts: The MIT Press. 1999, p. 38.

3 Karl Schriftgiesser. *The Lobbyists: The Art and Business of Influencing Lawmakers.* Boston: Little, Brown & Co. 1951, p. 59.

4 Senate Document 92, Part 71A, 70th Congress, 1st Session, p. 17.

5 Quoted in Schriftgiesser. *The Lobbyists.* pp. 59-60.

6 Carl D. Thompson. *Confessions of the Power Trust.* New York: E. P. Dutton & Co. 1932, p. 270.

7 Ibid., pp. 35, 38-9, 49, 51.

8 Lee Metcalf and Vic Reinemer. *Overcharge: How Electric Utilities Exploit and Mislead the Public.* New York: David McKay Company. 1967, p. 92.

9 Richard Munson. *Power Makers: The Inside Story of America's Biggest Business... And Its Struggle to Control Tomorrow's Electricity.* Emmaus, Pennsylvania: Rodale Press. 1985, pp. 65-6.

10 Hirsh. *Power Loss.*, p. 38.

11 Forrest McDonald, Insull biographer, quoted in Metcalf and Reinemer. *Overcharge.*, p. 93.

12 Hirsh. *Power Loss.*, p. 39; Richard Rudolph and Scott Ridley. *Power Struggle: The Hundred-Year War over Electricity.* New York: Harper & Row. 1986, p. 48.

13 Historian Arthur Schlesinger, quoted in Metcalf and Reinemer. *Overcharge.*, p. 94.

14 Rudolph and Ridley. *Power Struggle.*, p. 48; Thompson. *Confessions of the Power Trust.*, pp. 274, 281.

15 Quoted in Thompson. *Confessions of the Power Trust.*, p. 577.

16 Quoted in Ibid., p. 649.

17 Quoted in Munson. *Power Makers.*, pp. 66-7.

18 Jack Levin. *Power Ethics.* New York: Alfred A. Knopf. 1931, p. 30.

19 Schriftgiesser. *The Lobbyists.*, p. 59; Levin. *Power Ethics.*, chapter XVI; Thompson. *Confessions of the Power Trust.*, pp. 467-72.

20 Quoted in Levin. *Power Ethics.*, p. 45.

21 Ibid., pp. 46-7.

22 Thompson. *Confessions of the Power Trust.*, p. 442.

23 Quoted in Ibid., p. 437.

24 Ibid., pp. 444, 447-8.

25 Levin. *Power Ethics.*, p. 48; Thompson. *Confessions of the Power Trust.*, pp. 414-6.

26 Thompson. *Confessions of the Power Trust.*, pp. 416-7.

27 Alan R. Raucher. *Public Relations and Business 1900-1929.* Baltimore: The John Hopkins Press. 1968, pp. 86-7.

28 Quoted in Thompson. *Confessions of the Power Trust.*, p. 421.

29 A term used by H. Davis of the Nebraska Information Committee cited in Ibid., p. 458.

30 Quoted in Ibid., pp. 456-8.

31 Levin. *Power Ethics.*, pp. 101-2.

32 Thompson. *Confessions of the Power Trust.*, p. 310.

33 Schriftgiesser. *The Lobbyists.* p. 59.

34 Quoted in Levin. *Power Ethics.*, p. 104.

35 'What Happened to Hearst?' *San Francisco Bay Guardian.* 10 October 2001

36 Thompson. *Confessions of the Power Trust.*, pp. 284, 295-6.

37 Ibid., p. 299.

38 Ibid., pp. 296-9.

39 Ibid., p. 300..

40 Ibid., p. 301.

41 Ibid., pp. 304-5.

42 Quoted in Ibid., p. 411.

43 Quoted in Ibid., p. 322.

44 Ibid., p. 328.

45 Ibid., pp. 322-5.

46 Quoted in Levin. *Power Ethics.*, p. 50.

47 Quoted in Munson. *Power Makers.*, p. 67.

48 Schriftgiesser. *The Lobbyists.*, pp. 59-60.

49 Quoted in Thompson. *Confessions of the Power Trust.*, p. 331.

50 Quoted in Ibid., p. 389.

51 Ibid., pp. 390-1.

52 Quoted in Ibid., p. 390.

53 Ibid., p. 382.

54 Cited in Munson. *Power Makers.*, p. 67.

55 Levin. *Power Ethics.*, pp. 75-77; Daniel Berman. 'The Birth of the Public Power Movement.' Public Power Now. Accessed on

19 December 2001. http://www.publicpower-now.org/story/2001/6/21/0114/78378; Thompson. *Confessions of the Power Trust.*, pp. 377-9.

56 Berman. 'The Birth of the Public Power Movement.'; Levin. *Power Ethics.*, p. 80.

57 Quoted in Thompson. *Confessions of the Power Trust.*, p. 363.

58 Ibid., pp. 364-7.

59 Berman. 'The Birth of the Public Power Movement.'; Levin. *Power Ethics.*, p. 80; Thompson. *Confessions of the Power Trust.*, p. 378.

60 Quoted in Thompson. *Confessions of the Power Trust.*, p. 380.

61 Raucher. *Public Relations and Business 1900-1929.*, p. 87.

62 Quoted in Levin. *Power Ethics.*, p. 73.

63 Thompson. *Confessions of the Power Trust.*, p. 384.

64 Ibid., pp. 338, 351, 386-7

65 Ibid., p. 333.

66 Quoted in Ibid., p. 386.

67 Levin. *Power Ethics.*, pp. 81-2.

68 Thompson. *Confessions of the Power Trust.*, p. 341.

69 Chairman of the Rocky Mountain Committee on Public Utility Information quoted in Ibid., p. 335.

70 Ibid., p. 336; Levin. *Power Ethics.*, p. 83.

71 Quoted in Thompson. *Confessions of the Power Trust.*, p. 337.

72 Quoted in Levin. *Power Ethics.*, p. 84.

73 Munson. *Power Makers.*, p. 67; Thompson. *Confessions of the Power Trust.*, p. 349.

74 Quoted in Thompson. *Confessions of the Power Trust.*, p. 347.

75 Quoted in Ibid., p. 348.

76 Quoted in Ibid., p. 342.

77 Raucher. *Public Relations and Business 1900-1929.*, pp. 88-9.

78 Quoted in Thompson. *Confessions of the Power Trust.*, pp. 209-10.

79 Quoted in Ibid., p. 212.

80 Hirsh. *Power Loss.*, p. 39; Munson. *Power Makers.*, p. 67.

81 Thompson. *Confessions of the Power Trust.*, pp. 213-15.

82 Quoted in Ibid., p. 214.

83 Ibid., pp. 44, 204.

84 Quoted in Ibid., p. 205.

85 Ibid., p. 205.

86 Quoted in Ibid., pp. 207-8.

87 Rudolph and Ridley. *Power Struggle.*, p. 211, 213; Hirsh. *Power Loss.*, p. 34.

88 Rudolph and Ridley. *Power Struggle.*, p. 213.

89 Ibid., p. 10.

90 Thompson. *Confessions of the Power Trust.*, p. 198.

91 Quoted in Ibid., pp. 200-1.

92 Hockenbeamer quoted in Ibid., pp. 200-1.

93 Quoted in Ibid., pp. 202-3.

94 Rudolph and Ridley. *Power Struggle.*, p. 10; Thompson. *Confessions of the Power Trust.*, p. 274.

95 Thompson. *Confessions of the Power Trust.*, pp. 33, 43-4.

96 Rudolph and Ridley. *Power Struggle.*, p. 43; Thompson. *Confessions of the Power Trust.*, pp. 45, 48.

97 Thompson. *Confessions of the Power Trust.*, p. 48.

Chapter Three

1 Quoted in Richard Rudolph and Scott Ridley. *Power Struggle: The Hundred-Year War over Electricity.* New York: Harper & Row. 1986, p. 47.

2 Richard Munson. *Power Makers: The Inside Story of America's Biggest Business... And Its Struggle to Control Tomorrow's Electricity.* Emmaus, Pennsylvania: Rodale Press. 1985, p. 72.

3 Daniel M. Berman and John T. O'Connor. *Who Owns the Sun: People, Politics, and the Struggle for a Solar Economy.* White River Junction, Vermont: Chelsea Green Publishing Company. 1996, p. 72.

4 Quoted in Carl D. Thompson. *Confessions of the Power Trust.* New York: E. P. Dutton & Co. 1932, p. 10.

5 Richard F. Hirsh. *Power Loss: The Origins of Deregulation and Restructuring in the American Electric Utility System.* Cambridge, Massachusetts: The MIT Press. 1999, p. 49.

6 Thompson. *Confessions of the Power Trust.*, pp. 159-77, 441.

7 Rudolph and Ridley. *Power Struggle.*, p. 41; Thompson. *Confessions of the Power Trust.*, pp. 473-4.

8 Harvey Wasserman. *The Last Energy War: The Battle over Utility Regulation.* New York: Seven Stories Press. 1999, pp. 27-8.

9 Thompson. *Confessions of the Power Trust.*, p. 571; Berman and O'Connor. *Who Owns the Sun.*, p. 72.

10 Rudolph and Ridley. *Power Struggle.*, p. 43.

11 Wasserman. *The Last Energy War.*, p. 26.

12 Thompson. *Confessions of the Power Trust.*, pp. 475-9.

13 Ibid., p. 633.

14 Quoted in Ibid., p. 481.

15 Ibid., p. 473; Rudolph and Ridley. *Power Struggle.*, p. 44; Hirsh. *Power Loss.*, p. 30; Wasserman. *The Last Energy War.*, p. 22.

16 Thompson. *Confessions of the Power Trust.*, pp. 513, 527.

17 Quoted in Ibid., pp. 514-6.

18 Daniel A. Smith. 'Special Interests and Direct Democracy: An Historical Glance'. In *The Battle over Citizen Lawmaking.* ed M. Dane Waters. Durham: Carolina: Academic Press. 2001

19 Thompson. *Confessions of the Power Trust.*, p. 513-28.

20 Quoted in Ibid., p. 517.

21 Quoted in Ibid., p. 517.

22 Ibid., pp. 519-22.

23 Quoted in Ibid., p. 524.

24 Ibid., pp. 525-6.

25 Ibid., p. 515.

26 Ibid., p. 522.

27 Ibid., p. 518.

28 Quoted in Ibid., p. 518.

29 Ibid., p. 523.

30 Ibid., pp. 523-4.

31 Ibid., p. 521.

32 Ibid., pp. 212-3.

33 Thomas Hughes. *Networks of Power: Electrification in Western Society, 1880-1930.* Baltimore and London: John Hopkins University Press. 1983, pp. 297-313.

34 Ibid.,p. 302.

35 Ibid., pp. 302-3.

36 Ibid., p. 304.

37 Thompson. *Confessions of the Power Trust.*, p. 613.

38 Quoted in Ibid., p. 614.

39 Cited in Ibid., p. 616.

40 Hughes. *Networks of Power.*, p. 303.

41 Ibid. p, 299.

42 Ibid., p. 303.

43 Pinchot quoted in Thompson. *Confessions of the Power Trust.*, p. 615.

44 Hughes. *Networks of Power.*, p. 309.

45 Quoted in Thompson. *Confessions of the Power Trust.*, p. 618.

46 Quoted in Ibid., p. 619.

47 Hughes. *Networks of Power.*, pp. 310-12.

48 Thompson. *Confessions of the Power Trust.*, pp. 616-17, 624.

49 Hughes. *Networks of Power.*, p. 312.

50 Cited in Thompson. *Confessions of the Power Trust.*, p. 625.

51 Munson. *Power Makers.*, p. 78.

52 Rudolph and Ridley. *Power Struggle.*, p. 45;

Munson. *Power Makers.*, pp. 77-8, 80.

53 Rudolph and Ridley. *Power Struggle.*, p. 70; Munson. *Power Makers.*, p. 79.

54 Rudolph and Ridley. *Power Struggle.*, p. 47; Daniel Berman. 'The Birth of the Public Power Movement.' Public Power Now. Accessed on 19 December 2001. http://www.publicpowernow.org/story/2001/6/21/0114/78378

55 Thompson. *Confessions of the Power Trust.*, p. 5; Hirsh. *Power Loss.*, pp. 36-7.

56 Thompson. *Confessions of the Power Trust.*, pp. 80, 96.

57 Wasserman. *The Last Energy War.*, p. 22.

58 Richard Hirsh. 'Emergence of Electrical Utilities in America.' Smithsonian Museum. December 2001. http://americanhistory.si.edu/csr/powering/hirsh1/history.htm

59 Paul A. Gusmorino. 'Main Causes of the Great Depression.' *Gusmorino World.* 13 May 1996

60 Rudolph and Ridley. *Power Struggle.*, p. 55; Wasserman. *The Last Energy War.*, p. 23; Gusmorino. 'Main Causes of the Great Depression.'

61 Thompson. *Confessions of the Power Trust.*, p. 3.

62 Quoted in Karl Schriftgiesser. *The Lobbyists: The Art and Business of Influencing Lawmakers.* Boston: Little, Brown & Co. 1951, p. 58.

63 Ibid., p. 58.

64 Thompson. *Confessions of the Power Trust.*, pp. viii, 56, 60.

65 Rudolph and Ridley. *Power Struggle.*, pp. 56-8; Munson. *Power Makers.*, p. 70.

66 Berman. 'The Birth of the Public Power Movement.'

67 Thompson. *Confessions of the Power Trust.*, pp. 247-8; Lee Metcalf and Vic Reinemer. *Overcharge: How Electric Utilities Exploit and Mislead the Public.* New York: David McKay Company. 1967, p. 94; Rudolph and Ridley. *Power Struggle.*, p. 61.

68 Paul Gipe. 'History: California's Power Crisis, a Personal View.' *Juice.* 2 February 2001

69 Rudolph and Ridley. *Power Struggle.*, p. 61; Wasserman. *The Last Energy War.*, p. 25.

70 Munson. *Power Makers.*, pp. 70-1.

71 Franklin D. Roosevelt. 'FDR's 1932 Speech on Public Power.' Public Power Now. Accessed on 19 December 2001. http://www.publicpowernow.org/story/2001/6/21/03041/3752

72 Quoted in Charlie Higley. 'Disastrous Deregulation.' Public Citizen. December, 2000, p. 6.

73 Rudolph and Ridley. *Power Struggle.*, p. 63.

74 Munson. *Power Makers.*, p. 81; Berman and O'Connor. *Who Owns the Sun.*, p. 76.

75 Berman and O'Connor. *Who Owns the Sun.*, p. 76; Hirsh. *Power Loss.*, p. 53; Wasserman. *The Last Energy War.*, pp. 28-9.

76 Energy Information Agency. 'The Changing Structure of the Electric Power Industry 2000: An Update.' Department of Energy. October 2000, pp. 6-7.

77 Public Citizen. 'The PUHCA Primer.' Public Citizen. 29 January 1998. http://www.citizen.org/print_article.cfm?ID=4245

78 Higley. 'Disastrous Deregulation.', p. 7.

79 Rudolph and Ridley. *Power Struggle.*, pp. 194-5.

80 Ibid., p. 56.

81 Quoted in Ibid., pp. 78-9.

82 Munson. *Power Makers.*, p. 83.

83 Rudolph and Ridley. *Power Struggle.*, p. 77.

84 Ibid., p. 77.

85 Ibid., pp. 77-8, 214..

86 Schriftgiesser. *The Lobbyists.*, pp. 70-1; Rudolph and Ridley. *Power Struggle.*, p. 78

87 Ibid.

88 Wasserman. *The Last Energy War.*, p. 29.

89 Rudolph and Ridley. *Power Struggle.*, pp. 79, 215.

90 Wasserman. *The Last Energy War.*, p. 27.

91 Rudolph and Ridley. *Power Struggle.*, pp. 11, 195.

92 Ibid., p. 11.

Chapter Four

1 Lee Metcalf and Vic Reinemer. *Overcharge: How Electric Utilities Exploit and Mislead the Public.* New York: David McKay Company. 1967, p. 151.

2 Ibid., pp 6, 7, 110.

3 Richard F. Hirsh. *Power Loss: The Origins of Deregulation and Restructuring in the American Electric Utility System.* Cambridge, Massachusetts: The MIT Press. 1999, p. 46.

4 Metcalf and Reinemer. *Overcharge.*, pp. 95-6.

5 Ibid., p. 97.

6 Ibid., pp. 105, 112.

7 Quoted in Ibid., p. 147.

8 Ibid., p. 111.

9 Ibid., pp. 3, 21, 24.

10 Ibid., pp. 3, 4, 21, 24, 33.

11 Ibid., pp. 154, 155, 158.

12 Ibid., p. 158.

13 Ibid., p. 159.

14 Ibid., p. 164.

15 Ibid., p. 168.

16 Ibid., pp. 168, 170-8.

17 Ibid., pp. 181, 189.

18 Quoted in Ibid., pp. 185-6.

19 Ibid., pp. 186-7.

20 Richard Rudolph and Scott Ridley. *Power Struggle: The Hundred-Year War over Electricity.* New York: Harper & Row. 1986, p. 121.

21 J.E.Corette, President of the Montana Power Company (at 1959 EEI convention), quoted in Ibid., p. 121.

22 Quoted in Metcalf and Reinemer. *Overcharge.*, p. 98.

23 Ibid., p. 99.

24 Ibid., p. 100.

25 Ibid., p. 100.

26 Quoted in Ibid., pp. 100-1.

27 Quoted in Ibid., p. 149.

28 Ibid., p. 150.

29 Ibid., p. 132.

30 Ibid., p. 132.

31 Ibid., pp. 50-52.

32 Quoted in Ibid., p. 134.

33 Ibid., pp. 139-45.

34 Ibid., pp. 142-146.

35 Ibid., p. 137.

36 Rudolph and Ridley. *Power Struggle.*, p. 125.

37 Quoted in Ibid., p. 125.

38 Quoted in Metcalf and Reinemer. *Overcharge.*, p. 116.

39 Quoted in Ibid., p. 114.

40 Quoted in Ibid., p. 117.

41 Ibid., pp. 122-4.

42 A Time to Choose, 1974, quoted in Daniel M. Berman and John T. O'Connor. *Who Owns the Sun: People, Politics, and the Struggle for a Solar Economy.* White River Junction, Vermont: Chelsea Green Publishing Company. 1996, p. 3.

43 Ed Smeloff and Peter Asmus. *Reinventing Electric Utilities: Competition, Citizen Action, and Clean Power.* Washington, D. C.: Island Press. 1997, p. 19; 'California Orders Its Utilities to 'Unsell' Energy.' *Business Week.* 26 May 1980

44 Timothy J. Brennan, Karen L. Palmer, Raymond J. Kopp, Alan J. Krupnick, Vito Staglioano and Dallas Burtraw. *A Shock to the System: Restructuring America's Electricity Industry.* Washington D.C.: Resources for the Future. 1996, p. 26.

45 Smeloff and Asmus. *Reinventing Electric Utilities.*, p. 19; Harvey Wasserman. *The Last Energy War: The Battle over Utility Regulation.* New York: Seven Stories Press. 1999, p. 35.

46 Rudolph and Ridley. *Power Struggle.*, pp. 200-1; Brennan, Palmer, Kopp, Krupnick, Staglioano

and Burtraw. *A Shock to the System.*, p. 29.

47 Hirsh. *Power Loss.*, pp. 119, 123.

48 Rudolph and Ridley. *Power Struggle.*, pp. 3, 197; Wasserman. *The Last Energy War.*, p. 40; 'California Orders Its Utilities to 'Unsell' Energy.'

49 Rudolph and Ridley. *Power Struggle.*, pp. 7-8.

50 Steve Thomas. 'The Privatization of the Electricity Supply Industry'. In *The British Electricity Experiment.* ed John Surrey. London: Earthscan Publications. 1996, p. 48.

51 Rudolph and Ridley. *Power Struggle.*, p. 223.

52 Eugene Meyer, vice president of Kidder Peabody quoted in Berman and O'Connor. *Who Owns the Sun.*, p. 83.

53 Rudolph and Ridley. *Power Struggle.*, pp. 4, 13.

54 Berman and O'Connor. *Who Owns the Sun.*, p. 83; Rudolph and Ridley. *Power Struggle.*, p. 218.

55 Rudolph and Ridley. *Power Struggle.*, pp. 217-18, 223.

56 Ibid., pp. 13, 122.

57 Ibid., p. 201.

58 Ibid., p. 197; Smeloff and Asmus. *Reinventing Electric Utilities.*, p. 15.

59 1981 EEI advertisement reproduced in Hirsh. *Power Loss.*, figure 10.1.

60 1982 AEP advertisement reproduced in Ibid., figure 10.2.

61 1985 advertisement reproduced in Ibid., figure 10.3.

62 Arthur Hailey. *Overload.* London: Pan Books. 1980

63 Ibid., pp. 350-1.

64 'California Orders Its Utilities to 'Unsell' Energy.'

65 Daniel Seligman. 'They're Only Human.' *Fortune.* 12 February 1979

66 Rudolph and Ridley. *Power Struggle.*, p. 171.

67 Ibid., p. 172.

68 Ibid., p. 172.

69 Ibid., p. 191.

70 Ibid., pp. 14-5.

71 Berman and O'Connor. *Who Owns the Sun.*, pp. 109-110.

72 Sharon Beder. *The Nature of Sustainable Development*, 2nd edn. Melbourne: Scribe Publications. 1996, conclusion.

73 Savannah Blackwell. 'The Private Energy Elite.' *San Francisco Bay Guardian.* 8 October 1997

74 Berman and O'Connor. *Who Owns the Sun.*, pp. 110-1.

75 Ibid., pp. 107-8.

76 Wasserman. *The Last Energy War.*, p. 59.

77 Berman and O'Connor. *Who Owns the Sun.*,

p. 130.

78 Blackwell. 'The Private Energy Elite.'

79 Berman and O'Connor. *Who Owns the Sun.*, chapter 5.

80 Ibid., pp. 112, 120, 128.

81 Ibid., p. 112.

82 Hirsh. *Power Loss.*, p. 221.

83 David Howard Sinkman. 'California Green Groups Split over Power Policy.' *Planet Ark.* 1 February 2001

Chapter Five

1 Center for Responsive Politics. 'Power to the People? Money, Lawmakers, and Electricity Deregulation.' opensecrets.org. Accessed on 4 January 2001. http://www.opensecrets.org/pubs/cashingin_el ectric/contents.htm

2 Michael Kahn and Loretta Lynch. 'California's Electricity Options and Challenges: Report to Governor Gray Davis.' California Public Utilities Commission 2001

3 Joe Conason. 'Take It Public.' *Salon.com.* 19 June 2001

4 Sharon Beder. *Global Spin: The Corporate Assault on Environmentalism.* Devon: Green Books. 1997, chapter 5

5 Richard F. Hirsh. *Power Loss: The Origins of Deregulation and Restructuring in the American Electric Utility System.* Cambridge, Massachusetts: The MIT Press. 1999, p. 133; Richard Rudolph and Scott Ridley. *Power Struggle: The Hundred -Year War over Electricity.* New York: Harper & Row. 1986, p. 202

6 Rudolph and Ridley. *Power Struggle.*, p. 196.

7 Hirsh. *Power Loss.*, pp. 241, 244.

8 Charlie Higley. 'Disastrous Deregulation.' Public Citizen. December 2000

9 Ibid., p. 2; Ed Smeloff and Peter Asmus. *Reinventing Electric Utilities: Competition, Citizen Action, and Clean Power.* Washington, D. C.: Island Press. 1997, p. 2.

10 Timothy J. Brennan et. al. *A Shock to the System: Restructuring America's Electricity Industry.* Washington D.C.: Resources for the Future. 1996, p. 4; Higley. 'Disastrous Deregulation.', p. 2.

11 Paul Gipe. 'History: California's Power Crisis, a Personal View.' *Juice.* 2 February 2001; Hirsh. *Power Loss.*, p. 248.

12 Center for Responsive Politics. 'Power to the People?'

13 Martha M. Hamilton. 'Lobbyists Plug in to Debate over Electric Competition.' *Washington Post.* 25 January 1997

14 James Walsh. *The $10 Billion Jolt.* Los Angeles: Silver Lake Publishing. 2002, pp. 48, 53; Center for Responsive Politics. 'Power to the People?'; Eric Schmitt. 'Sides Square Off on Decontrolling Electricity Sales.' *New York Times.* 14 April 1997

15 Alliance of Energy Suppliers. 'Alliance of Energy Suppliers: About Us.' Edison Electric Institute. Accessed on 11 January 2002. http://eei.org/alliance/about/

16 Hirsh. *Power Loss.*, pp. 239, 243.

17 Kahn and Lynch. 'California's Electricity Options and Challenges.'

18 Schmitt. 'Sides Square Off.', p. A-1.

19 Harvey Wasserman. 'Power Struggle: California's Engineered Energy Crisis and the Potential of Public Power.' *Multinational Monitor* 22(6). 2001, p. 10; Higley. 'Disastrous Deregulation.', p. 3.

20 Hirsh. *Power Loss.*, p. 244.

21 Carl Deal. The Greenpeace Guide to Anti-Environmental Organizations. Berkeley, California: Odonian Press. 1993, pp. 57-9; David Helvarg. The War against the Greens: The "Wise-Use" Movement, the New Right, and Anti-Environmental Violence. San Francisco: Sierra Club Books. 1994, p. 20.

22 Adam Thierer. 'Energizing America: A Blueprint for Deregulating the Electricity Market.' *The Heritage Foundation Backgrounder* 23 January 1997

23 Hirsh. *Power Loss.*, p. 235.

24 Kahn and Lynch. 'California's Electricity Options and Challenges.'

25 Wasserman. 'Power Struggle.', p. 12; Kahn and Lynch. 'California's Electricity Options and Challenges.'; Merrill Goozner. 'Free Market Shock.' *The American Prospect.* 27 August 2001

26 Thomas DeLay. 'Bringing Consumer Choice to Electricity.' Paper presented at the Heritage Lecture No. 582, 8 April. 1997

27 Center for Responsive Politics. 'Power to the People?'

28 Ibid.; Center for Responsive Politics. 'Electricity Deregulation.' opensecrets.org. 30 January 2001. http://www.opensecrets.org/news/electricity.htm

29 Schmitt. 'Sides Square Off.'; Walsh. *The $10 Billion Jolt.* p. 54.

30 Walsh. *The $10 Billion Jolt.* pp. 54-5.

31 Ibid.; Citizens for a Sound Economy. 'Home Page.' Citizens for a Sound Economy. Accessed on 28 December 2001. http://www.cse.org/; Center for Responsive

Politics. 'Power to the People?'; Michael T. Maloney, Robert E. McCormick and Raymond D. Sauer. 'Customer Choice, Consumer Value: An Analysis of Retail Competition in America's Electric Industry.' Washington, DC: Citizens for a Sound Economy Foundation 1996

32 The Committee on Commerce. 'Bliley: Yet Another Study Endorses Electric 'Power to Choose'.' US House of Representative. 27 January 1997. http://www.house.gov/commerce/releases/pr012797.htm

33 Center for Responsive Politics. 'Power to the People?'

34 Agis Salpukas. 'In California, Enron Curbs Power Sales.' *New York Times.* 23 April 1998

35 Nancy Vogel. 'How State's Consumers Lost with Electricity Deregulation.' *LA Times.* 9 December 2000

36 David Morris. 'How to Solve the Electricity Crisis.' *Alternet* 5 September 2001

37 Higley. 'Disastrous Deregulation.', pp. 2-3.

38 Scott Sherman. 'Gimme an 'E;!' *Columbia Journalism Review* March/April, 2002

39 Gaston F. Ceron quoted in Ibid.

40 Robert Kuttner, *American Prospect* quoted in Ibid.

41 Mark Gladstone and Brandon Bailey. 'State's Long Road to Current Problem.' *Mercury News.* 30 November 2000

42 Goozner. 'Free Market Shock.'; Hamilton. 'Lobbyists Plug in to Debate over Electric Competition.'

43 Quoted in Hirsh. *Power Loss.*, pp. 252-3.

44 Smeloff and Asmus. *Reinventing Electric Utilities.*, p. 80; Vogel. 'How State's Consumers Lost.'; Gladstone and Bailey. 'State's Long Road to Current Problem.'

45 Erroll Davis, CEO Wisconson Power and Light Company, quoted in Hirsh. *Power Loss.*, p. 249.

46 David Bacon. 'USA: California's Deregulation Disaster.' *CorpWatch* 13 January 2001; Smeloff and Asmus. *Reinventing Electric Utilities.*, p. 77.

47 John Dunbar and Robert Moore. 'California Utilities' Donations Shed Light on Blackout Crisis.' The Center for Public Integrity. 30 May 2001. http://www.public-i.org/50states_01_053001.htm

48 Associated Press. 'Interactive Guide: California Power Woes.' Accessed on 4 April 2001. http://wire.ap.org/APpackages/california_power/; Smeloff and Asmus. *Reinventing Electric Utilities.*, p. 77.

49 Donella Meadows. 'Deregulation in California Didn't Help Consumers, or the Environment.' *Grist Magazine.* 22 January 2001

50 Harvey Wasserman. 'California's Deregulation Disaster.' *The Nation.* 12 February 2001, p. 11

51 Meadows. 'Deregulation in California.'

52 Wasserman. 'Power Struggle.', pp. 10-11.

53 Dunbar and Moore. 'California Utilities' Donations.'

54 'Pg&E's Web of Influence.' *San Francisco Bay Guardian.* 10 October 2001

55 Quoted in Ibid.

56 Vogel. 'How State's Consumers Lost.'; Dunbar and Moore. 'California Utilities' Donations.'

57 Dunbar and Moore. 'California Utilities' Donations.'

58 Environmental Action Foundation. 'Environmental Action Foundation's Position on Demand Side Management.' sfbg.com. 8 October 1997. http://www.sfbg.com/News/32/02/Documents/eafpos1.html; Kahn and Lynch. 'California's Electricity Options and Challenges.'; Hirsh. *Power Loss.*, p. 258.

59 Harvey Wasserman. *The Last Energy War: The Battle over Utility Regulation.* New York: Seven Stories Press. 1999, pp. 59-60.

60 Goozner. 'Free Market Shock.'

61 Harvey Wasserman. 'Deregulation Blackout: Manufacturing California's Fake Energy Crisis.' *Extra!* May/June, 2001, p. 23.

62 Walsh. *The $10 Billion Jolt.* p. 65.

63 Wasserman. *The Last Energy War.*, pp. 56-7.

64 Walsh. *The $10 Billion Jolt.* p. 82.

65 Quoted in Wasserman. 'Power Struggle.', p. 10.

66 Quoted in Hirsh. *Power Loss.*, p. 259.

67 Walsh. *The $10 Billion Jolt.* p. 84.

68 Gladstone and Bailey. 'State's Long Road to Current Problem.'; Paul Krugman. 'The Price of Power.' *New York Times.* 25 March 2001

69 Wasserman. 'Power Struggle.', pp. 10-11; Wasserman. 'California's Deregulation Disaster.', p. 12; 'PG&E's Web of Influence.'

70 Wasserman. 'Power Struggle.', pp. 10-12; Savannah Blackwell. 'The Private Energy Elite.' *San Francisco Bay Guardian.* 8 October, 1997.

71 The Foundation for Taxpayers & Consumer Rights. 'Prop 9 Supporters Confront Sen. Steve Peace's Propaganda Production against Prop. 9.' The Foundation for Taxpayers & Consumer Rights. 20 October 1998. http://www.consumerwatchdog.org/utilities/pr/pr000291.php3

72 Beth Snyder. 'Electricity Rivals Wary as Calif. Market Set to Reopen.' *Advertising Age* 30 March 1998, p. 28.

73 Beth Snyder. 'Electricity Utilities Rethink National Consumer Efforts.' *Advertising Age* 13 July 1998, p. 33.

74 Andrea Adelson. 'The $89 Million 'Plug in, California' Campaign Has Motivated Few Power Users to Switch Companies.' *New York Times.* 27 April 1998

75 Wasserman. *The Last Energy War.*, p. 59.

76 Vogel. 'How State's Consumers Lost.'

77 Ibid.; The Foundation for Taxpayer and Consumer Rights. 'Hoax: How Deregulation Let the Power Industry Steal $71 Billion from California.' Santa Monica, CA: FTCR. 17 January 2002, p. 6.

Chapter Six

1 Gregory Palast. 'Why the Lights Went out All over California.' *The Observer.* 1 July 2001, p. 4.

2 Nancy Vogel. 'How State's Consumers Lost with Electricity Deregulation.' *LA Times.* 9 December 2000; Doug Heller. 'Lesson of Enron: Deregulation Is a Disaster.' The Foundation for Taxpayer & Consumer Rights. 3 December 2001. http://www.consumer-watchdog.org/utilities/pr/pr002107.php3; Reuters. 'Calif. May Revive Utility Program to Save Electricity.' *Planet Ark.* 14 February 2001;

3 James Walsh. *The $10 Billion Jolt.* Los Angeles: Silver Lake Publishing. 2002, p. 45.

4 Savannah Blackwell. 'The Private Energy Elite.' *San Francisco Bay Guardian.* 8 October 1997

5 Timothy Egan. 'Once Braced for a Power Shortage, California Now Finds Itself with a Surplus.' *New York Times.* 4 November 2001

6 Vogel. 'How State's Consumers Lost.'; Aaron Glantz. 'No Power for the People.' *In These Times* 5 March 2001; Laura M. Holson and Richard A. Oppel. 'Trying to Follow the Money in California's Energy Mess.' *New York Times.* 12 January 2001; Harvey Wasserman. 'California's Deregulation Disaster.' *The Nation* 12 February 2001, p.12.

7 Glantz. 'No Power for the People.'

8 Marla Dickerson and Stuart Silverstein. 'Energy Crisis Spawns Business Feeding Frenzy.' *Los Angeles Times.* 23 January 2001, p. A-1.

9 Jerrold Oppenheim. 'US Electric Utilities: A Century of Successful Democratic Regulation of Private Monopolies; a Half-Decade of Failure of Experiments in Competition.' Brussels: European Federation of Public Service Unions. 12 December 2001, pp. 18-9.

10 Alex Berenson. 'Power Politics: New York Faces Prospect of Its Own Energy Troubles.'

New York Times. 25 February 2001

11 Ibid.

12 Michael Kahn and Loretta Lynch. 'California's Electricity Options and Challenges: Report to Governor Gray Davis.' California Public Utilities Commission 2001

13 Ibid.

14 Paul Krugman. 'The Unreal Thing.' *New York Times.* 18 February 2001; Kahn and Lynch. 'California's Electricity Options and Challenges.'

15 Vogel. 'How State's Consumers Lost.'; Timothy Egan and Sam Howe Verhovek. 'California's Panic Was Moneymaker for Energy Sellers.' *New York Times.* 11 February 2001

16 Kahn and Lynch. 'California's Electricity Options and Challenges.'

17 Vogel. 'How State's Consumers Lost.'

18 Paul Joskow and Edward Kahn. 'A Quantitative Analysis of Pricing Behavior in California's Wholesale Electricity Market During Summer 2000.' Southern California Edison. 21 November. Accessed on 11 January 2000 http://www.sce.com/005_regul_info/pdf/Josko wKahnPaper001121.pdf

19 Carl Blumstein, L. S. Friedman and R. J. Green. 'The History of Electricity Restructuring in California.' Berkeley, California: Center for the Study of Energy Markets. August, 2001, p. 26

20 Critical Mass Energy & Environment Program. 'Blind Faith: How Deregulation and Enron's Influence over Government Looted Billions from Americans.' Washington, D.C.: Public Citizen. December 2001, p. 21

21 Kahn and Lynch. 'California's Electricity Options and Challenges.'

22 Joskow and Kahn. 'A Quantitative Analysis of Pricing Behavior in California's Wholesale Electricity Market During Summer 2000.', p. 25

23 Steve Berry and Nicholas Riccardi. 'Generators Acted to Keep Prices Higher, Studies Show.' *Los Angeles Times.* 14 January 2001, p. A-1; Aaron Glantz. 'Few Lessons Learned from California's Energy Debacle.' *CorpWatch.* 15 March 2001

24 Berry and Riccardi. 'Generators Acted to Keep Prices Higher.'

25 William Marcus and Jan Hamrin. 'How We Got into the California Energy Crisis.' JBS Energy, Inc. Accessed on 19 February 2001. http://www.jbsenergy.com/Energy/Papers/Cali fornia_Energy_Crisis/california_energy_cri-sis.html; Kahn and Lynch. 'California's

Electricity Options and Challenges.'

26 Paul Gipe. 'History: California's Power Crisis, a Personal View.' *Juice.* 2 February 2001

27 Ibid.

28 Berry and Riccardi. 'Generators Acted to Keep Prices Higher.', p. A-1.

29 Marcus and Hamrin. 'How We Got into the California Energy Crisis.'; Egan. 'Once Braced for a Power Shortage.'; Critical Mass Energy & Environment Program. 'Blind Faith.', p. 21.

30 Wenonah Hauter and Tyson Slocum. 'It's Greed Stupid! Debunking the Ten Myths of Utility Deregulation.' Public Citizen. January 2001, p. 9.

31 Palast. 'Why the Lights Went out All over California.', p. 4.

32 Dunn & Rossi Barker. 'The Electric Summer: Symptoms — Options — Solutions.' Washington, DC: Edison Electric Institute. October, 2000, p. 3.

33 Hauter and Slocum. 'It's Greed Stupid!', p. 10; Marcus and Hamrin. 'How We Got into the California Energy Crisis.'; Gipe. 'History.'

34 Charlie Higley. 'Disastrous Deregulation.' Public Citizen. December, 2000, p. 1

35 Donella Meadows. 'Deregulation in California Didn't Help Consumers, or the Environment.' *Grist Magazine.* 22 January 2001

36 Greg Palast. 'Bush Energy Plan: Policy or Payback?' BBC News. 18 May 2001. http://news.bbc.co.uk/hi/english/world/ameri-cas/newsid_1336000/1336960.stm; Palast. 'Why the Lights Went out All over California.', p. 4; Editorial. 'California Culprits.' *New York Times.* 26 September 2002

37 Marcus and Hamrin. 'How We Got into the California Energy Crisis.'; Gipe. 'History.'

38 Berry and Riccardi. 'Generators Acted to Keep Prices Higher.', p. A-1.

39 Kahn and Lynch. 'California's Electricity Options and Challenges.'

40 Paul Krugman. 'The Price of Power.' *New York Times.* 25 March 2001

41 Vogel. 'How State's Consumers Lost.'

42 Mark Martin. 'Internal Memos Connect Enron to California Energy Crisis.' *San Francisco Chronicle.* 7 May 2002; Richard A. Oppel. 'How Enron Got California to Buy Power It Didn't Need.' *New York Times.* 8 May 2002

43 Quoted in Martin. 'Internal Memos Connect Enron to California Energy Crisis.'

44 Oppel. 'How Enron Got California to Buy Power It Didn't Need.'; Richard A. Oppel and Jeff Gerth. 'Enron Forced up California Energy Prices, Documents Show.' *New York*

Times. 7 May 2002

45 Richard W. Stevenson. 'Energy Trading Gave Prices Artificial Lift, Panel Is Told.' *New York Times.* 12 April, 2002

46 David Barboza. 'Former Officials Say Enron Hid Gains During Crisis in California.' *New York Times.* 23 June 2002

47 David Barboza. 'A Big Victory by California in Energy Case'. *New York Times.* 12 November 2002.

48 Gray Davis. 'Enron's Lessons for the Energy Market.' *New York Times.* 11 May 2002

49 Loren Fox. *Enron: The Rise and Fall.* Hoboken, New Jersey: John Wiley & Sons. 2003, p. 201.

50 Quoted in Nancy Dunne. 'Energy Groups Probed over California Trades.' *Financial Times.* 14 August 2002

51 Quoted in Joseph Kahn. 'Californians Call Enron Documents the Smoking Gun.' *New York Times.* 8 May 2002

52 Barboza. 'A Big Victory by California in Energy Case'.

53 Kevin Yamamura. 'Energy System Conflict Alleged.' *Sacramento Bee.* 6 June 2002

54 Carrie Peyton Dahlberg. 'Energy Firm Denies 'Wash' Trades.' *Sacramento Bee.* 6 June 2002

55 Palast. 'Why the Lights Went out All over California.', p. 4.

56 Kahn and Lynch. 'California's Electricity Options and Challenges.'

57 Hauter and Slocum. 'It's Greed Stupid!', p. 4; Public Citizen. 'Got Juice: Bush's Refusal to End California Electricity Price Gouging Enriches Texas Friends and Big Contributors.' Public Citizen. February, 2001, p. 6; Jeff Gerth and Lowell Bergman. 'Power Concern Offers California a Secret Deal.' *New York Times.* 2 May 2001; Glantz. 'Few Lessons Learned.'; Public Citizen. 'Got Juice.', p. 6; Vogel. 'How State's Consumers Lost.'; The Foundation for Taxpayer and Consumer Rights. 'Hoax: How Deregulation Let the Power Industry Steal $71 Billion from California.' Santa Monica, CA: FTCR. 17 January 2002, p. 30.

58 Walsh. *The $10 Billion Jolt.*, p.56.

59 Richard A. Oppel and Laura M. Holson. 'While a Utility May Be Failing, Its Owner Is Not.' *New York Times.* 30 April 2001

60 Tim Reiterman. 'Ex-Edison Chief Made Deregulation Pay Well.' *Los Angeles Times.* 26 January 2001, p. A-16; Carrie Peyton Dahlberg. 'Energy Rebate Program Approved.' *Sacramento Bee.* 7 June 2002

61 The Foundation for Taxpayer and Consumer Rights. 'Hoax.', p. 6; Holson and Oppel. 'Trying to Follow the Money.'; Wasserman. 'California's Deregulation Disaster.', p. 12.

62 Holson and Oppel. 'Trying to Follow the Money.'; Wasserman. 'California's Deregulation Disaster.', p. 12; Rachel Brahinsky. 'PG&E's Propaganda War.' *San Francisco Bay Guardian.* 3 January 2001; Michael A. Hiltzik. 'Part of Utilities' Windfall Went to Dividends, Parent Firms.' *LA Times.* 24 January 2001

63 Hiltzik. 'Part of Utilities' Windfall Went to Dividends, Parent Firms.'; Charlie Cray. 'Power Plays: Where Did the California Utilities Go?' *Multinational Monitor* 22(6). 2001, p. 13.

64 Glantz. 'Few Lessons Learned.'; Daniel Berman. 'The Confederate Cartel's War against California.' *San Francisco Bay Guardian.* 5 January, 2001; Ralph Nader. 'Deregulation Disaster: California Consumers Shouldn't Bailout PG&E.' *San Francisco Bay Guardian.* 15 January 2001

65 David Bacon. 'USA: California's Deregulation Disaster.' *CorpWatch* 13 January 2001

66 Glantz. 'Few Lessons Learned.'; Oppel and Holson. 'While a Utility May Be Failing, Its Owner Is Not.'

67 Public Citizen. 'Claiming Poverty in a Sea of Riches: New Investments by Parent Companies Belie California Utilities Claim of Bankruptcy.' Public Citizen. 16 January 2001. http://www.citizen.org/print_article.cfm?ID=4 407; Cray. 'Power Plays: Where Did the California Utilities Go?', p. 13; Brahinsky. 'PG&E's Propaganda War.'

68 Brahinsky. 'PG&E's Propaganda War.'

69 'Electric Executives on Deregulation Gravy Train', TURN. 2003. http://www.turn.org/turn/turnarticles/press_g ravytrain.htm.

70 Glantz. 'Few Lessons Learned.'

71 The Foundation for Taxpayer and Consumer Rights. 'Hoax.', p. 7; Nancy Rivera Brooks and Nicholas Riccardi. 'Energy 101: Power Exchange Marketplace to Close.' *LA Times.* 20 January 2001, p. A-25.

72 Cray. 'Power Plays: Where Did the California Utilities Go?', p. 13; Reuters. 'Californians Respond to Energy Conservation.' *Planet Ark.* 5 June, 2001; Mitchell Landsberg and Tim Reiterman. 'Utilities Scramble to Persuade Public of Need for Rate Hikes.' *Los Angeles Times.* 27 January 2001

73 Alison Mitchell. 'Ads brawl in a never-ending political season'. *The New York Times*. 3 July 2001.

74 Russell Mokhiber. 'Calif. Blackout Blackmail.' *Multinational Monitor* March, 2001, p. 29.

75 Quoted in Ibid., p. 29.

76 Cray. 'Power Plays: Where Did the California Utilities Go?', p. 13; Reuters. 'Californians Respond to Energy Conservation.'; Evelyn Nieves. 'Record Rate Hike Set in California.' *New York Times*. 28 March 2001; The Associated Press. 'California Spells out Rate Increase for Electricity.' *New York Times*. 16 May 2001

77 Nieves. 'Record Rate Hike Set in California.'

78 Laura M. Holson. 'California's Largest Utility Files for Bankruptcy.' *New York Times*. 7 April 2001

79 Glen Martin. 'Reorganized PG&E Could Sell Sierra Land.' *San Francisco Gate*. 16 January 2002

80 Southern California Edison. 'Public Information Campaigns.' Southern California Edison. Accessed on 11 January 2002. http://www.sce.com/005_regul_info/005c6q_campaign.shtml; Rachel Brahinsky. 'PG&E's Propaganda War, Part Two.' *San Francisco Bay Guardian*. 9 May 2001

81 Alex Berenson. 'California Plans to Buy Utility's Wires.' *New York Times*. 24 February 2001

82 Paul Krugman. 'The Power Perplex.' *New York Times*. 26 February 2002; The Foundation for Taxpayer and Consumer Rights. 'Hoax.', p. 14; Egan. 'Once Braced for a Power Shortage.'

83 Krugman. 'The Power Perplex.'

84 The Foundation for Taxpayer and Consumer Rights. 'Hoax.', pp. 8, 32.

85 Egan. 'Once Braced for a Power Shortage.'

86 The Foundation for Taxpayer and Consumer Rights. 'Hoax.', p. 35.

87 Ibid., p. 40.

88 Ibid., p. 38; Californians for Energy Action. 'Business Group Launches Advertising Campaign to Support Energy Competition, Jobs and California Economy.' CEA. 11 July 2001. http://www.piersystem.com/external/final_View.cfm?pressID=2504&CID=181

89 The Foundation for Taxpayer and Consumer Rights. 'Hoax.', p. 2.

Chapter Seven

1 Quoted in Nancy Vogel. 'How State's Consumers Lost with Electricity Deregulation.' *LA Times*. 9 December 2000

2 Aaron Glantz. 'Few Lessons Learned from California's Energy Debacle.' *CorpWatch*. 15 March 2001; Energy Information Agency. 'Current Federal Legislative Proposals.' Department of Energy. 21 February 2002; Wenonah Hauter and Tyson Slocum. 'It's Greed Stupid! Debunking the Ten Myths of Utility Deregulation.' Public Citizen. January, 2001, p. 15; Consumers Union. 'Deregulated.' *Consumer Reports* July, 2002, pp. 34-5; Jerrold Oppenheim. 'US Electric Utilities: A Century of Successful Democratic Regulation of Private Monopolies; a Half-Decade of Failure of Experiments in Competition.' Brussels: European Federation of Public Service Unions. 12 December 2001, p. 23.

3 See for example, Dunn & Rossi Barker. 'The Electric Summer: Symptoms—Options—Solutions.' Washington, DC: Edison Electric Institute. October, 2000, p. 1.

4 Eric Hirst. 'The California Electricity Crisis: Lessons for Other States.' Washington, D.C.: Edison Electric Institute. July, 2001, pp. 1, 11.

5 Hauter and Slocum. 'It's Greed Stupid!', p. 16; Merrill Goozner. 'Free Market Shock.' *The American Prospect*. 27 August 2001

6 Oppenheim. 'US Electric Utilities.', pp. 6, 11.

7 Charlie Higley. 'Disastrous Deregulation.' Public Citizen. December 2000, p. 3.

8 Goozner. 'Free Market Shock.'

9 Gary Locke. 'Caught in the Electrical Fallout.' *New York Times*. 2 February 2001

10 Ibid.

11 Paul Krugman. 'The Unreal Thing.' *New York Times*. 18 February 2001

12 Neela Banerjee and Richard Pérez-Pena. 'Power Politics: A Failed Energy Plan Catches up to New York.' *New York Times*. 1 June 2001; Alex Berenson. 'Power Politics: New York Faces Prospect of Its Own Energy Troubles.' *New York Times*. 25 February 2001

13 Gail Collins. 'Power Politics.' *New York Times*. 2 February 2001

14 Banerjee and Pérez-Pena. 'Power Politics.'; Berenson. 'Power Politics: New York Faces Prospect of Its Own Energy Troubles.'; Steven Pearlstein. 'On California Stage, a Cautionary Tale.' *The Washington Post*. 21 August 2001

15 Goozner. 'Free Market Shock.'; Banerjee and Pérez-Pena. 'Power Politics.'; Berenson. 'Power Politics: New York Faces Prospect of Its Own Energy Troubles.'; Editorial. 'The Turbine Mess.' *New York Times*. 20 March 2001

16 Reuters. 'Businesses Warn New York Needs More Power Plants.' *World Environment News*.

9 August 2002; Reuters. 'New York Again Asked to Cut Power Use in Heat Wave.' *Planet Ark*. 19 April 2002; Oppenheim. 'US Electric Utilities.', p. 23.

17 Jayson Blair. 'Power Problems Here to Stay, Experts Predict.' *New York Times*. 31 July 2002; Higley. 'Disastrous Deregulation.', p. 4; Oppenheim. 'US Electric Utilities.', p. 21.

18 Higley. 'Disastrous Deregulation.', p. 4; Oppenheim. 'US Electric Utilities.', p. 19.

19 Cited in Oppenheim. 'US Electric Utilities.', p. 20.

20 Quoted in Ibid., p. 21.

21 Ibid., p. 20.

22 Quoted in David M. Herszenhorn. 'Connecticut Utility Seeks More Money for Suppliers.' *New York Times*. 24 July 2002

23 Joseph Kahn. 'With Markets Flawed, Enron's Tactics Live On.' *New York Times*. 12 May 2002

24 Energy Information Agency. 'The Changing Structure of the Electric Power Industry 2000: An Update.' Department of Energy. October 2000, p. 85; Kahn. 'With Markets Flawed, Enron's Tactics Live On.'

25 Agis Salpukas. 'Subsidizing Competition in Utilities.' *New York Times*. 1 February 1997

26 Ibid.; Edward B. Flowers. *U.S. Utility Mergers and the Restructuring of the New Global Power Industry*. Westport, Connecticut: Quorum Books. 1998, p. 144.

27 Reuters. 'California Moving toward Reregulating Energy.' *New York Times*. 21 September 2001; 'California Power Crisis.' *E-Wire*. 8 February 2001; Consumers Union. 'Deregulated.', p. 35.

28 Banerjee and Pérez-Pena. 'Power Politics.'; Berenson. 'Power Politics: New York Faces Prospect of Its Own Energy Troubles.'

29 Hauter and Slocum. 'It's Greed Stupid!', p. 16.

30 Consumers Union. 'Deregulated.', p. 35; Pearlstein. 'On California Stage, a Cautionary Tale.'

31 American Public Power Association. 'Public Power Costs Less.' *2001 Annual Directory & Statistical Report*, 2001; Rachel Brahinsky. 'PG&E's Propaganda War, Part Two.' *San Francisco Bay Guardian*. 9 May 2001

32 Sarah Disbrow. 'Sitting on an Electric Fence: The Looming Threat to Nebraska Public Power.' Nebraskans for Peace. Accessed on 19 December 2001. http://www.nebraskansfor-peace.org/2000/o00.electricfence.html

33 Harvey Wasserman. 'Power Struggle: California's Engineered Energy Crisis and the Potential of Public Power.' *Multinational Monitor* 22(6). 2001, p. 20

34 Strategic Energy. 'Regulatory Update.' Strategic Energy. Accessed on 5 November 2002 http://www.sel.com/Supply/Electricity/states/Montana/montreg.htm; Matt Gouras. 'Montana Considers Going into the Electricity Business.' *The Morning Sun*. 21 September, 2002; Charles S. Johnson. 'Energy Bill in Hands of Voters.' *The Montana Standard*. 8 October 2002; Matt Gouras. 'Voters reject plan to buy dams.' *The Associated Press State & Local Wire*. 6 November 2002.

35 'State, Local Elections on Public Power Issues Produce Mixed Results.' *Public Power Weekly* 11 November, 2002, p. 1.

36 John Kelly. 'Electric Utility Industry Restructuring and Its Impact on Public Power.' Paper presented at the 25th Annual CIS Conference. Albuquerque, New Mexico, 15-18 May 2001; EEI. 'Electric Power—an Overview of the Industry and Its Impact, Section 1.' Edison Electric Institute. Accessed on 11 January 2002. http://www.eei.org/issues/comp_reg/key_facts/section1.pdf, p. 8.

37 'Manifesto on the California Electricity Crisis.' Haas School of Business, University of California Berkeley. 26 January 2001. http//haas.berkeley.edu/news/california_elec-tricity_crisis.html

38 Rachel Brahinsky. 'Mud Money.' *San Francisco Bay Guardian*. 8 August, 2001; Rachel Brahinsky. 'PG&E's Propaganda War, Part III.' *San Francisco Bay Guardian*. 17 October 2001

39 Energy Information Agency. 'Regulatory Changes by the Federal Energy Regulatory Commission.' Department of Energy. 21 February 2002; Kelly. 'Electric Utility Industry Restructuring.'

40 Hauter and Slocum. 'It's Greed Stupid!', p. 16.

41 Higley. 'Disastrous Deregulation.', p. 7.

42 EEI. 'Electric Power - an Overview of the Industry and Its Impact, Section 2.' Edison Electric Institute. Accessed on 11 January 2002. http://www.eei.org/issues/comp_reg/key_facts/section2.pdf, p. 15.

43 Joseph Kahn. 'Senate Committee Votes to Repeal Law Limiting Utilities.' *New York Times*. 25 April 2001

44 Public Citizen. 'Rep. Barton's Electricity Deregulation Bill Hurts Consumers.' Public Citizen. 12 December 2001. http://www.citi-zen.org/pressroom/print_release.cfm?ID=971

45 FTCR. 'Daschle Pushes Electricity

Deregulation Bill in Disguise.' Foundation for Taxpayer & Consumer Rights. 5 March 2002. http://www.consumerwatchdog.org/utilities/pr/pr002273.php3

46 EEI. 'Electric Power 1.'

47 Disbrow. 'Sitting on an Electric Fence.'

48 Cited in Mark Agnew. 'Mergers and Acquisitions: Reshaping the Investor-Owned Electric Utility Industry.' Bloomington, MN: Edison Electric Institute. 29 November 2001, p. 15.

49 Douglas M. Logan. 'Concentrated Transmission Asssets.' *Public Utilities Fortnightly*. 15 February 2002, p. 10.

50 Energy Information Agency. 'The Changing Structure of the Electric Power Industry 2000.', pp. 107-8.

51 Public Citizen. 'Got Juice: Bush's Refusal to End California Electricity Price Gouging Enriches Texas Friends and Big Contributors.' Public Citizen. February, 2001, p. 1.

52 Greg Palast. 'Bush Energy Plan: Policy or Payback?' BBC News. 18 May 2001. http://news.bbc.co.uk/hi/english/world/americas/newsid_1336000/1336960.stm; Joe Conason. 'Kenny Boy's Quiet, with Good Reason.' *New York Observer*. 10 February 2002

53 Palast. 'Bush Energy Plan: Policy or Payback?'; Public Citizen. 'Got Juice.', pp. 4-6.

54 Public Citizen. 'Got Juice.', p. 6.

55 Jeff Gerth and Joseph Kahn. 'Critics Say U.S. Energy Agency Is Weak in Oversight of Utilities.' *New York Times*. 23 March 2001

56 Paul Krugman. 'The Price of Power.' *New York Times*. 25 March 2001

57 Gerth and Kahn. 'Critics Say U.S. Energy Agency Is Weak in Oversight of Utilities.'

58 Nancy Dunne. 'FERC Head Faces Flak over US Energy Scandal.' *Financial Times*. 21 May 2002

59 Gerth and Kahn. 'Critics Say U.S. Energy Agency Is Weak in Oversight of Utilities.'

60 FERC. 'Commission Proposes to Reshape California's 'Seriously Flawed' Electricity Markets with Sweeping Changes.' Washington, D.C.: Federal Energy Regulatory Commission. 1 November 2000, p. 1.

61 Ibid., p. 2.

62 Cited in Alliance of Energy Suppliers. 'FERC Report on California Markets: Highlights.' Edison Electric Institute. 5 October 2000. http://eei.org/alliance/news/01101a.htm

63 Alliance of Energy Suppliers. 'EEI Alliance Asks FERC to Defer Action on Reporting Requirements, Postpone Energy Sales Conference.' Edison Electric Institute. 5 October 2001. http://eei.org/alliance/news/011005.htm

64 Ibid.

65 Hirst. 'The California Electricity Crisis.', p. 8.

66 Barker Dunn & Rossi. 'The Electric Summer: Symptoms—Options—Solutions.' Washington, DC: Edison Electric Institute. October 2000, pp. 1, 9, 12.

67 Ibid., p. 8.

68 Joe Conason. 'Take It Public.' *Salon.com*. 19 June 2001

69 'A Turning Point, Maybe.' *The Economist*. 23 June 2001, p. 39.

70 Stephanie Anderson Forest. 'The Power Party May Be Winding Down.' *Business Week*. 9 July 2001, p. 39.

71 Harvey Wasserman. 'Deregulation Blackout: Manufacturing California's Fake Energy Crisis.' *Extra!* May/June, 2001, p. 23; see for example Hirst. 'The California Electricity Crisis.', p. 5; Brahinsky. 'PG&E's Propaganda War, Part Two.', p. 23.

72 Alison Mitchell. 'Ads Brawl in Never-Ending Political Season.' *New York Times*. 3 July 2001

73 EEI. 'Electric Power 1.'; EEI. 'What's Happening in California.' Edison Electric Institute. Accessed on 11 January 2002. http://www.eei.org/futre/california/competion.htm

74 Paul Bernasconi, Oasis—the advertising agency that created the print ads – quoted in Laura Q. Hughes. 'Utilities Group Launches Ad Campaign.' *Advertising Age*. 21 May 2001, p. 39.

75 EEI. 'Advertising.' Edison Electric Institute. Accessed on 11 January 2002. http://www.eei.org/issues/news/ads_events.shtml

76 EEI advertisement, 'Believe it or not there is light at the end of the tunnel', Accessed on 11 January 2002. http://www.eei.org/issues/news/ads/print-tunnel.pdf.

77 Reprinted in *San Francisco Bay Guardian*. 3 January 2001, http://www.sfbg.com/News/35/14/14pgeletter.html

78 Wasserman. 'Deregulation Blackout.', p. 23.

79 Todd S. Purdum. 'California's Power Crisis Replays a Familiar Theme.' *The New York Times*. 25 January, 2001, p. A1.

80 Jackie Alan Giuliano. 'Energy Crisis or Greed Crisis?' *Environmental News Service*. 9 February 2001; Marla Cone and Gary

Polakovic. 'Bush's Idea of Easing Smog Rules Won't Help, Experts Say.' *Los Angeles Times*. 25 January 2001

81 Gary Polakovic. '2002 Spike in Air Pollution Reverses Downward Trend.' *Los Angeles Times*. 13 October 2002

82 Wasserman. 'Deregulation Blackout.', p. 24; Joseph Kahn. 'Energy Efficiency Programs Are Set for Bush Budget Cut.' *New York Times*. 5 April 2001; Glantz. 'Few Lessons Learned.'; Neela Banerjee. 'Energy Giants Push to Weaken a Pollution Rule.' *New York Times*. 13 April 2002

83 Cat Lazaroff. 'Power Plant Emissions Blamed for Premature Deaths.' *Environment News Service*. 18 April 2002; Katharine Q. Seelye. 'Senate to Examine Plans to Weaken Pollution Rules.' *New York Times*. 8 January 2002

84 Joseph Kahn. 'Cheney Promotes Increasing Supply as Energy Policy.' *New York Times*. 1 May 2001

85 Paul Krugman. 'Let Them Shovel.' *New York Times*. 15 April 2001

86 Michael Depp. 'US House Energy Chair Says Nation Faces Crisis.' *Planet Ark*. 5 June 2001; Vibeke Laroi. 'Most Californians Now Favor Nuclear Power—Poll.' *Planet Ark*. 24 May 2001

87 Center for Responsive Politics. 'Energy: Bush Energy Plan.' opensecrets.org. Accessed on 28 December 2001. http://www.opensecrets.org/payback/issue.asp?issueid=EN1

88 Cat Lazaroff. 'Energy Task Force Documents Show Industry Influence.' *Environment News Service*. 22 May, 2002

89 National Energy Policy Development Group. 'National Energy Policy: Reliable, Affordable, and Environmentally Sound Energy for America's Future.' Washington, DC: President of the United States. May, 2001, pp. 10, 78.

90 Ibid., p. 7.

91 Center for Responsive Politics. 'Energy: Bush Energy Plan.'

92 'More Enron Mischief.' *New York Times*. 8 May 2002

93 Paul Krugman. 'The Power Perplex.' *New York Times*. 26 February 2002

94 Editorial. 'Disturbing Numbers for Mr. Bush.' *New York Times*. 21 June 2001

95 James Walsh. *The $10 Billion Jolt*. Los Angeles: Silver Lake Publishing. 2002, p. 276.

Chapter Eight

1 Mark Mills and Peter Huber. 'Deregulation Will Survive Enron.' *The Wall Street Journal*. 6 December 2001

2 Quoted in Edwin Chen and Judy Pasternak. 'Bush's Ties to Enron Chief Attract Growing Scrutiny.' *LA Times*. 14 February 2001

3 Dan Morgan. 'Traders, Old Utilities Tangle over Wires.' *Washington Post*. 23 August 2001, p. A01.

4 Dan Morgan. 'From Maine to N.Y. By Way of Atlanta.' *Washington Post*. 23 August 2001, p. A15.

5 'Rise and Fall of an Energy Giant'. *BBC News Online*, 2001

6 Critical Mass Energy & Environment Program. 'Blind Faith: How Deregulation and Enron's Influence over Government Looted Billions from Americans.' Washington, D.C.: Public Citizen. December, 2001, p. 3.

7 'Business: Electric Avenues'. *The Economist*, 1998

8 Enron. 'Enron Wholesale Services.' Enron. Accessed on 2 January 2002. http://www.enron.com/corp/pressroom/factsheets/wholesale.html; Enron. 'Enron Global Services.' Enron. Accessed on 2 January 2002. http://www.enron.com/corp/pressroom/factsheets/egs/

9 'Rise and Fall of an Energy Giant',

10 Enron. 'Who We Are.' Enron. Accessed on 2 January 2002. http://www.enron.com/corp/whoweare.html

11 Enron. 'Company Snapshot.' Enron. Accessed on 2 January 2002. http://www.enron.com/corp/pressroom/factsheets/company.html; Steven Weiss. 'The Fall of a Giant: Enron's Campaign Contributions and Lobbying.' Centre for Responsive Politics. 9 November 2001. http://opensecrets.org/alerts/v6/alertv6_31.asp; Pratap Chatterjee. 'Enron: Pulling the Plug on the Global Power Broker.' *CorpWatch* 13 December, 2001; Kurt Eichenwald. 'Audacious Climb to Success Ended in Dizzying Plunge.' *New York Times*. 13 January, 2002; Jonathan D. Salant. 'Power Shortages Help Southern Utility Companies Make It Big.' *Grand Rapids Press*. 28 January 2001

12 Garry McWilliams. 'The Quiet Man Who's Jolting Utilities.' *Business Week*. 9 June 1997, p. 84; Edward Chancellor. 'The Trouble with Bubbles.' *New York Times*. 27 January 2002

13 'The Energetic Messiah', In *The Economist*, 2000

14 Chatterjee. 'Enron.'

15 Allan Sloan. 'Who Killed Enron.' *Newsweek* 21 January 2002, p. 18.

16 Quoted in Kurt Eichenwald. 'Web of Details Did Enron in as Warnings Went Unheeded.' *New York Times*. 10 February 2002

17 Chatterjee. 'Enron.'

18 Quoted in Steve Davies. 'Power Politics— Labour and Enron.' *Corporate Watch News Updates* 31 January 2002

19 Quoted in Eichenwald. 'Web of Details Did Enron in as Warnings Went Unheeded.'

20 Chancellor. 'The Trouble with Bubbles.'

21 Enron. 'Enron Named Most Innovative for Sixth Year.' Houston: Enron. 6 February 2001; 'Rise and Fall of an Energy Giant',

22 McWilliams. 'The Quiet Man Who's Jolting Utilities.', p. 84.

23 Steve Rosenfeld. 'How Enron's Chairman Changed the World.' Tom Paine.Com. 3 December 2001. http://www.tompained.com/features/2001/12/03/&e=42; Salant. 'Power Shortages.'; McWilliams. 'The Quiet Man Who's Jolting Utilities.', p. 84; Eichenwald. 'Audacious Climb to Success.'; Andrew Wheat. 'System Failure: Deregulation, Political Corruption, Corporate Fraud and the Enron Debacle.' *Multinational Monitor* January/February, 2002, p. 34; V Sridhar. 'Enron: A Business Model of the Times.' *Third World Resurgence*, 2002, p. 8.

24 Rosenfeld. 'How Enron's Chairman Changed the World.'

25 'A Brief Guide to Financial Derivatives.' Commonwealth of Pennsylvania. Accessed on 14 February 2002. http://sites.state.pa.us/PA_Exec/Securities/capital/derivatives.html

26 J. Gillard. 'Powercor Australia Ltd V Pacific Power.' Melbourne: Supreme Court of Victoria. 18 November 1999, p. 12.

27 Sridhar. 'Enron: A Business Model of the Times.', p. 8.

28 Enron. 'Weather.' Enron. Accessed on 2 January 2002. http://www.enron.com/wholesale/weather/

29 Eichenwald. 'Audacious Climb to Success.'

30 Enron. 'Maximizing Opportunities in Emissions Trading.' Enron. Accessed on 2 January 2002. http://www.enron.com.au/wholesale/emissions/

31 Enron. 'Enron Australia.' Enron. Accessed on 2 January 2002. http://www.enron.com.au/insideenron/;

Enron. 'Electricity Solutions.' Enron. Accessed on 2 January 2002. http://www.enron.com.au/ourservices/

32 Chatterjee. 'Enron.'; Wheat. 'System Failure.', p. 39; Eichenwald. 'Audacious Climb to Success.'; David Barboza. 'Despite Denial, Enron Papers Show Big Profit on Price Bets.' *The New York Times*. 12 December, 2002.

33 Bethany McLean. 'Why Enron Went Bust.' *Fortune*. 24 December 2001

34 Edmund Sanders and Richard Simon. 'Enron Role in Pricing Scrutinized.' *Los Angeles Times*. 30 January 2002

35 Wheat. 'System Failure.', p. 35.

36 Robert Scheer. 'Connect the Enron Dots to Bush.' *LA Times*. 11 December 2001; Salant. 'Power Shortages.'; Harvey Wasserman. 'Power Struggle: California's Engineered Energy Crisis and the Potential of Public Power.' *Multinational Monitor* 22(6). 2001, p. 16; Lowell Bergman and Jeff Gerth. 'Power Trader Tied to Bush Finds Washington All Ears.' *New York Times*. 25 May 2001; American Family Voices. 'Enron's Shadow Government.' American Family Voices. 12 March 2002, p. 3; David Corn. 'W.'s First Enron Connection.' *The Nation*. 4 March 2002; Public Citizen. 'Got Juice: Bush's Refusal to End California Electricity Price Gouging Enriches Texas Friends and Big Contributors.' Public Citizen. February, 2001, p. 6; Weiss. 'The Fall of a Giant.'; Peter Spiegel. 'Power Politics.' *Financial Times*. 11 January 2002.

37 Scheer. 'Connect the Enron Dots to Bush.'; Ed Vulliamy. 'Price of Power.' *The Observer*. 13 January 2002; Joe Stephens. 'Hard Money, Strong Arms and 'Matrix'.' *Washington Post*. 10 February 2002

38 Salant. 'Power Shortages.'; Greg Palast. 'Bush Energy Plan: Policy or Payback?' BBC News. 18 May 2001. http://news.bbc.co.uk/hi/english/world/americas/newsid_1336000/1336960.stm; Weiss. 'The Fall of a Giant.'; Chen and Pasternak. 'Bush's Ties to Enron Chief.'

39 Richard L. Berke. 'Enron Pursued Plan to Forge Close Ties to Gore Campaign.' *New York Times*. 18 February 2002

40 Weiss. 'The Fall of a Giant.'

41 Brendan Hightower and Peter Spiegel. 'Documents Show Enron Spend $4.6m on Lobbying.' *Financial Times*. 13 March 2002

42 Public Citizen. 'Got Juice.', p. 6.

43 David Corn. 'Enron End Run.' *The Nation* 18 February 2002

44 Ibid.; Lucy Shackelford. 'Enron Ties to the

Bush Administration.' *Washington Post.* Accessed on 20 January 2002. http://www.washingtonpost.com/wp-srv/onpolitics/articles/keyplayers_political.html

45 Quoted in Richard A. Oppel. 'White House Acknowledges More Contacts with Enron.' *New York Times.* 23 May 2002

46 Alex Berenson. 'Ex-Workers Say Unit's Earnings Were 'Illusory'.' *New York Times.* 25 January 2002

47 Ibid.; Scheer. 'Connect the Enron Dots to Bush.'; Vulliamy. 'Price of Power.'; John Hoefle. 'Bush Crew and Enron: Conflict of Interest and Reality.' *DifferentVoices.com,* 2001; Eichenwald. 'Audacious Climb to Success.'

48 Alison Mitchell. 'Enron's Ties to a Leader of House Republicans Went Beyond Contributions to His Campaign.' *New York Times.* 16 January 2002

49 American Family Voices. 'Enron's Shadow Government.', pp. 2-3.

50 Critical Mass Energy & Environment Program. 'Blind Faith.', pp. 10-12

51 Ibid., pp. 3, 12.

52 Ibid., p. 13.

53 Joe Conason. 'Whitewater Critic Quiet About Enron.' *New York Observer.* 1 January 2002

54 Stephens. 'Hard Money, Strong Arms and 'Matrix'.'

55 Ibid.

56 Center for Responsive Politics. 'Power to the People? Money, Lawmakers, and Electricity Deregulation.' opensecrets.org. Accessed on 4 January 2001. http://www.opensecrets.org/pubs/cashingin_electric/contents.htm; McWilliams. 'The Quiet Man Who's Jolting Utilities.', p. 84.

57 Tony Clarke. 'Enron: Washington's Number One Behind-the-Scenes Gats Negotiator.' *CorpWatch.* 25 October 2001

58 Enron. 'Enron Supports Electric Consumers' Power to Choose Act of 1996.' Houston: Enron. 6 February 1996

59 Enron. 'Enron Unveils New Advertising Campaign and Logo.' Houston: Enron. 14 January 1997

60 McWilliams. 'The Quiet Man Who's Jolting Utilities.', p. 84; Allen R. Myerson. 'Enron, Seeking to Be a Household Name, Plans to Start Its Campaign on Super Bowl Sunday.' *New York Times.* 14 January 1997

61 McWilliams. 'The Quiet Man Who's Jolting Utilities.', p. 84.

62 Wheat. 'System Failure.' p. 35; Nate Blakeslee. 'How Enron Did Texas.' *The Nation* 4 March 2002; Leslie Wayne. 'Enron, Preaching Deregulation, Worked the Statehouse Circuit.' *New York Times.* 9 February 2002

63 Blakeslee. 'How Enron Did Texas.'

64 Wayne. 'Enron, Preaching Deregulation.'; Barboza. 'Despite Denial.'; Mark Martin. 'Enron Helped Build Market, Then Exploited Weaknesses.' *San Francisco Chronicle.* 3 February 2002

65 Quoted in Wayne. 'Enron, Preaching Deregulation.'

66 Douglas Jehl. 'Freeing a Hydroelectric Giant, California Frets About Control.' *New York Times.* 19 July 2000

67 Critical Mass Energy & Environment Program. 'Blind Faith.', pp. 3-4, 17-19; Joseph Kahn and Jeff Gerth. 'Collapse of Enron May Reshape the Battlefield of Deregulation.' *New York Times.* 4 December 2001

68 Critical Mass Energy & Environment Program. 'Blind Faith.', pp. 3-4, 17-19; Robert L. Borosage. 'Enron Conservatives.' *The Nation* 4 February 2002.

69 Salant. 'Power Shortages.'; Palast. 'Bush Energy Plan: Policy or Payback?'

70 Critical Mass Energy & Environment Program. 'Blind Faith.', p. 4.

71 American Family Voices. 'Enron's Shadow Government.', p. 4; Joe Conason. 'Kenny Boy's Quiet, with Good Reason.' *New York Observer.* 10 February 2002

72 Clarke. 'Enron.'; Reuters. 'W. House Changed Draft Plant to Help Enron-Lawmaker.' *Yahoo!.News.* 26 January 2002

73 Bergman and Gerth. 'Power Trader Tied to Bush.'; Kahn and Gerth. 'Collapse of Enron.'; Mary Gordon. 'Enron Chair Gave List of Favored Names to White House.' *CorpWatch* 1 February 2002; Shackelford. 'Enron Ties to the Bush Administration.'

74 Bergman and Gerth. 'Power Trader Tied to Bush.'; Wheat. 'System Failure.', p. 36; Jeff Gerth and Joseph Kahn. 'Critics Say U.S. Energy Agency Is Weak in Oversight of Utilities.' *New York Times.* 23 March 2001; Blakeslee. 'How Enron Did Texas.'

75 Laurent Belsie. 'Enron's Ex-Role: Model of Ethics.' *The Christian Science Monitor* 4 March 2002, p. 20.

76 Bill Lickert and Christopher Morris. 'The Truth About Bush and Enron.' *National Review Online.* 8 February 2002

77 Bill Keller. 'Enron for Dummies.' *New York*

Times. 26 January, 2002; Enron. 'A Powerful Resource.' Enron. Accessed on 2 January 2002. http://www.enron.com.au/wholesale/emissions/resource.html

78 Quoted in Lickert and Morris. 'The Truth About Bush and Enron.'

79 Stephens. 'Hard Money, Strong Arms and 'Matrix'.'; Lickert and Morris. 'The Truth About Bush and Enron.'; Enron. 'Enron Australia.'

80 Quoted in Paul J. Georgia. 'Campaign ExxonMobil Caters to the Greens.' *National Review Online*. 29 May 2002

81 David Fleshler. 'Enron Corp. A Powerful Opponent.' *Sun-Sentinel*. 11 March, 2001; Sam Parry. 'Bush and Ken Lay: Slip Slidin' Away.' *Consortium News*. 6 February 2002

82 'Conservation Groups Questioned for Siding with Shell and Enron.' *Drillbits & Tailings*. 23 July 1999

83 Ibid; Jimmy Langman. 'Enron's Pipe Scheme.' *CorpWatch*. 9 May 2002; James V. Grimaldi. 'Enron Pipeline Leaves Scar on South America.' *Washington Post* 6 May. 2002, p. A01.

84 Anonymous quoted in 'Conservation Groups Questioned for Siding with Shell and Enron.'

85 Grimaldi. 'Enron Pipeline Leaves Scar on South America.'

86 Ibid.

87 Ibid.

88 Alexander Cockburn and Jeffrey St. Clair. 'Enron and the Green Seal.' *Counterpunch* 21 December 2001

89 Ibid; Lickert and Morris. 'The Truth About Bush and Enron.'

90 Grimaldi. 'Enron Pipeline Leaves Scar on South America.'; Corn. 'Enron End Run.'; Sustainable Energy and Economic Network. 'Enron's Pawns: How Public Institutions Bankrolled Enron's Globalization Game.' Washington, DC: Institute for Policy Studies. 22 March 2002, p. 18; Richard A. Oppel. 'For a Generous Donor and Bush, the Support Is a Two-Way Street.' *New York Times*. 30 June 2000; 'Chronology of Administrative Dealings with Enron's Dabhol Power Plant in India.' *Washington Post*. 22 January 2002

91 Sustainable Energy and Economic Network. 'Enron's Pawns.', pp. 9, 18.

92 Ibid., pp. 3-4, 21.

93 David Corn. 'Enron and the Bushes.' *The Nation*. 4 February 2002; Ron Callari. 'The Enron-Cheney-Taliban Connection?' *Albion Monitor*. 28 February 2002; Louis Dubose

and Carmen Coiro. 'Don't Cry for Bush, Argentina.' *Mother Jones* March/April, 2000.

94 Andrew Wheat. 'Enron Fries in Its Own Juices.' *The Texas Observer*. 7 December 2001; Sustainable Energy and Economic Network. 'Enron's Pawns.', p. 19.

95 'Rise and Fall of an Energy Giant',; Andrew Parker and Michael Peel. 'UK Government Pressed to Disclose Enron Links.' *Financial Times*. 28 January, 2002; 'Enron: UK Press Chief Stands Down.' *CNN.com*. 14 March 2002; Enron. 'Enron Energy Services.' Enron. Accessed on 2 January 2002. http://www.enron.com/corp/pressroom/factsheets/retail.html

96 Enron. 'Enron Global Services.'; Citizens for Safe Water. 'The Privatization Factor.' Citizens for Safe Water. October 31 2001. http://www.hevanet.com/safewater/enron.htm

97 Parker and Peel. 'UK Government Pressed to Disclose Enron Links.'; Hoefle. 'Bush Crew and Enron.'; Andrew Grice and Marie Woolf. 'Blair under Pressure over Government Links to Enron.' *The Independent*. 29 January 2002

98 Davies. 'Power Politics — Labour and Enron.'

99 Howard Hampton quoted in 'Electricity Privatization Brought to You by Enron.' *Canada Newswire*. 22 February 2002

100 Chatterjee. 'Enron.'; Clarke. 'Enron.'; Darrem Puscas. 'A Guide to the Enron Collapse: A Few Points for a Clearer Understanding.' Canada: Polaris Institute. 12 February 2002, pp. 11-12.

101 Clarke. 'Enron.'

102 Critical Mass Energy & Environment Program. 'Blind Faith.', p. 8.

103 Borosage. 'Enron Conservatives.'; Marjorie Kelly. 'Waving Goodbye to the Invisible Hand.' *San Francisco Chronicle*. 24 February 2002

Chapter Nine

1 Michael Aguirre quoted in Craig D. Rose. 'Enron Was Standard for Deregulation.' *Union-Tribune*. 29 November 2001

2 Marjorie Kelly. 'Waving Goodbye to the Invisible Hand.' *San Francisco Chronicle*. 24 February 2002

3 Pratap Chatterjee. 'Enron: Pulling the Plug on the Global Power Broker.' *CorpWatch* 13 December 2001; William Greider. 'Crime in the Suites.' *The Nation* 4 February, 2002; Arianna Huffington. 'Enron: Cooking the Books and Buying Protection.' Arianna Online. 3 December 2001. http://www.ariannaonline.com/columns/files/1

20301.html

4 Kurt Eichenwald. 'Audacious Climb to Success Ended in Dizzying Plunge.' *New York Times*. 13 January 2002

5 Darrem Puscas. 'A Guide to the Enron Collapse: A Few Points for a Clearer Understanding.' Canada: Polaris Institute. 12 February 2002, pp. 3, 5.

6 Erwin Seba. 'Companies Sue Enron, Anderson under Texas State Law.' *Dow Jones Energy Service*. 4 January 2002

7 Leslie Wayne. 'Before Debacle, Enron Insiders Cashed in $1.1 Billion in Shares.' *New York Times*. 13 January 2002; Madeleine Bunting. 'Enron: The End of Capitalism as We've Known It.' *The Age*. 29 January 2002

8 Eichenwald. 'Audacious Climb to Success.'

9 Floyd Norris. 'The Distorted Numbers at Enron.' *New York Times*. 14 December 2001; Allan Sloan. 'Who Killed Enron.' *Newsweek* 21 January 2002, p. 18; Andrew Wheat. 'System Failure: Deregulation, Political Corruption, Corporate Fraud and the Enron Debacle.' *Multinational Monitor* January/February, 2002, p. 34.

10 Gretchen Morgensen. 'A Bubble That Enron Insiders and Outsiders Didn't Want to Pop.' *New York Times*. 14 January 2002

11 Richard W. Stevenson. 'Energy Trading Gave Prices Artificial Lift, Panel Is Told.' *New York Times*. 12 April 2002; Richard A. Oppel. 'White House Acknowledges More Contacts with Enron.' *New York Times*. 23 May 2002; Alex Berenson. 'Ex-Workers Say Unit's Earnings Were 'Illusory'.' *New York Times*. 25 January 2002.

12 Paul Krugman. 'Two, Three, Many?' *New York Times*. 1 February 2002; Walter M. Cadette. 'How Stock Options Lead to Scandal.' *New York Times*. 12 July 2002; David Cay Johnston. 'Enron Avoided Income Taxes in 4 of 5 Years.' *New York Times*. 17 January 2002.

13 Cadette. 'How Stock Options Lead to Scandal.'; Kurt Eichenwald. 'Enron Paid Huge Bonuses in 'O1; Experts See a Motive for Cheating.' *New York Times*. 1 March 2002

14 Krugman. 'Two, Three, Many?'

15 Morgensen. 'A Bubble That Enron Insiders and Outsiders Didn't Want to Pop.'

16 Lucy Komisar. 'Enron and Al Qaeda's Shared Link.' *Alternet* 21 January 2002; Daniel Fisher. 'Shell Game: How Enron Concealed Losses, Inflated Earnings—and Hid Secret Deals.' *Forbes Magazine* 7 January 2002

17 Fisher. 'Shell Game.', p. 52.

18 William C. Powers, Raymond S. Troubh and Herbert S. Winokur. 'Report of Investigation.' Board of Directors of Enron. 1 February 2002, p. 10.

19 Floyd Norris. 'Panel Finds Rush to Hide Losses and Enrich a Few.' *New York Times*. 3 February 2002; Krugman. 'Two, Three, Many?'.

20 Fisher. 'Shell Game.', p. 52.

21 Johnston. 'Enron Avoided Income Taxes in 4 of 5 Years.'

22 Critical Mass Energy & Environment Program. 'Blind Faith: How Deregulation and Enron's Influence over Government Looted Billions from Americans.' Washington, D.C.: Public Citizen. December, 2001, p. 25; Komisar. 'Enron and Al Qaeda's Shared Link.'

23 Johnston. 'Enron Avoided Income Taxes in 4 of 5 Years.'; Mark Martin. 'Embattled Firm's Approach to State Tax Bill: Ignore It.' *San Francisco Chronicle*. 24 January 2002

24 Kurt Eichenwald. 'Web of Details Did Enron in as Warnings Went Unheeded.' *New York Times*. 10 February 2002

25 Molly Ivins. Creators Syndicate. 29 January 2002. http://www.creators.com/opinion_show.cfm?columnsName=miv

26 Fisher. 'Shell Game.', p. 52.

27 Alex Berenson and Johathan D. Glater. 'A Tattered Andersen Fights for Its Future.' *New York Times*. 13 January 2002

28 Ibid.; Wheat. 'System Failure.', p. 36; Norris. 'Panel Finds Rush to Hide Losses and Enrich a Few.'

29 Frank Partnoy, a former derivatives trade and now a Professor of Law at the University of San Diego in Stan Correy. 'Enron: The Musical.' *Background Briefing, ABC Radio National*. 17 February 2002

30 American Family Voices. 'Enron's Shadow Government.' American Family Voices. 12 March 2002, p. 5; Berenson and Glater. 'A Tattered Andersen Fights for Its Future.'; Arianna Huffington. 'The Enron Scandal—Why Was No One Minding the Store?' *Alternet* 21 December 2001; 'A Failure to Account.' *New York Times*. 14 January 2002; David Corn. 'Enron Is Only the Tip of the Iceberg.' *Alternet* 21 January 2002

31 Sloan. 'Who Killed Enron.', p. 18; Eichenwald. 'Web of Details Did Enron in as Warnings Went Unheeded.'; 'Enron and the Role of the Banks.' *Financial Times*. 16 January 2002.

32 Greider. 'Crime in the Suites.'

33 Edward Chancellor. 'The Trouble with Bubbles.' *New York Times*. 27 January 2002; Kurt Eichenwald. 'Investors Lured to Enron Deals by inside Data.' *New York Times*. 25 January 2002

34 Sloan. 'Who Killed Enron.', p. 18; David Leonhardt. 'How Will Washington Read the Signs?' *New York Times*. 10 February 2002; 'Wall Street's 'Big Lie'.' *Washington Post*. 11 April 2002, p. A28.

35 Theresa Amato. 'Enron-Omics at a Glance.' Citizen Works. 21 January 2002. http://www.citizenworks.org/enronomics.html

36 Richard A. Oppel. 'Merrill Replaced Research Analyst Who Upset Enron.' *New York Times*. 30 July 2002

37 Quoted in 'Wall Street's 'Big Lie'.', p. A28.

38 Associated Press. 'Senate Investigates Investment Banks' Role in Enron.' *New York Times*. 23 July 2002

39 William Greider. 'The Enron Nine.' *The Nation* 13 May 2002

40 Daniel Altman. 'Enron Had More Than One Way to Disguise Rapid Rise in Debt.' *New York Times*. 17 February 2002; 41 'Enron and the Role of the Banks.'; Greider. 'The Enron Nine.'

41 Associated Press. 'Senate Investigates Investment Banks' Role in Enron.'

42 Huffington. 'The Enron Scandal.'

43 Richard Blow. 'Enron Paid Off Top Journalists in Return For ... What?' *Alternet* 6 February 2002; Howard Kurtz. '...And the Enron Pundits.' *Washington Post*. 30 January 2002; Howard Kurtz. 'Enron-N.Y.Times Co. Deal Highlights Media's Dilemma.' *Washington Post*. 18 July 2002, p. C01.

44 Critical Mass Energy & Environment Program. 'Blind Faith.', p. 24.

45 Chatterjee. 'Enron.'; Wayne. 'Before Debacle, Enron Insiders Cashed in $1.1 Billion in Shares.'

46 Quoted in Bob Herbert. 'Silencing the Alarm.' *New York Times*. 14 January 2002

47 Sherron S. Watkins. 'Text of a Letter to Enron's Chairman after Departure of Chief Executive.' *New York Times*. 16 January 2002

48 Floyd Norris and David Barboza. 'Lay Sold Shares for $100 Million.' *New York Times*. 16 February 2002

49 Berenson and Glater. 'A Tattered Andersen Fights for Its Future.'; Kurt Eichenwald. 'Andersen Guilty in Effort to Block Inquiry on Enron.' *New York Times*. 16 June 2002; Puscas. 'A Guide to the Enron Collapse.', p. 2.

50 Quoted in David Wastell and Mary Fagan. 'Enron: 'Crimes Were Committed'.' *Electronic Telegraph*. 20 January 2002

51 Enron. 'Enron Reports Recurring Third Quarter Earnings of $0.43 Per Diluted Share.' Enron. 16 October 2001

52 Eichenwald. 'Audacious Climb to Success.'; 'Probe Sends Enron Shares Tumbling'. *BBC News Online*, 2001

53 Enron. 'Enron Provides Additional Information About Related Party and Off-Balance Sheet Transactions.' Enron. 8 November 2001

54 Bethany McLean. 'Why Enron Went Bust.' *Fortune* 24 December 2001

55 Lawrence White. 'Credit and Credibility.' *New York Times*. 24 February 2002

56 Richard A. Oppel and Kurt Eichenwald. 'Enron Paid out 'Retention' Bonuses before Bankruptcy Filing.' *New York Times*. 6 December 2001; Herbert. 'Silencing the Alarm.'

57 Cadette. 'How Stock Options Lead to Scandal.'

58 'Earnings Overstated.' *Sydney Morning Herald*. 3-4 August 2002

59 Quoted in Wheat. 'System Failure.', p. 39.

60 David Barboza. 'Enron Offered Management Aid to Companies.' *New York Times*. 10 April 2002

61 Associated Press. 'Senate Investigates Investment Banks' Role in Enron.'; Reuters. 'Abb Says Sacked Executives over Hiding Loss.' iwon. 9 July 2002. http://money.iwon.com/

62 Mark Mills and Peter Huber. 'Deregulation Will Survive Enron.' *The Wall Street Journal*. 6 December 2001

63 V Sridhar. 'Enron: A Business Model of the Times.' *Third World Resurgence*, 2002, p. 8; 'Book Explains Shared Financial Risk.' University of Waterloo. 2 August 2001. http://www.bulletin.uwatrloo.ca/2001/aug/02 th.html

64 'Enron Admits Inflating Profits'. *BBC News Online*, 2001

65 Joseph Kahn. 'With Markets Flawed, Enron's Tactics Live On.' *New York Times*. 12 May 2002; Riva D. Atlas. 'Dynegy Faces New Questions over 'Debt' of Partnership.' *New York Times*. 14 May 2002; David Barboza. 'Ex-Executive Says Dynegy Asked His Help to Cheat.' *New York Times*. 5 August 2002

66 Reuters. 'Dynegy's Chief Executive Quits Amid Investigation of Trades.' *New York*

Times. 28 May 2002; Alex Berenson and Neela Banerjee. 'Energy Trader Cancels Deal; Shares Tumble.' *New York Times.* 11 May 2002; Neela Banerjee. 'Energy Trader Admits Faking Transactions.' *New York Times.* 14 May 2002; Nancy Dunne. 'Ferc Head Faces Flak over US Energy Scandal.' *Financial Times.* 21 May 2002; Associated Press. 'S.E.C. Investigates Mirant Accounting.' *New York Times.* 5 August 2002

67 Alex Berenson. 'Power Giants Have Trouble Raising Cash for Plants.' *New York Times.* 16 May 2002

68 Gregory Palast. 'Enron, Not the Only Bad Apple.' *The Guardian.* 1 February 2002

69 Wayne Madsen. 'Williams Companies: Enron II.' *CorpWatch* 14 February, 2002; Neela Ranerjee. 'A Collision on Risk of Energy Trading.' *New York Times.* 2 June 2002.

70 Ranerjee. 'A Collision on Risk of Energy Trading.'

71 Joseph Weber. 'Arthur Andersen: How Bad Will It Get?' *Business Week.* 24 December 2001; Becky Gaylord. 'For Months, Australia Has Had an Enron of Its Own.' *New York Times.* 22 February 2002; David S. Hilzenrath and Kathleen Day. 'PwC to Pay $5 Million to Settle SEC Case.' *Washington Post.* 17 July 2002; Greider. 'Crime in the Suites.'

72 Quoted in Leonhardt. 'How Will Washington Read the Signs?'

73 Robert L. Borosage. 'Enron Conservatives.' *The Nation.* 4 February 2002

74 FTCR. 'Daschle Pushes Electricity Deregulation Bill in Disguise.' Foundation for Taxpayer & Consumer Rights. 5 March 2002. http://www.consumerwatchdog.org/utilities/pr/pr002273.php3; EEI. 'Electric Power—an Overview of the Industry and Its Impact, Section 2.' Edison Electric Institute. Accessed on 11 January 2002. http://www.eei.org/issues/comp_reg/key_facts/section2.pdf

75 Kelly. 'Waving Goodbye to the Invisible Hand.'

76 Ibid.; Editorial. 'Preparing for the Next Enron.' *Multinational Monitor* January/February, 2002, p. 5; Kelly. 'Waving Goodbye to the Invisible Hand.'; Loren Fox. *Enron: The Rise and Fall.* Hoboken, New Jersey: John Wiley & Sons. 2003, p. 217.

77 Leslie Wayne. 'Tighter Rules for Options Fall Victim to Lobbying.' *New York Times.* 20 July 2002

78 Alison Mitchell. 'Companies Use Ex-Lawmakers in Fight on Offshore Tax Break.'

New York Times. 10 August 2002

79 Nancy Dunne. 'Energy Bill Amendment Hits Senate Opposition.' *Financial Times.* 20 March 2002; Kahn. 'With Markets Flawed, Enron's Tactics Live On.'

80 Kelly. 'Waving Goodbye to the Invisible Hand.'

Chapter Ten

1 Steve Thomas. 'The Wholesale Electricity Market in Britain—1990-2001.' London: PSIRU, University of Greenwich. August 2001, p. 3.

2 Leslie Hannah. *Electricity before Nationalisation: A Study of the Development of the Electricity Supply Industry in Britain to 1948.* London: Macmillan. 1979, p. 27.

3 James Foreman-Peck. *Public and Private Ownership of British Industry 1820-1990.* Oxford: Clarendon Press. 1994, p. 169.

4 Ibid., p. 168; Hannah. *Electricity before Nationalisation.*, pp 22-3.

5 Balfour Committee quoted in Foreman-Peck. *Public and Private Ownership of British Industry.*, p. 165.

6 Thomas Hughes. *Networks of Power: Electrification in Western Society, 1880-1930.* Baltimore and London: John Hopkins University Press. 1983, p. 60; Foreman-Peck. *Public and Private Ownership of British Industry.*, pp. 163-5.

7 Hannah. *Electricity before Nationalisation.*, p. 23.

8 Quoted in Hannah. *Electricity before Nationalisation.*, p. 23.

9 Quoted in Foreman-Peck. *Public and Private Ownership of British Industry.*, p. 167.

10 Ibid., p. 24.

11 Ibid., pp. 25-7.

12 Hughes. *Networks of Power.*, pp. 230-1.

13 Hannah. *Electricity before Nationalisation.*, pp. 42, 44.

14 Hughes. *Networks of Power.*, p. 227.

15 Ibid., p. 257; Hannah. *Electricity before Nationalisation.*, pp. 52-3.

16 Hughes. *Networks of Power.*, pp. 259-60, 361.

17 Hannah. *Electricity before Nationalisation.*, p. 27.

18 Quoted in Ibid., p.. 47.

19 Quoted in Ibid., p. 49.

20 Ibid., p. 50; Dexter Whitfield. *Making It Public: Evidence and Action against Privatisation.* London: Pluto Press. 1983, p. 72; Hannah. *Electricity before Nationalisation.*, pp. 43, 50.

21 Hannah. *Electricity before Nationalisation.*, pp. 53-62.

22 Hughes. *Networks of Power.*, p. 350.

23 Hannah. *Electricity before Nationalisation.*, pp. 63-72.

24 Ibid., pp. 73-86; Foreman-Peck. *Public and Private Ownership of British Industry.*, p. 258.

25 Hannah. *Electricity before Nationalisation.*, pp. 90-2.

26 Ibid., pp. 91, 93; Foreman-Peck. *Public and Private Ownership of British Industry.*, p. 258; John Chesshire. 'UK Electricity Supply under Public Ownership'. In *The British Electricity Experiment.* ed. John Surrey. London: Earthscan Publications. 1996, p. 15.

27 Quoted in Hannah. *Electricity before Nationalisation.*, p. 94.

28 Ibid., pp. 96-7.

29 Quoted in Ibid., pp. 330-1.

30 Ibid., pp. 96-8; 331.

31 Hughes. *Networks of Power.*, p. 354.

32 Hannah. *Electricity before Nationalisation.*, p. 101.

33 Ibid., pp. 94, 122; Hughes. *Networks of Power.*, pp. 355- 60.

34 Foreman-Peck. *Public and Private Ownership of British Industry.*, pp. 258-9.

35 Hannah. *Electricity before Nationalisation.*, pp. 122, 213; Foreman-Peck. *Public and Private Ownership of British Industry.*, p. 281.

36 Leslie Hannah quoted in Hughes. *Networks of Power.*, pp. 261-2.

37 Foreman-Peck. *Public and Private Ownership of British Industry.*, p. 281.

38 William Ashworth. *The State in Business 1945 to the Mid-1980s.* London: Macmillan. 1991, p. 5.

39 Foreman-Peck. *Public and Private Ownership of British Industry.*, p. 281.

40 Hannah. *Electricity before Nationalisation.* pp. 214, 217, 226.

41 Ibid., p. 225.

42 Ibid., pp. 223-7, 234; Foreman-Peck. *Public and Private Ownership of British Industry.*, p. 259.

43 Hannah. *Electricity before Nationalisation.*, pp. 223, 227.

44 Ibid., p. 228.

45 Ibid., p. 228.

46 Ibid., pp. 229, 232.

47 Ibid., pp. 226-7.

48 Foreman-Peck. *Public and Private Ownership of British Industry.*, p. 275.

49 Steve Thomas. 'Strategic Government and Corporate Issues'. In *The British Electricity Experiment.* ed. Surrey, p. pp. 255, 9.

50 Foreman-Peck. *Public and Private Ownership of British Industry.*, pp. 276-8; Walt Patterson. *Transforming Electricity: The Coming Generation of Change.* London: Royal Institute of International Affairs and Earthscan. 1999, p. 55.

51 Foreman-Peck. *Public and Private Ownership of British Industry.*, p. 289.

52 Hannah. *Electricity before Nationalisation.*, pp. 345-50.

53 Foreman-Peck. *Public and Private Ownership of British Industry.*, pp. 295-7.

54 Ibid., p. 290; Hannah. *Electricity before Nationalisation.*, p. 334.

55 Foreman-Peck. *Public and Private Ownership of British Industry.*, pp. 296-7.

56 Ashworth. *The State in Business.*, pp. 24-5.

57 Chesshire. 'UK Electricity Supply under Public Ownership'., pp. 16-7.

58 Hannah. *Electricity before Nationalisation.*, pp. 347, 351; Ashworth. *The State in Business.*, p. 24.

59 Hannah. *Electricity before Nationalisation.*, p. 353.

60 Patterson. *Transforming Electricity.*, pp. 55-6.

61 Chesshire. 'UK Electricity Supply under Public Ownership'., p. 19.

62 Ashworth. *The State in Business.*, p. 44; Foreman-Peck. *Public and Private Ownership of British Industry.*, pp. 293-4.

63 Jane Roberts, David Elliott and Trevor Houghton. *Privatising Electricity: The Politics of Power.* London and New York: Belhaven Press. 1991, p. 42.

64 Colin Robinson. 'Pressure Groups and Political Forces in Britain's Privatisation Programme.' Paper presented at the Japan Public Choice Society International Conference. Chiba University of Commerce, 22-23 August. 1997, p. 10.

65 Ashworth. *The State in Business.*, p. 54.

66 Thomas. 'Strategic Government and Corporate Issues'., p. 279.

67 Chesshire. 'UK Electricity Supply under Public Ownership'., pp. 37-8.

68 Foreman-Peck. *Public and Private Ownership of British Industry.*, p. 318.

69 Ashworth. *The State in Business.*, pp. 47-8.

70 Chesshire. 'UK Electricity Supply under Public Ownership'., p. 38, l 17.

71 Ashworth. *The State in Business.*, p. 56.

Chapter Eleven

1 John Surrey. 'Introduction'. In *The British Electricity Experiment.* ed. John Surrey. London: Earthscan Publications. 1996, p. 5.

2 James Foreman-Peck. *Public and Private Ownership of British Industry 1820-1990.*

Oxford: Clarendon Press. 1994, pp. 319-20.

3 Matt Warner. 'Power to the People.' *Accountancy*. 5 December 2001, p. 32.

4 Foreman-Peck. *Public and Private Ownership of British Industry.*, p. 333.

5 Cited in Peter M Jackson and Catherine M Price. 'Privatisation and Regulation: A Review of the Issues'. In *Privatisation and Regulation: A Review of the Issues.* ed. Peter M Jackson and Catherine M Price. London and New York: Longman. 1994, p. 15; Michael G. Pollitt. 'A Survey of Liberalisation of Public Enterprises in the UK since 1979.' University of Cambridge. January, 1999, p. 7.

6 Dexter Whitfield. *Making It Public: Evidence and Action against Privatisation*. London: Pluto Press. 1983, pp. 44, 49.

7 Richard Cockett. *Thinking the Unthinkable: Think-Tanks and the Economic Counter-Revolution 1931-1983*. Harper Collins. 1994, p. 140; R. Desai. 'Second-Hand Dealers in Ideas: Think-Tanks and Thatcherite Hegemony.' *New Left Review* 203(Jan-Feb). 1994, p. 29.

8 Cockett. *Thinking the Unthinkable.*; Simon James. 'The Idea Brokers: The Impact of Think Tanks on British Government.' *Public Administration* 71(Winter). 1993, p. 495; Desai. 'Second-Hand Dealers in Ideas.', p. 30.

9 CPS. 'Mission Statement.' Centre for Policy Studies. Accessed on 27 October 2002. http://www.cps.org.uk/mission.htm

10 Maurice Samuelson. 'Proud to Be Harnessed to Defend the Future.' *Financial Times*. 25 January 1988, p. 15.

11   Desai. 'Second-Hand Dealers in Ideas.'; 'Of Policy and Pedigree.' *The Economist* 6 May 1989; Desai. 'Second-Hand Dealers in Ideas.'; James. 'The Idea Brokers.', p. 53.

12 Nigel Ashford. 'Politically Impossible? How Ideas Not Interests and Circumstances, Determine Public Policies.' *Policy*. Autumn, 1997, p. 24.

13 Robin Oakley. 'Privatized Policy-Making for the Tory Right.' *The Times*. 17 February 1989; Alan Rusbridger. 'A Thought for Tomorrow.' *The Guardian*. 22 December 1987

14 Rusbridger. 'A Thought for Tomorrow.'

15 Barry Spicer, David Emanuel and Michael Powell. *Transforming Government Enterprises: Managing Radical Organisational Change in Deregulated Environments*. St Leonards, NSW: Centre for Independent Studies. 1996, p. 10.

16 Major Energy Users' Council. 'History'. MEUC. Accessed 19 October 2002.

http://www.meuc.co.uk/about/history/index.htm; Energy Intensive Users Group. 'About the EIUG'. EIUG. 1 April 2001. http://www.eiug.org.uk/about.htm

17 John Hooper. 'BR Warns of Power Sale Hazard.' *The Guardian*. 26 May 1988; Michael Harrison. 'British Coal Plans Financial Reconstruction.' *The Independent*. 27 July 1989, p. 26.

18 Whitfield. *Making It Public.*, p. 19.

19 Foreman-Peck. *Public and Private Ownership of British Industry.*, p. 321; Irwin Stelzer. 'A Review of Privatization and Regulation Experience in Britain.' Institute of Economic Affairs. 7 November 2000. http://www.iea.org.uk/record.php?type=article&ID=54

20 David Parker. 'Nationalisation, Privatisation, and Agency Status within Government: Testing for the Importance of Ownership'. In *Privatisation and Regulation: A Review of the Issues*. ed. Peter M Jackson and Catherine M Price. London and New York: Longman. 1994, p. 151; Jackson and Price. 'Privatisation and Regulation'., p. 4.

21 Julia O'Connell Davidson. 'Metamorphosis? Privatisation and the Restructuring of Management and Labour'. In *Privatisation and Regulation*. ed. Jackson and Price, p. 170.

22 Steve Thomas. 'The Privatization of the Electricity Supply Industry'. In *The British Electricity Experiment*. ed. John Surrey. London: Earthscan Publications. 1996, p. 43.

23 Ibid., p. 40.

24 Quoted in Foreman-Peck. *Public and Private Ownership of British Industry.*, p. 322.

25 Jackson and Price. 'Privatisation and Regulation'., p. 24.

26 Quoted in Jane Roberts, David Elliott and Trevor Houghton. *Privatising Electricity: The Politics of Power*. London and New York: Belhaven Press. 1991, p. 65.

27 Jackson and Price. 'Privatisation and Regulation'., p. 11; Whitfield. *Making It Public.*, p. 37.

28 Foreman-Peck. *Public and Private Ownership of British Industry.*, p. 323.

29 Steve Thomas. 'Strategic Government and Corporate Issues'. In *The British Electricity Experiment*. ed Surrey, p. 257.

30 Pollitt. 'A Survey of Liberalisation of Public Enterprises.', p. 3.

31 Foreman-Peck. *Public and Private Ownership of British Industry.*, pp. 331, 335.

32 Jackson and Price. 'Privatisation and

Regulation'., p. 14; Foreman-Peck. *Public and Private Ownership of British Industry*., p. 334; Thomas. 'The Privatization of the Electricity Supply Industry'., pp. 41, 51.

33 Steve Thomas. 'Has Privatisation Reduced the Price of Power in Britain?' UNISON. November Accessed on 14 March 1999. http://www.unison.org.uk/polres/esd/sthomas 1.htm and sthomas2.htm.

34 Pollitt. 'A Survey of Liberalisation of Public Enterprises.', p. 7.

35 Davidson. 'Metamorphosis?' In. ed., p. 172.

36 Thomas. 'The Privatization of the Electricity Supply Industry'., pp. 42.

37 Ibid., pp. 52-4.

38 Pollitt. 'A Survey of Liberalisation of Public Enterprises.', p. 8.

39 John Cryer. 'Utilities (Foreign Ownership).' House of Commons Hansard Debates. 25 February 1998. http://www.parliament.the-stationery-office.co.uk/pa/cm199798/cmhansard/vo9002 25/debtext/80225-12.htm

40 Foreman-Peck. *Public and Private Ownership of British Industry*., p. 335.

41 John Moore, Tory Minister, quoted in Jackson and Price. 'Privatisation and Regulation'., p. 14.

42 'View from City Road: Making Share Ownership Work.' *The Independent*. 18 December 1990, p. 19.

43 Whitfield. *Making It Public*., pp. 27-30.

44 Ibid., pp. 24, 28.

45 Pollitt. 'A Survey of Liberalisation of Public Enterprises.', p. 5.

46 Thomas. 'The Privatization of the Electricity Supply Industry'., pp. 41, 52; Jackson and Price. 'Privatisation and Regulation'., p. 15.

47 Cryer. 'Utilities (Foreign Ownership).'

48 Roberts, Elliott and Houghton. *Privatising Electricity*., pp. 51-2.

49 Surrey. 'Introduction'., p. 3; Pollitt. 'A Survey of Liberalisation of Public Enterprises.', p. 18.

50 Gordon MacKerron and Jim Watson. 'The Winners and Losers So Far'. In *The British Electricity Experiment*. ed. John Surrey. London: Earthscan Publications. 1996, pp. 186, 192-3.

51 Thomas. 'The Privatization of the Electricity Supply Industry'., pp. 51, 59; Steve Thomas. 'The Development of Competition'. In *The British Electricity Experiment*. ed. Surrey, p. 68.

52 Thomas. 'The Privatization of the Electricity Supply Industry'., pp. 54-6.

53 Colin Hughes. 'Electricity Bill Faces Tory Revolt.' *The Independent*. 3 April 1989

54 Thomas. 'The Privatization of the Electricity Supply Industry'., p. 56.

55 Ibid., pp. 56-7; Roberts, Elliott and Houghton. *Privatising Electricity*., p. 66.

56 Thomas. 'The Development of Competition'., p. 76; 'Where to We Get Our Energy?' In *The Observer*, 1999.

57 Thomas. 'Strategic Government and Corporate Issues'., p. 267; 'Where to We Get Our Energy?'

58 Electricity Association. 'Trade & Industry Committee Report - EA Welcomes Support for Liberalised Energy Markets.' Electricity Association. 7 February 2002. http://www.electricity.org.uk

59 Thomas. 'Strategic Government and Corporate Issues'., p. 274; Roberts, Elliott and Houghton. *Privatising Electricity*., p. 73.

60 Thomas. 'Strategic Government and Corporate Issues'., p. 285.

61 Thomas. 'The Development of Competition'., p. 68; Walt Patterson. *Transforming Electricity: The Coming Generation of Change*. London: Royal Institute of International Affairs and Earthscan. 1999, pp. 80, 133.

62 OFFER. 'Review of Electricity Trading Arrangements: Background Paper 1.' Office of Electricity Regulation. February 1998, p. 4.

63 Thomas. 'The Development of Competition'., p. 69.

64 Thomas. 'The Privatization of the Electricity Supply Industry'., p. 48.

65 Mary Fagan. 'Government Adviser to Be Electricity Watchdog.' *The Independent*. 23 May 1989, p. 22; David Hencke. 'The Think-Tank Engine.' *The Guardian*. 10 March 1989

66 Gordon MacKerron and Isabel Boira-Segarra. 'Regulation'. In *The British Electricity Experiment*. ed. Surrey, p. 119.

67 Pollitt. 'A Survey of Liberalisation of Public Enterprises.', pp. 1, 3.

68 Stelzer. 'A Review of Privatization and Regulation Experience in Britain.'

Chapter Twelve

1 Steve Thomas. 'The Wholesale Electricity Market in Britain 1990-2001.' London: PSIRU, University of Greenwich. August, 2001, p. 2.

2 John Surrey. 'Introduction'. In *The British Electricity Experiment*. ed. John Surrey. London: Earthscan Publications. 1996, p. 7.

3 Theo MacGregor. 'Electricity Restructuring in Britain: Not a Model to Follow.' *IEEE Spectrum* June, 2001, p. 19.

4 Reuters. 'Britain Pushing Electric Stocks.' *The New York Times*. 9 October 1990; Steve Thomas. 'The Privatization of the Electricity Supply Industry'. In *The British Electricity Experiment*. ed. Surrey, pp. 54, 58.

5 'Flogging the Family Silver.' *Charter* February, 1997; Gordon MacKerron and Jim Watson. 'The Winners and Losers So Far'. In *The British Electricity Experiment*. ed. Surrey, pp. 197-9.

6 MacGregor. 'Electricity Restructuring in Britain.', p. 15.

7 MacKerron and Watson. 'The Winners and Losers So Far'., pp. 200-212; Colin Robinson. 'Pressure Groups and Political Forces in Britain's Privatisation Programme.' Paper presented at the Japan Public Choice Society International Conference. Chiba University of Commerce, 22-23 August 1997, p. 22.

8 Gregory Palast. 'A High Price to Pay for the Power and the Glory.' *The Observer*. 4 February 2001

9 'Flogging the Family Silver.'; Andrew Lorenz. 'Power Plays.' *The Sunday Times*. 24 September 1995, p. 3.

10 'Flogging the Family Silver.'

11 MacKerron and Watson. 'The Winners and Losers So Far'., p. 204.

12 OFFER. 'Review of Electricity Trading Arrangements: Background Paper 1.' Office of Electricity Regulation. February 1998, p. 3.

13 Palast. 'A High Price to Pay for the Power and the Glory.'

14 Steve Thomas. 'The Development of Competition'. In *The British Electricity Experiment*. ed. Surrey, pp. 80-1; Thomas. 'The Wholesale Electricity Market.', p. 5.

15 Thomas. 'The Development of Competition'., p. 80.

16 Robinson. 'Pressure Groups and Political Forces in Britain's Privatisation Programme.', p. 21; Thomas. 'The Privatization of the Electricity Supply Industry'., p. 55.

17 Thomas. 'The Wholesale Electricity Market.', p. 3; Thomas. 'The Development of Competition'., p. 82.

18 Thomas. 'The Development of Competition'., p. 74.

19 OFFER. 'Review of Electricity Trading Arrangements: Proposals.' Office of Electricity Regulation. July, 1998, p. 19.

20 Matt Warner. 'Power to the People.' *Accountancy* 5 December 2001, p. 32.

21 Thomas. 'The Development of Competition'., p. 82.

22 Thomas. 'The Wholesale Electricity Market.', pp. 8-9; David Buchan. 'Reforms That Have Failed to Work a Power of Good.' *Financial Times*. 7 September 2002.

23 OFFER. 'Background Paper 1.', p. 42; OFFER. 'Proposals.', p. 21.

24 Callum McCarthy. 'Statement by Callum Mccarthy, Director General of OFGEM Addressing the Scope for, and Experience of, the Abuse of Market Power by the Generators under the Wholesale Electricity Pool in England & Wales.' Office of Gas and Electricity Markets 2000, p. 4; OFGEM. 'Introduction of a Market Abuse Condition into the Licences of Certain Generators.' Office of Gas and Electricity Markets. May 2000, pp. 5-7; Thomas. 'The Development of Competition'., p. 83; OFFER. 'Background Paper 1.', pp. 46-7.

25 Thomas. 'The Wholesale Electricity Market.', p. 5-6; OFGEM. 'Introduction of a Market Abuse Condition.', p. 5.

26 Electricity Association. 'Introduction to the UK Electricity Industry.' Electricity Association,. February, 2002. http://www.electricity.org.uk/uk_inds/industry_2001.html

27 OFFER. 'Proposals.', p. 4.

28 Ibid., pp. 17-8.

29 OFGEM. 'Introduction of a Market Abuse Condition.', pp. 8-10.

30 Thomas. 'The Wholesale Electricity Market.', p. 7.

31 McCarthy. 'Statement.', pp. 2, 4.

32 Ibid., pp. 4-5, 7; OFGEM. 'Introduction of a Market Abuse Condition.', p. 2.

33 MacGregor. 'Electricity Restructuring in Britain.', p. 16.

34 Warner. 'Power to the People.', p. 32.

35 MacGregor. 'Electricity Restructuring in Britain.', p. 16.

36 Thomas. 'The Wholesale Electricity Market.', pp. 4, 10.

37 Ibid., p. 10.

38 OFGEM. 'Introduction of a Market Abuse Condition.', pp. 1-2; Andrew Taylor. 'Increase in Energy Competition Prompts End to All Price Controls.' *Financial Times*. 26 November 2001, p. 4.

39 Robinson. 'Pressure Groups and Political Forces in Britain's Privatisation Programme.', p. 12.

40 Ibid., p. 12; 'Flogging the Family Silver.'; Thomas. 'The Development of Competition'., p. 70.

41 Electricity Association. 'Introduction to the UK Electricity Industry.'

42 Thomas. 'The Development of Competition'., p. 71.

43 Robert Bacon. 'Lessons from Power Sector Reform in England and Wales.' *Public Policy for the Private Sector* October, 1995, p. 4.

44 John Cryer. 'Utilities (Foreign Ownership).' House of Commons Hansard Debates. 25 February 1998. http://www.parliament.the-stationery-office.co.uk/pa/cm199798/cmhansard/vo9002 25/debtext/80225-12.htm

45 Ibid.

46 Andrew Taylor. 'European Utilities Dominate Deals.' *Financial Times.* 21 January 2002, p. 21; Lucinda Kemeny. 'UK Energy and Water Firms Fall to Invaders.' *Sunday Times.* 24 February 2002; Electricity Association. 'Who Owns Whom.' Electricity Association. 18 January 2002. http://www.electricity.org.uk/about_ea/bic_pu b/who_owns_whom.pdf

47 Warner. 'Power to the People.', p. 32.

48 Lucinda Kemeny. 'Energy Firms Headed for Power Struggle.' *Sunday Times.* 9 December 2001

49 Lorenz. 'Power Plays.', p. 3.

50 Michael Harrison. 'National Grid Merger with Lattice Will Create £30bn Utilities Powerhouse.' *The Independent.* 23 April 2002

51 Michael G. Pollitt. 'A Survey of Liberalisation of Public Enterprises in the UK since 1979.' University of Cambridge. January, 1999, pp. 17-18.

52 Thomas. 'The Wholesale Electricity Market.', p. 9.

53 Kemeny. 'Energy Firms Headed for Power Struggle.'

54 Suzanne Kapner. 'British Reopening the Debate over Privatization.' *The New York Times.* 29 August 2002; Andrew Taylor and Dan Roberts. 'Banks Warned of Power Station Loan Loss.' *Financial Times.* 19 May 2002

55 Kapner. 'British Reopening the Debate over Privatization.'; Michael Harrison. 'British Energy at Record Low on Reactor Closure.' *The Independent.* 14 August 2002

56 James Blitz, David Buchan and Dan Roberts. 'UK May Overhaul Wholesale Electricity Market.' *Financial Times.* 25 August 2002

57 Michael Harrison. 'British Energy Rescue to Cost Taxpayers £3bn.' *The Independent.* 29 November 2002; Christine Buckley. 'New Lifeline for Energy Attacked.' *The Times.* 27 September 2002; Philip Howard. 'Belgium Files Formal EU Complaint over British Energy

Aid Package.' *Business a.m.* 1 October 2002.

58 Michael Harrison. 'Generators Exposed after Collapse of TXU Europe'. *The Independent.* 20 November 2002; Suzanne Kapner. 'TXU's Abrupt Exit Roils Britain's Energy Market.' *New York Times.* 15 October 2002.

59 Michael Harrison. 'Powergen Closures Send Shock Waves through Energy Market.' *The Independent.* 10 October 2002; Michael Harrison. 'Powergen Takes Pole Position after £1.6bn Acquisition of TXU.' *The Independent.* 22 October 2002.

60 Jane Roberts, David Elliott and Trevor Houghton. *Privatising Electricity: The Politics of Power.* London and New York: Belhaven Press. 1991, p. 75.

61 Editorial. 'Power Politics: Britain Needs a New Energy Strategy.' *The Guardian.* 30 September 2002; 'UK Faces Battle to Meet 2010 Co2 Emissions Cut.' *World Environment News.* 23 July 2002; 'UK Energy Market Thrives, But CO2 on the Rise', *Edie Weekly Summaries,* 1 November 2002.

62 'Energy Minister Admits That Renewable Energy Is Suffering under NETA.' *Edie Weekly Summaries.* 19 October 2001; Margaret Orgill. 'UK's New Electricity Market Drives up Co2 Emissions.' *World Environment News.* 15 July 2002; Eva Sohlman. 'Britain May Rejig Power Market to Help CHP.' *World Environment News.* 15 May 2002

63 Lisa Sykes. 'The Power to Choose.' *New Scientist* 6 September 1997, pp. 16-17; 'Tony Blair's Energy Review Urges Promotion of Renewables.' *Edie Weekly Summaries.* 15 February 2002; Oliver Bullough. 'Consumers Pay for UK Govt's Green Power Plan.' *World Environment News.* 21 March 2002

64 Bullough,' Consumers Pay for UK Govt's Green Power Plan'; 'Companies Buying Green Energy Need to Be Beware.' *Edie Weekly Summaries.* 6 September 2002

65 Mary O'Mahony and Michela Vecchi. 'The Electricity Supply Industry: A Study of an Industry in Transition.' National Institute of Economic and Social Research. July, 2001. http://www.niesr.ac.uk/review/177/Mary.pdf

66 Thomas. 'The Wholesale Electricity Market.', p. 12.

67 David M. Newbery and Michael G. Pollitt. 'The Restructuring and Privatisation of the UK Electricity Supply—Was It Worth It?' *Public Policy for the Private Sector* September, 1997, p. 4.

68 MacGregor. 'Electricity Restructuring in

Britain.', p. 16; Thomas Walkom. "the Real Winners ... Are the Places That Stayed Regulated'.' *The Toronto Star*. 2 April, 2001; Thomas. 'The Development of Competition'., p. 88.

69 Neil Hirst. 'Consumer Protection in a Deregulated Market.' Paper presented at the IEA Regulatory Forum: Competition in Energy Markets. Paris, 7-8 February 2002, p. 12.

70 Matthew Jones and Andrew Taylor. 'Energy Regulator to Press on with End to Price Curbs.' *Financial Times*. 16 February 2002, p. 5.

71 Cryer. 'Utilities (Foreign Ownership).'

72 John E. Besant-Jones. 'The England and Wales Electricity Model—Option or Warning for Developing Countries?' *Public Policy for the Private Sector* June, 1996, p. 3.

73 Ralph Atkins. 'Privatisation Experts Offer Advice Abroad.' *Financial Times*. 12 July 1989, p. 9.

Chapter Thirteen

1 State and Commonwealth privatisations in the 1990s have totalled over $95 billion. Bob Walker and Betty Con Walker. *Privatisation: Sell of or Sell Out? The Australian Experience*. Sydney: ABC Books. 2001, pp. 17-18; Adele Ferguson. 'Merrill Goes for Growth.' *Business Review Weekly*. 29 June 1998, p. 22.

2 IEA. 'Energy Policies of IEA Countries: Australia 2001.' International Energy Agency. Accessed on 8 June 2001. http://www.iea.org/public/reviews/australia2001.htm

3 Hans Van Leeuwen. 'The Great Australian Sell-Off: RBA Verdict.' *Australian Financial Review*. 17 December 1997, p. 9.

4 Robert R. Booth. *Warring Tribes: The Story of Power Development in Australia*. West Perth: The Bardak Group. 2000, p. 29.

5 World Energy Council. 'Electricity Market Design and Creation in Asia Pacific.' World Energy Council, London. Accessed on 9 June 2001. http://www.worldenergy.org/wec-geis/publications/reports/emd/status/australia/default.asp; Booth. *Warring Tribes.*, pp. 14-18.

6 John Quiggin. 'Market-Oriented Reform in the Australian Electricity Industry.' Canberra: School of Economics, ANU. 15 March 2001, p. 24.

7 John Spoehr. 'Commission Needed to Head Off Electricity Problems.' *The Advertiser*. 28 December 2001, p. 18; Booth. *Warring Tribes.*, p. 103; John Spoehr. 'Power Struggles:

Privatisation and the Electricity Industry.' *Australian Options* February, 2000, p. 21.

8 World Energy Council. 'Electricity Market Design and Creation in Asia Pacific.'; Booth. *Warring Tribes.*, p. 16.

9 Booth. *Warring Tribes.*, p. 15; Quiggin. 'Market-Oriented Reform in the Australian Electricity Industry.', p. 1.

10 World Energy Council. 'Electricity Market Design and Creation in Asia Pacific.'

11 Tim Duncan and Anthony McAdam. 'New Right: Where Is Stands and What It Means.' *The Bulletin* 10 December 1985, p. 38.

12 W. Max Corden. 'Comment'. In *The Political Economy of Policy Reform*. ed. John Williamson. Washington, DC: Institute for International Economics. 1994, pp. 112-13.

13 Cited in Booth. *Warring Tribes.*, pp. 164-5 and Access Economics. 'Impact on Victoria of the Privatisation of the State's Electricity and Gas Assets.' Canberra: Access Economics. June, 2001, p. 10.

14 Quoted in Access Economics. 'Impact on Victoria of the Privatisation of the State's Electricity and Gas Assets.', p. 14.

15 Booth. *Warring Tribes.*, p. 165.

16 World Energy Council. 'Electricity Market Design and Creation in Asia Pacific.'

17 Stewart Russell and Andrea Bunting. 'Privatisation, Electricity Markets and New Energy Technologies'. In *Technology Studies and Sustainable Development*. Ed. A. Jamison and H. Rohracher. München: Profil. 2002

18 Paul Kelly. *The End of Uncertainty: The Story of the 1980s*. St Leonards, NSW: Allen & Unwin. 1992, p. 224.

19 Trevor Matthews. 'Employers' Associations, Corporatism and the Accord: The Politics of Industrial Relations'. In *State, Economy and Public Policy*. ed. Stephen Bell and Brian Head. Oxford University Press: Melbourne. 1994, p. 205.

20 Tony Daniels. 'Benchmarking and Microeconomic Reform in Major Infrastructural Services'. In *Managing Microeconomic Reform*. ed. Brian Galligan, Bob Lim and Kim Lovegrove. Canberra: Federalism Research Centre, ANU. 1993, p. 61.

21 Russell and Bunting. 'Privatisation, Electricity Markets'.

22 Daniels. 'Benchmarking and Microeconomic Reform in Major Infrastructural Services'., pp. 60, 63.

23 Ibid., pp. 66-7.

24 Brian Loton. 'Introduction'. In *Managing*

Microeconomic Reform. ed. Galligan, p. 4.

25 Daniels. 'Benchmarking and Microeconomic Reform in Major Infrastructural Services'., p. 67.

26 Tom Dusevic. 'The Idea Factories.' *Australian Financial Review.* 25 May 1990, p. 3; Susan Oliver. 'Where Do Governments Get Their Advice—Lobby Groups Think Tanks the Universities and the Media.' *Canberra Bulletin of Public Administration* December, 1993; Georgina Murray and Douglas Pacheco. 'Think Tanks in the 1990s.' Australian National University. Accessed on 23 January 2001. http://www.anu.edu.au/polsci/marx/interventions/thinktanks.htm; Bernie Taft. 'The New Right in Practice'. In *The New Right's Australian Fantasy.* ed. Ken Coghill. Fitzroy, Victoria: McPhee Gribble and Penguin Books. 1987, p. 28.

27 Marsh cited in Murray and Pacheco. 'Think Tanks in the 1990s.'

28 Marsh cited in Ibid.; Wilson Da Silva. 'The New Social Focus.' *Asutralian Financial Review Magazine.* May, 1996, p. 21.

29 IPA Report, Institute of Public Affairs Ltd, 1991, p. 1.

30 Tasman Institute. 'Tasman Institute Annual Review.' Melbourne: Tasman Institute Pty. Ltd. and Tasman Economic Research Pty. Ltd. December 1991; Dusevic. 'The Idea Factories.', p. 3; Da Silva. 'The New Social Focus.', p. 26.

31 Bette Moore and Gary Carpenter. 'Main Players'. In *The New Right's Australian Fantasy.* ed, Coghill, p. 151.

32 Edwin J. Feulner. 'Ideas, Think-Tanks and Governments: Away from the Power Elite, Back to the People.' *Quadrant* November, 1985, p. 25.

33 Tasman Institute. 'Tasman in Australia & New Zealand.' Tasman Institute. Accessed on 20 July 2001. www.tasman.com.au/Review/page11.html

34 Booth. *Warring Tribes.*, p. 45.

35 Michael G. Porter. 'Government and State Enterprise in Victoria.' H. R. Nicholls Society. Accessed on 20 July 2001. http://www.hrnicholls.com.au/nicholls/nichvo10/vol105go.htm

36 Des Moore and Michael Porter, eds. *Victoria: An Agenda for Change.* Melbourne: The Tasman Institute and the Institute of Public Affairs for Project Victoria. 1991, preface; Tasman Institute. 'About Us/Projects.' Tasman Institute. Accessed on 20 July 2001. http://www.tasman.com.au/main/a_nz.html

37 Tasman Institute. 'About Us/Projects.'

38 Alan Kohler. 'The Radical Right Wing Speeds the Kennett Revolution.' *The Age.* 14 February 1997, p. 15.

39 Moore and Porter, eds. *Victoria: An Agenda for Change.*, pp. 4-4, 4-5; Porter. 'Government and State Enterprise in Victoria.'

40 Cited in Karl Miller. 'The Truth About Privatisation.' *Green Left Weekly*, 1995, p. 6 and 'Independent Inquiry Recommends Halt to Electricity Privatization.' *Frontline* September, 1995, p. 4.

41 Booth. *Warring Tribes.*, p. 45; Rod Myer. 'Now It's Time for Stockdale Inc.' *The Age.* 8 May 1999; Tim Colebatch. 'His Crusade over, a Warrior Withdraws.' *The Age.* 2 June 1999

42 Nicole Lindsay and Brett Clegg. 'Stockdale Quits Politics for Macquarie.' *The Australian Financial Review.* 7 October 1999, p. 3.

43 Booth. *Warring Tribes.*, p. 46.

44 Mark Skulley. 'Private Power, Public Interest.' *Sydney Morning Herald.* 11 March 1995, p. 32.

45 Cited in 'Independent Inquiry Recommends Halt to Electricity Privatization.', p. 4.

46 Moore and Porter, eds. *Victoria: An Agenda for Change.*, p. 4-6.

47 Ibid., p. 4-6.

48 Cited in Access Economics. 'Impact on Victoria of the Privatisation of the State's Electricity and Gas Assets.', p. 12 and Moore and Porter, eds. *Victoria: An Agenda for Change.*, p. 4-6.

49 Tasman Institute. 'Tasman Institute Annual Review.', pp. 11, 13.

50 Kohler. 'The Radical Right Wing Speeds the Kennett Revolution.', p. 15; Jane Kelsey. *Economic Fundamentalism.* London: Pluto Press. 1995, pp. 47-8.

51 Robert Murray. 'Power without Glory.' *The Independent Monthly.* October, 1995, p. 46.

52 David Walker. 'Selling Electricity and Staying in Power.' *Sydney Morning Herald.* 31 May 1997, p. 39.

53 Booth. *Warring Tribes.*, p. 49.

54 Ibid., pp. 50-1.

55 Bronwyn Beechey. 'Power Sell-Off: Bad News for Victorians.' *Green Left Weekly*, 1995, p. 11; Skulley. 'Private Power, Public Interest.', p. 32.

56 Booth. *Warring Tribes.*, pp. 52-3, 57.

57 Ibid., p. 51.

58 Ibid., p. 60.

59 Ibid., pp. 56-7.

60 Quiggin. 'Market-Oriented Reform in the Australian Electricity Industry.', p. 27.

61 EIA. 'Privatization and the Globalization of

Energy Markets.' US Dept of Energy. Accessed on 21 March 2001. http://www.eia.doe.gov/emeu/pgem/ch5f.html ; Booth. *Warring Tribes.*, p. 62

62 Booth. *Warring Tribes.*, p. 56; 'Independent Inquiry Recommends Halt to Electricity Privatization.', p. 4.

63 Robert R. Booth. 'California's Electrifying Experience—Lessons for Australia.' West Perth: Bardak Group. 27 August 2001, p. 5.

64 Booth. *Warring Tribes.*, pp. 61-2.

65 Ibid., p. 63.

66 Ibid., pp. 64-8.

67 Ibid., pp. 68-70.

68 Walker. 'Selling Electricity and Staying in Power.', p. 39; Booth. *Warring Tribes.*, p. 72 Kenneth Davidson cited in Beechey. 'Power Sell-Off.', p. 11.

69 Booth. *Warring Tribes.*, p. 72.

70 Murray Massey. 'Power Politics.' *Business Review Weekly.* 3 March 2000, p. 68.

71 Booth. *Warring Tribes.*, p. 73.

72 David Walker. 'Victoria's Reforms Hold a Lesson for All the Knockers.' *Sydney Morning Herald.* 11 March 1998

73 Coopers & Lybrand survey quoted in Ewin Hannan. 'Privatised Power Less Reliable, Say Providers.' *The Australian.* 2 July 1997

74 Quoted in Booth. *Warring Tribes.*, p. 76.

75 Peter Hunt. 'Huge Energy Hikes Feared.' *Weekly Times.* 4 April 2001, p. 20; James Thompson. 'High-Voltage Hard Ship.' *Business Review Weekly.* 28 February 2002, p. 32; 'The Game of Power.' *Business Review Weekly* 25 January 2001, p. 54; Claire Konkes. 'US Blackouts Send Warning.' *The Australian.* 3 February 2001

76 Stephen Bartholomeusz. 'Power Consumers in for a Shock from Full Contestability.' *The Age.* 7 June 2001, p. 3; 'Can Farmers Keep Their Cool?' *The Age.* 12 November 2001, p. 16; Thompson. 'High-Voltage Hard Ship.', p. 32.

77 Philip Hopkins. 'Powercor Underpins Origin's 10% Surge.' *The Age.* 19 February 2002, p. 2; Ian Haberfield. 'Rural Power Bill Fury.' *Sunday Herald Sun.* 17 February 2002, p. 33.

78 Rod Myer. 'Consumers Declare 'No Contest' as Energy Industry Regroups.' *The Age.* 6 July 2002, p. 3.

79 John Durie. 'Energy Heading for Consolidation Fast.' *Australian Financial Review.* 22 March 2002, p. 84; Myer. 'Consumers Declare 'No Contest'.', p. 3; Thompson. 'High-Voltage Hard Ship.', p. 32; Nigel Wilson. 'Li Wins New Citipower Play

with $1.56 Bn Bid.' *The Weekend Australian.* 20 July 2002, p. 28.

80 Myer. 'Consumers Declare 'No Contest'.', p. 3.

81 Thompson. 'High-Voltage Hard Ship.', p. 32.

82 Myer. 'Consumers Declare 'No Contest'.', p. 3.

83 AGL spokesperson quoted in Ibid., p. 3; Rod Myer. 'AGL Thrives on a fresh Pulse'. *Sydney Morning Herald.* 28 November 2002, p. 25..

84 Ibid., p. 3; 'Independent Inquiry Recommends Halt to Electricity Privatization.', p. 4.

85 'ALP Blames Kennett for Looming Electricity Crisis.' *The Age.* 2 January 2002, p. 1; Skulley. 'Private Power, Public Interest.', p. 32; Josh Gordon. 'Business the Main Beneficiary of Reforms.' *The Age.* 29 May 2002, p. 3.

Chapter Fourteen

1 John Spoehr. 'Commission Needed to Head Off Electricity Problems.' *The Advertiser.* 28 December 2001, p. 18.

2 Cited in Claire Konkes. 'US Blackouts Send Warning.' *The Australian.* 2 March 2001

3 Murray Massey. 'Power Politics.' *Business Review Weekly.* 3 March 2000, p. 68.

4 Robert R. Booth. *Warring Tribes: The Story of Power Development in Australia.* West Perth: The Bardak Group. 2000, p. 171; 'The Game of Power.' *Business Review Weekly* 25 January 2001, p. 54.

5 Booth. *Warring Tribes.*, p. 191; Mark Searle. 'Will We Have the Californian Experience.' *Engineers Australia.* May, 2001, p. 24.

6 NEMMCO. 'An Introduction to Australia's National Electricity Market.' Melbourne and Sydney: National Electricity Market Management Company Limited. March, 2001, p. 21.

7 'Let There Be Light.' *Australian Financial Review.* 1 June 2001, p. 80.

8 Mike Sexton. 'National Electricity Grid Welcomes Tasmania.' *7.30 Report, ABC TV.* 3 April 2001; 'The Game of Power.', p. 54; Colin James. 'Pushing the Right Buttons.' *The Advertiser.* 3 May 2001, p. 19; Nigel Wilson. 'Market Reform Fails to Deliver.' *The Australian.* 19 April 2001, p. 8.

9 See for example Owens cited in Nigel Wilson. 'Regulator Aims to Generate Competition.' *The Australian.* 1 March 2001 and Konkes. 'US Blackouts Send Warning.'

10 Quoted in Booth. *Warring Tribes.*, pp. 175-6.

11 Ibid., pp. 177-8.

12 Quoted in Ibid., pp. 182-3.

13 Rod Myer. 'Call for Reform as Power Crisis

Looms.' *The Age*. 13 January 2001

14 ABARE. 'Competition in the Australian National Electricity Market.' *ABARE Current Issues* January, 2002, p. 1.

15 Ibid., pp. 7-8.

16 Ibid., pp. 8-10.

17 'The Game of Power.', p. 54.

18 ACCC. 'Amendments to the National Electricity Code: Changes to Bidding and Rebidding Rules.' Australian Competition and Consumer Commission. 2 July 2002, p. 49.

19 Ibid., pp. 77-8.

20 Ibid., pp. 11-12, 14-5.

21 Colin James. 'Power Brokers.' *The Advertiser*. 28 April 2001, p. 63.

22 Robert R. Booth. 'California's Electrifying Experience—Lessons for Australia.' West Perth: Bardak Group. 27 August 2001, p. 16.

23 Malcolm Knox. 'Power to the People? You Must Be Kidding, Pal.' *Sydney Morning Herald*. 23 January 2001

24 Keith Orchison. 'California Experience: A Warning Not a Prediction.' *Australian Energy News* March, 2001, p. 18.

25 Quoted in Claire Konkes. 'US Blackouts Send Warning.' *The Australia*. 3 February 2001

26 Searle. 'Will We Have the Californian Experience.', p. 24.

27 James Thomson. 'Electricity Market's Final Notice.' *Business Review Weekly*. 20 June 2002, p. 66.

28 Rod Myer. 'Rebidding Pushes Power Prices up 400%.' *The Age*. 5 June 2002; Brian Robins. 'High Power Prices Referred to ACCC.' *Sydney Morning Herald*. 31 May 2002

29 ACCC. 'Amendments to the National Electricity Code.' pp. 4, 54.

30 ACCC. 'National Electricity Market - Rebidding Code Changes: Draft Determination.' Australian Competition and Consumer Commission. 4 July 2002; ACCC. 'Amendments to the National Electricity Code.', p. 53.

31 Booth. *Warring Tribes*., pp. 107-9.

32 Ibid., pp. 110-11.

33 John Spoehr, 'Market Power'. *In Power Politics: The Electricity Crisis and You*. ed. John Spoehr. Kent Town, SA: Wakefield Press. 2003, pp. 30-32.

34 'Victory as ETSA Sale Stopped.' *The Guardian*. 1 July 1998; Peter Ward. 'How Much Heat Can Olsen Take?' *The Australian*. 22 August 2001, p. 12; Tom Morton. 'Power Games—the Politics of Electricity.' *Background Briefing, Radio National*. 19 March, 2000; 'Campaign

to Stop SA Power Sell-Off.' *The Guardian*. 10 June 1998.

35 John Spoehr. 'Power Struggles: Privatisation and the Electricity Industry.' *Australian Options* February, 2000, p. 16.

36 Ibid., p. 17; Rohan Gowland. 'Power Sale Bonanza for Advisors.' *The Guardian*. 24 June 1998; 'Victory as ETSA Sale Stopped.'; Quiggan cited in Spoehr. 'Power Struggles.', p. 20.

37 Quoted in 'Victory as ETSA Sale Stopped.'

38 Greg Kelton and Kim Wheatley. 'Pulling the Plug.' *The Advertiser*. 10 February 2001, p. 23

39 Richard Blandy. 'Cost of Power to the People.' *The Australian*. 4 February 2002, p. 11.

40 John Quiggin. 'Market-Oriented Reform in the Australian Electricity Industry.' Canberra: School of Economics, ANU. 15 March 2001, p. 28.

41 Paul Holloway. 'Why Olsen Is Wrong on ETSA.' *The Advertiser*. 24 March 1999

42 John Spoehr, 'Market Power'., pp. 32-39.

43 Ibid., pp. 40-43.

44 SA Auditor-General. 'Electricity Businesses Disposal Process in South Australia: Report by the Auditor-General Pursuant to Section 22(2) of the Electricity Corporations (Restructuring and Disposal) Act 1999 on Relevant Long Term Leases.' South Australia: House of Assembly. 27 March 2001, pp. ii-iii; Booth. *Warring Tribes*., pp. 112-13; Nigel Wilson. 'Li Wins New Citipower Play with $1.56 Bn Bid.' *The Weekend Australian*. 20 July 2002, p. 28; Bronwyn Beechey. 'Privatisation Leads to SA Power Crisis.' *Green Left Weekly*. 6 June 2001, p. 16; Booth. *Warring Tribes*., p. 113.

45 Booth. *Warring Tribes*., pp. 112-13.

46 Quoted in Carol Altmann. 'Hospitals in Generator Power Crisis.' *Sydney Morning Herald*. 21 March 2001

47 Morton. 'Power Games.'; Beechey. 'Privatisation Leads to SA Power Crisis.', p. 16; Blandy. 'Cost of Power to the People.', p. 11; Wilson. 'Market Reform Fails to Deliver.', p. 8.

48 James. 'Power Brokers.', p. 63; Greg Kelton and Kim Wheatley. 'The Big Switch.' *The Advertiser*. 20 July 2001, p. 19; Wilson. 'Market Reform Fails to Deliver.', p. 8; Konkes. 'US Blackouts Send Warning.'

49 Blandy. 'Cost of Power to the People.', p. 11; Sexton. 'National Electricity Grid Welcomes Tasmania.'

50 'Power Crisis: Heat Turned on Advisers.' *Australian Financial Review*. 23 July 2001, p. 7; Kelton and Wheatley. 'The Big Switch.', p. 19.

51 Kelton and Wheatley. 'The Big Switch.', p. 19.

52 Booth. *Warring Tribes.*, pp. 191-2.

53 Morton. 'Power Games.'; Peter Haran. 'Warnings of More Power Blackouts.' *Sunday Mail.* 5 November 2000, p. 17.

54 Kim Wheatley. 'Fortunes Made While SA in Dark.' *The Advertiser.* 4 November 2000, p. 12.

55 Quoted in Ibid., p. 12.

56 Beechey. 'Privatisation Leads to SA Power Crisis.', p. 16.

57 James. 'Power Brokers.', p. 63; Ward. 'How Much Heat Can Olsen Take?', p. 12; Kelton and Wheatley. 'Pulling the Plug.', p. 23; Beechey. 'Privatisation Leads to SA Power Crisis.', p. 16.

58 Beechey. 'Privatisation Leads to SA Power Crisis.', p. 16; Kelton and Wheatley. 'Pulling the Plug.', p. 23.

59 Tom Miller, Mechanical engineer, personal communication, 8 February 2001.

60 Laura Kendall and Matthew Bowman. 'Power Cut to 750 Homes as Record Falls.' *The Advertiser.* 8 February 2001, p. 8; Anna Cock. 'Power-Hungry Appliances at Fault.' *The Advertiser.* 12 February 2000, p. 14.

61 Kelton and Wheatley. 'Pulling the Plug.', p. 23.

62 Altmann. 'Hospitals in Generator Power Crisis.'; Craig Clarke. 'The Power Crunch.' *Sunday Mail.* 25 November 2001, p. 12.

63 Bryan Littley and Sean Fewster. 'Low-Voltage Damage Soars.' *The Advertiser.* 20 March 2001

64 Morton. 'Power Games.'; Quiggin. 'Market-Oriented Reform in the Australian Electricity Industry.', p. 5.

65 Blandy. 'Cost of Power to the People.', p. 11.

66 Ibid., p. 11; Ward. 'How Much Heat Can Olsen Take?', p. 12; Greg Kelton. 'Rann Makes Power Play.' *The Advertiser.* 4 February 2002, p. 1; Kelton. 'Rann Makes Power Play.', p. 1.

67 Quoted in Ward. 'How Much Heat Can Olsen Take?', p. 12.

68 Terry Plane. 'When Cost of Power Hits the Fan.' *The Australian.* 25 June 2002

69 SAIIR. 'Electricity Retail Price Justification: Final Report.' Adelaide: Office of the South Australian Independent Industry Regulator. September 2002, p. iii; Leanne Craig and David Eccles. 'Power Bills to Rise $300 Million.' *The Advertiser.* 3 September 2002

70 SAIIR. 'Electricity Retail Price Justification.', pp iii, 3.

71 Plane. 'When Cost of Power Hits the Fan.', p. 24.

72 Craig and Eccles. 'Power Bills to Rise $300 Million.', p. 1; David Nankervis. 'Power Price Plea for Help from Canberra.' *Sunday Mail.* 15 September 2002, p. 17; Kim Wheatley. 'Extra $276 for Power.' *The Advertiser.* 6 April 2002, p. 1; Nankervis. 'Power Price Plea for Help from Canberra.', p. 17.

73 Essential Services Commission of South Australia. 'Commission Trims AGL's Planned Prices and Revenue for New S.A. Electricity Market'. Media Release. 31 October 2002; Andrew McGarry. 'AGL Defends Power Hikes.' *The Australian.* 1 October 2002, p. 6; Spoehr. 'Commission Needed to Head Off Electricity Problems.', p. 18.

74 Patrick Conlon. 'Higher Electricity Bills the Price of Privatisation.' *The Advertiser.* 5 October 2002, p. 20; Wheatley. 'Extra $276 for Power.', p. 1; Conlon. 'Higher Electricity Bills the Price of Privatisation.', p. 20.

75 Conlon. 'Higher Electricity Bills the Price of Privatisation.', p. 20.

76 Quoted in Leanne Craig. 'Contracts Unfair, Says Business.' *The Advertiser.* 24 June 2002

77 Mike Sexton. 'SA Consumers Face Skyrocketing Electricity Prices.' *7.30 Report* (ABC TV). 15 January 2003.

78 Terry Plane. 'Crises Conspire to Give Privatisation a Bad Name.' *The Advertiser.* 20 December, 2002, p. 2; 'Station's $4.5m Gas Bill Paid by US Company.' *The Advertiser.* 21 December, 2002, p. 4.; Elizabeth Rowe. 'Electricity at $54 a Unit One Moment, $3102 the Next.' *The Advertiser.* 21 December, 2002, p. 4.

Chapter Fifteen

1 Quoted in David Leser. 'Lights Out!' *Good Weekend.* 18 April 1998

2 World Energy Council. 'Electricity Market Design and Creation in Asia Pacific.' World Energy Council, London. Accessed on 9 June 2001. http://www.worldenergy.org/wec-geis/publications/reports/emd/status/australia/default.asp; Colin James. 'Power Brokers.' *The Advertiser.* 28 April 2001, p. 63.

3 Cited in Karl Miller. 'The Truth About Privatisation.' *Green Left Weekly*, 1995, p. 6.

4 Robert R. Booth. *Warring Tribes: The Story of Power Development in Australia.* West Perth: The Bardak Group. 2000, p. 86; Stewart Russell and Andrea Bunting. 'Privatisation, Electricity Markets and New Energy Technologies'. In *Technology Studies and Sustainable Development.* ed. H. Rohracher. München: Profil. 2002

5 Karen Maley. 'Arguments Rage over the Fate of Pacific Power.' *Sydney Morning Herald*. 26 June 1995

6 Russell and Bunting. 'Privatisation, Electricity Markets'.

7 OFFER. 'Review of Electricity Trading Arrangements: Background Paper 2.' Office of Electricity Regulation. February, 1998, p. 6; J. Gillard. 'Powercor Australia Ltd V Pacific Power.' Melbourne: Supreme Court of Victoria. 18 November 1999, p. 9; Anthony Hughes. 'All Charged and Ready to Go.' *Sydney Morning Herald*. 11 March 1998

8 Cited in Mark Skulley. 'Private Power, Public Interest.' *Sydney Morning Herald*. 11 March 1995, p. 32.

9 Christopher Sheil. 'History Puts Powerful Argument.' *Australian Financial Review*. 3 August 2001, p. 63.

10 Milton Cockburn and Mark Riley. 'Power Failure.' *Sydney Morning Herald*. 4 October 1997, p. 29; Hughes. 'All Charged and Ready to Go.'

11 David Humphries. 'Part Sale of Pacific Power 'to Save Jobs'.' *Sydney Morning Herald*. 7 December 1996, p. 2; Margaret Gleeson. 'Privatisation Report Ignores Rank and File Opposition.' *Green Left Weekly*, 1997, p. 4; David Humphries. 'Power Struggles.' *Sydney Morning Herald*. 11 October 1997, p. 40; David Walker. 'Power Sell-Off Could Raise $25bn.' *Sydney Morning Herald*. 23 May,1997

12 Mark Riley. 'Power and Passion.' *Sydney Morning Herald*. 28 June 1997, p. 37.

13 Gleeson. 'Privatisation Report Ignores Rank and File Opposition.', p. 4; Humphries. 'Power Struggles.', p. 40; Cockburn and Riley. 'Power Failure.', p. 29.

14 Humphries. 'Power Struggles.', p. 40.

15 Gleeson. 'Privatisation Report Ignores Rank and File Opposition.', p. 4; Humphries. 'Power Struggles.', p. 40; G Lloyd. 'The Price of Power.' *Courier-Mail*. 11 October 1997, p. 26.

16 Cockburn and Riley. 'Power Failure.', p. 29; Hughes. 'All Charged and Ready to Go.'; Trudy Harris. 'Carr Switches Off Private Electricity.' *The Australian*. 28 August 1998, p. 8.

17 Robert Wainwright and Paola Totaro. 'Brogden's Switch over Power Plans.' *Sydney Morning Herald*. 6-7 April 2002; Lloyd. 'The Price of Power.', p. 26.

18 David Humphries. 'Unplugged.' *Sydney Morning Herald*. 20 February 1999, p. 36.

19 Ibid., pp. 33, 36.

20 Wainwright and Totaro. 'Brogden's Switch over Power Plans.'; David Humphries. 'Shock Switch on Private Electricity.' *Sydney Morning Herald*. 27 February 2002, p. 9.

21 Brian Robins. 'Carr May Pay the Price of Power.' *Sydney Morning Herald*. 16 April 2001, p. 4.

22 Gillard. 'Powercor Australia Ltd V Pacific Power.', p. 6.

23 Ibid., p. 15.

24 Ibid., p. 14; Ben Hills. 'A Big Power Bill.' *Sydney Morning Herald*. 4 December 1999, p. 39

25 Ibid., p. 39.

26 Ibid., p. 39.

27 'It's Full Steam Ahead for NSW's Power Generators.' *Sydney Morning Herald*. 10 January 2002, p. 25; Paola Totaro. 'Time to Celebrate 10 Years of Ensuring the Price Is Right.' *Sydney Morning Herald*. 6 July 2002, p. 13; Nigel Wilson. 'Power Price Blow-Out.' *The Australian*. 15 October 2001, p. 36.

28 Pacific Power. 'About Pacific Power.' Pacific Power. 6 March 2001. http://www.pp.nsw.gov.au/about.html

29 Brian Robins. 'Electricity Reform Plan to Control Price Surges.' *Sydney Morning Herald*. 7 October 2002

30 Brian Robins. 'Banks See Big Chance in Trading Electricity.' *Sydney Morning Herald*. 5-6 October 2002, p. 45.

31 Booth. *Warring Tribes.*, pp. 97-9.

32 Ibid., p. 97.

33 Ibid., p. 191.

34 Ibid., p. 98.

35 Ibid., p. 100.

36 G Lloyd. 'Power Play.' *Courier-Mail*. 3 June 1997, p. 9.

37 Cited in Nigel Wilson. 'Grid and Bear It.' *The Australian*. 5 October 2001, p. 34.

38 Mark Skulley. 'Crisis in Power Policy Looming.' *Australian Financial Review*. 13 March 2002, p. 3; Danny Rose. 'State Gives Formal Ok to Basslink.' *The Hobart Mercury*. 6 August 2002

39 Andrew Darby. 'Eat Your Greens.' *Sydney Morning Herald*. 29 August 1998, p. 41; Kirsty Simpson. 'Tasmania's HEC Set for Privatisation.' *The Age*. 25 April 1998, p. 3.

40 Lester Michael. 'Warning against Hasty Sell-Off of HEC.' *Hobary Mercury*. 12 November 1996

41 John Quiggin. 'Market-Oriented Reform in the Australian Electricity Industry.' Canberra: School of Economics, ANU. 15 March 2001, p. 27; Darby. 'Eat Your Greens.', p. 41.

42 Booth. *Warring Tribes.*, p. 117.

43 The Australia Institute. 'Privatising Electricity:

A Modern Cargo Cult?' *The Australia Institute* December, 1998, p. 9.

44 James Vassilopoulos. 'ACTEW Privatisation Victory.' *Green Left Weekly*, 1999, p. 5.

45 David McLennan. 'Electricity Bills Set to Increase.' *The Canberra Times*. 13 July 2002, p. 1.

46 Mark Drummond. 'Barnett in About-Face on Power.' *Australian Financial Review*. 13 August 2002, p. 5.

47 'Both Sides Put a Lot of Energy into Reform Debate.' *Australian Financial Review*. 29 August 2001, p. 15.

48 Booth. *Warring Tribes.*, pp. 75, 201; Rod Myer. 'Now It's Time for Stockdale Inc.' *The Age*. 8 May 1999; Luke Collins. 'Rear Window.' *Australian Financial Review*. 22 October 1999, p. 91.

49 Rohan Gowland. 'Power Sale Bonanza for Advisors.' *The Guardian*. 24 June 1998; 'Power Crisis: Heat Turned on Advisers.' *Australian Financial Review*. 23 July 2001, p. 7.

50 David Walker. 'The Power in Power Plays.' *The Age*. 25 October, 1997, p. 16.

51 Tasman Economics. 'Initiatives: Project Victoria.' Tasman Economics. Accessed on 12 February 2001. http://www.tasman.com.au/main/initiatives.html

52 Tasman Economics. 'Our Founders.' Tasman Economics. Accessed on 26 June 2002. http://www.tasman.com.au/founders/founders.htm

53 Tasman Economics. 'About Us.' Tasman Economics. Accessed on 26 June 2002. http://www.tasman.com.au/aboutus/abt_london.htm; Tasman Economics. 'Our Founders.'

54 Tasman Economics. 'Our Founders.'; Alan Kohler. 'The Radical Right Wing Speeds the Kennett Revolution.' *The Age*. 14 February, 1997, p. 15.

55 Tasman Economics. 'Expertise.' Tasman Economics. Accessed on 26 June 2002. http://www.tasman.com.au/expertise/exp_cba.htm

56 Tasman Economics. 'Our People.' Tasman Economics. Accessed on 26 June 2002. http://www.tasman.com.au/people/people.htm; Tasman Economics. 'Our Clients.' Tasman Economics. Accessed on 26 June 2002. http://www.tasman.com.au/clients/clients.htm

57 Miles Kemp. 'Out of Service.' *The Advertiser*. 29 July 2000, p. 65.

58 SA Auditor-General. 'Electricity Businesses Disposal Process in South Australia: Arrangements for the Disposal of ETSA Utilities Pty Ltd and ETSA Power Pty Ltd: Some Audit Observations.' South Australia: House of Assembly. 30 November 2000, p. ii.

59 Booth. *Warring Tribes.*, p. 194.

60 Bob Lim and Co, The Bardak Group and Headberry Partners. 'Submission to the Council of Australian Governments Energy Market Review.' Holden, WMC Limited, Visy Paper Limited, OneSteel Limited, BHP Billiton Limited. April, 2002, p. 15.

61 Rod Myers. 'Consumers Declare 'No Contest' as Energy Industry Regroups.' *The Age*. 6 July 2002

62 John Quiggan, 'Free market reform and the South Australian electricity supply industry'. In *Power Politics: The Electricity Crisis and You*. ed. John Spoehr. Kent Town, SA: Wakefield Press. 2003, p. 66

63 Booth. *Warring Tribes.*, p. 193; David Walker. 'Shocks for NSW as Electricity Selling Goes National.' *Sydney Morning Herald*. 7 August 1996, p. 28; John Garnaut. 'Curb on Emissions Feasible'. *Sydney Morning Herald*. 21 October 2002; David Wroe. 'Farmers Win Power Subsidies.' *The Age*. 20 December 2001, p. 2; The Australia Institute. 'Submission to the COAG Energy Market Review.' Canberra: The Australia Institute. 18 April 2002.

64 Reuters. 'Australia Wasting a $1bln on Greenhouse Efforts -Report.' *Planet Ark*. 24 July 2002

65 'Australia renewable power sector condemns report'. *World Environment News*. 30 December 2002.

66 Editorial. 'Paying the Price for "Green Power".' *Sydney Morning Herald*. 4-5 January, 2003.

67 Stephanie Peatling. 'Coal Remains King.' *Sydney Morning Herald*. 18 December, 2002, p. 14.

68 Alan Mitchell. 'Don't Pull the Plug on Energy Reform.' *Australian Financial Review*. 23 March 2002, p. 54.

69 Wilson. 'Grid and Bear It.', p. 34.

70 AAP. 'Consumers Carry Can for Power Guzzling Smelters.' *The Australian*. 2 January, 2002, p. 17.

71 EUAA. 'Time to Link Greenhouse Policy to Energy Market Reform.' Energy Users Association of Australia. 25 November 2001; EUAA. 'EUAA Services.' Energy Users Association of Australia. Accessed on 14 October 2002. http://www.euaa.com.au/euaa_services.htm

72 Bob Lim and Co, The Bardak Group and Headberry Partners. 'Submission to the

Council of Australian Governments Energy Market Review.', pp. 14-19.

73 EUAA. 'Business Plan 2002/03.' Energy Users Association of Australia. March 2002, p. 6.

74 EUAA. 'Time to Link Greenhouse Policy to Energy Market Reform.'

75 Mitchell. 'Don't Pull the Plug on Energy Reform.'

76 Ibid.

77 COAG. 'Towards a Truly National and Efficient Energy Market - Draft Report.' Council of Australian Governments. November, 2002, pp. 6, 8.

78 Anna Reynolds. 'What you need to know about the Oz Energy Review'. Climate Action Network Australia. 30 April 2002.

79 Ibid., pp. 11-12, 17-19.

80 Ibid., pp. 12-13, 18.

81 Ibid., p. 20.

82 ACCI. 'Energy Market Review.' ACT: Australian Chamber of Commerce and Industry. April, 2002, p. 16.

83 Ibid., p. 9.

84 Ibid., pp. 12, 25.

Chapter Sixteen

1 Gregory Palast. 'IMF's Four Steps to Damnation.' Observer. 29 April 2001, p. 7.

2 Quoted in Natalie Avery. 'Stealing from the State.' Multinational Monitor September, 1993

3 Sustainable Energy and Economic Network. 'Enron's Pawns: How Public Institutions Bankrolled Enron's Globalization Game.' Washington, DC: Institute for Policy Studies. 22 March 2002, p. 10.

4 Palast. 'IMF's Four Steps to Damnation.', p. 7

5 'Malaysia Needs $9.7 Bil over Next 10 Years to Meet Electricity Capacity Requirements.' Power Engineering International November, 2001, p. 32.

6 John Williamson. 'In Search of a Manual for Technopols'. In The Political Economy of Policy Reform. ed. John Williamson. Washington, DC: Institute for International Economics. 1994, p. 17.

7 Frank Stilwell. 'Economic Rationalism: Sound Foundations for Policy?' In Beyond the Market: Alternatives to Economic Rationalism. ed. Stuart Rees, Gordon Rodley and Frank Stilwell. Leichhardt, NSW: Pluto Press. 1993, p. 36; Williamson. 'In Search of a Manual for Technopols'., p. 17.

8 Vincent Lloyd and Robert Weissman. 'Against the Workers: How IMF and World Bank Policies Undermine Labor Power and Rights.'

9 Jeffrey Davis et. al. . 'Fiscal and Macroeconomic Impact of Privatization.' IMF Occasional Paper 22 June, 2000; Susan Hawley. 'Exporting Corruption: Privatisation, Multinationals and Bribery.' The Corner House Briefing, 2000.

Multinational Monitor September, 2001

10 Walden Bello and Shea Cunningham. 'Disciplining the Third World: The Role of the World Bank in US Foreign Policy.' CovertAction Winter, 1991-2

11 John Weeks. 'Credit Where Discredit Is Due.' Third World Resurgence April, 1994, p. 32.

12 Lloyd and Weissman. 'Against the Workers: How IMF and World Bank Policies Undermine Labor Power and Rights.'

13 Weeks. 'Credit Where Discredit Is Due.', p. 32.

14 Walden Bello and Shea Cunningham. 'The World Bank & the IMF.' Z Magazine July, 1994

15 Weeks. 'Credit Where Discredit Is Due.', p. 33.

16 Avery. 'Stealing from the State.'

17 Hawley. 'Exporting Corruption.'

18 Ibid.; Kate Bayliss. 'Privatisation and the World Bank: A Flawed Development Tool.' Global Focus June, 2001

19 World Bank. 'Privatization and Enterprise Reform.' World Bank. 2002. http://www.worldbank.org/html/fpd/private-sector/priv-ent.htm

20 Hawley. 'Exporting Corruption.'

21 Friends of the Earth. 'International Monetary Fund 101.' Multinational Monitor January/February, 1998

22 Masood Ahmed, Timothy Lane and Marianne Schulze-Ghattas. 'Refocusing IMF Conditionality.' Finance & Development December, 2001

23 Ibid.

24 Sue Shaw. 'Dicing with Debt: The Third World Dilemma.' New Internationalist November, 1988, p. 16.

25 Wayne Ellwood. 'Pinstripes and Poverty: Inside the World Bank.' New Internationalist December, 1990, p. 6.

26 Ahmed, Lane and Schulze-Ghattas. 'Refocusing IMF Conditionality.'

27 Davis et. al.. 'Fiscal and Macroeconomic Impact of Privatization.'

28 Gabriel Kolko. 'Ravaging the Poor: IMF Indicted by Its Own Data.' Multinational Monitor June, 1998, p. 21.

29 Michel Chossudovsky. 'The Global Creation of Third World Poverty.' Third World Resurgence January, 1992, p. 16.

30 Kolko. 'Ravaging the Poor.', p. 21.

31 Ibid., p. 20; Chris Adams. 'Privatising Infrastructure in the South.' *Focus on Trade* May, 2001

32 Ahmed, Lane and Schulze-Ghattas. 'Refocusing IMF Conditionality.'; Davis, Ossowski, Richardson and Barnett. 'Fiscal and Macroeconomic Impact of Privatization.'

33 Bruce Rich. 'The Cuckoo in the Nest: Fifty Years of Political Meddling by the World Bank.' *The Ecologist* January/February, 1994, p. 10.

34 Adams. 'Privatising Infrastructure in the South.'

35 Asian Development Bank. 'The Bank's Policy Initiatives for the Energy Sector.' Philippines: Asian Development Bank. May 1995

36 Ibid.

37 Ibid.

38 Ibid.

39 Sean Healy. 'Papua New Guinea: People Rebel against World Bank.' Green Left Weekly. Accessed on 5 August 2001. http://www.scoop.co.nz/mason/stories/HL010 7/S00010.htm; Craig Skehan. 'Passions Will Be Hard to Cool.' *Sydney Morning Herald*. 27 June, 2001; 'Papua New Guinea to Press on with Privatisations.' 18 July 2001. http://urn: bigchalk:US;Lib&dtype=0~0&dinst=

40 AusAID. 'AusAID Country Information: Papua New Guinea.' AusAID. 19 December. http://www.ausaid.gov.au/country/png/gover-nance.cfm; 'Aust Meeting on PNG Assets Sale.' Post-Courier Online. Accessed on 5 August 2000. http://www.postcourier.com.pg/ 20000713/business01.htm; 'Hutchinson to Sell PNG Post, Telikom.' *Sydney Morning Herald*. 30 March 2001

41 Skehan. 'Passions Will Be Hard to Cool.'; Facts of Life. 'Why Would Anyone Want Privatisation in PNG?' www.niugini.com. Accessed on 5 August 2001. http://www.niug-ini.com/wwwboard/messages/84007.html

42 Mark Forbes. 'World Bank Becomes the Bogeyman in PNG.' *The Age*. 27 June 2001

43 Paul Blustein. 'IMF's 'Consensus' Policies Fraying.' *Washington Post*. 26 September, 2002, p. E01; Richard Lapper. 'Piling on the Pressure.' *Financial Times*. 5 October 2002, p. 1; Juan Forero. 'Still Poor, Latin Americans Protest Push for Open Markets.' *The New York Times*. 19 July 2002, p. A-1.

44 Forero. 'Still Poor, Latin Americans Protest Push for Open Markets.', p. A-1.

45 Chossudovsky. 'The Global Creation of Third World Poverty.', p. 13.

46 Adams. 'Privatising Infrastructure in the South.'; Tony Clarke. 'Enron: Washington's

Number One Behind-the-Scenes Gats Negotiator.' *CorpWatch* 25 October 2001

47 Quoted in Avery. 'Stealing from the State.'

48 Global Exchange. 'World Bank / IMF Questions and Answers.' Global Exchange. 13 February 2002. http://www.globalexchange. org/wbimf/faq.html

49 Davison Budhoo and Claude Alvares. 'Why the IMF Is a Threat to the South.' *Third World Resurgence* June, 1992

50 Larry Rohter. 'In Free-Market Slump, Brazil's Voters Look for Change.' *The New York Times*. 5 October 2002; Juan Forero. 'As Bolivians Vote, Populism Is on the Rise.' *The New York Times*. 30 June 2002; Forero. 'Still Poor, Latin Americans Protest Push for Open Markets.', p. A-1; Lapper. 'Piling on the Pressure.', p. 1. Juan Forero. 'Still Poor, Latin Americans Protest Push for Open Markets.' *The New York Times*. 19 July, 2002

51 Chris Kraul. 'Protests Stymie Peru's Drive to Raise Capital.' *Los Angeles Times*. 14 July 2002, p. 3-1; Herald Wire Services. 'Peruvian Protests of Privatization Spread.' *The Miami Herald*. 20 June 2002, p. A3; Reuters. 'Troops Deployed in Peru's 2nd-Largest City.' *Chicago Tribune*. 18 June, 2002, p. 4; Richard Lapper. 'Latin America Turns Left.' *Financial Times*. 29 July 2002, p. 19.

52 Quoted in Tony Smith. 'Brazil's 10-Year Effort to Privatize State Assets a Real Deal.' *Chicago Tribune*. 4 February 2001, p. 8C.

53 Sustainable Energy and Economic Network. 'Enron's Pawns.' p. 3

54 Rachel L. Swarns. 'In South Africa, Leaders Face Blacks' Ire.' *New York Times*. 2 October 2002, p. A10; Jon Jeter. 'For South Africa's Poor, a New Power Struggle.' *The Washington Post*. 6 November, 2001, p. A01; Nick Mathiason. 'Turning Off the Tap for Poor.' *The Observer*. 18 August 2002, p. 4

55 Ibid., p. A01; John Murphy. 'Unions in South Africa Strike over Selling of State Industries.' *The Baltimore Sun*. 30 August 2001, p. 18A.

56 Quoted in Blustein. 'IMF's 'Consensus' Policies Fraying.', p. E01.

57 Ibid., p,. E01.

58 Editorial. 'Argentina's Model Crash.' *The Washington Post*. 24 December 2001, p. A16.

59 John E. Besant-Jones and Bernard W. Tenenbaum. 'The California Experience with Power Sector Reform: Lessons for Developing Countries.' Energy and Mining Sector Board, The World Bank. April, 2001, p. 2.

60 Ibid., pp. 4-8.

Chapter Seventeen

1 'Electricity: Power Crazy.' *The Economist* 10 October 1998

2 Asian Development Bank. 'The Bank's Policy Initiatives for the Energy Sector.' Philippines: Asian Development Bank. May 1995; R. David Gray and John Schuster. 'The East Asian Financial Crisis—Fallout for the Private Power Projects.' *The World Bank Group—Public Policy for the Private Sector* August, 1998, p. 1.

3 Ada Karina Izaguirre. 'Private Participation in Energy.' *The World Bank Group - Public Policy for the Private Sector* May, 2000, pp. 3-5.

4 Ibid., pp. 1-3.

5 The Regulatory Assistance Project. 'Best Practices Guide: Implementing Power Sector Reform.' Gardiner, Maine and Montpelier, Vermont: Energy and Environment Training Program, Office of Energy, Environment and Technology and Global Bureau, Center for the Environment, United States Agency for International Development, pp. 2-3.

6 Izaguirre. 'Private Participation in Energy.', p. 5.

7 Yves Albouy and Reda Bousba. 'The Impact of IPPs in Developing Countries—out of the Crisis and into the Future.' *The World Bank Group - Public Policy for the Private Sector* December, 1998, pp. 1-2.

8 Kate Bayliss and David Hall. 'Independent Power Producers: A Review of the Issues.' University of Greenwich, London: Public Services International Research Unit (PSIRU). November, 2000, p. 5; Fernando Y. Roxas. 'The Importance and the Changing Role of the Independent Power Producers (IPPs) in the Proposed Competitive Power Market in the Philippines.' Paper presented at the APEC 8th Technical Seminar & 7th Coal Flow Seminar. Bangkok, 30 October-1 November 2001, p. 1; Mizuho Research. 'Credit Comment: National Power Corporation.' Mizuho Research. 28 September 2001

9 Asian Development Bank. 'The Bank's Policy Initiatives for the Energy Sector.'

10 Albouy and Bousba. 'The Impact of IPPs in Developing Countries.', p. 5.

11 Bayliss and Hall. 'Independent Power Producers.', p. 8.

12 ECA - Watch. 'Export Credit Agencies: International NGO Campaign.' Export Credit Agency Watch. Accessed on 15 February 2002. http://www.eca-watch.org/Home/index1.html

13 Bruch Rich. 'Exporting Destruction.' *The Environmental Forum* September/October, 2000, p. 32; Doug Norlen. 'Export Credit Agencies Explained.' Export Credit Agency Watch. Accessed on 23 February 2002. http://www.eca-watch.org/ECAs_Explained_Rev. htm

14 Ibid.

15 Rich. 'Exporting Destruction.', p. 35.

16 Ibid., p. 36.

17 Ibid., p. 33.

18 Ibid., p. 34.

19 Navroz K. Dubash. 'The Changing Global Context for Electricity Reform'. In *Power Politics: Equity and Environment in Electricity Reform.* ed. Navroz K. Dubash. Washington D.C.: World Resources Institute. 2002, p. 19.

20 The Regulatory Assistance Project. 'Best Practices Guide.', p. 12.

21 Gray and Schuster. 'The East Asian Financial Crisis.', pp. 2-3.

22 Albouy and Bousba. 'The Impact of IPPs in Developing Countries.', p. 2; The Regulatory Assistance Project. 'Best Practices Guide.', p. 13.

23 Mizuho Research. 'Credit Comment: National Power Corporation.'; Bayliss and Hall. 'Independent Power Producers.', p. 9.

24 Albouy and Bousba. 'The Impact of IPPs in Developing Countries.', p. 5.

25 Bayliss and Hall. 'Independent Power Producers.', pp. 3, 5.

26 Albouy and Bousba. 'The Impact of IPPs in Developing Countries.', p. 3; Mizuho Research. 'Credit Comment: National Power Corporation.'; Albouy and Bousba. 'The Impact of IPPs in Developing Countries.', p. 3.

27 Albouy and Bousba. 'The Impact of IPPs in Developing Countries.', p. 2; Gray and Schuster. 'The East Asian Financial Crisis.', p. 3; Roxas. 'The Importance and the Changing Role of the IPPs.', p. 2.

28 Albouy and Bousba. 'The Impact of IPPs in Developing Countries.', p. 2; Bayliss and Hall. 'Independent Power Producers.', p. 4.

29 The Regulatory Assistance Project. 'Best Practices Guide.', p. 12.

30 Albouy and Bousba. 'The Impact of IPPs in Developing Countries.', p. 4.

31 Roxas. 'The Importance and the Changing Role of the IPPs.', p. 1; Bayliss and Hall. 'Independent Power Producers.', p. 4.

32 Chakravarthi Raghavan. 'FDI Is No Panacea for South's Economic Woes.' *Third World Resurgence* October/November, 1999

33 Ibid.

34 Chris Adams. 'Privatising Infrastructure in the

South.' *Focus on Trade* May, 2001

35 Bayliss and Hall. 'Independent Power Producers.', p. 4.

36 Adams. 'Privatising Infrastructure in the South.'

37 Michel Chossudovsky. 'Financial Warfare.' 21 September 1998. http://www.interlog.com/~cjazz/chossd.htm

38 Bayliss and Hall. 'Independent Power Producers.', p. 7.

39 Kate Bayliss and David Hall. 'A PSIRU Response to the World Bank's "Private Sector Development Strategy: Issues and Options".' University of Greenwich, London: Public Services International Research Unit (PSIRU). October 2001, p. 8.

40 Ibid., p. 9.

41 Albouy and Bousba. 'The Impact of IPPs in Developing Countries.', p. 3.

42 John Javetski. 'The Lure of Latin America.' *Electrical World* September, 1996, p. 23.

43 Martin Khor. 'What Is MAI?' *Third World Resurgence*, 1998, p. 7; Oliver Hoedeman and et. al. 'MAIgalomania: The New Corporate Agenda.' *The Ecologist* 28(3). 1998

44 International Forum on Globalization. 'Should Corporations Govern the World?' *Third World Resurgence*, 1998; Hoedeman and al. 'MAIgalomania.'; International Forum on Globalization. 'Should Corporations Govern the World?'

45 Marjorie Griffin Cohen. 'From Public Good to Private Exploitation: Electricity Deregulation, Privatization and Continental Integration.' Nova Scotia: Canadian Centre for Policy Alternatives. July 2002, pp. 10-11.

46 Tony Clarke. 'Enron: Washington's Number One Behind-the-Scenes Gats Negotiator.' *CorpWatch* 25 October 2001

47 Ibid.

48 World Development Movement. 'The Missing Link: Debt and Trade.' World Development Movement. 3 February 2001. http://www.wdm.org.uk/cambriefs/Debt/missl ink.pdf, p. 3.

49 Bayliss and Hall. 'Independent Power Producers.', p. 6.

50 Izaguirre. 'Private Participation in Energy.', p. 6.

51 Elliot Roseman and Anil Malbotra. 'The Dynamics of Independent Power: IPPs Seed Top-to-Bottom Reform.' *The World Bank Group - Public Policy for the Private Sector* June, 1996, p. 1.

52 Asian Development Bank. 'The Bank's Policy Initiatives for the Energy Sector.'

53 Mizuho Research. 'Credit Comment: National

Power Corporation.'; Bayliss and Hall. 'Independent Power Producers.', p. 4.

54 Bayliss and Hall. 'Independent Power Producers.', p. 6.

55 Sustainable Energy and Economic Network. 'Enron's Pawns: How Public Institutions Bankrolled Enron's Globalization Game.' Washington, DC: Institute for Policy Studies. 22 March 2002, p. 3.

56 Canute James. 'Leader Acts to Tackle Power Shortage.' *Financial Times*. 18 June 2002, p. 9; Herald Wire Services. 'Latin American Roundup.' *The Miami Herald*. 16 September 2002, p. A11.

Chapter Eighteen

1 Darryl D'Monte. 'Enron Sheds No Light on Consumer.' *The Times of India*. 12 December 2000

2 Lawrence Saez and Joy Yang. 'The Deregulation of State-Owned Enterprises in India and China.' *Comparative Economic Studies* 43(3). 2001, p. 69.

3 Navroz K. Dubash. 'India: Electricity Reform under Political Constraints'. In *Power Politics: Equity and Environment in Electricity Reform*. ed. Navroz K. Dubash. Washington D.C.: World Resources Institute. 2002, pp. 51-3.

4 Michel Chossudovsky. 'India under IMF Rule.' *The Ecologist* November/December 1992, pp. 271, 275; Sustainable Energy and Economic Network. 'Enron's Pawns: How Public Institutions Bankrolled Enron's Globalization Game.' Washington, DC: Institute for Policy Studies. 22 March 2002, p. 11.

5 Kenneth J. Cooper. 'Wattage to India.' *Washington Post* 5 February 1996, p. A12; Cabinet of Maharashtra Sub-Committee. 'Report of the Cabinet Sub-Commitee to Review the Dabhol Power Project'. In *The Enron Corporation: Corporate Complicity in Human Rights Violations*. Ed. Human Rights Watch. Human Rights Watch. 1999; Abhay Mehta. *Power Play: A Study of the Enron Project*. Mumbai: Orient Longman. 2000, p. 24; Dubash. 'India'., p. 56; Dubash. 'India'., p. 55.

6 Ranjit Devraj. 'Enron Saga a Lesson against Globalisation.' *Third World Resurgence* January/February, 2002, p. 41.

7 Sanjeev Srivastava. 'Enron "Desperate" to Sell India Assets.' *BBC News Online* 10 January 2002; Sandip Roy. 'Enron in India: The Giant's First Fall.' *Alternet* 8 February 2002

8 Asian Development Bank. 'The Bank's Policy Initiatives for the Energy Sector.' Philippines:

Asian Development Bank. May 1995

9 Sub-Committee. 'Report'.; Devraj. 'Enron Saga a Lesson against Globalisation.', p. 42; 'Enron Scandal Touches Even Ordinary Taxpayer—and the Environment.' Environmental Defense. 5 February 2002. http://www.environmentaldefense.org/article.cfm?ContentID=1246; Timothy J. Burger. 'VP Tried to Aid Enron in India.' *New York Daily News* 18 January 2002; Dana Milbank and Paul Blustein. 'White House Aided Enron in Dispute.' *Washington Post* 20 January 2002

10 Sub-Committee. 'Report'.; Russell Mokhiber and Andrew Wheat. 'Shameless: 1995's Ten Worst Corporations.' *Multinational Monitor* December, 1995; Sanjeev Srivastava. 'Enron Cashes in India Power Bill.' *BBC News Online* 6 February 2001

11 John-Thor Dahlburg. 'This Power Game Has High Stakes for India.' *The Times of India.* 22 June 1995; D'Monte. 'Enron Sheds No Light on Consumer.'

12 Sub-Committee. 'Report'.; Cooper. 'Wattage to India.', p. A12; Srivastava. 'Enron Cashes in India Power Bill.'; Mehta. *Power Play.*, p. 22.

13 Sub-Committee. 'Report'., Ch 11; Devraj. 'Enron Saga a Lesson against Globalisation.', p. 42; Ron Callari. 'The Enron-Cheney-Taliban Connection?' *Albion Monitor* 28 February 2002; Sub-Committee. 'Report'., ch 2.

14 D'Monte. 'Enron Sheds No Light on Consumer.'; Pratap Chatterjee. 'Enron Deal Blows a Fuse.' *Multinational Monitor* July/August 1995

15 Sub-Committee. 'Report'.

16 Ibid.

17 Callari. 'The Enron-Cheney-Taliban Connection?'

18 Cited in Ibid.

19 Sub-Committee. 'Report'., Ch 11; Mehta. *Power Play.*, p. 29.

20 Sub-Committee. 'Report'., Ch 2.

21 Ibid., ch 2.

22 Ibid., ch 2; Devraj. 'Enron Saga a Lesson against Globalisation.', p. 42; Jonathan Rugman. 'Power Failure.' *Channel 4 News* 21 June 2000

23 Sub-Committee. 'Report'., ch. 2; Kate Bayliss and David Hall. 'Independent Power Producers: A Review of the Issues.' University of Greenwich, London: Public Services International Research Unit (PSIRU). November, 2000, p. 4.

24 Mehta. *Power Play.*, p. 4.

25 Sub-Committee. 'Report'., ch 2; Mehta.

Power Play., p. 4.

26 Sub-Committee. 'Report'., ch 2.

27 Ibid.

28 Rugman. 'Power Failure.'; Roy. 'Enron in India: The Giant's First Fall.'

29 Dahlburg. 'This Power Game Has High Stakes for India.'; Cooper. 'Wattage to India.', p. A12.

30 David E. Sanger. 'How Washington Inc. Makes a Sale.' *The New York Times.* 19 February 1995

31 Ibid.

32 Arundhati Roy. 'Shall We Leave It to the Experts?' *The Nation* 18 February 2002

33 Sub-Committee. 'Report'.; quoted in Mokhiber and Wheat. 'Shameless.'

34 Dahlburg. 'This Power Game Has High Stakes for India.'

35 Mokhiber and Wheat. 'Shameless.'; Dahlburg. 'This Power Game Has High Stakes for India.'

36 Quoted in Chatterjee. 'Enron Deal Blows a Fuse.'

37 Daniel Chavez. 'Lights Off! Debunking the Myths of Power Liberalisation.' Amsterdam: Transnational Institute (TNI). May, 2002, p. 15.

38 Mehta. *Power Play.*, p. 3; Sub-Committee. 'Report'.; Devraj. 'Enron Saga a Lesson against Globalisation.', p. 41; Roy. 'Shall We Leave It to the Experts?'; D'Monte. 'Enron Sheds No Light on Consumer.'; Celia W. Dugger. 'High-Stakes Showdown: Enron's Fight over Power Plant Reverberates Beyond India.' *The New York Times.* 20 March 2001.

39 Roy. 'Shall We Leave It to the Experts?'

40 Devraj. 'Enron Saga a Lesson against Globalisation.', p. 41; Roy. 'Enron in India: The Giant's First Fall.'

41 Roy. 'Enron in India: The Giant's First Fall.'; Rugman. 'Power Failure.'; Cooper. 'Wattage to India.'

42 Amnesty International. 'The "Enron Project" in Maharashtra—Protests Suppressed in the Name of Development.' Amnesty International. 17 July 1997. http://www.web.amnesty.org/aidoc/aidoc_pdf.nsf/index/ASA200311997ENGLISH/$File/ASA2003197.pdf, pp. 1-4.

43 Sub-Committee. 'Report'.

44 Ibid.

45 Roy. 'Enron in India: The Giant's First Fall.'

46 Rugman. 'Power Failure.'; Roy. 'Shall We Leave It to the Experts?'; Associated Press. 'US Official: Cutoff of Aid to India Possible If Enron Project Deemed 'Expropriated'.' *wtowatchact* 8 April 2002

47 Devraj. 'Enron Saga a Lesson against

Globalisation.', p. 42; Rugman. 'Power Failure.'; Cooper. 'Wattage to India.'; Roy. 'Shall We Leave It to the Experts?'; Rugman. 'Power Failure.'

48 Rugman. 'Power Failure.'

49 Kate Bayliss and David Hall. 'A PSIRU Response to the World Bank's 'Private Sector Development Strategy: Issues and Options'.' University of Greenwich, London: Public Services International Research Unit (PSIRU). October, 2001, p. 10.

50 Roy. 'Shall We Leave It to the Experts?'; Srivastava. 'Enron "Desperate" to Sell India Assets.'

51 Quoted in Sheila McNulty and Khozem Merchant. 'Enron Issues Veiled Sanction Threat to India.' *The Financial Times* 24 August 2001, p. 6.

52 Dana Milbank and Alan Sipress. 'NSC Aided Enron's Efforts.' *Washington Post* 25 January 2002, p. A18.

53 Callari. 'The Enron-Cheney-Taliban Connection?'; Milbank and Blustein. 'White House Aided Enron in Dispute.', p. A12; 'Chronology of Administrative Dealings with Enron's Dabhol Power Plant in India.' *Washington Post* 22 January, 2002; Milbank and Sipress. 'NSC Aided Enron's Efforts.', p. A18.

54 Roy. 'Enron in India: The Giant's First Fall.'

55 Callari. 'The Enron-Cheney-Taliban Connection?'; Associated Press. 'US Official.'

56 Roy. 'Enron in India: The Giant's First Fall.'

57 Bayliss and Hall. 'Independent Power Producers.', p. 6.

58 Dubash. 'India'., p. 56.

Chapter Nineteen

1 Quoted in César Benjamin. 'The Reason for the Energy Crisis in Brazil.' Paper presented at the III Conferência Regional Energética de la ICEM. Rio de Janeiro, 10-13 September 2001, p. 18.

2 Nilder Costa. 'IMF and Energy Pirates Made Brazil's Electricity Crisis, "California Style".' *Executive Intelligence Review* 20 July 2001

3 Benjamin. 'The Reason for the Energy Crisis in Brazil.', pp. 1-2.

4 Ibid., p. 2.

5 Ibid., p. 4; Walt Patterson. *Transforming Electricity: The Coming Generation of Change.* London: Royal Institute of International Affairs and Earthscan. 1999, p. 31.

6 Barbara N. McKee. 'Independent Power Production and the New Model of the Electric Sector.' Paper presented at the IV

International Workshop Independent Power Production in Brazil: Creating the New Reality. Sao Paolo, Brazil, 24 June 1996.

7 Kate Frey. 'Brazil's New Economic Reforms, Liberalization Measures Open Doors to Expansion of Opportunities for U.S. Firms.' *Business America* June, 1998, p. 17.

8 Brazil-US Business Council. 'Brazil Information: The Brazilian Electrical Energy Sector.' Brazil-US Business Council,. Accessed on 9 January 2002. http://www.brazilcouncil.org/brazilinformation/brazilinfo_energysector.html

9 M2 Communications. 'Wilson Challenges the Best of British to Capture Brazilian Opportunities.' *M2 Presswire.* 15 October 2001

10 John Javetski. 'The Lure of Latin America.' *Electrical World* September, 1996, p. 23.

11 Noronha Advogados. 'Brazil's Move toward Privatization.' *Inter-American Trade* 5(11). 1998, p. 1.

12 Infrastructure Brazil. 'Privatization.'; Roberto Macedo. 'Privatization and the Distribution of Assets and Income in Brazil.' Economic Reform Project, Carnegie Endowment for International Peace. July 2000, pp. 8-9.; BNDES. 'Foreign Investors.' BNDES. 12 April 2001. http://www.bndes.gov.br/english/Priv4.htm

13 Patterson. *Transforming Electricity.*, p. 32.

14 Theo MacGregor. 'Electricity Restructuring in Britain: Not a Model to Follow.' *IEEE Spectrum* June, 2001, p. 16.

15 'Lights out across Rio? World Bank Is to Blame.' *Observer.* 6 December 1998

16 Benjamin. 'The Reason for the Energy Crisis in Brazil.', p. 3.

17 Infrastructure Brazil. 'Privatization.'

18 Marta Alvim. 'Privatization: No More a Dirty Word.' *Brazzil.* November, 2000.

19 Noronha Advogados. 'Brazil's Move toward Privatization.', p. 1.

20 Benjamin L. Israel and Ivor Heyman. 'Brazil in Transition.' *Independent Energy* 28(7). 1998.

21 Costa. 'IMF and Energy Pirates.'; Benjamin. 'The Reason for the Energy Crisis in Brazil.', p. 5.; Israel and Heyman. 'Brazil in Transition.'

22 'Lights out across Rio?', p. 6.

23 Israel and Heyman. 'Brazil in Transition.'; Brazil-US Business Council. 'Brazil Information.'; San Beatty. 'Brazil: Electricity.' Energy Division, U.S. Department of Commerce. April 2001. http://www.ita.doc.gov/td/energy/brazil1.html

24 Infrastructure Brazil. 'Energy Sector

Restructuring.' Infrastructure Brazil. Accessed on 9 November 2002. http://www.infraestru-turabrasil.gov.br/english/perfis/ene1.asp; David Watts and Rafael Ariztia. 'The Electricity Crises of California, Brazil and Chile: Lessons to the Chilean Market.' Catholic University of Chile. Accessed on 9 November 2002. http://www2.ing.puc.cl/~power/paperspdf/wattsariztia.pdf, p. 2; Israel and Heyman. 'Brazil in Transition.'

25 McKee. 'Independent Power Production.'; Benjamin. 'The Reason for the Energy Crisis in Brazil.', p. 5; Costa. 'IMF and Energy Pirates.'

26 'Brazil's Rationing-Related Rate Hike Means 7.9% Increase for Industrials.' *Electric Utility Week*. 24 December 2001, p. 28.

27 Benjamin. 'The Reason for the Energy Crisis in Brazil.', p. 6; 'Lights out across Rio?', p. 6.

28 Jean-Paul Prates. 'Brazil's Energy Crisis Complicates Progress in Gas, Power Markets, but Outlook Brightening.' *The Oil and Gas Journal* 15 October 2001.

29 Benjamin. 'The Reason for the Energy Crisis in Brazil.', p. 6.

30 'Lights out across Rio?', p. 6.

31 Costa. 'IMF and Energy Pirates.'; Benjamin. 'The Reason for the Energy Crisis in Brazil.', p. 4.

32 Ibid., p. 4.

33 Costa. 'IMF and Energy Pirates.'

34 Charles Roth. 'Necessity Mother of Deregulation in Power Hungry Brazil.' *Dow Jones News Service*. 3 July 2001, 2001

35 Benjamin. 'The Reason for the Energy Crisis in Brazil.', p. 3.

36 'Embracing the Gas Turbine.' *Power Engineering International*. June, 1999, p. 22.

37 Ibid., p. 7.

38 'Enron: The Global Gospel of Gas.' Project Underground. 27 November 1997. http://www.moles.org/ProjectUnderground/mohterload/enron.html

39 'Embracing the Gas Turbine.', p. 22.

40 Kari Hemmerschlag. 'Bolivia Brazil Natural Gas Pipeline.' Bank Information Center. Accessed on 9 January 1999. http://www.bicusa.org/lac/bol_brazil.htm; 'Enron: The Global Gospel of Gas.'; 'The Bolivia-Brazil Gas Pipeline.' Bankwatch. 21 May 2001. http://www.bankwatch.org/publications/issue_papers/2001/eib-bolivia-brazil.html

41 Benjamin. 'The Reason for the Energy Crisis in Brazil.', pp. 15, 17.

42 Costa. 'IMF and Energy Pirates.'

43 Benjamin. 'The Reason for the Energy Crisis in Brazil.', pp. 16-17.

44 Ibid., pp. 7-8; 'The Brazilian Crisis.' *CNM-CUT Internacional* 1 August 2001, p. 1.

45 Roth. 'Necessity Mother of Deregulation.'

46 Watts and Ariztia. 'The Electricity Crises of California, Brazil and Chile: Lessons to the Chilean Market.', p. 4; Benjamin. 'The Reason for the Energy Crisis in Brazil.', pp. 8-11.

47 'Enron Suspends Investments in Brazil.' *O Globo*. 15 May 2001; 'The Brazilian Crisis.', p. 1; Roth. 'Necessity Mother of Deregulation.'

48 Benjamin. 'The Reason for the Energy Crisis in Brazil.', p. 8; 'The Brazilian Crisis.', p. 1; Costa. 'IMF and Energy Pirates.'

49 Benjamin. 'The Reason for the Energy Crisis in Brazil.', p. 9.

50 Ibid., pp. 9-11.

51 Fernando Henrique Cardoso in 1997 quoted in Costa. 'IMF and Energy Pirates.'

52 Costa. 'IMF and Energy Pirates.'; Anthony Faiola. 'Brazil Dimming the Lights.' *The Washington Post*. 29 May 2001, p. A9; Prates. 'Brazil's Energy Crisis.', p. 77; Cheryl E. Richer. 'Brazil Energy Crisis Raises Utility Credit Concerns.' *Standard & Poor's Ratings Direct* 24 May 2001

53 'Will Brazil Want All That Gas When Hydro Comes Back?' *World Gas Intelligence* 24 October 2001, p. P7; 'Brazil's Power Crisis Is Due to Bad Regulations, Market Participants Say.' *Global Power Report* 30 March 2001, p. 10.

54 'Companies Lobby for Higher Rate, Clearer Rules — Brazil.' *Business News Americas* 22 August 2000.

55 'Will Brazil Want All That Gas When Hydro Comes Back?', p. P7.

56 Quoted in Sustainable Energy and Economic Network. 'Enron's Pawns: How Public Institutions Bankrolled Enron's Globalization Game.' Washington, DC: Institute for Policy Studies. 22 March 2002, p. 28.

57 'Brazil's Rationing-Related Rate Hike.', p. 28.

58 Benjamin. 'The Reason for the Energy Crisis in Brazil.', p. 17.

59 See for example, Janet Matthews. 'Brazil: Review.' *Americas Review World of Information* 10 August 2001

60 Roth. 'Necessity Mother of Deregulation.'

61 Alvim. 'Privatization.'

62 'Lights out across Rio?', p. 6.

63 Macedo. 'Privatization and the Distribution of Assets and Income in Brazil.', p. 3.

64 Daniel Chavez. 'Lights Off! Debunking the Myths of Power Liberalisation.' Amsterdam: Transnational Institute (TNI). May, 2002, p. 7.

Conclusion

1 James Walsh. *The $10 Billion Jolt*. Los Angeles: Silver Lake Publishing. 2002, p. 37.

2 Ibid., p. 5.

3 Ibid., p. 285.

4 Energy Information Agency. 'The Changing Structure of the Electric Power Industry 2000: An Update.' Department of Energy. October, 2000, pp. 97-8.

5 Ibid., p. 98.

6 Daniel Berman. 'The Confederate Cartel's War against California.' *San Francisco Bay Guardian*. 5 January, 2001; Merrill Goozner. 'Free Market Shock.' *The American Prospect*. 27 August 2001

7 ABARE. 'Competition in the Australian National Electricity Market.' *ABARE Current Issues*. January, 2002, p. 11.

8 Quoted in Walsh. *The $10 Billion Jolt*., p. 282.

9 Cited in Anthony Hughes. 'All Charged and Ready to Go.' *Sydney Morning Herald*. 11 March 1998

10 Julia O'Connell Davidson. 'Metamorphosis? Privatisation and the Restructuring of Management and Labour'. In *Privatisation and Regulation: A Review of the Issues*. ed. Peter M Jackson and Catherine M Price. London and New York: Longman. 1994, p. 173.

11 Ibid. In. ed., p. 177.

12 John Quiggan. 'Crossed Wires in the Privatisation Debate.' *Australian Financial Review*. 17 May 1999, p. 34.

13 Quoted in Consumers Union. 'Deregulated.' *Consumer Reports* July, 2002, p. 34.

14 Quoted in Navroz K. Dubash. 'The Changing Global Context for Electricity Reform'. In *Power Politics: Equity and Environment in Electricity Reform*. ed. Navroz K. Dubash. Washington D.C.: World Resources Institute. 2002, p. 21.

15 Kate Bayliss and David Hall. 'Independent Power Producers: A Review of the Issues.' University of Greenwich, London: Public Services International Research Unit (PSIRU). November 2000.

16 Peter Martin. 'Failure is an option'. *The Financial Times* (London). 11 October 2001, p. 15.

17 Bayliss and Hall. 'Independent Power Producers.'

18 Gráinne Ryder. 'Creating Poverty: The ADB in Asia: Focus on the Global South.' Probe International. 3 May 2000. http://www.probeinernational.org/index.cfm?DSP=content&ContentID=712

19 Jonathan Lash. 'Foreword'. In *Power Politics* ed. Dubash, p. vii.

20 Charlie Higley. 'Disastrous Deregulation.' Public Citizen. December, 2000, p. 5.

21 'Pollution up Down Under.' *Earth Island Journal*. Spring, 2001, p. 3.

22 Robert Melnbardis. 'Power Deregulation Fueled Pollution—NAFTA Agency.' *World Environmental News*. 19 June 2002.

23 Dubash. 'The Changing Global Context for Electricity Reform'. In. ed., p. 19.

24 Nicholas Hildyard. 'Snouts in the Trough: Export Credit Agencies, Corporate Welfare and Policy Incoherence.' *The CornerHouse Briefing*. 1999

25 'California Passes Strong Renewables Standard.' *Environmental News Service*. 16 September 2002.

26 'Growth Slows in Independent Power Market.' *Oil and Gas Journal* 97(9). 1999

27 'US Renewable Energy Use Falls to 12-year Low'. *World Environment News*. 25 November 2002; 'Energy, the New Convergence.' *The Economist*. 29 May 1999

28 Dexter Whitfield. *Making It Public: Evidence and Action against Privatisation*. London: Pluto Press. 1983, p. 49.

29 Walsh. *The $10 Billion Jolt*., pp. 288-9; Brian Robins. 'Banks See Big Chance in Trading Electricity.' *Sydney Morning Herald*. 5-6 October 2002, p. 45.

30 Quiggan. 'Crossed Wires in the Privatisation Debate.', p. 34.

31 Walsh. *The $10 Billion Jolt*., pp. 275-6.

Index

Note: italicised page numbers refer to a figure or table within the text.

DATE DUE

GAYLORD			PRINTED IN U.S.A.